PAUL's ESCHATOLOGICAL &
PASTORAL EPISTLES

Cover Photo Description

This course covers five letters of Paul, including 1 & 2 Thessalonians, with 1 & 2 Timothy, and Titus (Paul's three pastoral epistles). A common theme in all five of these letters is *eschatology*—a Greek word that refers to "last things."

Our cover shows a pastor caring for one of Father's lambs, as he walks toward our Savior's Second Coming—represented by rays of light shining through the clouds in the upper right corner.

Components That Complement This Book

Visit www.FaithAndActionSeries.org to see components with this book:

eVisuals—all figures in color with captions for projection in classroom. Download from our website.

2 Kindle versions available from Amazon:

Version on right is a typical Kindle format. Suitable for your tablet or phone or computer

Teacher's Guides—To purchase a TG a person must submit our online form and be approved as a teacher, pastor, or administrator.
www.faithandactionseries.org/teachers.html

To find us on Amazon search Faith & Action Team.
www.amazon.com (search Faith & Action Team)

Contact Information

Order your copy online from:

Web: www.FaithAndActionSeries.org

Faith & Action
429 U.S. Hwy 65
Walnut Shade, Missouri 65771 U.S.A.

E-mail: Info@FaithAndActionSeries.org

Telephone: (417) 881-4698

PAUL'S ESCHATOLOGICAL &
PASTORAL EPISTLES

Student Manual

by Dr. Quentin McGhee, Dr. Steve D. Eutsler, and Dr. Johnny Ford

Instructional Design by
Dr. Quentin McGhee, Senior Editor

PUT YOUR FAITH TO WORK!

Faith & Action Series

Faith & Action
429 U.S. Hwy 65
Walnut Shade, Missouri 65771 U.S.A.

Copyright Information

Cover layout and logo design: Imaginational; www.Imaginational.biz, 406 W. Commercial St., Springfield, MO 65803

The Holy Bible: New International Version, International Bible Societies, Grand Rapids, Michigan: Zondervan Publishing House, ©1984.

The Holy Bible: King James Version, Cleveland and New York: The World Publishing Company.

The Holy Bible: New King James Version, Nashville, Tennessee: Thomas Nelson Inc., Publishers, ©1979.

The Holy Bible: New American Standard Bible, Philadelphia and New York: A. J. Holman Company, ©1973.

Noted Scripture quotations [   ] are from the New Revised Standard Version Bible, copyright © 1989 the Division of Christian Education of the National Council of the Churches of Christ in the United States of America. Used by permission. All rights reserved.

Figure 2.10 By Classical Numismatic Group, Inc. http://www.cngcoins.com, CC BY-SA 3.0, https://commons.wikimedia.org/w/index.php?curid=2155073

Faith & Action Team purchased graphics through Imaginational, or from art stock sources. All tables, questions, and exercises are by the Faith & Action Team unless endnotes indicate otherwise. All photos are used by license or permission. All stories and illustrations are created by the authors from research of public documents, personal creativity or experiences, and contributors, unless endnotes indicate otherwise.

First Edition 2017

Faith & Action Series—Paul's Eschatological & Pastoral Epistles
First Edition ©2017 Faith & Action Team

Course # BIB3012
ISBN: 978-1-60382-118-6
Item # 4411-31E0

Table of Contents

Cover Photo Description 2

Contact Information 2

Copyright Information 4

Table of Contents 5

Chapter—Lesson

Unit 1:
The Eschatological Letters (1 & 2 Thessalonians)

1 Live Ready for the Lord's Coming 18

   1 Introduction to the Thessalonian Letters 20

   2 Live Ready: Be an Encourager as You Wait for the Lord (1 Thess. 1:1-10) 24

   3 Live Ready: Be a Fruitful Servant as You Wait for the Lord—Part 1 (1 Thess. 2:1-16) 29

   4 Live Ready: Be a Fruitful Servant as You Wait for the Lord—Part 2
      (1 Thess. 2:17–3:13) 33

   5 Live Ready: Grow as You Wait for the Lord (1 Thess. 4:1-10) 35

   6 Live Ready: Prepare as You Wait for the Lord (1 Thess. 4:11–18) 41

   7 Live Ready: Understand as You Wait for the Day of the Lord
      (1 Thess. 5:1-11) 44

   8 Live Ready: Obey as You Wait for the Lord (1 Thess. 5:12-28) 51

2 Be Steadfast as You Wait for the Lord's Return 60

   9 Make the Most of Your Suffering (2 Thess. 1) 61

  10 The Comings of Christ and Antichrist—Part 1 (2 Thess. 2:1-8) 65

  11 The Comings of Christ and Antichrist—Part 2 (2 Thess. 2:9–3:8) 71

Unit 2:
The Pastoral Letters (1 Timothy)

3 Be True and Wise in God's Household 82

  12 False Teachers of the Law (1 Tim. 1:1-11) 83

  13 Inspiration: The Worst Sinner Became One of the Best Servants
      (1 Tim. 1:12-20) 90

  14 Objects and Attitudes of Prayer—Part 1 (1 Tim. 2:1-7) 97

  15 Objects and Attitudes of Prayer—Part 2 (1 Tim. 2:8-15) 101

  16 Qualifications for Pastors and Deacons—Blameless in Five Ways
      (1 Tim. 3:1-16; Titus 1:6-9) 108

  17 Qualifications for Pastors and Deacons: Respected for Seven Reasons
      (1 Tim. 3:1-16; Titus 1:6-9) 114

4 Be Strong and Faithful Serving the Lord 122

   18 The Pastor's Responsibilities in the Family of God (1 Tim. 4:1-16) 123

   19 Relating to Widows in the Family of God (1 Tim. 5:1-16) 130

   20 Overcoming the Threat of Sexual Sins 135

   21 Relating to Elders in the Family of God (1 Tim. 5:17-25). 141

   22 Relating to Slaves, False Teachers, Self, and the Rich in the Family of God (1 Tim. 6:1-21) 145

Unit 3:
The Pastoral Letters (Titus and Second Timothy)

5 Live in the Light of What Grace Teaches 156

   23 Silence False Teachers (Titus 1:1-16) 157

   24 Teach the A, B, C's of Grace (Titus 2:1-15) 162

   25 Discern the Past, Present, and Future Aspects of Salvation (Titus 3:1-15) 170

6 Be Faithful and Fruitful as You Finish the Race 176

   26 Encouraging Yourself in Hard Times—Part 1 (2 Tim. 1:1–2:13) 177

   27 Encouraging Yourself in Hard Times—Part 2 (2 Tim. 1:1–2:13) 183

   28 Choosing to Be a Vessel of Honor in the Last Days (2 Tim. 2:14–3:9) 190

   29 Finishing the Race Well—Part 1 (2 Tim. 3:10-17) 199

   30 Finishing the Race Well—Part 2 (2 Tim. 4:1-22) 203

Appendix A 212

Appendix B 213

Definitions 214

God's Plan of Salvation 217

Scripture List. 218

Bibliography 222

Endnotes 226

Figure 0.1   At the Rapture, all who believe in Christ will be united with Him and glorified.

Figure 0.1 (also Figure 1.21)   Artwork by Pat Marvenko Smith, ©2005 - www.revelationillustrated.com

List of Figures

Figure 0.1　At the Rapture, all who believe in Christ will be united with Him and glorified. 7

Figure 1.1　Map showing Thessalonica, Corinth, Rome, and Philippi 18
Figure 1.2　Eschatological Epistles 20
Figure 1.3　Groups, sub-groups, dates, and authors of New Testament books 20
Figure 1.5　Events related to Paul's ministry to the Thessalonians 21
Figure 1.4　This great city was on the Egnatian Way. 21
Figure 1.6　Outline that shows the purposes of 1 Thessalonians. 22
Figure 1.9　Thessalonica was a major city on the Egnatian Way. 24
Figure 1.11　Missionary David Grams showed appreciation to all. 25
Figure 1.12　Encourage each other. 26
Figure 1.13　References to the gospel in 1 and 2 Thessalonians 28
Figure 1.14　Until we share money or the gospel, neither will help anyone. 30
Figure 1.15　References to free will in relation to salvation 32
Figure 1.16　Three aspects of holiness in Christ 36
Figure 1.19　How can I get the air out of a glass? 38
Figure 1.20　The Jordan River connects two seas in Israel. 40
Figure 1.22　At the Rapture, all who believe in Christ will be united with Him and glorified. 42
Figure 1.23　Verses related to the Day of the Lord. 45
Figure 1.24　The Day of the Lord will bring wrath to some and reward to others (1 Thess. 5:1-11). 47
Figure 1.26　The volcano of Mount Vesuvius 48
Figure 1.28　Contrasts between children of darkness and children of light (1 Thess. 5:1-11) 49
Figure 1.29　Parallels that show Matthew 24 influenced 1 and 2 Thessalonians 50
Figure 1.30　15 principles for children of light awaiting the Day of the Lord 51
Figure 1.32　One man thought the whole world stunk, but the problem was cheese on his moustache. 53
Figure 1.34　Paul and Silas prayed and sang in prison at Philippi. 54
Figure 1.35　Scripture warns against two spiritual extremes: no fire and wild fire. (Lev. 10:1). 55

Figure 2.1　Sabio warns: "Do not buy everything that wiggles." 60
Figure 2.2　There is a mineral called iron pyrite that looks like gold. 60
Figure 2.6　Two mountains or events may blend into one ... from a great distance. 66
Figure 2.7　Contrasts of values in different cultures 67
Figure 2.8　Daniel, Matthew, John, and Paul all describe the resurrections of the righteous and wicked. 69
Figure 2.9　Contrasts between the Antichrist and Christ (2 Thess. 2:1-12). 70
Figure 2.10　Ancient coin showing the image of Antiochus IV Epiphanes in the form of the Greek god Zeus . . 71
Figure 2.12　Second Thessalonians 2:13—3:5 is an encouragement between two tough topics. 76
Figure 2.13　Paul seeks to correct the problem of idleness among believers (2 Thess. 3:6-15). 78

Figure 3.1　We may divide Paul's 13 letters into four groups. 82
Figure 3.2　Timothy was from Lystra, a small city in Galatia. 83
Figure 3.3　Part of an old Roman amphitheater at Ephesus 83
Figure 3.4　Outline of 1 Timothy 84
Figure 3.5　The main street at Ephesus led to the harbor. 85
Figure 3.6　Paul's pastoral instructions to Timothy (2 Tim. 1–4) 86
Figure 3.7　Seven comparisons of a pastor in 2 Timothy 2 87
Figure 3.10　Aspects of the gospel in the Pastoral Epistles 89
Figure 3.11　Rembrandt's Decent From the Cross 91
Figure 3.13　When a ship at sea wrecks, this usually results in the loss of many lives. 95
Figure 3.15　Five warnings in the book of Hebrews 96
Figure 3.16　In 1 Timothy 2.1 the Greek word *oun* is like a bridge. 97
Figure 3.18　The smallest human has more worth in God's eyes than the biggest animal. 99
Figure 3.19　Only Jesus can save us from the penalty and power of sin. 100
Figure 3.22　Paul urged men to lift up holy hands in prayer. 102
Figure 3.24　Our horizontal relationships on earth affect our vertical relationship to the God of heaven. 104

Figure 3.25   The Pastoral Epistles contrast godly and ungodly women. 108
Figure 3.27   Qualifications for overseers and deacons (1 Tim. 3; Titus 1) 109
Figure 3.29   The skunk earns a bad reputation, so people do not like to be near it. 112
Figure 3.30   Remember the disillusioned the woodpecker. 113
Figure 3.32   Seven laws of a good teacher. 117
Figure 3.33   First Timothy 3:16 is part of an old hymn. 118

Figure 4.1   The family of God includes young and old, male and female, rich and poor. 122
Figure 4.3   Biblical warnings of apostasy—abandoning our faith in Christ 124
Figure 4.6   Four lists of gifts in the New Testament 128
Figure 4.7   Some churches have as many as 200 different ministries that church members are doing! 129
Figure 4.8   Paul gives four guidelines for helping older widows. 131
Figure 4.9   Paul recognizes three groups: believers, unbelievers, and apostates. 132
Figure 4.12   Satan, like a roaring lion, seeks to destroy people. 135
Figure 4.13   Beware when you see outward signs that warn of sexual danger. 136
Figure 4.14   Beware when you see inward signs that warn of sexual danger. 137
Figure 4.15   The steps down to adultery are many and small. 137
Figure 4.16   Five needs of most men and women. How well do you know your spouse's needs? 139
Figure 4.17   Preaching and Teaching elders are worthy of double honor. 142
Figure 4.18   In biblical times, people used an oxen to grind grain. 142
Figure 4.19   Don't be like a greedy dog. 148
Figure 4.20   Steps to apostasy and spiritual suicide 149
Figure 4.21   Two roads run through both the old covenant and the new covenant. 150
Figure 4.23   Statements about God in the doxology of 1 Timothy 6:15-16. 152

Figure 5.1   Map showing places where Titus ministered (Jerusalem, Crete, Corinth, Dalmatia). 156
Figure 5.2   Outline of Titus 156
Figure 5.4   Knossos Palace on the island of Crete. 158
Figure 5.6   Characteristics for leaders to avoid and pursue (Titus 1:7-8) 160
Figure 5.8a   The vulture saw a dead animal. 162
Figure 5.8b   The honey bee saw a flower. 162
Figure 5.12   The process of sanctification (holiness) begins at regeneration (the new birth). 167

Figure 6.1   Nero declared in public that he was number one among God's chief enemies. 176
Figure 6.2   Paul encourages Timothy through our relationships with people and with God. 177
Figure 6.3   Geese are a common sight on many farms. 179
Figure 6.5   Paul often contrasts the human spirit with the divine Spirit. 184
Figure 6.6   Don't be a one-man band, trying to do everything yourself. 185
Figure 6.8   Ephesus was a strategic center for missions. 187
Figure 6.11   Paul uses four "if–then" statements to summarize our relationship to Christ (2 Tim. 2:11-13). ... 189
Figure 6.12   Two kinds of vessels—one for honor and one for dishonor 190
Figure 6.13   Paul contrasts vessels of honor and vessels of dishonor (2 Tim. 2:14–3:9) 191
Figure 6.15   Never argue with a fool—people might not notice the difference. 196
Figure 6.16   In the beginning, God made Adam from the ground. 198
Figure 6.17   Paul compares the Christian life to a race that ends in heaven or hell. 199
Figure 6.18   Paul summarizes these six themes in light of false teachers. 200
Figure 6.22   Pastors should preach a topical series on 16 basic truths of the Bible. 203
Figure 6.23   Seven benefits of preaching a series of expository sermons 204
Figure 6.25   The snake was mad because the wasp was stinging his head. 206
Figure 6.26   Paul and Silas prayed and sang in prison at Philippi. 208

Figure 7.1   Key questions to answer on the letter to 1 & 2 Timothy. 212
Figure 7.2   Key questions to answer on the letter to Titus. 213

Faith & Action Series Overview

Bible	Theology	Church Ministries
Survey of the Old Testament	God & the Bible (Theology 1)	Evangelism & Discipleship
Survey of the New Testament	Angels, Man, & Sin (Theology 2)	Marriage & Family
Pentateuch	Christ & Salvation(Theology 3)	Pastoral Ministry
Historical Books	The Holy Spirit & the Church (Theology 4)	Ministerial Ethics
Poetic Books	General Principles for Interpreting Scripture (Hermeneutics 1)	Preach the Word (Homiletics 1)
Major Prophets	Hermeneutics 2	Homiletics 2
Minor Prophets	Unlocking the Treasures of Your Fire Bible	Principles of Teaching
Life & Teachings of Christ (Synoptic Gospels)		Biblical Counseling
Gospel of John		Children's Ministry
Acts of the Holy Spirit		Youth Ministry
Romans & Galatians		Missions 1
First & Second Corinthians		Cross-Cultural Communications (Missions 2)
Prison Epistles		Teaching Literacy
Paul's Eschatological & Pastoral Epistles		Leadership
Hebrews		Church Government & Administration
General Epistles		Church History 1
Revelation & Daniel		Church History 2

Faith & Action Series Three-Year Bible School Plan
(103 credits)

First Year

First Semester

Course #	Title	Credits
BIB1013	Survey of the New Testament	3
BIB1023	Pentateuch	3
BIB1033	Synoptic Gospels	3
THE1012	God & the Bible (Theology 1)	2
THE1022	Hermeneutics 1	2
MIN3023	Children's Ministry	3
		16

Second Semester

Course #	Title	Credits
BIB1043	Survey of the Old Testament	3
BIB1052	Gospel of John	2
BIB1063	Acts	3
THE1032	Angels, Man, and Sin (Theology 2)	2
MIN1013	Homiletics 1	3
MIN1033	Evangelism & Discipleship	3
		16

Second Year

First Semester

Course #	Title	Credits
BIB2013	Romans & Galatians	3
BIB2023	Historical Books	3
BIB2072	Hebrews	2
MIN2012	Church History 1	2
MIN2023	Missions 1	3
THE2013	Christ & Salvation (Theology 3)	3
THE2032	Hermeneutics 2	2
		18

Second Semester

Course #	Title	Credits
BIB2043	Corinthians	3
BIB2052	Prison Epistles	2
BIB2063	Poetic Books	3
MIN2032	Church History 2	2
THE2042	The Holy Spirit & the Church (Theology 4)	2
THE2052	Leadership	2
MIN3073	Marriage & Family	3
		17

Third Year

First Semester

Course #	Title	Credits
BIB3012	Paul's Eschatological & Pastoral Epistles	2
BIB3022	General Epistles	2
BIB3033	Major Prophets	3
MIN3013	Pastoral Ministry	3
MIN3022	Church Government & Administration	2
MIN3033	Cross-Cultural Communications (Missions 2)	3
MIN3043	Homiletics 2	3
		18

Second Semester

Course #	Title	Credits
BIB3043	Revelation & Daniel	3
MIN1032	Teaching Literacy	2
MIN3053	Biblical Counseling	3
BIB3053	Minor Prophets	3
MIN3063	Principles of Teaching	3
MIN3072	Ministerial Ethics	2
MIN3082	Youth Ministry	2
		18

About This Book

1. **The Lesson Headings** divide each chapter into several parts. Each of these lessons focuses on principles related to one theme. We number the lessons consecutively throughout the book.

2. **The Lesson Goals** are listed at the beginning of each chapter. Also, when a lesson begins, the goal for that lesson is printed there. You will find that there is at least one goal for each lesson.

3. **Key Words** are defined in a section called "Definitions" at the end of the book. The symbol * comes before all words that are defined. To help some students, we have also defined a few words that are not key words.

4. **Teaching Method:** These courses are designed for the *guided discovery* method of learning. This method focuses on the student, rather than the teacher. When this course is used in a classroom, lectures are not intended. Rather, most of the class time should be used for students to discuss the questions in the margins and related questions from the teacher and other students. At least 25 percent of the student's grade should be on how faithfully the student has tried to answer questions *before* class.

   It is VERY important for each student to own his or her book. We encourage Bible schools to require students to buy their texts at the time they pay tuition. It is a shame for students to leave school without their books, because they need them for a lifetime of ministry. Owning the book enables a student to write notes in it and underline important ideas. Also, when students own their books, they do not waste class time by copying things that are already written in the text. Rather, they spend their time discussing questions related to the Bible and ministry.

   In a classroom the teacher and students should discuss key questions together. The best teachers never answer their own questions. Some students will complain at first when the teacher requires them to think, read, and search for answers. But a good teacher knows that children who are always carried never learn to walk. And students who are always told the answer learn to memorize, but not to think and solve problems. In many ways, a good teacher is like a coach—guiding others to succeed.

   The questions in this course are like a path that leads straight to the goal. If the questions are too hard for a student, the teacher can ask easier questions that are like stairs toward harder questions. Also, the teacher should ask questions that guide students to apply the text to local issues. Often, a good teacher will add a story or illustration that emphasizes a truth for students.

5. **Schedule:** This *Faith & Action Series* course is for two credits. For a Bible school course, it is good to plan 26 contact hours between the teacher and students. This allows one lesson for a class hour.

6. **The Questions:** Most questions in the margins are identified by the hammer ➤ and nail ➤ symbols. Questions are steps toward a goal. As a student answers the questions, he or she is sure to reach the goals. The hammer introduces *content questions* and the nail precedes *application questions*. Our logo for this book includes the hammer hitting the nail. A student must grasp content before being able to apply it. The answers to all content questions are in the text, near the question. We encourage students to answer nail or application questions from their local settings.

   In some books there is the symbol of a shovel ➤ before certain questions. Questions beside the shovel symbol are inductive questions. The word *induce* means "to lead." These questions lead students to discover truth for themselves.

7. *Sabio* is a Spanish word that means "wise man." This symbol in the margin signifies a proverb or wise saying.

8. **The Illustrations**, such as stories and examples, are preceded by the candle symbol.

9. **Figures** include pictures, photos, charts, and maps. We number the figures in order throughout the chapter. For example, the first three figures in chapter one are numbered 1.1, 1.2, and 1.3. There is a list of significant figures near the front of the book.

10. **The Test Yourself** questions come at the end of each chapter and are indicated by the balance symbol ⚖. There are always ten of these questions. As a rule, there are two test questions for each goal in the chapter. If students miss any of these questions, they need to understand why they missed them. Knowing why an answer is right is as important as knowing the right answer.

11. **Essay Test Topics** are at the end of each chapter, indicated by the pencil symbol ✎. Note that these essay topics are the lesson goals of the chapter. A student should be able to summarize these goals, writing 50-100 words on each one. These essay topics test students at a much higher level than the multiple choice, Test Yourself questions.

12. **Sample Answers** to the hammer questions, some comments on the nail questions, and answers for the Test Yourself questions and Essay Topics are in the Teacher's Guide. Students should answer questions so they will grow and become strong in their mental skills.

13. **Bible quotations** are usually from the New International Version (NIV). We also use the New American Standard Bible (NASB) and the King James Version (KJV). We encourage students to compare biblical passages in several versions of the Bible.

14. **The Scripture List** includes key Scripture references in this course. It is located near the back of the book.

15. **The Bibliography** is near the endnotes page. It is a complete list of books to which the authors refer in this course. Some students will want to do further research in these books.

16. **Endnotes** identify the sources of thoughts and quotes. They are listed by chapter at the end of the book.

17. **The Unit Exams and Final Exam** are in the Teacher's Guide. In the Teacher's Guide there are also other useful items for the teacher and potential projects for the students.

18. **Course Description (BIB3012):** The Eschatological and Pastoral Epistles. A thorough study of five of Paul's letters, from 1 Thessalonians through Titus. Examining each of the five letters includes an analysis of the biblical author, date, readers, historical and cultural setting, purpose, themes, special features, and outlines. Also, studying each epistle involves the exegesis and analysis of each paragraph in its literary context, with an emphasis on the two main hermeneutical questions: What did this paragraph mean to the first readers? And what does it mean to us today? Continuing to the top of the hermeneutical ladder, each lesson identifies timeless, cross-cultural principles for every paragraph of these five letters. Interactive questions, case studies, and illustrations guide students to evaluate and apply these principles to the situations believers face today. (This workbook by itself is designed for 2 credits, based on 16 class hours per credit.)

19. **Global Goals:**

F&A Chapter	Pastoral Epistles	Global Goals
1	1 Thess. 1–5	Summarize Paul's ministry to the Thessalonians, and explain four reasons why he wrote to them.
		Define *eschatology,* and summarize its emphasis in the Thessalonian Epistles.
		Identify and apply three ways Paul encouraged Thessalonian believers.
		Explain what Paul means by *the gospel.*
		Explain how fruitful ministry depends on boldness, love, endurance, and the response of listeners. (1 Thess. 2:1-16).
		Explain three aspects of holiness, and explain reasons why Paul wants all believers to grow in personal responsibility.
		Summarize the first Thessalonian question and Paul's answer.
		Explain the five commands about spiritual gifts in 1 Thessalonians 5:19-22.
2	2 Thess. 1–3	Analyze the *"day of the Lord"*—its purpose, scope, events, and valleys.
		Analyze the rise of the Antichrist to power, and the length of his rule.
		Explain how danger and safety relate to our response to truth

3	1 Tim. 1–3	Summarize the background, setting, date, and purpose of First Timothy. Analyze the problem, result, and methods of false teachers at Ephesus. Contrast the need for law among the unrighteous and the righteous. Define *the gospel,* and identify topics it spans. Contrast the penalty and power of sins from which Jesus saves us. Explain how salvation is from the penalty and power of sin, and how it inspires us to care for our faith–not wreck it. Explain why Paul wants believers to pray for all people, and how we can have holy hands. Interpret Paul's words on dress, teaching, and motherhood, in the context of the influence of false teachers on a few Ephesian women. Explain the meanings and relationships of overseer and deacon, and summarize their qualifications.
4	1 Tim. 4–6	Explain a balanced position between eternal insecurity and eternal security. Identify three ways a leader models good behavior. Give illustrations. Explain ways a leader can help believers identify and use their spiritual gifts. Explain four criteria of caring for older widows: relatives, need, godliness, age. Explain and apply principles to protect your family from sexual sins. Summarize ways to treat elderly believers as fathers, showing honor without favoritism. Summarize Paul's attitudes and values for employees and employers. Summarize the keys to being a faithful minister (1 Tim. 6).
5	Titus 1–3	Explain key words and phrases of the introduction to Titus. Contrast characteristics of false teachers at Crete, with characteristics of godly leaders. Explain ways for a pastor to overcome false teaching. Analyze the relationship of godly behavior to the gospel in Titus 2:1-14. Summarize how grace brings salvation, and enables holy living. Analyze the past, present, and future aspects of salvation in Titus.
6	2 Tim. 1–4	Analyze the setting of 2 Timothy, including circumstances and challenges. Explain and illustrate how we encourage ourselves through relationships with believers and the Father, Son, and Spirit. List advantages of training and involving others in ministry. Summarize five examples Paul uses in 2 Timothy 2 to motivate believers. Explain how God is faithful to Himself, in dealing with saints and sinners. Explain the context of two types of vessels in 2 Timothy 2, and contrast these on four topics. Define inspiration, inerrancy, and infallibility, and explain how belief in these guides us. Analyze why pastors must preach the Word, and explain four guidelines for preaching it. Summarize and apply Paul's attitudes toward persecutors, deserters, unmet expectations, and God.

20. Authors

Dr. Quentin McGhee is the founder and senior editor of the *Faith & Action Series*. He earned a B.A. from Southwestern College in Oklahoma City, and a B.S. from Oral Roberts University (ORU). Later he completed an M.Div. at the Assemblies of God Theological Seminary, where he taught beginning Greek. He earned a D.Min. from ORU in 1987. Dr. McGhee and his wife, Elizabeth, pioneered a church in Oklahoma. They went on to serve as missionaries in Kenya for 15 years. There they helped start many churches, developed an extension Bible school for full-time ministers, and assisted in curriculum development. Currently, Dr. McGhee serves as Director for the *Faith & Action Series*, while Elizabeth assists with graphics, desk-top publishing, website development, translations, and sales.

Dr. Johnny Ford has a rich background of academics and practics. He has a B.A. from Southwestern Assemblies of God University, an M.Div. from Southwestern Baptist Theological Seminary, and a D.Min. from Fuller Theological Seminary. Johnny and his wife, Medina, have served in full-time ministry for 26 years, including 8 years training pastors and planting churches in Tanzania, and 6 years in New York City pastoring in Queens and directing Bible Institutes. The Fords have three grown children: Wesley, Kendell, and Davida. They currently pastor a growing church they planted in Houston, Texas.

Dr. Steve D. Eutsler has a rich ministerial background as a teacher, pastor, preacher, and writer. He serves as a mentor for students of Global University in the areas of Bible and Practical Theology. Also, he has served as adjunct professor at Central Bible College and Evangel University for 12 years, teaching courses on Bible, practical ministry, and preaching. Steve has pastored 18 years. He is the author of four books, *Light for the Darkened Heart, Clothing the Mind, Planning Pentecostal Preaching,* and *The Prison Epistles.* Steve is known for being an outstanding expository preacher. He has contributed sermons to *Preaching On-Line* and illustrations to *PreachingToday.com.* His sermon outlines often appear in *Enrichment Journal* and *Pulpit Helps.* Also, he serves as a Dale Carnegie trainer. He contributed significant research and notes for this *Faith & Action* course on *Paul's Eschatological & Pastoral Epistles.* He earned his Doctor of Ministry degree at the Assemblies of God Theological Seminary in Springfield, Missouri, where he and his wife, Jackie reside. They have two grown children, Tabitha and Jeremy.

21. Contributors and Reviewers

Pastor Ron Woods is a 1988 graduate of Central Bible College in Springfield, Missouri. He also holds a Master's degree in Ministerial Leadership from Southeastern University.

Ron became the lead pastor of The Assembly at Broken Arrow in 2009. This church has sponsored two *Faith & Action* courses: *Acts of the Holy Spirit,* and *Paul's Eschatological & Pastoral Epistles.* Pastor Ron has also served churches in Pine Bluff, Arkansas and Memphis, Tennessee. His visionary leadership and dynamic preaching style have motivated others to excellence in ministry and purpose in life. Ron is a speaker at conferences across the United States and has become a regular guest at the Dream Center in Los Angeles. He has a great passion to lead the local church in community and global impact through servant leadership and Spirit-filled living.

Dr. Warren Bullock is the author of *"When the Spirit Speaks: Making Sense of Tongues, Interpretation & Prophecy"* (Amazon.com). His past ministry includes: Senior pastor for 25 years in four churches, Dean of the College of Ministry at Northwest University, Superintendent of the Northwest Ministry Network [District]. He presently serves as: General Council Executive Presbyter for the Northwest Region; adjunct faculty member for Northwest University and for Assemblies of God Theological Seminary; board member of Northwest University and of AGTS; writer, preacher, and teacher in the US and various nations. Warren and his wife, Judi, have two children and five grandchildren.

Dr. James Hernando has earned the following degrees: B.S. in Education (State University of New York), B.A. in Bible (Northeast Bible College), M.S. in Education (State University of New York), M.Div. (Assemblies of God Theological Seminary), M.Phil. and Ph.D. (Drew University, 1990). Jim and his wife, Moira, have three sons: Matthew, Eric, and Daniel.

Jim taught at Trinity Bible College and served as Chair of Biblical Studies (1980–1986). He has been Associate Professor of New Testament at AGTS from 1990–2014, and Chairs the Biblical Theology Department. Jim has preached and taught Hermeneutics and New Testament Theology in Ukraine and Costa Rica.

His recent publications are: 2 Corinthians in *Full Life Bible Commentary to the New Testament* (Zondervan), *Dictionary of Hermeneutics: A Concise Guide to Terms, Names, Methods and Expressions* (Gospel Publishing House), *Studies in the Letters of Paul* (Global University), and *First and Second Corinthians* (Faith & Action Series).

Jim has been awarded many honors, such as: Who's Who in American High Schools, Who's Who in American Colleges and University, FTE Hispanic Doctoral Scholarship, Outstanding Alumnus of Valley Forge Christian College, Member of the Advisory Board for the Foundation of Pentecostal Scholarship, and Assemblies of God Distinguished Educator's Award for 25 years of service.

Dr. French L. Arrington has ministered in evangelical and Pentecostal circles around the world. He has served as a pastor and for 17 years at Lee University, where he was chairman of the Bible and Theology Dept., Professor of New Testament Greek and Pauline Studies; and received the Excellence in Teaching Award. He has lectured in seminaries in Korea, Puerto Rico, Guatemala, Philippines, Indonesia, Ecuador, Virgin Islands, China and Russia. He also ministers at seminars, conferences, and local churches. Dr. Arrington is an ordained bishop in the Church of God; and served as Professor of New Testament Greek and Exegesis at the Pentecostal Theological Seminary from 1981-2002, where he is now Professor Emeritus. In 2017 he was asked to serve full time again at the Church of God Pentecostal Theological Seminary, as the first Chair of the Restoration of the Tabernacle of David.

His education includes BA degrees from Lee College and the Univ. of Chattanooga; an M. Div. and a Th. M. from Columbia Theologica Sem.; and a Ph. D in biblical languages from St. Louis University. He has authored and edited too many books to list here. Pathway Press published his three-volume work Christian Doctrine: a Pentecostal Perspective. His latest commentary is: T*he Greatest Letter Ever Written: A Study of Romans*. He was a general editor of the *Life in the Spirit New Testament Commentary*.

Dr. George O. Wood has contributed pastoral insights on 1 & 2 Timothy. His insights and illustrations were vital to this course. He is co-author of the *Faith & Action* book, *Acts of the Holy Spirit*. Dr. Wood has authored a number of books including a college textbook on Acts. He is the son of missionary parents to China and Tibet. He completed his undergraduate degree from Evangel College (now Evangel University). Later, he earned a doctorate in theology from Fuller Theological Seminary, and a juris doctorate from Western State University College of Law. He was assistant district superintendent of Southern California for 4 years and pastored Newport-Mesa Christian Center in Costa Mesa for 17 years. Dr. Wood served as General Secretary of the Assemblies of God from 1993, until he was elected as General Superintendent in 2007.

Unit 1:
The Eschatological Letters (1 & 2 Thessalonians)

Welcome to this study on five of Paul's letters: the Thessalonian and Pastoral Epistles. Our prayer is that you will open your heart and enjoy God's presence, time after time as you study truth in the 30 lessons of this course. Those who love the truth and walk in its light are secure and have fellowship with God. But the Antichrist will deceive those who do not love the truth (2 Thess. 2:9-10).

Sometimes, we love people and would like to see them. But circumstances prevent us from being close. This was the case with Paul and the new believers at Thessalonica. Acts 17:1-9 gives us the background of Paul's letters to the Thessalonians. Paul arrived in Thessalonica, a large city of about 200,000 people, on his second missionary trip. Silas and Timothy were with him. Things went well for these three missionaries until some of the Jews became jealous and angry. With loud voices, they accused Paul and his friends. *"They are all defying Caesar's decrees, saying that there is another king, one called Jesus"* (Acts 17:7). These bitter Jews forced Paul and his friends to leave Thessalonica. After they left, the Jews persecuted the new believers there (1 Thess. 2:14). Later, Paul sent Timothy to Thessalonica to see how they were doing (1 Thess. 3:2, 5). Timothy returned to Paul with good news about their faith and love (1 Thess. 3:6-10). Paul wanted to return to them, but he could not. So he wrote letters from Corinth to encourage them, about A.D. 51. When we cannot be close to those we love, sending a letter expresses our love from a distance. In this Unit, you will explore both of Paul's letters to believers in Thessalonica.

In Chapter 1, 1 Thessalonians 1–5, we will help you to:
- *Summarize Paul's ministry to the Thessalonians, and explain four reasons why he wrote to them.*
- *Define eschatology, and summarize its emphasis in the Thessalonian Epistles.*
- *Identify and apply three ways Paul encouraged Thessalonian believers.*
- *Explain what Paul means by 'the gospel.'*
- *Explain how fruitful ministry depends on boldness, love, endurance, and the response of listeners.*
- *Explain three aspects of holiness, and explain reasons why Paul wants all believers to grow in personal responsibility.*
- *Summarize the first Thessalonian question and Paul's answer.*
- *Explain the five commands about spiritual gifts in 1 Thessalonians 5:19-22.*

In Chapter 2, 2 Thessalonians 1–3, you will learn to:
- *Analyze 'the day of the Lord'—its meaning, purpose, scope, events, and valleys.*
- *Summarize the rise of the Antichrist to power, and the length of his rule.*
- *Explain how spiritual danger and safety depend on our response to truth.*

Chapter 1:
Live Ready for the Lord's Coming
(1 Thess. 1–5)

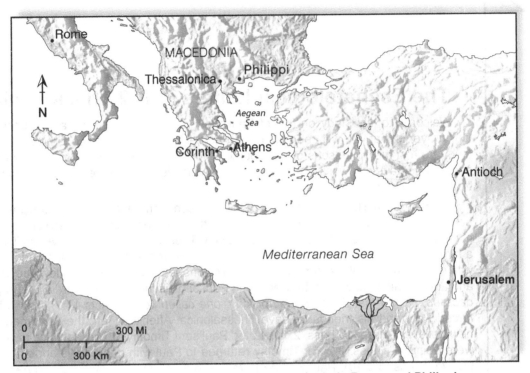

Figure 1.1   Map showing Thessalonica, Corinth, Rome, and Philippi

Q 1 ✎ *How do the words "our Lord Jesus" emphasize our faith in Christ's return? Complete Figure 1.2.*

Words	Your Summaries
Lord	
Jesus	
Our	

Figure 1.2   Practice analyzing the relationship of *"our Lord Jesus"* to faith in Christ's return.

Paul uses the phrase **our Lord Jesus** 24 times in the short letters of 1 and 2 Thessalonians. In contrast, Acts, which contains 28 chapters, refers to the *Lord Jesus* 17 times. And Romans refers to the *Lord Jesus* 16 times.[1] Paul's frequent use of **our Lord Jesus** in 1 and 2 Thessalonians matches his emphasis on **the Lord's coming**.

- The title **Lord** reminds us that Christ is above all powers and principalities.

- Likewise, the name **Jesus** means Savior (Matt. 1:21). Jesus is our Savior, who saved us from our sins and from the wrath of God coming on the disobedient (2 Thess. 1:8).

- The One coming back is **our Lord Jesus.** He is Lord of lords; He is **our Lord**—the One we obey.

Our Lord Jesus—how sweet the sound of these words to God's children. **Our Lord Jesus**, the One coming back for us. Enjoy these beautiful words 24 times in the short letters of 1 and 2 Thessalonians.

Lessons:

Introduction to the Thessalonian Letters

Goal A: *Summarize Paul's ministry to the Thessalonians—its beginning, interruption, and continuation.*

Goal B: *Explain 5 reasons why Paul wrote to Thessalonian believers.*

Goal C: *Define eschatology, and summarize its emphasis in the Thessalonian Epistles.*

Live Ready: Be an Encourager as You Wait for the Lord (1 Thess. 1:1-10)

Goal A: *Summarize the challenges that believers in Thessalonica faced.*
Goal B: *Identify and apply 3 ways Paul encouraged Thessalonian believers.*
Goal C: *Explain what Paul means by 'the gospel.'*

Live Ready: Be a Fruitful Servant as You Wait for the Lord—Part 1 (1 Thess. 2:1-16)

Goal A: *Explain and illustrate how fruitful ministry depends on daring commitment (1 Thess. 2:1-16).*
Goal B: *Analyze and illustrate the role of loving commitment in fruitful ministry (1 Thess. 2:1-16).*
Goal C: *Examine the relationship of fruitful ministry to the hearers' response (1 Thess. 2:1-16). Illustrate this.*

Live Ready: Be a Fruitful Servant as You Wait for the Lord—Part 2 (1 Thess. 2:17–3:13)

Goal A: *Summarize and illustrate the importance of endurance for fruitful servants.*
Goal B: *Explain and illustrate that fruitful service depends on God's love flowing through us.*

Live Ready: Grow as You Wait for the Lord (1 Thess. 4:1-10)

Goal A: *Explain and illustrate 3 aspects of growing in holiness.*
Goal B: *Summarize how our cooperation with the Holy Spirit is God's plan for holy living.*
Goal C: *Contrast the love of a young believer and a mature believer.*
Goal D: *Identify and illustrate 2 reasons why Paul wants all believers to grow in personal responsibility.*

Live Ready: Prepare as You Wait for the Lord (1 Thess. 4:11-18)

Goal: *Summarize the Thessalonian question and Paul's answer on the Lord's return (1 Thess. 4:13-18).*

Live Ready: Understand as You Wait for the Day of the Lord (1 Thess. 5:1-11)

Goal A: *Explain what Paul means by 'the Day of the Lord.' Include at least 4 key biblical references.*
Goal B: *Contrast the sad and glad aspects of the Day of the Lord.*

Live Ready: Obey as You Wait for the Lord (1 Thess. 5:12-28)

Goal A: *Illustrate and practice each of the 15 principles in 1 Thessalonians 5:12-28.*
Goal B: *Explain the 5 commands about spiritual gifts in 1 Thessalonians 5:19-22.*

Key Words

eschatology—a study about last things, including teachings on the Second Coming, the Rapture, and the rise and fall of the Antichrist; the biblical study of the last things, with an emphasis on the Day of the Lord

dead in Christ—believers who died before the return of Christ; at His return, the souls of those who died in Christ will return with Him, a loud command will call the bodies of the dead in Christ from their graves, so those souls will be united with their new, glorified bodies and will rise first.

Rapture—an event in the Day of the Lord when living believers are *caught up* to meet Christ in the clouds

Blessed Hope—the expectation of all believers of their joyful meeting with Jesus at the Rapture

imminent—an event, like the Coming of Christ, that could happen at any moment

Day of the Lord—Old Testament: a time that God judges the evil and rewards the righteous. New Testament: a period of time when God breaks into human history, so that His kingdom comes, and His will is done on earth, as it is in heaven—bringing judgment to the disobedient, but salvation, glorification, and reward to the obedient. The Day of the Lord includes such things as the Rapture, judgment of the Antichrist and his followers, Christ's reign on earth, and the Great White Throne judgment. Scholars agree that the Day of the Lord and its events extend beyond a normal day.

Lesson ## Introduction to the Thessalonian Letters

Goal A: *Summarize Paul's ministry to the Thessalonians—its beginning, interruption, and continuation.*
Goal B: *Explain 5 reasons why Paul wrote to Thessalonian believers.*
Goal C: *Define eschatology, and summarize its emphasis in the Thessalonian Epistles.*

Group	Book Title	Sub-group	Date+	Author
1. Historical Books (5)	Matthew	Synoptic Gospels	55-70	Matthew
	Mark		50-68	Mark
	Luke		60	Luke
	John		85-95	John
	Acts		62	Luke
2. Paul's Epistles (13)	Romans	Salvation Epistles	55-56	Paul
	1 Corinthians		55	
	2 Corinthians		56	
	Galatians		48-49	
	Ephesians	Prison Epistles	60-61	
	Philippians		61	
	Colossians		60-61	
	Philemon		60-61	
	1 Thessalonians	Eschatological Epistles	50-51	
	2 Thessalonians		51	
	1 Timothy	Pastoral Epistles	63	
	2 Timothy		67	
	Titus		65	
3. Hebrews and the General Epistles (8)	Hebrews	Epistles to suffering believers	65-70	Unknown
	James		45-49	James
	1 Peter		63-65	Peter
	2 Peter	Epistles to correct false teachings	65-67	Peter
	1 John		85-90	John
	2 John		85-90	John
	3 John		85-90	John
	Jude		67-80	Jude
4. Prophecy	Revelation		90-95	John

Figure 1.3   Groups, sub-groups, dates, and authors of New Testament books

Q 2 ➤ *How many letters did Paul write?*

Q 3 ➤ *Which of Paul's letters are eschatological? Which are pastoral?*

Q 4 ➤ *Which 2 Greek words help us understand the word 'eschatology'? Explain each.*

We may divide Paul's 13 letters into four groups. In this course we are studying five of Paul's letters:

- The Eschatological Epistles: 1 and 2 Thessalonians;
- The Pastoral Epistles: 1 and 2 Timothy, and Titus.

The first two chapters of this *Faith & Action* book cover 1 and 2 Thessalonians, the *Eschatological* Letters.

The word *eschatology* is based on two Greek words. *Eschatos* means "last," and *logos* means "word." *Eschatology* is a *word* (a study) about *last things*. In 1 and 2 Thessalonians, Paul writes a lot about eschatology, including teachings on the Second Coming, the Rapture, and the rise and fall of the Antichrist (See Figure 1.3).

+ Bible scholars differ on the exact dates of New Testament books.

A. Paul's relationship to believers at Thessalonica

Acts 17:1-9 gives us the background of Paul's first letter to the Thessalonians. Paul arrived there on his second missionary trip. Silas and Timothy were with him. Things went well for these missionaries until some of the Jews became jealous and angry. With loud voices, they accused Paul and his friends. *"They are all defying Caesar's decrees, saying that there is another king, one called Jesus"* (Acts 17:7). These bitter Jews forced Paul and his friends to leave Thessalonica. Paul traveled from Thessalonica to Athens, and on to Corinth (Acts 18). After he left Thessalonica, the Jews persecuted believers there (1 Thess. 2:14). Later, Paul sent Timothy to Thessalonica to see how they were doing (1 Thess. 3:5). Timothy returned to Paul with good news about the Thessalonian believers. Timothy praised the Thessalonians for their faith and love (1 Thess. 3:6-10).

Q 5 *Where was the city of Thessalonica?*

Q 6 *What city in your nation is about the size that Thessalonica was?*

Q 7 *Why did some Jews in Thessalonica accuse Paul of defying Caesar?*

Paul wanted to return to them, but he could not. So he wrote a letter from Corinth to encourage them, about A.D. 51.

Q 8 *What prevented Paul from returning to believers at Thessalonica?*

Q 9 *Have circumstances ever kept you from visiting those you love? Explain.*

Often, we love people, and would like to see them. But circumstances prevent us from being close to them. Writing a letter is like cooking something, and sending it to someone we love. Paul could not return to visit the Thessalonians. So he did what he could. He prayed for them, and he sent two letters to encourage them.[2]

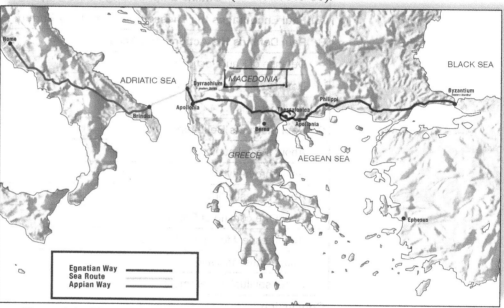

Figure 1.4   Thessalonica was the capital of Macedonia. This great city was on the Egnatian Way—a road that stretched from Dyrrachium to Byzantium, and connected the city of Rome with the eastern part of the Roman Empire. Note that another road, the Appian Way, stretches from Rome to Brindisi, at the west shore of the Adriatic Sea.

Reference	Events
Acts 16	1. Paul travelled from Philippi to Thessalonica, after his beating and release from prison in Philippi.
Acts 17:10	2. Paul and Silas fled from Thessalonica to Berea.
Acts 17:14	3. Paul fled from Berea to Athens (leaving Timothy and Silas in Berea).
Acts 17:15	4. Paul sent word from Athens for Timothy and Silas to join him there.
1 Thess. 3:1-5	5. Paul sent Timothy to Thessalonica, to see how the young believers were doing.
Acts 18:1	6. Paul moved from Athens to Corinth.
Acts 18:5; 1 Thess. 3:6	7. Timothy traveled from Thessalonica to join Paul in Corinth.
	8. Paul wrote 1 Thessalonians from Corinth and sent it to the church.
	9. Paul wrote 2 Thessalonians from Corinth, about 6 months later, after receiving more information about the young church.

Figure 1.5   Events related to Paul's ministry to the Thessalonians[3]

B. Paul's purposes for writing 1 and 2 Thessalonians

Paul left Thessalonica abruptly, after a brief ministry of a few weeks (Acts 17:5-10). His young converts from Judaism and paganism remained in Thessalonica. With little support, these young believers were left to face persecution from unbelieving Jews, and other hostile people (1 Thess. 2:14-16). Paul wrote two letters to the church at Thessalonica for at least five reasons:[4]

Q 10 *Summarize 5 reasons why Paul wrote to the Thessalonians.*

- To encourage the new converts in their trials (1 Thess. 1:3-12; 3:1-5; 2 Thess. 1:4-10; 2:13-17);
- To defend his actions and absence (1 Thess. 2:1-16; 2:17–3:10);
- To give teachings about godly living (1 Thess. 4:1-8; 5:1-24);
- To urge the lazy to work, and the working to avoid the lazy (1 Thess. 4:11-12; 2 Thess. 3:6-15);
- To give assurance and teachings on eschatology (1 Thess. 4:13-18; 2 Thess. 1:5-10; 2:1-12). Look ahead to Figure 1.7 on the seven references to the Lord's coming in 1 and 2 Thessalonians.

Outline Emphasizing Paul's Purposes	1 Thess.
A. Paul Encourages the Thessalonians as They Endure Persecution	**1**
B. Paul Defends His Actions and Absence	**2–3**
Defense of Paul's actions	2:1-16
Defense of Paul's absence	2:17–3:10
Paul's prayer	3:11-13
C. Paul Instructs Believers	**4–5**
About sexual purity	4:1-8
About brotherly love	4:9-10
About honest work	4:11-12
About the coming of Christ	4:13–5:11
About respect for spiritual leaders	5:12-13
About Christian living	5:14-18
About spiritual discernment	5:19-22
Conclusion	**5:23-28**

Figure 1.6   Outline that shows the purposes of 1 Thessalonians

Q 11 ✎ *How is Scripture like an anvil?*

In some places we can still find an anvil—a heavy piece of iron, perhaps 45 kilos (100 pounds), on which a metal worker hammers to shape pieces of hot metal. *As an anvil outlasts hammers, the Bible lasts longer than its enemies.*

A preacher stood before a hostile crowd. They yelled so loudly that no one could hear his voice. So he stopped talking, and bent down. It looked as if he were whispering to someone near the platform. The people became curious, and began trying to hear the preacher. Looking at the crowd the preacher said: "Yell as loudly as you want. I do not need your ears. Through my writings, millions will hear my message." This great truth quieted the crowd, and for the rest of his message, no one in the crowd spoke a word. Likewise, Paul had many enemies in Thessalonica. Through persecution, they tried to silence his voice. But for 20 centuries, millions have heard the message of Paul's *letters to the church.* [5] As an anvil lasts longer than the hammers that pound it, the Word of God endures beyond the attacks of its critics.

C. Eschatology: the theme of 1 and 2 Thessalonians

Q 12 ↗ *Which theme appears often throughout 1 and 2 Thessalonians?*

As the outline shows, Paul covers several topics in the Thessalonian letters (Figure 1.6). But the topic of eschatology, the last things, occurs often in these two letters. Every chapter in 1 Thessalonians ends with a reference to the Lord's coming (See Figure 1.7). And 1 Thessalonians 4:13–5:11 is a lengthy teaching on the return of Christ. Likewise, 2 Thessalonians 1 and 2 contain passages about the Lord's return. In 2 Thessalonians, 18 of the 47 verses (38 percent) are about the end times. So we may say that the second coming of Christ is the theme of 1 and 2 Thessalonians, often called the Eschatological Epistles.

Q 13 ✎ *Complete Figure 1.7 by summarizing references to the Second Coming in 1 and 2 Thessalonians.*

Reference	Your Summaries of Verses on the Second Coming of Christ
1 Thess. 1:9-10	
1 Thess. 2:19-20	
1 Thess. 3:13	
1 Thess. 4:13-18	
1 Thess. 5:23-24	
2 Thess. 1:5-10	
2 Thess. 2:1-12	

Figure 1.7 **Practice summarizing references to the second coming of Christ in 1 and 2 Thessalonians.**

The second coming of Jesus Christ is one of the greatest themes in Scripture. Near the end of His ministry on earth, Jesus told four parables to emphasize His return. All four of these parables stress the coming or return of an important person. And all four emphasize reward for those who are ready, and loss for those unprepared.

Q 14 ✎ *Complete Figure 1.8 as you analyze four parables related to the second coming of Christ.*

Reference	Parable	Rewards for the Faithful	Loss/Judgment for the Unfaithful
Matt. 21:33-44			
Matt. 25:1-13			
Matt. 25:14-30			
Matt. 25:31-46			

Figure 1.8 **Practice analyzing parables on the second coming of Christ.**

- **The parable of the tenants** stresses the return of a wealthy landowner. He had leased his vineyard to tenants before he went away on a long journey. The renters enjoyed the privileges and profits the owner made possible. But over time, their perspective became twisted. At first they were grateful for the blessing the owner gave them. But their freedom and prosperity changed their hearts. They became greedy and rebelled against the one who gave them everything. In the end, the owner returned and destroyed those he had chosen to bless (Matt. 21:33-44). Jesus spoke this parable as a warning to Jewish leaders. But the lesson of the parable applies to all of us. A day is coming when the Lord will return to reward or punish each person.

- **The parable of the ten virgins** emphasizes the coming Christ, the Bridegroom. Five foolish virgins did not plan ahead. They were not ready when the Bridegroom came. In contrast, five wise virgins were prepared. They entered into the eternal joys of the feast. Jesus summarized the lesson in one sentence: *"Therefore keep watch, because you do not know the day or the hour"* (Matt. 25:13). When the Lord returns, some will rejoice, and others will mourn forever.

- **The parable of the talents** underlines the same truth a third time. It is certain that Jesus will return to earth. He will reward those servants who were faithful and obedient to Him. But He will punish those who lived in disobedience, and throw them into darkness—condemned to weeping and grinding of teeth (Matt. 25:14-30).

- **The parable of the sheep and goats** is the fourth parable on the Lord's return. Jesus told four parables *to assure us* that He is coming back. He will welcome those who served Him into eternal joys. And He will send the disobedient into the eternal fires of hell (Matt. 25:31-46).

Q 15 *How does every chapter in 1 Thessalonians end?*

Q 16 *What percentage of 2 Thessalonians is on eschatology?*

Like Jesus, Paul emphasizes that our Lord will surely return. Every chapter in 1 Thessalonians ends with a reference to the return of Christ. And about 40 percent of 2 Thessalonians is on *eschatology*—the end times. When Christ returns in blazing fire, He will punish those who do not know and obey Him (2 Thess. 1:8), and He will reward His holy people who honored Him with faith and obedience (1 Thess. 4:1-8; 2 Thess. 1:10). As you study 1 and 2 Thessalonians, notice how much of these letters emphasize the coming of Christ to judge the disobedient, and reward the holy and faithful.

Lesson 2

Live Ready: Be an Encourager as You Wait for the Lord (1 Thess. 1:1-10)

Goal A: *Summarize the challenges that believers in Thessalonica faced.*
Goal B: *Identify and apply 3 ways Paul encouraged Thessalonian believers.*
Goal C: *Explain what Paul means by 'the gospel.'*

Figure 1.9   Thessalonica was a major city on the Egnatian Way—a famous stone road that connected Rome to the eastern parts of the Roman Empire. Life for believers in Thessalonica was as hard as the stones in the Egnatian Way.

Q 17 *In what sense was life for Thessalonian believers as hard as the stones of the Egnatian Way?*

A. The Challenge: Believers face many trials in life.

Q 18 *What was life like for Paul in almost every city where he preached? (Complete Figure 1.10.)*

Q 19 *In what ways did believers at Thessalonica imitate Paul (1 Thess. 1:6)?*

Acts	City	Your Summaries of the Response Paul Received for Preaching the Gospel
14:1-7	Iconium	
14:8-20	Lystra	
16:16-24	Philippi	
17:10	Thessalonica	
17:13-14	Berea	

Figure 1.10   Practice summarizing the persecution Paul faced as he told people about God's love through Christ.

Explanation. Following Jesus in Thessalonica was like climbing up a steep, rocky road. From the beginning, believers at Thessalonica accepted Christ at the cost of severe suffering (1 Thess. 1:6). They became imitators of Paul, who suffered for Christ everywhere he went. At Iconium he escaped at night, when there was a plot to stone him. At Lystra, he did not have time to escape, and they stoned him and left him for dead. Paul was beaten and jailed in Philippi, just *before* he came to Thessalonica (1 Thess. 2:2). Soon after Paul arrived in Thessalonica, the brothers there sent Paul away at night, after a riot threatened his safety (Acts 17:10). And at Berea, once again, Paul fled by night toward Athens (Acts 17:13-14). For Paul, and those who received his gospel, persecution was certain. So in Thessalonica, the apostle Paul warned believers that we are *destined* for trials (1 Thess. 3:3). The path of following Jesus is paved with persecution (1 Thess. 3:1-4).

Q 20 *Which of the 4 types of persecution do believers face where you live? Illustrate.*

All people on earth face trials. In addition to normal trials of life, we may identify four types of trials that followers of Jesus face:

- Physical persecution, such as beatings and prison (Matt. 25:36-40; Acts 16:16-24; 1 Thess. 2:2).

- Social/emotional/mental insults (1 Thess. 2:2); rejected, despised, ridiculed; excluded (family rejection, Matt. 10:34-36).

- Spiritual warfare (1 Thess. 2:18); Satan hindered us.

- Financial loss. At Thessalonica, because Jason and others welcomed Paul, they had to post bond, giving money to the court. It is likely that this money was not returned to them after Paul left that night (Acts 17:9). In the early church, and in many parts of the world today, choosing Jesus leads to losing money and property, and even life at times (Acts 8:1; Heb. 10:32-34; James 5:1-6).

(We will study more on the theme of trials in Lesson 4, point A.)

Missionary Adoniram Judson was a missionary to Burma. He suffered much in a filthy prison, where his hands were scarred from the beatings. Afterward, Judson appeared before the king of Burma and asked permission to go preach in a certain city. The king replied, "I am willing for a dozen preachers to go, but not you—not with those hands! My people are wise enough to ignore your preaching. But those scarred hands will have great influence on them." Persecution adds its testimony as believers suffer for the gospel. When believers are willing to suffer for their faith, this emphasizes that the message is true.[6]

Q 21 *Does following Jesus always lead to peace and prosperity? Explain.*

Definitely not... but →we can have peace and joy in the Lord through our trials and suffering

B. Partial Solution: Let us encourage believers with the evidence of salvation we see in them (1 Thess. 1:2-3; 3:9).[7]

Paul encouraged believers in Thessalonica with the progress he saw. The apostle wrote:

[2]*We always thank God for all of you, mentioning you in our prayers.* [3]*We continually remember before our God and Father your work produced by faith, your labor prompted by love, and your endurance inspired by hope in our Lord Jesus Christ* (1 Thess. 1:2-3).

Dr. George Wood calls his sermon on this chapter: "Please Pass the Praise!"[8] Life can be difficult. At times, we all grow weary from our trials. Sincere praise for our progress encourages us. We all have a need to be appreciated. So when someone expresses honest praise about our progress, we feel encouraged—because one of our inner needs has been met. As a thirsty person feels better after a drink, those persevering through trials feel better after a word of appreciation. A word of encouragement helps us lift up our heads and tired hands that hang down. Sincere praise refuels us. It bring out the best in all of us.

Q 22 *How does sincere praise encourage people?*

Figure 1.11 Missionary David Grams showed appreciation to all—to those over nations and those over kitchens.

For 50 years of ministry, Missionary David Grams practiced showing appreciation. As a teacher across 20 nations in Latin America, Missionary Grams taught people at every level of authority. He talked with those over nations and those over kitchens. Grams was a master at paying his dues in society. Wherever he went, he left a trail of encouragement. Those who served in the kitchen still remember him, because after each seminar, he had his picture taken with them, and then sent them their photo with a thank you note on the back of it. A *small gift* of appreciation to a living person, means 100 times more to him than a *truck full of gifts* at the grave. Appreciation is always appreciated. Sabio says: "Be an encourager. Share *sincere* appreciation with people, and you will strengthen them."

Why do we show appreciation to people? Show appreciation because it is one of our greatest needs. As humans, we all have many needs. Physically, we need air to breath, bread to eat and water to drink. Each day we need several hours of rest for our

Q 23 *How long do you remember the good things someone says about you? Explain.*

bodies. Likewise, we have emotional and spiritual needs. God has created every person with the need to feel appreciated and worthwhile. Life can be tough, and people can be cruel. A word of appreciation brightens the heart and lifts the head. Appreciation is free, but worth a fortune. As you take the time to show appreciation, you will encourage people, and lift their spirits. How long do you remember the appreciation others have shown you? For some, receiving appreciation is so rare, that they may remember it for a month—or even a lifetime. Also, people will love and appreciate you for noticing their hard work, sacrifices, perseverance and faithfulness. Criticism discourages, but gratitude inspires. Learn to notice the hard work and progress other are making. And when you notice, open your mouth and tell people what you have seen. Otherwise, they may think that neither you nor anyone else even notices or cares.

Q 24 ↖ *What is the difference between flattery and honest appreciation? Illustrate.*

Do not confuse honest appreciation with flattery. What is the difference? Flattery is shallow, selfish, and insincere. Those who flatter have wrong motives—to manipulate or deceive others. Scripture warns, *"Whoever flatters his neighbor is spreading a net for his feet"* (Prov. 29:5). Most people can discern flattery. But unlike flattery, showing sincere appreciation is honest, comes from a pure heart, and is for a good purpose. As we noted above, the Bible teaches us to show honor and appreciation because it is a debt we owe people for their sacrifices, hard work, and faithfulness. Speaking words of appreciation is a way to edify and encourage one another, which Scripture exhorts us to do (Rom. 14:19; 1 Cor. 14:26; Heb. 3:13). Avoid flattery, but be eager to express honest appreciation. Practice speaking a word of appreciation to every person you meet—and others will walk away standing a little taller.

Show appreciation in a way that speaks to the receiver. If a person's love language is kind words, then show appreciation through kind words. Show appreciation by sharing a meal, giving some time, recognizing a person's title, or giving a gift. (In Japan, the wrapping is as important as the gift.). And if a person's greatest need is financial, and you want to show appreciation, give an offering.

Application.   Pastors should encourage their people. Parents should encourage family members. Teachers and mentors should practice encouraging those under them. Friends and siblings should encourage each other. Christians should encourage unbelievers, as Paul encouraged those in a storm with him (Acts 27). All of us believers should watch and pray for ways to encourage others.

"Good job!"

Figure 1.12   Encourage each other.

Paul encouraged the Thessalonian believers by calling attention to evidence of salvation he saw in them. He says that he always thanks God for them. But notice that Paul is not praying when he writes to the Thessalonians. Rather, he is telling the Thessalonians some reasons why he thanks God for them. In this manner, Paul lets the Thessalonian believers *overhear* the good things he tells God about them. This is a subtle, indirect way of praising them. Paul compliments these young believers for three types of salvation—evidence in their lives.

1. Paul encouraged believers by their spiritual motivation (1 Thess. 1:2-3).

Q 25 ↖ *As Paul looked for ways to encourage the Thessalonians, how did he use their motivation?*

Paul mentions three motivators in the Thessalonians: faith, hope, and love.[9]

²*We always thank God for all of you, mentioning you in our prayers.* ³*We continually remember before our God and Father your work produced by **faith**, your labor prompted by **love**, and your endurance inspired by **hope** in our Lord Jesus Christ* (1 Thess. 1:2-3).

We can learn a lot about people by identifying the reasons why they work. Some people only do their best if they think someone is watching—*if* their work is being inspected. We call these workers "eye pleasers." Others work mostly for money, greed, or selfish reasons. Still others work because of duty, recognition, or some form of fear.

In contrast, believers at Thessalonica did good works, *motivated* by faith and love. Whatever good things they did were done *"in the name of the Lord Jesus"* (Col. 3:17). They became known for serving others through good works (1 Thess. 1:9).

Jesus used 18 verses to teach that if we pray, fast, or give alms so people will notice, then we already have our brief reward—the mere praise of people. But if we pray, fast, and give to please God, we have a permanent reward in heaven for our good deeds (Matt. 6:1-18).

Q 26 *Who can you encourage by complimenting them for reasons why they do good deeds?*

As people work for different reasons, they also endure trials in various ways. Some endure trials by trusting in their own abilities, education, strength, and resources. Others endure trials by trusting in their employer, or government. Scripture says those who trust in man hope in a spider's web (Job 8:14). But the endurance of trials by the Thessalonians grew from the seed of hope *"in our Lord Jesus Christ."* Their trust in God motivated them to endure trials. The arm of flesh will fail us. The only hope that will not disappoint us is hope in our Lord.

Q 27 *Why was Paul able to praise the Thessalonians for their hope? How did this praise reinforce their hope?*

Paul praised the Thessalonians for work prompted by faith and love for God; and endurance inspired by hope in our Lord Jesus Christ (1 Thess. 1:2-3). Let us be sure that our work grows from the right roots—faith, love, and hope! As we fix our eyes on Jesus, we are preparing for eternity.

> [29] *He gives strength to the weary and increases the power of the weak.* [30] *Even youths grow tired and weary, and young men stumble and fall;* [31] *but **those who hope in the LORD** will renew their strength. They will soar on wings like eagles; they will run and not grow weary, they will walk and not be faint* (Isa. 40:29-31).

2. Paul encouraged believers by their conversion (1 Thess. 1:4-5a).

> [4] *For we know, brothers loved by God, that he has chosen you,* [5] *because our gospel came to you not simply with words, but also with power, with the Holy Spirit and with deep conviction. You know how we lived among you for your sake* (1 Thess. 1:4-5a).

Q 28 *How did Paul know that believers at Thessalonica were true followers of Jesus?*

The gospel came with *power* and *deep conviction* of the Holy Spirit—working in the speaker and the listeners (1 Thess. 1:4-5a; Rom. 1:16). There was evidence of change in their lives. They did not just pray and go on living as usual. No! The new believers *"turned to God from idols to serve the living and true God"* (1 Thess. 1:9)

Like a smile, praise encourages us. Someone has said that a smile is a hug from a distance. Praise is like a verbal hug or pat on the back. It is a way to tell someone you love and appreciate them. Paul made it a habit to praise believers often. **We never tire of hearing that someone has noticed good things about us.** When the hills of life are the steepest, we can encourage ourselves with the good things people have said about us. Recalling encouraging words is like getting a hug when you need it most.

One great leader endured much criticism. As with all leaders, some appreciated him, but many did not. One grandmother sent him a letter of encouragement. She thanked him for doing what was right, and for living to serve and help others. This one letter of gratitude was such a strength, that the leader carried it with him, in the pocket of his coat. In his most discouraging hours, he often read the letter and was uplifted. He only received the letter once, but he read it more than a hundred times. At the death of President Abraham Lincoln, someone found the letter in his pocket.

Application. Pay attention to the progress and faithfulness of those you meet. Speak words of appreciation, and do small deeds to show that you appreciate others. The strength others receive from your kindness will be 100 times what it costs you. Words and deeds of appreciation are like seeds that multiply into a harvest of inspiration for others.

3. Paul encouraged believers with their continuing transformation.

You became imitators of us and of the Lord; in spite of severe suffering, you welcomed the message with the joy given by the Holy Spirit (1 Thess. 1:6).

The new believers changed their behavior—they became disciples! They began *imitating* Paul and the Lord (1 Thess. 1:6). Paul praised them for the evidence he saw in their emotions. The new believers welcomed the gospel with *joy* from the Holy Spirit (1 Thess. 1:6). He praised the new disciples for their *reputation*. People all over the region were talking about the new faith of believers at Thessalonica (1 Thess. 1:7-9). And as we mentioned above, Paul praised them for serving others—while waiting for the Son from heaven (1 Thess. 1:3, 6, 9).

Application.   We should make it a habit to point out the progress we see in people. We should underline and call to attention the good things God is doing in believers. Never flatter people (1 Thess. 2:5). But look for genuine compliments to give people for godly qualities in their lives. Sincere praise inspires all of us. For every one word of "criticism" we should speak at least seven words of praise and thanks for the good fruit we see. When we praise people for the good they are and do, they become even better.

Whenever two believers meet, each should be asking himself, "How can I encourage you?" (1 Cor. 14:12).

In the seven letters to the churches, Jesus praised believers *before* He mentioned any areas they needed to improve (Rev. 2–3). A spoon full of sugar makes the medicine taste sweeter.

The gospel.   It is important to understand what Paul means by *the gospel*. Paul said his gospel came with *power* and deep conviction of the Holy Spirit (1 Thess. 1:5). As you study the five letters of Paul in this course, pay attention to the word *gospel*, and *synonyms of the gospel. In these five letters of Paul, the word *gospel* refers to the entire message and teachings of Paul. For Paul, the word *gospel* refers to all of the good news about Jesus, and our relationship with Him now and in the future. Paul's gospel *includes* Christ's incarnation, life, teachings, ministry, death, resurrection, ascension, second coming, and judgments. His gospel *includes* salvation from the *penalty* and *power* of sin. It *includes* a righteous relationship with God as family members, *and* in our daily living. Paul's gospel *includes* instructions on how to live holy lives as we wait for Jesus to return. His gospel *includes* teachings on how to live with each other and our neighbors. His gospel *includes* atonement for our sins, forgiveness, adoption into God's family, freedom in the Holy Spirit from sin's slavery. Paul's gospel *includes* justification, sanctification (holy living), and glorification. It *includes* the punishment of sinners at the final judgment and the reward of those who obey God by faith. We will study more on what Paul means by gospel when we come to Dr. Fee's helpful comments on 1 Timothy 1:10-11 in Lesson 11.

Q 29 ➚ *What words of praise did Paul give the Thessalonians for their actions and attitudes?*

Q 30 ✎ *How is genuine praise different from flattery? Give an example.*

Q 31 ➚ *What were the 3 reasons for which Paul praised believers at Thessalonica?*

Q 32 ✎ *Encourage someone this week by showing appreciation. Share the result in class.*

Q 33 ➚ *In Paul's writings, to what does the word 'gospel' refer?*

Q 34 ✎ *What are at least 10 things that Paul's gospel includes?*

Q 35 ✎ *Complete Figure 1.13 by summarizing references to the gospel in 1 and 2 Thessalonians.*

Reference	Verses About Paul's Gospel
1 Thess. 1:5	
1 Thess. 2:2	
1 Thess. 2:4	
1 Thess. 2:8	
1 Thess. 2:9	
1 Thess. 2:13	
1 Thess. 3:2	
1 Thess. 3:6	
2 Thess. 1:8	
2 Thess. 2:14	

Figure 1.13   References to the gospel in 1 and 2 Thessalonians

Live Ready: Be a Fruitful Servant as You Wait for the Lord—Part 1
Lesson 3 (1 Thess. 2:1-16)

Goal A: *Explain and illustrate how fruitful ministry depends on daring commitment (1 Thess. 2:1-16).*
Goal B: *Analyze and illustrate the role of loving commitment in fruitful ministry (1 Thess. 2:1-16).*
Goal C: *Examine the relationship of fruitful ministry to the hearers' response (1 Thess. 2:1-16). Illustrate this.*

Bible teachers refer to 1 and 2 Thessalonians as *the Eschatological Epistles.* Eschatology is the biblical study of the last things. Recall that the Greek word *eschatos* means "last." Living ready for the second coming of Christ in the last days is a major theme of the Thessalonian letters. Some young believers in Thessalonica were idle. So Paul emphasizes that we need to do more than just look up at the clouds as we wait for Jesus to come back. God wants us to be active, about the Master's business, while we await His return.

Q 36 *What is eschatology?*

Paul states that his time in Thessalonica was *"not a failure"* (1 Thess. 2:1). He was successful and fruitful. The apostle mentions **three commitments related to being a fruitful servant of Christ**.

Q 37 *What problem at Thessalonica was related to eschatology? Explain.*

A. Fruitfulness depends on a *daring commitment* to share the *pure gospel* by *God's help* (1 Thess. 2:1-6a).

*¹ You know, brothers, that our visit to you was not a failure. ² We had previously suffered and been insulted in Philippi, as you know, but with the help of our God we **dared** to tell you his gospel in spite of strong opposition. ³ For the appeal we make does not spring from error or impure motives, nor are we trying to trick you. ⁴ On the contrary, we speak as men approved by God to be entrusted with the gospel. We are not trying to please men but God, who tests our hearts. ⁵ You know we never used flattery, nor did we put on a mask to cover up greed—God is our witness. ⁶ We were not looking for praise from men, not from you or anyone else* (1 Thess. 2:1-6a).

Q 38 *Why did Paul's preaching in Thessalonica require daring and boldness?*

Paul dared to share the gospel in Thessalonica after he had been beaten for sharing it in Philippi. Let us follow this bold commitment to testify of Christ, even as we face certain persecution.

Let us also dare to share the gospel to the worst sinners. When Paul came to Thessalonica, he did not greet saints—he faced pagans. Like all big cities of Paul's day, Thessalonica was a sewer for every kind of evil. Paul reminds his readers, *"you turned to God from idols"* (1 Thess. 1:9). Idolatry is just one of the sins of darkness. Wherever there are slaves of sin, we find every form of sin. Yet as a doctor lives to treat the sick, Paul rejoiced to find slaves of sin.

Q 39 *In Thessalonica, what are some things that might have discouraged Paul from preaching the gospel?*

Paul dared to preach the gospel with confidence to the vilest sinners. His gospel was not just for those who had tasted sin. He looked for those who enjoyed dining at the table of sin year after year. Paul was fearless as he preached the gospel. He lived with full assurance that his gospel could change the dirtiest sinner into the purest saint. Paul believed in the power of redeeming grace. His letters contain lists of depraved sinners, headed for hell. On his list of sinners to the Corinthians, Paul includes the sexually immoral, idolaters, adulterers, prostitutes, homosexuals, thieves, the greedy, drunkards, slanderers, and swindlers. Then he reminds the believers, *"And that is what some of **you were**, but you were washed"* (1 Cor. 6:11)! And for Paul, *washed* includes getting rid of filthy stains as well as filthy habits and desires. Jesus washes away the guilt and the slavery. He cleanses from the penalty and the power of sin. He delivers us from the guilt and the grip of sin. Our Lord frees the sinner from the slavery of sin. Jesus sets the captive free to live a new life of holiness and righteousness. This is a major part of Paul's

Q 40 *In Corinth, from what types of sins did Jesus save people?*

gospel! It has the power to transform the worst sinner. Paul's gospel offers pardon to the most guilty. He offers white clothes to the dirtiest offender. This is the gospel Paul dared to share.

Q 41 *What is remarkable about the salvation of Manasseh, Paul, and John Newton?*

Jesus came to save sinners. Some religious leaders criticized Him because He ate with the most evil people of society—tax collectors and prostitutes. Jesus answered: *"It is not the healthy who **need a doctor**, but the sick. I have not come to call the righteous, but sinners"* (Mark 2:17). Our Lord called Matthew, a national traitor, to be an apostle. He cast seven demons out of Mary Magdalene, and freed her from the chains of sin. John Newton was one of the vilest sinners on earth. He filled his pockets with the money of slaves he bought in Africa, and sold in the Americas. Then Newton met the Savior, who forgave his sins, and guided him to walk on a righteous path. Filled with love and new life. Newton wrote the words of a famous hymn, "Amazing grace, how sweet the sound, that saved a wretch like me. I once was lost, but now I'm found; was blind but now I see." The list of those whom God has forgiven and saved include some of the worst sinners who ever lived, including King Manasseh, who filled Jerusalem with innocent blood and sacrificed his own son to an idol. History records that Manasseh put the prophet Isaiah between two planks, and then sawed him in half (2 Chron. 33:1-20). But when the evil king repented, God forgave him. Isaiah's greatest surprise in heaven may be seeing Manasseh there! So let us dare to preach the gospel to the worst of sinners. And let us not give up on evil people. Remember, the apostle Paul was once a blasphemer, a persecutor of believers, a violent man, and the worst of sinners (1 Tim. 1:12-15). Think of the worst sinner you know and remind yourself that the grace of God can save and transform even this person. Share the gospel with the least sinners you can find, and the greatest.

Q 42 *From what kinds of sins has Jesus saved you or people you know?*

When Satan accused Joshua the high priest of sin, the Lord told an angel to take off Joshua's dirty clothes and put rich clean ones on him (Zech. 3:1-10). Paul often instructs his converts to change clothes—to put off the old clothes that sinful flesh prefers and to put on the new clothes that their spiritual nature prefers.

Q 43 *Do you dare to share the gospel with all who need it? Explain.*

Application.   Do we dare to share the full gospel to the worst sinners of society? Do we speak boldly with confidence that Jesus can save the porn king and the queen of harlots? Or do we preach a weak gospel? Do we roar to tiny sinners, but whisper to the giants? Do we whimper and tremble with doubt when we proclaim the good news to the bad boys? Or is our speech bold, with assurance that Jesus Christ is the Savior of *all* who repent and put their trust in Him? There is great power and persuasion in the gospel when we declare it with authority and certainty! Faith is contagious. If we fully believe what we preach, our boldness helps others dare to believe.[10]

If a person walks around with money, but never uses it, that money is just a piece of paper in his pocket. It is valuable paper, but it does not help until a person uses it. Likewise, until we share the gospel with others, it will not help them.[11]

Figure 1.14
Until we share money or the gospel, neither will help anyone.

B. Fruitfulness depends on *a loving commitment to share the gospel and our lives as well* (1 Thess. 2:6b-12).

*6b As apostles of Christ we could have been a burden to you, 7but we were gentle among you, **like a mother** caring for her little children. 8We loved you so much that we were delighted to share with you not only the gospel of God but our lives as well, because you had become so dear to us. 9Surely you remember, brothers, our toil and hardship; we worked night and day in order not to be a burden to anyone while we preached the gospel of God to you. 10You are witnesses, and so is God,*

Q 44 *How was Paul like a mother to those he helped be born spiritually?*

of how holy, righteous and blameless we were among you who believed. [11]*For you know that we dealt with each of you **as a father** deals with his own children,* [12]*encouraging, comforting and urging you to live lives worthy of God, who calls you into his kingdom and glory* (1 Thess. 2:6b-12).

Paul's commitment did not end with proclamation. He did not preach the gospel, and then walk away from those who received it. His journeys were not littered with dead babies he helped to birth, and then abandoned. He did not believe in evangelism without discipleship. When Paul helped someone be born again, he lived like the parent of a new child. The apostle Paul was responsible to his spiritual children.

As a mother watches over her infant children day and night, Paul cared for the young believers at Thessalonica. God puts love in the hearts of mothers for their beloved children. Likewise, God gives spiritual parents this type of love for their new converts.

As a father nurtures his children, Paul cherished baby believers at Thessalonica. He set a holy, righteous example for them. He left footprints on the road to heaven. And he encouraged and urged them to live godly lives (1 Thess. 2:10-12).

C. Fruitfulness depends on a *personal commitment* by the hearers—to welcome and obey the gospel (1 Thess. 1:6; 2:13-17; 3:10).

[13]*And we also thank God continually because, when you received the word of God, which you heard from us, **you accepted it** not as the word of men, but as it actually is, the word of God, which is at work in you who believe.* [14]*For you, brothers, became imitators of God's churches in Judea, which are in Christ Jesus: You suffered from your own countrymen the same things those churches suffered from the Jews,* [15]*who killed the Lord Jesus and the prophets and also drove us out. They displease God and are hostile to all men* [16]*in their effort to keep us from speaking to the Gentiles so that they may be saved. In this way they always heap up their sins to the limit. The wrath of God has come upon them at last* (1 Thess. 2:13-16).

This paragraph shifts from *we* to *you,* as Paul continues to encourage young believers at Thessalonica (1 Thess. 2:13). Paul turns from how *he* behaved to how *the Thessalonians* behaved. No matter how holy and faithful God's speaker is, the harvest depends on the response of the listeners. God's Word is always good seed that we sow. But the fate of the seed depends on the soil. In the parable of the sower, there was only one sower, and only one type of seed (Matt. 13). Yet the results were varied. Likewise, when godly believers share the gospel, the results depend on the responses of the listeners.

God gives each person the gift of choice. Each of us has the right to choose his or her own destiny. Some respond like Cain, and others are like Abel. Great prophets like Jeremiah wept, because their listeners would not repent and obey the message from God. Many in Thessalonica rejected Paul's gospel, and persecuted those who received it. In contrast, the [11] *"... Bereans were of more noble character than the Thessalonians, for they received the message with great eagerness and examined the Scriptures every day to see if what Paul said was true.* [12]*Many of the Jews believed as did also a number of prominent Greek women and many Greek men"* (Acts 17:11-12).

Spiritual success depends on the free will of the listeners. Even the apostle Paul was not very successful at Athens. People mocked him, and ridiculed his message. And Jesus Christ could not do many miracles at Nazareth, because the citizens there refused to believe (Matt. 13:53-58).

God Himself succeeds at redeeming only those who cooperate! He scattered about two million Israelites in wilderness graves, *after* He freed them from Egypt (Heb. 3:16-17). Why? Because they *chose* to stop trusting Him.

Q 45 *How was Paul like a father to those he led to Christ?*

Q 46 *Is evangelism without discipleship biblical? Explain.*

Q 47 *How must you be like a mother or father to those you lead to Christ?*

Q 48 *Does the fate of the seed depend on the sower, the seed, or the soil? Explain.*

Q 49 *If the Bereans were more noble and open to the gospel than many at Thessalonica, why did Paul flee from Berea (Acts 17:10-14)?*

Q 50 *Has your ministry been fruitful? Why or why not?*

Q 51 ➤ *What great concern did Paul have for young believers at Thessalonica?*

Q 52 ➤ *How is salvation like an election?*

Paul knew that the fate of the young Thessalonian believers depended on their choices to accept the Word of God and continue following Jesus (1 Thess. 2:13-16). He was thankful for their response. When he left suddenly at night, he feared that his ministry in Thessalonica might be useless (1 Thess. 3:5). But he was delighted with the good report that Timothy brought. The Thessalonians were standing firm in the faith as they waited for Christ to return (1 Thess. 2:8).

Fathers and mothers can live godly examples and lead their children on the path to heaven. But each child must decide whether to accept or reject Jesus as Savior and Lord. Salvation is like an election that requires two out of three votes. God votes for all to be saved. He is not willing for any to perish. The Heavenly Father does not want one child, one youth, or one adult to be lost (1 Tim. 2:4; Matt. 18:14; 2 Pet. 3:9). God sent His Son to pay the pardon for every sinner (1 Tim. 4:10). In contrast, the devil votes against the salvation of each person. From Eden in Genesis to the rebellions of Revelation, the desire of Satan is to deceive and destroy. God votes for all to be saved, and the devil votes for all to be lost. So the election to salvation favors all who vote for themselves. We are chosen for salvation when we answer God's call, like someone answering a phone call (1 Thess. 1:4). A person may choose to call anyone. But a relationship is only possible when someone answers a call. Many are called, but few are chosen, because they refuse to answer the call (Matt. 22:14). Whosoever will may come and drink of the water of life freely (Rev. 22:17). God votes for all, and calls to all. But He only chooses to save those who choose to answer and obey His call to salvation.

Application.   Salvation has past, present, and future aspects. We were saved from past sins. We are being saved from present sins and temptations. We will be fully saved when Jesus returns. All aspects of salvation are by the grace of God. Yet from the beginning of the race to the end, we must use our free will to trust, obey, and choose God.

A teacher asked students to give examples of people in the Bible who made a bad choice. Here were some examples from the students.

- Adam and Eve made a bad choice with Satan, trading paradise for a bite of forbidden fruit.
- Esau made a bad choice when he sold his birthright for a bowl of stew.
- Samson made a bad choice when he traded his eyes for Delilah.
- Judas made a bad choice when he sold his Lord and his soul for 30 pieces of silver.
- Ananias and Sapphira made a bad choice when they traded their salvation and lives for the applause of people.
- It is a bad choice whenever anyone trades his soul, even if he gains the whole world.
- It is bad to choose the mark of the Antichrist, and thus reject heaven.

Let us be careful with our freedom. God allows us to choose anything we desire. But some bad choices last forever. Let us not miss heaven for the world.

Q 53 ➤ *What are some examples of good and bad choices made by people in the Bible?*

Q 54 ➤ *Complete Figure 1.15 by summarizing references to free will in the process of salvation.*

Reference	Your Summary on Passages Emphasizing Our Free Will in the Process of Salvation
1 Thess. 4:1-8	
1 Thess. 5:1-10	
2 Thess. 2:13-15	
2 Thess. 3:6, 14	
1 Cor. 10:1-13	
Heb. 3:7-11	
Heb. 10:26-27	
Heb. 10:35-39	
2 Pet. 1:3-11	

Figure 1.15   References to free will in relation to salvation

Lesson 4 — Live Ready: Be a Fruitful Servant as You Wait for the Lord—Part 2 (1 Thess. 2:17–3:13)

Goal A: *Summarize and illustrate the importance of endurance for fruitful servants.*
Goal B: *Explain and illustrate that fruitful service depends on God's love flowing through us.*

In the last lesson we emphasized that fruitfulness depends on a daring commitment to share the gospel, a loving commitment to share life with others, and a personal commitment from the hearers to welcome and obey the gospel. In this lesson we look at two more keys to fruitfulness.

D. Fruitfulness depends on *persevering through trials* (1 Thess. 1:6; 3:3-7, 11).

*¹You became imitators of us and of the Lord; in spite of **severe suffering**, you welcomed the message with the joy given by the Holy Spirit* (1 Thess. 1:6).

*¹So when we could stand it no longer, we thought it best to be left by ourselves in Athens. ²We sent Timothy, who is our brother and God's fellow worker in spreading the gospel of Christ, to strengthen and encourage you in your faith, ³**so that no one would be unsettled by these trials**. You know quite well that we were **destined for them**. ⁴In fact, when we were with you, **we kept telling you that we would be persecuted. And it turned out that way, as you well know.** ⁵For this reason, when I could stand it no longer, I sent to find out about your faith. I was afraid that in some way the tempter might have tempted you and our efforts might have been useless ... ¹¹Now may our God and Father himself and our Lord Jesus clear the way for us to come to you* (1 Thess. 3:1-5, 11).

Q 55 *In the parable of the sower, those who began to follow Christ, but fell away because of trouble and persecution, were like which kind of seed (Matt. 13:20-21)?*

Q 56 *What fear did Paul have about believers in Thessalonica (1 Thess. 1:5)?*

Trials for believers are as certain as thorns, thieves, moths, and rust. Everyone has trials. And all followers of Christ face persecution for their faith. The Holy Spirit testified to Paul that bonds, chains, and afflictions waited for him in every city (Acts 20:23). Paul was beaten at Philippi *before* he went to Thessalonica. He was chased from Berea *after* he left Thessalonica. And *during* the few weeks he was in Thessalonica, Paul warned the young believers that trials are a normal part of following Jesus. Paul wrote that we are destined for trials (1 Thess. 3:3). *"In fact, everyone who wants to live a godly life in Christ Jesus will be persecuted"* (2 Tim. 3:12).

Q 57 *Can we avoid trials if we have strong faith? Explain.*

Time after time, Jesus warned His followers that persecution was certain (John 15:18-21).

¹⁸"If the world hates you, keep in mind that it hated me first. ¹⁹If you belonged to the world, it would love you as its own. As it is, you do not belong to the world, but I have chosen you out of the world. That is why the world hates you. ²⁰Remember the words I spoke to you: 'No servant is greater than his master.' If they persecuted me, they will persecute you also. If they obeyed my teaching, they will obey yours also. ²¹They will treat you this way because of my name, for they do not know the One who sent me" (John 15:18-21).

Q 58 *What did Jesus promise about persecution?*

God uses trials for many reasons.

- Suffering produces patience and Christian maturity (James 1:2-4).
- Suffering is like a fire that purifies (1 Pet. 1:6-7).
- Suffering causes us to lose our desire for sin (1 Pet. 4:1-2).
- Suffering can discipline and perfect us (1 Cor. 11:30-32; Heb. 12:3-11).
- Suffering may prevent us from sinning and help us be holy (2 Cor. 12:7).
- Suffering gives an opportunity for a powerful testimony for Christ (Acts 9:15-16).
- Suffering enables us to fellowship with and follow the footsteps of Jesus (Col. 1:24).

Q 59 *What warning did Jesus give in Matthew 10:17-22? Summarize it.*

Q 60 *What are some purposes of trials?*

Q 61 ⬉ *What are 2 keys to remaining steadfast through trials?*

But Paul's main point is not why God allows trials. Rather, Paul's point is that we believers must expect persecution and be ready for it. Otherwise, trials may cause us to be *unsettled,* confused, and blown away (1 Thess. 3:3). Some fall away from Christ when trials and persecution come (Matt. 13:21). In contrast, let us put down roots deep into the love of God, and stand firm in the Holy Spirit when trials come.

Beware of any gospel or teacher that says believers are exempt from trials and persecution on earth. Nothing could be further from the truth! People who hear a hurricane is coming prepare for it, so they do not get blown away. Likewise, let us make up our minds to follow Jesus, whatever the cost!

Q 62 ⬉ *What types of persecution do believers face where you live?*

More than 43 million Christians have been killed for their faith since the crucifixion of Jesus. It is estimated that more Christians have been martyred in the past century than in all the past 1900 years combined. There are millions of recorded cases of martyrdom in this century alone. More than 200 million Christians in over 60 nations face persecution each day, and 60 percent of these are children. Each year over 160,000 followers of Jesus are martyred. Christians today are the most persecuted group in the world.[12] Hundreds of thousands of people today are being killed, beaten, sold as slaves, imprisoned, tortured, threatened, discriminated against, and arrested—only because they follow Jesus Christ.

E. Fruitfulness depends on *God's love* flowing through us (1 Thess. 2:17–3:13).

As technology, education, and progress increase, it is easy to forget the more fundamental keys to fruitful ministry. In Lessons 3 and 4 we have been reviewing the foundation blocks of all spiritual ministry. The final point of this lesson focuses on the necessity of love. As a wise man said, "People do not care how much you know, until they know how much you care." Without love, all of the gifts in the world are meaningless (1 Cor. 13).

Q 63 ↗ *Why does fruitful ministry depend more on love than human ability?*

[17] *But, brothers, when we were torn away from you for a short time (in person, not in thought), out of our intense longing we made every effort to see you.* [18] *For we wanted to come to you—certainly I, Paul, did, again and again—but Satan stopped us.* [19] *For what is our hope, our joy, or the crown in which we will glory in the presence of our Lord Jesus when he comes? Is it not you?* [20] *Indeed, you are our glory and joy* (1 Thess. 2:17-20).

[6] *Timothy has just now come to us from you and has brought good news about your faith and love. He has told us that you always have pleasant memories of us and that you long to see us, just as we also long to see you.* [7] *Therefore, brothers, in all our distress and persecution we were encouraged about you because of your faith.* [8] *For now we really live, since you are standing firm in the Lord.* [9] *How can we thank God enough for you in return for all the joy we have in the presence of our God because of you?* [10] *Night and day we pray most earnestly that we may see you again and supply what is lacking in your faith.* [11] *Now may our God and Father himself and our Lord Jesus clear the way for us to come to you.* [12] *May the Lord make your love increase and overflow for each other and for everyone else, just as ours does for you.* [13] *May he strengthen your hearts so that you will be blameless and holy in the presence of our God and Father when our Lord Jesus comes with all his holy ones* (1 Thess. 3:6-13).

Q 64 ⬉ *What do you think Paul's critics said when persecution forced him to leave Thessalonica?*

Paul was in Thessalonica for only a few weeks. In the synagogue for three Sabbaths, he reasoned from the Scriptures that Jesus is the Christ. Then jealous Jews stirred up the whole city against Paul. So the brothers at Thessalonica sent Paul and Silas away at night (Acts 17:1-10). After Paul left, we can hear his enemies attacking his reputation: "If this missionary really cared for you, why did he abandon you? Surely Paul is a fraud!

He is more concerned about his own skin than he is about you. If he truly loved you, surely he would come back."[13]

So Paul was forced to defend himself. Note the tender feelings and strong emotions he felt for his young converts at Thessalonica. Paul emphasized his love, concern, and emotions for his spiritual children:

- I was like a mother (1 Thess. 2:2-7).
- I was like a father (1 Thess. 2:11).
- My heart was torn and desperate: When I left, I felt like a parent torn from a small child—[Greek: *orphaned*] (1 Thess. 2:17). *"Out of our intense longing—we made every effort to see you... again and again"* (2:17-18a).
- My heart was heavy with anxiety: *"When we could stand it no longer..."* (1 Thess. 3:1); *"Night and day we pray most earnestly that we may see you again and supply what is lacking in your faith"* (1 Thess. 3:10).
- My heart was bound to your welfare: *"For now we really live, since you are standing firm in the Lord"* (1 Thess. 3:8). You are *our hope, joy, and crown* when Jesus comes (1 Thess. 2:19).
- My heart was interceding for God's help (1 Thess. 3:9-13). Let us never take for granted the spiritual power we have through prayer. Even when we are separated from those we love, we can pray for them.

Q 65 *Why did Paul have to defend his absence from Thessalonica?*

Q 66 *What are some ways Paul showed his love for the Thessalonians?*

 My mother prayed 3 or 4 hours a day for me, after I went as a missionary to Africa. Her heart was filled with the love of God for her son. Likewise, the love Paul felt for his spiritual children was the love of God flowing through him.

Paul loved people everywhere. To the Romans he wrote: *"I speak the truth in Christ—I am not lying, my conscience confirms it in the Holy Spirit— [2] I have great sorrow and unceasing anguish in my heart. [3] For I could wish that I myself were cursed and cut off from Christ for the sake of my brothers, those of my own race— [4] the people of Israel"* (Rom. 9:1-4a).

Q 67 *How do you know if a pastor or teacher cares about you?*

The good shepherd leaves the 99 to seek the 1 lost sheep. He feels a special love and concern for each member of his flock. He is filled with joy when he finds his lost sheep. Likewise, when the love of God fills our hearts, we will seek to help those who are lost.

The wind and sun had a contest to make a man remove his coat. The wind used its violence and force, trying to get the coat off. It blew with all its might. But the man clung to the coat with all his strength. In contrast, the sun shined its warm rays on the man. And in time, the man removed his coat with a smile. Likewise, the gentle and warm love of Christ opens the hearts of people when force fails.

Q 68 *What kind of love and emotions do you communicate toward those you serve?*

If we try to open the bud of a flower, we will leave its petals in the dust. Only God can open a flower, with His love, gentleness, and timing. When our lives reflect the love of God, the hearts of people open to the Savior.

Q 69 *How do you show your love, emotions, and concern for those who receive your ministry?*

Lesson 5

Live Ready: Grow as You Wait for the Lord (1 Thess. 4:1-10)

Goal A: *Explain and illustrate 3 aspects of growing in holiness.*
Goal B: *Summarize how our cooperation with the Holy Spirit is God's plan for holy living.*
Goal C: *Contrast the love of a young believer and a mature believer.*
Goal D: *Identify and illustrate 2 reasons why Paul wants all believers to grow in personal responsibility.*

---

[1] *Finally, brothers, we instructed you **how to live in order to please God**, as in fact you are living. Now we ask you and urge you in the Lord Jesus to **do this more and more**. [2] For you know what instructions we gave you by the authority of the*

Lord Jesus. [3] It is God's will that you should be sanctified: that you should avoid sexual immorality; [4] that each of you should learn to control his own body in a way that is holy and honorable, [5] not in passionate lust like the heathen, who do not know God; [6] and that in this matter no one should wrong his brother or take advantage of him. The Lord will punish men for all such sins, as we have already told you and warned you. [7] For God did not call us to be impure, but to live a holy life. [8] Therefore, he who rejects this instruction does not reject man but God, who gives you his Holy Spirit. [9] Now about brotherly love we do not need to write to you, for you yourselves have been taught by God to love each other. [10] And in fact, you do love all the brothers throughout Macedonia. Yet we urge you, brothers, to **do so more and more**. *[11] Make it your ambition to lead a quiet life, to mind your own business and to work with your hands, just as we told you, [12] so that your daily life may win the respect of outsiders and so that you will not be dependent on anybody* (1 Thess. 4:1-12).

As we wait for our Lord Jesus Christ to return, God calls us to grow in three ways (A–C).

A. God calls us to grow in holiness.

Q 70 ➤ *What are 3 aspects or sides of holiness?*

Please read 1 Thess. 4:1-8 again. *It is God's will that you should be sanctified* [holy]: *that you should avoid sexual immorality* (1 Thess. 4:3).

God wants us to be holy, because He is holy (1 Pet. 1:16). Our Heavenly Father is holy in three ways, holy in his position, actions, and condition. Let us quickly review these three aspects of God's holiness. [14]

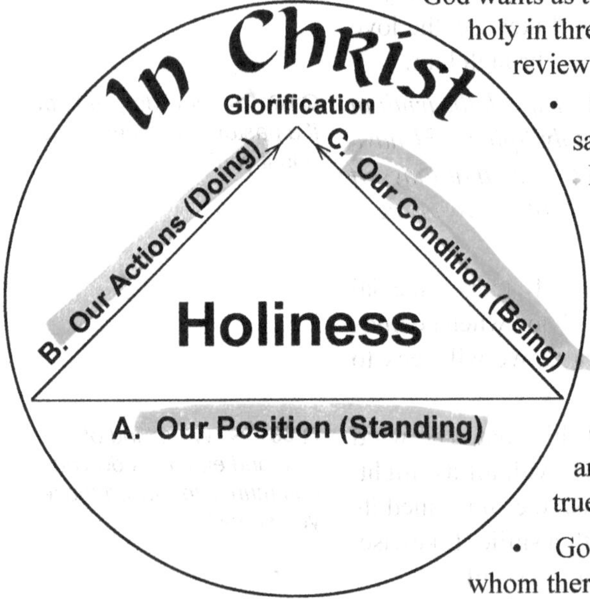

Figure 1.16 Three aspects of holiness in Christ

- God is holy in His **position**. *Holy* is the opposite of common. We say that God is holy because He is separate—high above all else. He is holy because there is none like Him. In His position, God is Holy—divine, supreme, exalted, glorious above all creation. God's holiness is His might that makes people tremble and nation's dread (Exod. 15:11-18; 1 Sam. 6:20; Ps. 68:35). [15] In His position above all, at the top, God alone is holy, for He alone is God (Rev. 15:4)! (English speakers, for an inspiring song on God's holiness, visit http://www.youtube.com/watch?v=9zl6Sf3Rt0s.)

- God is holy in His **actions**—holy in all He does. His decrees and actions are completely holy—altogether just, righteous, and true.

- God is holy in His **condition**—His essence and nature. He is light in whom there is no darkness. His character is 100 percent pure, unmixed with any trace of evil.

Throughout the New Testament, the many references to the Holy Spirit emphasize that God is holy.

Q 71 ➤ *Complete Figure 1.17, explaining 3 aspects of holiness in believers.*

Aspect of Holiness	Your Explanations	Illustrations
Position		
Actions		
Condition		

Figure 1.17 **Practice explaining and illustrating three aspects of holiness in believers.**

Q 72 ➤ *What warning does Paul give to those who do not practice holy living (1 Thess. 4:6-7)?*

Like God, His children are also holy in three ways: holy in position, actions, and condition. Paul urges believers *"to please God… more and more"* (1 Thess. 4:1). The **bottom of the holiness triangle** refers to holiness in **position**. Like the Thessalonians, we become holy at conversion, when we welcome the gospel and turn from our sins to serve God, as we wait for His Son from heaven (1 Thess. 1:6-10). Linked with holiness of position are words such as regeneration, adoption, and justification. This aspect of holiness is complete in Christ. There is a sense in which our holiness of position in Christ will never increase. And yet even our holiness of position will shine with more glory when we reach heaven, and receive our full inheritance.

When we see holiness in the Bible, it is important to understand which of the three aspects of holiness is in focus. God gives us holiness of position. Then He asks us to practice holiness in our actions. In 1 Thessalonians 4:1-8, Paul urges believers to grow in **holiness of action.** Note in these verses Paul is emphasizing the **left** side of the holiness triangle. He instructs believers to *practice holy living.* Paul says each believer must *"learn to control his own body, in a way that is holy and honorable,* [5]*not in passionate lust like the heathen who do not know God;* [6]*and that in this matter no one should wrong his brother or take advantage of him"* or her (1 Thess. 4:4-6). We refer to this aspect of holiness as *sanctification.* Many Scriptures teach us to grow in this aspect of holiness.

Q 73 *Complete Figure 1.18 by summarizing verses about growing in holy actions and holy living.*

Reference	Your Summary of Growing in Holiness
Rom. 12:1	
2 Cor. 7:1	
Heb. 12:14	
1 Pet. 1:15-16	
1 Thess. 4:3-7	
2 Tim. 2:21	

Figure 1.18   Practice summarizing verses that teach us to grow in holy living.

All of our holiness is *in Christ*, and through Christ (1 Cor. 1:30). At the new birth, God's Holy Spirit brings us new life, and comes to live in us. And as we are filled with the Holy Spirit, day by day, God enables us to please Him by living holy lives.

Charles Spurgeon, a famous preacher, loved to teach on holiness. He said that holy living is always present in guests at the King's banquet. For without holy living no one will see the Lord (Heb. 12:14). Spurgeon said many false Christians claim they possess *only *imputed righteousness (justification, Rom. 3–5). Such hypocrites care little about the sanctifying work of the Holy Spirit (Rom. 6–8). These fake followers of Christ refuse to put on the garment of obedience. They reject the white linen which is the righteous acts of the saints (Rev. 19:8). Thus they reveal their self-will, their enmity to God, and their lack of submission to His Son and His Spirit. Such people talk about justification by faith, and salvation by grace, but they are rebels at heart. Like the self-righteous, they do not wear a wedding garment (Matt. 22:11). The fact is that if we want the blessings of grace, we must submit to the rules of grace—without picking and choosing. It is foolish to argue whether the wedding garment is faith, love, righteous deeds, or holy living. For all the graces of the Spirit are woven together in the new covenant. No one ever had the imputed righteousness of Christ (justification) without receiving the *imparted righteousness (sanctification)—which comes as we submit to the Holy Spirit. Justification by faith is not contrary to the fruit of good works: God forbid. The faith by which we are justified is the faith which produces holy living. And those whom God justifies by faith, He sanctifies and delivers from the love of sin in this life. [16]

God gives us power to live holy lives through the Holy Spirit.   Paul connects holy living to God's gift of the Holy Spirit. In 1 Thessalonians 4:1-8, Paul's final emphasis about holiness is: *"God, who gives you his Holy Spirit"* (1 Thess. 4:8). In our struggle against desires of the flesh, God does not leave us alone. As at the Jerusalem Pentecost (Acts 2), Samaria (Acts 8), Caesarea (Acts 10–11), and Ephesus (Acts 19), God desires to fill all believers with the Holy Spirit. For being filled with the Spirit and led by the

Q 74 *What does the Bible teach about the relationship between justification and holy living?*

Q 75 *Which verse in 1 Thessalonians 4 links holy living to the Holy Spirit?*
Q 76 *Are you walking in God's plan and power to overcome unholy desires of the flesh? Explain.*

Spirit are God's solution to overcoming unholy desires of the flesh. In Romans 7–8, Paul contrasts the flesh and Spirit about 20 times. In 1 Thessalonians 4:1-8, Paul is writing about living holy lives *"to please God"* (1 Thess. 4:1). Those led by unholy desires of the flesh cannot please God (Rom. 8:8). Rather, those led by the flesh are slaves of the flesh and servants of sin, not servants of God. Unholy desires of the flesh are hostile to God, and those who follow the flesh will die spiritually (Rom. 8:6, 13). In contrast, those led by the Spirit are God's true children, and will live forever (Rom. 8:13-14). Paul summarizes the conflict between flesh and Spirit in Galatians 5. He says that unholy desires of the flesh are in conflict with the Spirit. But the solution is to *"live by the Spirit, and you will not gratify the desires of the sinful nature"* (Gal. 5:16). So brothers and sisters in Christ, let us be filled and refilled with the Spirit, day by day. Let us be filled with the Spirit, edifying ourselves with spiritual songs, giving thanks, praying, and singing in our hearts (Eph. 5:18-20). For as we are filled and led by the Spirit, unholy desires of the flesh become like an annoying insect that we either ignore, swat, or dismiss. And thus we enjoy constant fellowship with our Holy Father. So let us, like believers at Thessalonica, live holy lives that please the Lord, more and more (1 Thess. 1:6; 4:1, 10).

We should always rest in the fact that our holiness is a gift God gives us as we abide in Christ. And we should live to please our Heavenly Father, by being holy as He is holy. For as Paul warns, God will punish those who do not live holy lives (1 Thess. 4:6). Let us remind ourselves that *"God did not call us to be impure, but to live a holy life"* (1 Thess. 4:7). Anyone who rejects this Scriptural teaching on holy living rejects God, who gives the Holy Spirit (1 Thess. 4:8). So let us live to please God, and not live like those who reject the Heavenly Father, the Lord Jesus Christ, and the Holy Spirit. Adam and Eve learned the cost of rejecting God's will (1 Thess. 4:8).[17] Can we practice rejecting God's call, and remain among the called (1 Thess. 4:7; Rom. 8:28-30)? Impossible! Justification without holy living is fiction.

B. God calls us to grow in love for each other (1 Thess. 4:9-10).

9 Now about brotherly love we do not need to write to you, for you yourselves have been taught by God to love each other. 10 And in fact, you do love all the brothers throughout Macedonia. Yet we urge you, brothers, to do so more and more (1 Thess. 4:9-10).

As Paul urges believers to grow, he shifts from holiness to love. He reminds them that God has already taught them to love one another. And they *"do love all the brothers throughout Macedonia"* (1 Thess. 4:9-10). Notice that their love reached beyond their own homes, church, and community into the broad region of Macedonia. Still, as Paul guided them to grow in holiness, he exhorts them to grow in love *"more and more"* (1 Thess. 4:10). **Believers should grow in love throughout life.** A believer who is 10 years old should love more than a believer who has known Christ for only 2 years. The more we mature in Christ, the more we should love others, as we love ourselves. The Holy Spirit helps us grow in love as we depend on Him. The more we grow in holiness and love, the more we are being transformed to the likeness of Jesus. As we practice love, all people know we are disciples of Christ—learning to love as He loves (John 13:34-35).

Evangelist Dwight L. Moody used a glass to teach that the love of God overcomes fleshly desires in our lives. He asked his listeners, "How can I get the air out of this glass?" He listened to some suggestions. Then he picked up a pitcher of water and filled the glass. "There," he said, "the air is gone from the glass." We cannot overcome evil, bitterness, and temptation by only fighting against them.

Q 77 *What can we say about those who do not live holy lives that please God?*

they are slaves
of sin
they disobey and
reject God.

Q 78 *Would you expect a believer who has been following Jesus for 5 years to be more holy and more loving than a new believer? Explain.*

Q 79 *How does love help us win the battle over temptations?*

Figure 1.19   How can I get the air out of a glass?

Rather, let us permit the Holy Spirit to fill our hearts. Let Him pour in love until it overflows. As this happens, God's love replaces the things we do not want in our hearts. [18] So Paul emphasizes, *"Be filled with the Spirit"* (Eph. 5:18).

C. God calls us to grow in personal responsibility (1 Thess. 4:11-12).

In his **first letter** to the Thessalonians, after many words of praise and encouragement, Paul touched gently on the problems of gossip, laziness, and idleness. He wrote:

> [11] *Make it your ambition to lead a quiet life, to mind your own business and to work with your hands, just as we told you,* [12] *so that your daily life may win the respect of outsiders and so that you will not be dependent on anybody* (1 Thess. 4:11-12).

Paul contrasts the gossips with those who mind their own business. And he contrasts the lazy with those who work with their own hands. Perhaps some were so focused on end time matters, such as the Antichrist and the Lord's return, that they worked less and less and talked more and more. Paul touches on these problems of speculation, gossip, and laziness in his first letter to the Thessalonians.

But a few months later, these problems were worse. In his **second letter** to believers at Thessalonica, Paul's words were more plentiful and stronger on these topics:

> [6] *In the name of the Lord Jesus Christ, we command you, brothers, to keep away from every brother who is idle and does not live according to the teaching you received from us.* [7] *For you yourselves know how you ought to follow our example. We were not idle when we were with you,* [8] *nor did we eat anyone's food without paying for it. On the contrary, we worked night and day, laboring and toiling so that we would not be a burden to any of you.* [9] *We did this, not because we do not have the right to such help, but in order to make ourselves a model for you to follow.* [10] *For even when we were with you, we gave you this rule: "If a man will not work, he shall not eat."* [11] *We hear that some among you are idle. They are not busy; they are busybodies.* [12] *Such people we command and urge in the Lord Jesus Christ to settle down and earn the bread they eat.* [13] *And as for you, brothers, never tire of doing what is right* (2 Thess. 3:6-13).

Baby birds and baby children are born with their mouths open, crying to be fed. But little by little, both must grow up and learn to carry responsibilities. Even small children begin to learn responsibilities, as they pick up, and clean up, doing chores, studies, and small tasks, mixed with play. Older children learn skills of responsibility by feeding, helping, or carrying smaller children. It is a tragedy to see youth and young adults, and even older adults, who are irresponsible. Like infants in a crib, these think only of themselves. But it is a beautiful thing to watch a child grow into a responsible adult, in the home, the church, and the community. Christianity teaches hard work, paying our own bills, helping the church pay its bills, and earning enough to share with those in need.

Paul urges believers to grow in responsibility for two reasons: *"so that your daily life may win the respect of outsiders and so that you will not be dependent on anybody"* (1 Thess. 4:12). Let us consider each of these briefly.

1. Responsibility is a bridge to fruitful witness. The respect of others is not automatic. Respect is something we must earn or win. Often, we must *win the respect of outsiders* **before** we can win their hearts to Christ. People notice who works hard at home and helping others. They hear the reputation of those who pay their bills. Neighbors notice who cares about others, and who cares only about self.

Jim and Alice were cheerful believers at church, when they attended. But they did not pay tithes nor give generous offerings. They were takers, not givers. They were a debit, rather than a credit. If there was a special meal or event, they showed up to enjoy

Q 80 *How do Paul's words about idleness differ in 1 and 2 Thessalonians? Why?*

Q 81 *How are young Christians like small children?*

Q 82 *What are some differences between an irresponsible believer and a mature, responsible believer—in the home, the church, and the community?*

Print # 1
We are called to
be good stewards

Q 83 *How can you earn influence and respect by being responsible? Illustrate.*

Q 84 *What percentage of the people in your church are responsible, dependable members?*

it—not to help plan or prepare it. And when the church scheduled a work day of any kind, Jim and Alice did not come. The church could not depend on them to teach a class, or help with any of the many tasks that are necessary for a good church. In fact, if everyone in the church had been like Jim and Alice, there would not have been a church. But thankfully, there were several faithful and responsible families who worked hard and made it possible for there to be a church with a good reputation. Jim and Alice were like the immature believers at Thessalonica who needed to grow up. They wanted to eat physically and spiritually without working (2 Thess. 3:10).

Q 85 *What is the balance between having fun and working? What does a good work ethic look like?*

Q 86 *Do you carry a fair share of the load—at home, at church, and in the community? Explain.*

2. **Working and being responsible enables us not to depend on others.** A sponge is known for soaking in whatever is around it. Likewise, parasites attach themselves to healthy things, and suck life from them. A welfare system is made up of people who live like sponges or parasites—always wanting to receive something without sore muscles, tired feet, or an aching back. Such people want food, shelter, and money without sweat, calluses, or blisters. People like this lack self-respect, and have a poor reputation. In the church, a lazy person gives the gospel a bad reputation. In contrast, God's plan is for believers to earn their own bread. Accidents, disasters, and circumstances prevent some from working. These may provide a biblical reason for charity and compassion. But the Bible cites laziness as an enemy of Christianity. Sabio says, "An idle mind and idle hands are the devil's tools."

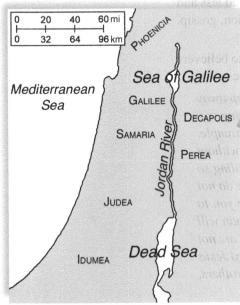

Figure 1.20   **The Jordan River connects two seas in Israel.**

Q 87 *How do the 2 seas in Israel represent 2 types of people?*

"There are two seas in Israel that are not far from each other. The Jordan River feeds both seas. But they are as different as day and night. The Sea of Galilee in the north is alive and fresh. It has sweet, pure water and is the home of many fish. Green trees and plants grow along its beautiful shores. This sea gives as much as it receives and seems happy to give. After receiving the waters of the Jordan, it is generous, and sends water on again—into a valley toward the Dead Sea. But the Dead Sea is dead and still. There are no fish in its salty waters. No vegetation grows along its barren shores. It swallows all the water that flows into it. But it does not share any water. Not one drop flows out. So the Dead Sea remains what it has been for centuries—a lifeless, barren, grave of water. These two seas contrast two types of people. The same stream of God's blessings feeds both. Some people take, but do not give. Their empty hand is always reaching out to grasp or receive. These bring a curse of death and barrenness upon themselves. Others enjoy God's blessings, and become good stewards. These work hard and allow the living water to flow through them. These become sources of joy and good things to others."[19] So let us be gracious faithful stewards of all the blessings God gives us, including love, mercy, time, health, and opportunities to work and share.

Q 88 *What are 3 areas of growth that show we are following Jesus?*

Growing in holiness, love, and responsibility are evidence that we are following Jesus, and being transformed into His image (Rom. 8:28).

Figure 1.21   **Romans 3:21–5:21 emphasizes <u>justification</u>—holiness and righteousness of position that God imputes (credits to us) through faith in Christ (see the base of the holiness triangle in Figure 1.16). Likewise, Romans 6–8 emphasizes <u>sanctification</u>—holiness and righteous doing and being (see the sides of the holiness triangle in Figure 1.16).**

Romans 6–8 stresses the process of growing in the likeness of Christ. The imparted holiness of sanctification begins at regeneration, and reaches its highest level at glorification. In between the new birth and the new body, we perfect holiness—we increase in holy actions, holy attitudes, and holy character.

Some children of righteousness are babies in Christ, while others have grown to be more mature. Our glorious destiny is to become completely holy, like God the Son! Even now, the Spirit enables us to become more and more like our Savior (Rom. 8:29; 2 Cor. 3:18).[20]

Lesson 6

Live Ready: Prepare as You Wait for the Lord (1 Thess. 4:11–18)

Goal: *Summarize the Thessalonian question and Paul's answer on the Lord's return (1 Thess. 4:13-18).*

Setting. The Thessalonian believers were young Christians. Paul led them to Christ, but deadly persecution forced him to flee within a short time—perhaps only *three Sabbaths* (Acts 17:2). In these few weeks Paul taught the basics of the gospel—from the Incarnation to the Second Coming, and the judgments and rewards that follow. But imagine trying to learn everything about Christianity in 3 weeks! Impossible! So in Paul's letters to the Thessalonians, it is not surprising that he needs to review and clarify some teachings. In this lesson we will examine his review on eschatology!

A. The coming of the Lord includes believers who died in Christ (1 Thess. 4:13-14).

¹³Brothers, we do not want you to be ignorant about those who fall asleep, or to grieve like the rest of men, who have no hope. ¹⁴We believe that Jesus died and rose again and so we believe that God will bring with Jesus those who have fallen asleep in him (1 Thess. 4:13-14).

The question. Some believers at Thessalonica were confused. Perhaps they thought all followers of Jesus would live until the Lord's return. When some believers died, from persecution or natural causes, the question arose, "Will believers who have died miss the great and glorious *Day of the Lord's return?

Q 89 ⟋ *What question troubled believers at Thessalonica (1 Thess. 4:13)?*

The answer. Paul assures the Thessalonians that death will not prevent any believer from being with the Lord in the air. In 1 Thessalonians 4:13-15 as in 1 Corinthians 15, Paul refers to death as *sleep* (1 Thess. 4:13-15; 5:10; 1 Cor. 15:51).

Q 90 ⟋ *What was Paul's answer to the question that troubled the Thessalonians?*

Sleep is a fitting way for believers to think of death—because death is not final. As we rise from sleep, believers will rise from death at the Resurrection. So when a loved one dies, we do not *"grieve like the rest of men, who have no hope"* (1 Thess. 4:13). When death comes, those outside of Christ mourn with no hope—only sorrow, emptiness, anger, and perhaps fear. In contrast, our hope burns brightly when a believer falls asleep in Christ. For when Jesus returns, *"whether we are awake or asleep, we* [will] *live together with him* [our Lord]"(1 Thess. 5:10).

Q 91 ⟋ *Why is sleep a fitting metaphor to talk with believers about death?*

B. The coming of the Lord follows a sequence and three signs (1 Thess. 4:15-18).

¹⁵According to the Lord's own word, we tell you that we who are still alive, who are left till the coming of the Lord, will certainly not precede those who have fallen asleep. ¹⁶For the Lord himself will come down from heaven, with a loud command, with the voice of the archangel and with the trumpet call of God, and the dead in Christ will rise first. ¹⁷After that, we who are still alive and are left will be caught up together with them in the clouds to meet the Lord in the air. And so we will be with the Lord forever. ¹⁸Therefore encourage each other with these words (1 Thess. 4:15-18).

When Christ returns, the new bodies of believers who have died rise first to meet the Lord. One wink later, believers alive on earth will be transformed and caught up together with them to meet the Lord in the air.

Q 92 ⟑ *If departed believers come from heaven with Christ, how can they rise?*

Elsewhere, Paul writes that to be away from the body is to be present with the Lord (Phil. 1:20-23). So although the body may *sleep* at death, the believer's soul is in the presence of God. We understand little about the state of departed believers. But Scripture assures us that they are conscious, and very much alive in the presence of God (see Rev. 6:9-11). For those who live by faith in God, death is not a termination, but a graduation—a promotion from earth to heaven. When Christ returns, He will bring with Him believers who have already passed from this life to the next. In a moment, these departed souls will be glorified—united with their new bodies that *rise first* (1 Cor. 15:51-53).

C. The coming of the Lord follows three signs (1 Thess. 4:16).

Q 93 ⟑ *What are the 3 loud signs that announce the Lord's sudden return?*

Three loud signs announce the sudden return of Christ. *"For the Lord himself will come down from heaven, with a loud command, with the voice of the archangel and with the trumpet call of God, and the dead in Christ will rise first"* (1 Thess. 4:16).

First, "a loud command" announces Christ's return and calls forth the bodies of believers from the grave. This reminds us of the time Jesus called in a loud voice, *"Lazarus, come out!"* (John 11:43). At that command, the dead believer came to life, and came out of the tomb. Likewise, Jesus said, *"a time is coming when all who are in their graves will hear his voice [29] and come out—those who have done good will rise to live, and those who have done evil will rise to be condemned"* (John 5:28-29; Dan. 12:2). Prophetic passages like John 5:28-29 often combine events. In light of John's words in Revelation 20:4-5, we see that a thousand years separate the resurrection of the righteous and the wicked. But a point that Paul emphasizes in 1 Thessalonians 4, Philippians 3, and 1 Corinthians 15, is that when Christ returns, *all* believers will receive new bodies.

[20] *But our citizenship is in heaven. And we eagerly await a Savior from there, the Lord Jesus Christ,* [21] *who, by the power that enables him to bring everything under his control, will transform our lowly bodies so that they will be like his glorious body* (Phil. 3:20-21).

Q 94 ⟑ *At Christ's coming, how is a loud command related to our new bodies?*

When the Lord Jesus returns, there will be a resurrection for those who died in Christ. A loud command calls the bodies of the *dead in Christ from their graves. In that moment it will not matter whether a believer was buried in the earth, buried at sea, or burned like many martyrs. In Corinthians, Paul likens our earthly body to a seed that we plant at death (1 Cor. 15:36-37). At the Lord's return, the souls of those who died in Christ will be united with their new bodies. Living believers on earth will be transformed and *caught up,* raptured (1 Thess. 4:17). The Greek word for caught up is *harpazo.* Of the 13 times that *harpazo* occurs in the New Testament, only 1 Thessalonians 4:17 refers to the second coming of

Figure 1.22   At the Rapture, all who believe in Christ will be united with Him and glorified.

Christ. The Latin form of *caught up* comes from the verb *rapere*, which is the root of the popular word *Rapture.[21] At the Rapture, living believers are *caught up* to meet Christ in the clouds (1 Thess. 4:17). This joyful meeting with Jesus is the *Blessed Hope of all believers (Titus 2:13). There are several events related to the coming of the Lord, including a great apostasy, the Rapture, the Great Tribulation, the rise and fall of the Antichrist and his followers, Christ's reign on the earth, and the Great White Throne judgment. The sequence of these events is a matter of debate—even among Pentecostals. But Scripture does not give us a detailed timeline. Rather, it just emphasizes that we should live ready for the Lord's return. For a fuller discussion of the coming of the Lord, see the first few pages of *Lesson 10* in this book. Also see the *Faith & Action* course: *Revelation & Daniel*.

After the Rapture comes the best part—the highest hope and honor of all believers: *"And so we will be with the Lord forever"* (1 Thess. 4:17). Beyond the promise of resurrection, new bodies, and the Rapture is the unspeakable joy of being with our Lord and Savior evermore! After the Lord first came to earth, the hearts of His disciples were filled with sorrow at His death and departure. But at His second coming we will be with Him forever. Never again will He leave us (Rev. 7:9-17).

The ***second sign*** of Christ's return is ***"the voice of the *archangel"*** (1 Thess. 4:16). The word *archangel* comes from a Greek word that combines *angel* with *arche* (which means "beginning, first, or chief"). So an *archangel* is a chief angel.[22] Scripture does not tell us what the archangel says, nor give us his name. In Scripture, only Michael is referred to as an archangel (Jude 9). But Jewish tradition recognized seven archangels by name.[23] At the first coming of Jesus into the world, an angel announced His birth to the shepherds. And a host of angels praised God at that glorious event (Luke 2:9-14). So at the second coming of the King of kings, it is fitting for an angel to announce the joyful news.

The ***third sign*** of Christ's *return* [Greek: *Parousia*] is ***"the trumpet call of God"*** (1 Thess. 4:16). Jesus taught that all the nations will see the Son of Man coming on the clouds with power and great glory. At that time *"he will send his angels with **a loud trumpet call, and they will gather his elect"** from* every direction (Matt. 24:31). Note that this verse in Matthew refers to what Paul calls the Rapture [Greek: *harpazo*, "caught up"].

Encourage yourself with this great biblical promise as you read Paul's famous passage in Corinthians:

> [51] *Listen, I tell you a mystery: We will not all sleep, but we will all be changed—* [52] *in a flash, in the twinkling of an eye, at the last trumpet. For the trumpet will sound, the dead will be raised imperishable, and we will be changed.* [53] *For the perishable must clothe itself with the imperishable, and the mortal with immortality.* [54] *When the perishable has been clothed with the imperishable, and the mortal with immortality, then the saying that is written will come true: "Death has been swallowed up in victory."* [55] *"Where, O death, is your victory? Where, O death, is your sting?"* [56] *The sting of death is sin, and the power of sin is the law.* [57] *But thanks be to God! He gives us the victory through our Lord Jesus Christ.* [58] *Therefore, my dear brothers, stand firm. Let nothing move you. Always give yourselves fully to the work of the Lord, because you know that your labor in the Lord is not in vain* (1 Cor. 15:51-58).

Application.   Meeting Jesus in the air is the *Blessed Hope* of believers of all generations (Titus 2:13). His coming is a spring of encouragement. When a great leader comes to a nation, a group of people often go out to meet him. Then they escort him to the place he is going. Likewise, we will meet Jesus in the air, and then escort Him to heaven—and live together with Him forever. His first coming, at the Incarnation, was for only

Q 95 ⟩ *What does the Blessed Hope of all believers include?*

Q 96 ⟨ *What is the highest hope of all believers?*

Q 97 ⟩ *What is an archangel?*

Q 98 ⟨ *Why might we expect an angel to announce the second coming of Jesus?*

Q 99 ⟩ *Besides 1 Thessalonians 4:16, which Gospel mentions a loud trumpet at Christ's return?*

Q 100 ⟨ *What will happen to believers when the trumpet of God sounds?*

Q 101 ⟨ *What do you look forward to the most at the Lord's coming?*

a few years. But at the *Parousia* [Greek for the Second Coming], never again will there be any separation between us. He will be our God and we will be His people for eternity. Like the Thessalonians, we feel sorrow when our loved ones die. Likewise, our hearts are saddened as perhaps 160,000 believers become martyrs this year, and thousands of others suffer persecution. But when Jesus returns He will wipe all tears from our eyes (Rev. 7:17). And we will enter into the joys of our Lord forever. So let us lift up the hands that hang down (Heb. 12:12). *"Therefore encourage each other with these words"* (1 Thess. 4:18). Let us be ever watchful, looking for those we can encourage with a smile, a greeting, a listening ear, a kind deed, and above all, the promise of our Lord's return.

Lesson 7

Live Ready: Understand as You Wait for the Day of the Lord (1 Thess. 5:1-11)

Goal A: *Explain what Paul means by 'the Day of the Lord.' Include at least 4 key biblical references.*
Goal B: *Contrast the sad and glad aspects of the Day of the Lord.*

Q 102 ⟋ *In the Old Testament, what is the Day of the Lord?*

A. What is the Day of the Lord (1 Thess. 5:1-2)?

*¹Now, brothers, about times and dates we do not need to write to you, ²for you know very well that **the day of the Lord** will come like a thief in the night* (1 Thess. 5:1-2).

Paul has assured believers that those asleep in Christ will not miss the Lord's glorious appearing. Next, Paul contrasts two groups of people on earth when Jesus returns (1 Thess. 5:1-11). As we begin to look at this passage, it is important to understand the key phrase of eschatology, *"the day of the Lord"* (1 Thess. 5:2).

In the Old Testament *"the day of the LORD"* refers to a time that God judges the evil and rewards the righteous. The prophet Amos saw the day of the Lord when Assyria would slaughter and enslave Israel.

Q 103 ⟍ *Why did Amos tell the Israelites to stop looking forward to the Day of the Lord?*

¹⁸Woe to you who long for the day of the LORD! Why do you long for the day of the LORD? That day will be darkness, not light. ¹⁹It will be as though a man fled from a lion only to meet a bear, as though he entered his house and rested his hand on the wall only to have a snake bite him. ²⁰Will not the day of the LORD be darkness, not light—pitch-dark, without a ray of brightness? ²¹"I hate, I despise your religious feasts; I cannot stand your assemblies. ²²Even though you bring me burnt offerings and grain offerings, I will not accept them. Though you bring choice fellowship offerings, I will have no regard for them. ²³Away with the noise of your songs! I will not listen to the music of your harps. ²⁴But let justice roll on like a river, righteousness like a never-failing stream! ²⁵Did you bring me sacrifices and offerings forty years in the desert, O house of Israel? ²⁶You have lifted up the shrine of your king, the pedestal of your idols, the star of your god—which you made for yourselves. ²⁷Therefore I will send you into exile beyond Damascus," says the LORD, whose name is God Almighty (Amos 5:18-27).

Q 104 ⟋ *Was 722 B.C. the final "Day of the Lord", or just a shadow of it? Explain.*

Sometime the Old Testament prophets, such as Amos, spoke of the Day of the Lord as a time that was near. Within 30 years of Amos 5:18-27, in 722 B.C., Assyria destroyed the Northern Kingdom. It was a very dark day. But even a judgment such as Amos prophesied was only a shadow of the final Day of the Lord. Several prophets of the Old Testament predicted a Day when God will judge the whole earth. On that Day He will punish all sinners for their evil deeds (Isa. 13:9-11; Zeph. 1:14–2:3). All nations will receive what they deserve (Obad. 15). Yet there is no need for the righteous to fear the Day of the Lord. For this is also a Day of deliverance and reward for God's children (Joel 2:28-32; Obad. 16-21).

In the New Testament, Christians recognized that the Day of the Lord begins when the Lord Jesus returns. But the *"Day"* of the Lord includes such things as the Rapture, judgment of the Antichrist and his followers, Christ's reign on earth, and the Great White Throne judgment. Scholars agree that the Day of the Lord and its events extend beyond a normal day. The *Day* of the Lord is a *period of time* when God breaks into human history. On the *Day* of the Lord, His kingdom comes, and His will is done on earth, as it is in heaven. The *Day of the Lord* brings *judgment* to the disobedient, *but salvation, glorification, and reward* to the obedient. Other phrases that refer to this same Day are: *"the day of Christ Jesus"* (Phil. 1:6) and *"the day of the Lord Jesus"* (2 Cor. 1:14). In its shortest form the Day of the Lord is simply *"the day"* (2 Thess. 2:3). Thus Paul writes: *"This will take place on **the day** when God will judge men's secrets through Jesus Christ, as my gospel declares"* (Rom. 2:16).

Q 105 *How long is the Day of the Lord? What events does it include?*

Q 106 *What are the positive and negative aspects of the Day of the Lord?*

Note that the gospel does not end at Calvary, the empty tomb, or the resurrection and ascension of Christ. Rather, the gospel includes both the first *and* second comings of Jesus, and the judgments or rewards that follow. Many err these days by ending Paul's gospel at Romans 5, although Romans 6–8, and 9–16 are a vital part of the gospel Paul preached.[24]

Q 107 *In the New Testament, what are 3 synonyms for "the Day of the Lord"?*

Q 108 *What does "the gospel" include?*

Take a few minutes to explore some key passages on *"the day of the Lord"* (Figure 1.23). Then we will study some principles in 1 Thessalonians 5:1-11.

Q 109 *Complete Figure 1.23 by summarizing verses related to "the day of the Lord".*

Reference	Your Summary of Verses Related to *"the Day of the Lord"*
Matt. 24:42-44	Keep watch and be ready; for as with a thief, you don't know when he is coming.
John 6:39	Jesus will raise up all believers at the last day.
Rom. 2:5	Stubbornness and refusing to repent store up wrath for the day of judgment.
1 Cor. 1:8	
Eph. 4:30	
Phil. 1:6	
1 Thess. 5:2	
2 Thess. 1:7-10	
2 Thess. 2:1-3	
2 Pet. 2:9	God rescues the righteous but holds the unrighteous for the day of judgment.
2 Pet. 3:10-12	On the Day of the Lord, God destroys the heavens with fire, and the elements melt.
1 John 3:2-3	When Christ appears, we will be like Him.
Jude 6	
Rev. 16:15	Jesus is coming like a thief; blessed are the alert and those clothed with righteousness.

Figure 1.23   Verses related to the Day of the Lord—the climax of all things when Jesus Christ returns to punish the wicked and reward the righteous

The **first eschatological question** of the Thessalonians was, "Will those who have died in Christ miss the coming of the Lord?" Paul explained that the dead in Christ will return with Him and rise first in their new bodies. Then living believers will be transformed and *caught up* to meet the Lord. Any mention of the Rapture leads to **the next question:** "When?" Like people of every generation, Thessalonian believers wanted to know *when* the Lord was returning to bring justice, relief, and reward. Even the apostles were eager to know the timing of the Kingdom.

Q 110 *What were the 2 questions of the Thessalonians about eschatology?*

After the resurrection, the apostles asked Jesus if it was time for the King to rule on the earth. Christ's answer was something like: "God's timing is God's business. Your business is to receive the Spirit and witness about Me."

*[6]So when they met together, they asked him, "Lord, are you at this time going to restore the kingdom to Israel?" [7]He said to them: **It is not for you to know the times or dates the Father has set by his own authority.** [8]But you will*

receive power when the Holy Spirit comes on you; and you will be my witnesses in Jerusalem, and in all Judea and Samaria, and to the ends of the earth (Acts 1:6-8).

So in 1 Thessalonians 5:1, we see that the phrase Paul uses (*times or dates*) is the same phrase Jesus used just before He ascended. Jesus turned their attention from the dates on God's calendar in heaven to our responsibilities of daily living on earth.

There are always some in every generation who want to focus on the time or date of Christ's coming (Acts 1:7; Rev. 6:10). But Scripture declares that God has *concealed* the time of the Lord's return. So let us turn away from curiosity about the timing of Christ's return. While Christians are debating about eschatology, many believers are being entangled in sin, and half of the world is headed for hell. The great concern of Christians should not be the time of the Lord's return, nor the rule of the Antichrist. Rather, let us focus on being ready to meet God at any moment—by avoiding the seduction of the world. Sabio says: *"Only one generation* will be alive when the Lord returns. But *every generation* must either overcome the world, or be overcome by it."

In our *Faith & Action* course *Cross-Cultural Communication* by Dr. Judy Graner, we contrast eight pairs of values in cultures. One of the pairs we study in *Cross-Cultural Communication* is *time* versus *event*. Some societies, like North America and Europe, emphasize time more than events. In these Western societies, people keep a close eye on the clock. Stores open on a certain minute, and close on another minute. Buses and trains follow a strict schedule. Meetings and church services start at one time and end at another. Most members of society wear a watch or carry a cell phone that tells them the time of the day, all through the day. If you are 5 minutes late in the West, you are *very* late! So as you might imagine, people in Western societies are very concerned about the time Jesus will return—since they are concerned about the time for everything! In Western societies, there are many theological debates about the *time* Jesus will return—whether pre-Trib, mid-Trib, or post-Trib. In contrast, most of the rest of the world focuses more on events than on time. For example in Africa or much of Latin America, people pay less attention to the clock, and more attention to people and the events that bring them together. Buses and trains are a popular way to travel, but they may not run on a strict schedule. A meeting or church service may begin around 9 in the morning, but many people will still be coming to the meeting at 9:15, 9:30, 9:45, and even 10 o'clock. And if the meeting is very important, it might last an hour or more longer than expected. If a special church service lasts 3 hours instead of 2, no one will be upset—because the event, and the people involved, are more important than the time! So when we study eschatology, let us remember that biblical writers were from the East, not the West. They were more concerned about events than about time. When Paul and others write about the Day of the Lord, they focus on the event, not the timing. And when Jesus Himself taught about His coming, His main point was always to live ready for the event. He avoided giving details about the day and the hour (Matt. 24:36).

Peter, Paul, and John each wrote about the return of Christ. But consider the unique context and perspective of each. **Peter** wrote near the time of his own crucifixion. Thirty years earlier, the Lord had prophesied about Peter's death (John 21:18-19). As the time of Peter's execution drew near, the Holy Spirit revealed to him that his departure was at hand (2 Pet. 1:14-15). Take a moment to review Peter's final chapter of Scripture (2 Pet. 3:10-17). As Peter writes on the Second Coming, he does not mention the Antichrist, the Tribulation, or the Rapture. Rather, his emphasis is on our responsibility to live holy, godly lives—**living ready** for the event of meeting Jesus. In contrast to Peter, **Paul** mentions both the Rapture (1 Thess. 4:17) and the Antichrist (2 Thess. 2:1-12). Still, Paul's main emphasis to the Thessalonians is to **live ready** for the coming of

---

Point #2

Q 111 *What should be our focus about the Lord's coming?*

What I tell Damaris, if you're sure that you're sure that Jesus is coming in our life time.

Q 112 *How do the values of time or event affect the study of eschatology?*

Q 113 *After waiting 30 years for Christ to return, why do you think Peter does not mention the Antichrist, the Tribulation, or the Rapture?*

Christ—as *"sons of the light,... alert and self-controlled"* (1 Thess. 5:1-11), cooperating with the sanctifying work of the Spirit (2 Thess. 2:13).

Unlike Peter and Paul, the apostle **John** writes over 20 chapters on details of the end times. John was dying the slow death of a martyr on the island of Patmos. And throughout his final letter, he emphasizes that believers must overcome the world and be willing to be martyrs for Christ (Rev. 1:9; 2:10; 7:9-14; 11:7; 12:11; 13:7; 14:13; 17:6; 20:4; 21:7). John urges us to renew our first love for Christ (Rev. 2:4-5); be faithful to death (2:10); repent or face the sword of His mouth (2:16, 21); wake up and clean up (3:2-4); warm up spiritually (3:14-18). Peter, Paul, and John do not answer all of our questions on the coming of the Lord. But they all urge us to live holy lives, stand firm, and be ready for the **event** of meeting Jesus at any moment. And *living ready* is the very truth that Jesus Himself emphasized (Matt. 24–25). Get the message?

Q 114 ✎ *What do Peter, Paul, and John emphasize about the Lord's return?*

In Point A, we have looked at the background and context of the phrase, the Day of the Lord. When that great Day dawns, there will be two groups of people on earth: the surprised and the prepared. Let us study the characteristics of each group (Points B and C).

B. The Day of the Lord will bring sudden judgment on the disobedient—those who live in darkness.

[1] *Now, brothers, about times and dates we do not need to write to you,* [2] *for you know very well that the day of the Lord will come like a thief in the night.* [3] *While people are saying, "Peace and safety," destruction will come on them suddenly, as labor pains on a pregnant woman, and they will not escape* (1 Thess. 5:1-3).

Figure 1.24 The Day of the Lord will bring wrath to some and reward to others (1 Thess. 5:1-11). Left group: Children of darkness, dullness, destruction, self-indulgence, wrath. Right group: Sons of Light, alertness, self-control, salvation

Q 115 ✎ *Explain the two sides of God's justice.*

Q 116 ✎ *Complete Figure 1.25 on the topic of judgment or retribution.*

Person	Your Summary of Feelings About the Judgment of the Unrighteous
Jeremiah	
Ezekiel	
Jesus	
Paul	
You	

Figure 1.25   Practice summarizing the feelings of God's people about the judgment of the unrighteous.

The Day of the Lord has a sad side and a glad side. It brings wailing for some and rejoicing for others.

Let us look first at the sad side of justice—sometimes called *retribution*. The Day of the Lord will bring weeping and wailing for those outside of Christ. This is sad news, not only to the disobedient, but to believers. We grieve as we think about the fate of those out of fellowship with God. Jesus felt great sorrow for the sad side of God's justice. It caused him to weep over Jerusalem (Luke 19:41-44). Likewise, Paul wrote about his feelings towards unbelieving Jews:

²I have great sorrow and unceasing anguish in my heart. ³For I could wish that I myself were cursed and cut off from Christ for the sake of my brothers, those of my own race, ⁴the people of Israel (Rom. 9:2-4).

> GOD HAS NO PLEASURE IN THE DEATH OF THE WICKED, AND NEITHER DO WE.

God has no pleasure in the death of the wicked, and neither do we, His children (Ezek. 18:32; 33:11). Jeremiah expressed the sorrow that we feel for those God must punish. The weeping prophet wrote:

¹Oh, that my head were a spring of water and my eyes a fountain of tears! I would weep day and night for the slain of my people (Jer. 9:1).

Figure 1.26   The volcano of Mount Vesuvius growled for days, and then exploded, covering the city of Pompeii, Italy with boiling lava that flowed like liquid fire. The city was suddenly destroyed by poisonous gas and falling ash and pumice from the volcano.

Q 117 ↗ *What happened at Pompeii? What does this illustrate?*

The volcano of Mount Vesuvius rumbled for days before it exploded. Still, most people in Pompeii, the city below the volcano, paid no attention as the mountain smoked and growled. Then one day, in a moment, the mountain overflowed with fiery lava. Thousands were buried alive in lava and ash. Like Lot's wife, they became monuments of people unprepared for judgment day. Jesus promised that He is coming back to earth in blazing fire to take vengeance on those who do not know God, and those who do not obey the Scriptures (2 Thess. 1:7-8). He has warned us for centuries. His coming will be as sudden as the snap of a trap (Luke 21:34). When the Lord returns to earth, there will be no time to repent and prepare for His coming. The Day of the Lord will bring sudden justice for the disobedient. (Review the four parables that open this chapter.)

When we teach, preach, or study about the sad side of God's justice, there should be tears in our eyes. And yet we know that to remain just, God must punish those who reject His rule. He must judge all who rebel against their Creator. So Paul writes that we agree with what must happen—though the sad side of justice fills our hearts with sorrow.

⁶God is just: He will pay back trouble to those who trouble you ⁷and give relief to you who are troubled, and to us as well. This will happen when the Lord Jesus is revealed from heaven in blazing fire with his powerful angels. ⁸He will punish those who do not know God and do not obey the gospel of our Lord Jesus. ⁹They will be punished with everlasting destruction and shut out from the presence of the Lord and from the majesty of his power ¹⁰on the day he comes to be glorified in his holy people and to be marveled at among all those who have believed. This includes you, because you believed our testimony to you (2 Thess. 1:6-10).

God is just. So much sadness and joy in only three words.

Q 118 ✎ *Complete Figure 1.27 by summarizing verses on the sad and glad sides of justice.*

Reference	Sad Side of Justice	Glad Side of Justice
Matt. 25:31-46		
Mark 12:1-11		
Luke 13:28		
John 5:28-29		
Rom. 2:6-11		
Rom. 11:22-23		
2 Thess. 1:6-10		
2 Thess. 1:6-10		
Heb. 10:39		
Rev. 20:11-15		

Figure 1.27   Practice summarizing New Testament verses on the sad side and the glad side of the Day of the Lord.

Paul says sudden justice will surprise the disobedient. The Day of the Lord will come *"like a thief in the night. ³While people are saying, 'Peace and safety,' destruction will come on them suddenly, as labor pains on a pregnant woman, and they will not escape"* (1 Thess. 5:2-3).

Jesus said the Day of the Lord will surprise the disobedient. He will come with sudden justice:

- Like the flood (Matt. 24:36-41).
- Like a thief (Matt. 24:42-44).
- Like a master, returning from a journey (Matt. 24:45-51).
- Like a midnight bridegroom (Matt. 25:1-13).
- Like a trap snapping shut (Luke 21:34-36).

Q 119 ➚ *To which 5 things did Jesus compare the Day of the Lord?*

Application.   Paul describes the sudden changes at the Lord's coming as *"a flash, in the twinkling of an eye"* (1 Cor. 15:52). The Greek word translated *flash, moment,* or *instant* is *atomo.* The word *atom* comes from this Greek word *atomo.* To the Greeks, *atomo* meant the smallest amount of time one can imagine. The changes that will happen on the Day of the Lord will be sudden. At His coming, changes will be quicker than you can clap your hands, blink your eyes, or snap your fingers. His coming is without warning. People will have no time to repent or change the way they are living. So let us live ready. His coming is *imminent—he could come at any minute.

Q 120 ✎ *How does believing in the imminent return of Jesus affect our lifestyle?*

C. The Day of the Lord will bring salvation to the obedient—the sons of light (1 Thess. 5:4, 9).

*¹Now, brothers, about times and dates we do not need to write to you, ²for you know very well that the day of the Lord will come like a thief in the night. ³While people are saying, "Peace and safety," destruction will come on them suddenly, as labor pains on a pregnant woman, and they will not escape. ⁴**But you, brothers, are not in darkness so that this day should surprise you like a thief.** ⁵You are all sons of the light and sons of the day. We do not belong to the night or to the darkness. ⁶So then, let us not be like others, who are asleep, but let us be alert and self-controlled. ⁷For those who sleep, sleep at night, and those who get drunk, get drunk at night. ⁸But since we belong to the day, let us be self-controlled, putting on faith and love as a breastplate, and the hope of salvation as a helmet. ⁹**For God did not appoint us to suffer wrath but to receive salvation through our Lord Jesus Christ.** ¹⁰He died for us so that, whether we are awake or asleep, we may live together with him. ¹¹Therefore encourage one another and build each other up, just as in fact you are doing* (1 Thess. 5:1-11).

The flood did not surprise Noah. And the return of Jesus will not shock the children of light. Since we live in the light, we will not be in the dark when our Lord returns.

Q 121 What are some characteristics of children of light?

Sometimes we can discern the children of light by their talk. But we can always identify God's children by their walk. The contrast between the disobedient and obedient is like darkness and light.

1 Thess.	Children of Darkness; Sons of the Night	Children of the Light; Sons of the Day	1 Thess.
5:1-11	Referred to as: people, them, they, others, those	Referred to as: you, brothers, we, us	5:1-11
5:1-3	Destruction will come on **them** like a thief in the night. **They** will not escape.	Not in darkness, NOT surprised by the Day of the Lord like a thief in the night. We do not belong to the night or the darkness.	5:4 5:5
5:7	Sleep in the night; get drunk in the night	Let us be alert and self-controlled. We belong to the day, are self-controlled, walking in faith, love, and hope.	5:6 5:8
5:9	They have an appointment with wrath.	We are appointed to salvation.	5:9
4:13	Without hope	Encouraging one another; building each other up	5:11

Figure 1.28   Contrasts between children of darkness and children of light as the Day of the Lord approaches (1 Thess. 5:1-11)

Q 122 When God pours out His wrath, how will it affect His children of light?

When Christ returns, He will pour out His wrath on those who live in darkness. In contrast, the children of light are exempt from the wrath of God (1 Thess. 5:9-11; compare Luke 21:36; Rev. 3:10). God has not appointed us to wrath, but to salvation (1 Thess. 5:9). On earth, we may suffer persecution. Like the Thessalonians, we may face suffering and trials—the wrath of Satan and humans. But when the wrath of God boils over, not one drop will fall on His children. The plagues of Revelation will come to earth, but God has promised to protect His children. On the Day of the Lord, God will give us relief from all our trials. And He will repay those who have troubled us (2 Thess. 1:6-9).

God protected Noah and his family. Inside the ark, they were safe from God's wrath. God rescued Lot and his daughters when the fire of judgment fell on Sodom. In Egypt, the ten plagues came upon the Egyptians, but did not harm the Israelites. Thank God! He has promised to protect His people from suffering His wrath. *"For God did not appoint us to suffer wrath but to receive salvation through our Lord Jesus Christ"* (1 Thess. 5:9).

The World Assemblies of God Fellowship is a body of over 140 self-governing Assemblies of God national groups of churches; with 300,000 ministers and outstations in over 212 countries and territories—serving over 66 million members worldwide. Here is a section from their statement of beliefs:

Q 123 What does the World Assemblies of God Fellowship believe about the Day of the Lord?

"WE BELIEVE IN THE PRE-MILLENIAL, IMMINENT, AND PERSONAL RETURN OF OUR LORD JESUS CHRIST TO GATHER HIS PEOPLE UNTO HIMSELF. HAVING THIS BLESSED HOPE AND EARNEST EXPECTATION, WE PURIFY OURSELVES, EVEN AS HE IS PURE, SO THAT WE MAY BE READY TO MEET HIM WHEN HE COMES (JOHN 14:1-3; TITUS 2:13; 1 THESS. 4:15-17; 1 JOHN 3:2-3; REV. 20:1-6).

WE BELIEVE IN THE BODILY RESURRECTION OF ALL HUMANITY, THE EVERLASTING CONSCIOUS BLISS OF ALL WHO TRULY BELIEVE IN OUR LORD JESUS CHRIST, AND THAT EVERLASTING CONSCIOUS PUNISHMENT IS THE PORTION OF ALL WHOSE NAMES ARE NOT WRITTEN IN THE BOOK OF LIFE (JOHN 5:28-29; 1 COR. 15:22-24; REV. 20:10-15)."[25]

Jesus is coming back to punish the disobedient and reward the obedient. So let us encourage each other, and not mourn as those with no hope. Let us have no fear of the future, as we live as children of the day. Whether we are asleep (dead in Christ) or awake when Christ comes, we will live together with Him (1 Thess. 4:17-18; 5:10-11).

Matthew	Words in Matthew	Words in Paul	1 and 2 Thess.
24:8	Birth pains	Labor pains	1 Thess. 5:3
24:9	Persecution and death	Destruction	1 Thess. 5:3
24:10	Turning away from the faith	Deception, rebellion	2 Thess. 2:3
24:11	False prophets	Alarmed by some prophecy	2 Thess. 2:2
24:11	Deception	Deceives those who are perishing	2 Thess. 2:10-11
24:12	Increase of wickedness	Delighted in wickedness	2 Thess. 2:12
24:13	Stand firm	Stand firm and hold to the teachings	2 Thess. 2:15
24:15	Abomination that causes desolation	Sets himself up as God in God's temple	2 Thess. 2:4
24:24	False christs and prophets, signs and miracles	Counterfeit miracles, signs, and wonders	2 Thess. 2:9
24:30-31	Send forth his angels with a loud trumpet	Loud command, voice of archangel, trumpet	1 Thess. 4:16
24:42, 44	Keep watch! Be ready!	Be sober! Be alert! Be self-controlled!	1 Thess. 5:6, 8
24:43	Thief	Thief	1 Thess. 5:2, 4
24:49	Drink with drunkards	Drunkenness	1 Thess. 5:7
24:51	Assigned a place with hypocrites; Weeping and gnashing of teeth	Everlasting destruction; Shut out from the presence of the Lord	2 Thess. 1:8-9

Figure 1.29   Parallels that show Matthew 24 influenced 1 and 2 Thessalonians [26]

Lesson 8 — Live Ready: Obey as You Wait for the Lord (1 Thess. 5:12-28)

Goal A: *Illustrate and practice each of the 15 principles in 1 Thessalonians 5:12–28).*
Goal B: *Explain the 5 commands about spiritual gifts in 1 Thessalonians 5:19-22.*

Every pastor should preach each of the 15 principles in Figure 1.30. In this lesson we will identify these principles, explain them, and guide students to illustrate and apply each. Also, we will spend extra time on 1 Thessalonians 5:19-22, a key passage.

1 Thess.	Principles to Live by as We Await the Lord's Coming	Illustrations of Principles
5:12	1 Respect church leaders who work hard, are over you in the Lord, and admonish you.	Contrast: Diotrephes, who opposed the apostle John
5:13	2 Live in peace with each other.	Isaac walked away from two wells he dug (Gen. 26:17-22).
5:14	3 Warn those who are idle.	
5:14	4 Encourage the timid.	
5:14	5 Help the weak.	
5:14	6 Be patient with everyone.	
5:15	7 Never pay back wrong for wrong, but always try to be kind to each other and to everyone else!	Romans 12:17-21
5:16	8 Be joyful always.	Paul at Philippi (Acts 16:25); 2 Corinthians 7:4
5:17	9 Pray continually.	
5:18	10 Give thanks in all circumstances, for this is God's will for you in Christ Jesus.	
5:19-22	11 Encourage spiritual gifts in the light of Scripture.	2 Thessalonians 2:2 (See point H in this lesson.)
5:23	12 Allow God to make you holy—body, soul, and spirit.	
5:25	13 Pray for church leaders.	
5:26	14 Be friendly to other believers.	
5:28	15 Enjoy God's grace and presence.	

Figure 1.30   15 principles for children of light awaiting the Day of the Lord

Paul closes his first letter to the Thessalonians with a series of about 15 commands:

[12]Now we ask you, brothers, to respect those who work hard among you, who are over you in the Lord and who admonish you. [13]Hold them in the highest regard in love because of their work. Live in peace with each other. [14]And we urge you, brothers, warn those who are idle, encourage the timid, help the weak,

be patient with everyone. ¹⁵*Make sure that nobody pays back wrong for wrong, but always try to be kind to each other and to everyone else.* ¹⁶*Be joyful always;* ¹⁷*pray continually;* ¹⁸*give thanks in all circumstances, for this is God's will for you in Christ Jesus.* ¹⁹*Do not put out the Spirit's fire;* ²⁰*do not treat prophecies with contempt.* ²¹*Test everything. Hold on to the good.* ²²*Avoid every kind of evil.* ²³*May God himself, the God of peace, sanctify you through and through. May your whole spirit, soul and body be kept blameless at the coming of our Lord Jesus Christ.* ²⁴*The one who calls you is faithful and he will do it.* ²⁵*Brothers, pray for us.* ²⁶*Greet all the brothers with a holy kiss.* ²⁷*I charge you before the Lord to have this letter read to all the brothers.* ²⁸*The grace of our Lord Jesus Christ be with you* (1 Thess. 5:12-28).

In this lesson we will highlight 12 of Paul's 15 commands (A–I).

A. Show respect to church leaders who deserve it (1 Thess. 5:12).

¹²*Now we ask you, brothers, to respect those who work hard among you, who are over you in the Lord and who admonish you.* ¹³*Hold them in the highest regard in love because of their work* (1 Thess. 5:12-13a).

Q 124 ➚ *When did the Israelites give Moses the most and the least respect?*

Thessalonica was a difficult place for Christians to live. At the edge of the city, someone could have put a warning: "Christians: Welcome to Hard Times! " Paul often reminded believers to show respect and honor to spiritual leaders who deserved it—such as Timothy, Titus, Epaphroditus, and Trophimus. But in difficult times, we need more reminders to be polite and respectful. The harder life gets, the more people grumble and complain. By the Red Sea, the Israelites saw Egyptian soldiers floating dead in the water and lying lifeless on the shore. So they sang, danced, and cheered for Moses (Exod. 15). But in the wilderness, when the sun was hot and water was scarce, they criticized Moses for leading them there (Exod. 17:1-3). The Thessalonians were as human as the rest of us. So Paul reminded them that even when our hills are steep to climb—we need to show respect to church leaders who work.

Christians: Welcome to Hard Times!

Q 125 ✎ *How do you show respect to spiritual leaders at home, at school, and at church?*

Q 126 ✎ *Why did Paul emphasize showing respect to spiritual leaders?*

David showed respect to King Saul even when he deserved it the least, because Saul was an anointed leader. Likewise, the writer of Hebrews admonished: Do yourself a favor—

Obey your leaders and submit to their authority. They keep watch over you as men who must give an account. Obey them so that their work will be a joy, not a burden, for that would be of no advantage to you (Heb. 13:17).

B. Live in peace with each other (1 Thess. 5:13b, 26).

Q 127 ✎ *Why is it harder to live in peace in difficult times? How is it possible?*

Believers in Thessalonica were like the rest of us—prone to grumble when life was tough. The Israelites criticized Moses when they had to make bricks without straw. They complained when the sun was hot and water was scarce. And they murmured when there was no meat to eat in the wilderness. Likewise, it would not surprise us if believers at Thessalonica complained and criticized when they lost their jobs, got kicked out of certain groups, were beaten or jailed. The pressures of life can bring out the worst in us.

Nothing is easier than for people to cause trouble. It is normal human behavior to slander, criticize, complain, be rude, and to spread gossip. These evils are common fruits of the flesh. Sinful forms of human behavior require no talent, no self-denial, no brains, and no character. They require no prayer, no spiritual life, and no effort. But in contrast to those who live by the flesh, the Bible emphasizes that God's children are led by the Spirit. And a major fruit of the Spirit is living in peace. So let us practice living in ways that sow seeds of peace, not discord.

Faults are like the lights of an approaching car: they seem to glare more than our own.[27]

Q 128 Summarize what each verse teaches about peace (Figure 1.31).

Scripture	Your Summaries About Peace
Matt. 5:9	
Gal. 5:22	
James 3:17	

Figure 1.31   Practice summarizing verses about peace.

C. Be patient with everyone (1 Thess. 5:14).

Love is patient, because it thinks about and values the feelings of others (1 Cor. 13:4). In contrast, when we lack love we may be rude. Consider the unloving, rude behavior of an impatient person. A parent yells or growls at a spouse or children. The rude tone of the voice reveals thinking only of self. A driver honks a horn, because someone has caused him to wait an extra second or two. A customer who has waited for a few minutes talks harshly to an employee. A child grabs a toy from another child, instead of waiting for his or her turn. All of these fleshly actions betray a focus on self. Most forms of sinful behavior reveal a lack of love for others. So when we feel impatient, let us whisper a prayer for more of God's love. *"By this all men will know that you are my disciples, if you love one another"* (John 13:35). Followers of Christ are known by their love. And love is known by its patience.

A man eating Limburger cheese, which has a strong smell, got some on his moustache. He walked from the dining room to the living room, sniffed the air and said, "Wife, your living room stinks." Afterward, he sniffed the air in the bedroom and declared, "Wife, your bedroom stinks." Later, in front of the house he sniffed the air and said, "Wife, the whole world stinks." Moral of the story: When others seem slow, dull, stupid, or incompetent, check your moustache! The problem may be closer to home than you realize.

Q 129 When is it hardest for you to be patient? How is patience possible?

Point #3 We need to analyze ourselves when we are lacking patience.

Q 130 What caused a man to think the whole world stunk?

Figure 1.32   One man thought the whole world stunk, but the problem was cheese on his moustache.

D. Never pay back wrong for wrong (1 Thess. 5:15).

"Make sure that nobody pays back wrong for wrong, but always try to be kind to each other and to everyone else" (1 Thess. 5:15). New believers at Thessalonica suffered greatly. No doubt their persecutions were like other believers of the New Testament. Recall the words of Hebrews to those suffering:

> [32]*Remember those earlier days after you had received the light, when you stood your ground in a great contest in the face of suffering.* [33]*Sometimes you were publicly exposed to insult and persecution; at other times you stood side by side with those who were so treated.* [34]*You sympathized with those in prison and joyfully accepted the confiscation of your property, because you knew that you yourselves had better and lasting possessions* (Heb. 10:32-34).

Persecution for following Christ has always been fierce. It includes beatings and imprisonment (Acts 16:22-24; 18:17), rejection by friends and family members (Matt. 10:34-36), having wages stolen (James 5:1-6), and even death (Acts 22:4).

So when we read Paul's words to Thessalonian Christians, let us recall that their sufferings included tears, heartache, bruises, and blood. To these believers Paul wrote:

Q 131 What types of persecution did believers at Thessalonica face?

Q 132 How is it possible to avoid returning evil for evil?

"Make sure that nobody pays back wrong for wrong, but always try to be kind to each other and to everyone else" (1 Thess. 5:15).

This type of attitude is too high for humans to reach in their own strength. But this is Christianity. Notice that the verse tells us to *"always **try** to be kind to each other and to everyone else"* (1 Thess. 5:15). And as we try and ask God to help us, He will give us grace that enables us to be like Jesus.

Perhaps the question we need to ask ourselves is: "Am I trying to be kind when others hurt me?"

One man struggled to forgive those who persecuted him and others of his ethnic group. As he saw the injuries and insults to his people, he hated the persecutors. He hated them until his soul dried up. Then one day he tried to forgive. He took his hatred to Jesus Christ, and asked for help. At once the Savior took the hatred from his heart. New life flowed into his dry soul. Jesus taught him how to forgive and love his enemies. This is the path to forgiveness. Whether someone has insulted you, cheated you, lied about you, or hurt you, your family, or your friends, kneel and remember the cross. Look to the risen One and ask Him to give you His love.

Q 133 ⬃ *Have you ever wanted to forgive, but lacked the strength? Explain.*

Q 134 ⬃ *Summarize what each verse teaches about forgiveness* (Figure 1.33).

Scripture	Your Summaries
Gen. 50:19-21	
Rom. 12:19-21	
1 Pet. 2:20b-23	

Figure 1.33   Practice summarizing verses about forgiveness, and leaving vengeance to God.

Q 135 ⬃ *How can we guide ourselves to joy, when we feel sad?*

E. Be joyful always (1 Thess. 5:16).

In Thessalonica, trials and troubles were trying to bend the heads of believers down. But Paul teaches them that Christians can sing in the storms. And Paul practiced what he preached. In Philippi, at midnight, Paul and Silas were in prison after a severe beating (Acts 16:19-25). No need trying to sleep in jail with their backs bleeding, and their feet in the stocks. So they began singing hymns! It was not likely that they felt like singing at first. But more often than not, when we start singing, we soon feel like singing some more.

Christianity is the most encouraging and the most joyful of all religions. We believers have our tears and sorrows. And we train ourselves to practice what is right, even when emotions lag behind. But the end of our journey is not a burial, but a resurrection—not a funeral, but a festival. And whenever we encourage it, the life of Christ bubbles up within us, providing a song in the night, and a candle in the dark.

Figure 1.34   Paul and Silas prayed and sang in prison at Philippi.

F. Pray continually (1 Thess. 5:17).

General Jackson was famous for his constant prayer in human and spiritual battles. Jackson said, "I have so fixed the habit of prayer in my mind, that I never raise a glass of water to my lips without asking God's blessing. I never seal a letter without putting a word of prayer under the seal. I never take a letter from an envelope without sending a prayer toward heaven. I never walk from one classroom to teach in another without a minute of prayer for the students who are coming in and going out."

Q 136 ⬀ *Is it possible to pray all day? Explain.*

Q 137 ⬃ *Do you practice praying with your eyes open—as you go through the day?*

Likewise, the apostle Paul urges us to make prayer a way of life. Earth is a battlefield between good and evil (Eph. 6:12-20). Through constant prayer, we stay in touch with our Spiritual Commander.[28]

John Wesley liked to greet believers with: "Do I meet you praying?"

G. Give thanks in all circumstances (1 Thess. 5:18).

Give thanks in all circumstances, for this is God's will for you in Christ Jesus (1 Thess. 5:18).

Imagine, Paul wrote 1 Thessalonians 5:18 to believers who were in the midst of intense suffering! Praise to our Father is always a fitting garment for God's children to wear. So let us wrap ourselves with the robe of thanksgiving. Earth has its sorrows for everyone. But Jesus died to cleanse us from sin and shame. Our sins and our chains are gone. We have been chosen to spend eternity as God's children. His Spirit lives within us. We are children of the King, and it is His delight to share His kingdom with us forever. We have so much for which to be thankful!

Q 138 *How was it possible for the Thessalonians to give thanks while suffering?*

The prophet Habakkuk lived in the days of Jeremiah, about 640–609 B.C. Habakkuk was grieved over the sins of Judah. He asked God why Judah's sins were not punished. God replied that He would indeed send the Babylonians to conquer and punish Judah. Then Habakkuk asked God how he could use the Babylonians, who were more evil than Judah, to punish Judah. God answered that in time He would also punish the Babylonians. As the book of Habakkuk closes, the prophet realizes that his nation will soon be destroyed. Still, with deep roots of faith, He rejoices in God, our Savior. Recall his prayer:

Q 139 *In what circumstances did Habakkuk give thanks?*

> ¹⁷*Though the fig tree does not bud and there are no grapes on the vines, though the olive crop fails and the fields produce no food, though there are no sheep in the pen and no cattle in the stalls,* ¹⁸*yet I will rejoice in the LORD, I will be joyful in God my Savior.* ¹⁹*The Sovereign LORD is my strength; he makes my feet like the feet of a deer, he enables me to go on the heights* (Hab. 3:17-19).

> LOCK ME UP IN A PRISON, AND THROW AWAY THE KEY.
> TAKE AWAY THE VISION, FROM THESE EYES THAT NOW CAN SEE.
> DEPRIVE ME OF THE FOOD I EAT,
> AND EVEN BIND MY HANDS AND FEET.
> FOR AS LONG AS I KNOW JESUS, I CAN STILL GO FREE.
> WHAT KIND OF MAN
> WOULD REACH DOWN HIS HAND AND DO THIS FOR ME?
> UNWORTHY TO LIVE AND NOT FIT TO KILL;
> YET A MAN ON THE CROSS PUT ME IN HIS WILL
> AND SAID THAT I COULD STILL GO FREE.²⁹

Q 140 *What enabled Paul to give thanks in any situation?*

H. Encourage spiritual gifts in the light of Scripture (1 Thess. 5:19-22).

Paul gives five verbs as commands in 1 Thessalonians 5:19-22. At first, a reader might think these five *imperatives (commands) are unrelated. But as Stronstad shows, **all five commands are connected to the ministry of prophecy.**³⁰ Let us look briefly at these five commands.

Q 141 *What happens when there is wildfire in a church? Illustrate.*

- The *first* command is a warning. Paul says in the Greek: *"Do not put out* [extinguish or quench] *the Spirit"* (1 Thess. 5:19). Some translations, like the NIV, add the word *fire,* which is sometimes a symbol of the Spirit (Acts 2:3; 2 Tim. 1:6).³¹ Elsewhere Paul cautions against *wildfire*—confusion and disorder (1 Cor. 14:39-40). But here he warns against *"no fire,"* which results when leaders want too much order and control.

Q 142 *Why do some pastors try to exclude spiritual gifts from the church? What is the balance?*

Wildfire		Strange		Fire of the		No
fire		fire		Holy Spirit		fire

Figure 1.35   Scripture warns against two spiritual extremes: no fire and wild fire. Elsewhere, Scripture warns about *strange fire* (Lev. 10:1), which we may liken to teachings that do not come from God. What the Church needs is the pure fire of the Holy Spirit among us.

Q 143 *How are earthly and spiritual fires a blessing to us?*

Two men out hiking got lost in mountains on a cold, rainy night. Wet, tired, and chilled, they gathered a few pieces of wood. After several tries, they succeeded in lighting a fire. Carefully they tended that fire, watching over it until they were certain it would keep burning. As it grew brighter, it provided the comfort of light in the darkness—and the necessity of heat to warm their cold, weary bodies. That night they realized as never before what a friend fire is to man. Even more, we need to keep the fire of the Spirit burning!

Q 144 *How does 1 Thessalonians 5:20 relate to 1 Thessalonians 5:19?*

Q 145 *What are 3 forms of prophecy? Illustrate each.*

- The **second** command is a warning that clarifies the first one. *"Do not treat prophecies with contempt"* (1 Thess. 5:20). Paul is concerned that believers should not show contempt for the spiritual gift of prophecy (1 Cor. 12:10; 14:1-4), or its equivalent, tongues and interpretation. He does not want them to throw water on the Spirit's fire.

God desires to bless the Church with the gift of prophecy, and all spiritual gifts, until Christ's return (1 Cor. 1:7). The spiritual gift of prophecy may come in three forms: *forth-telling, foretelling,* and *heart telling.* As *forth-telling,* prophecy proclaims the anointed Word of God in a specific situation. Peter's message on the Day of Pentecost was prophetic in the sense of forth-telling. As *foretelling,* prophecy declares the future. When Agabus prophesied a famine in Jerusalem, he was *foretelling* the future (Acts 11:27-28). As *heart telling,* prophecy reveals the secrets of a person's heart. Jesus showed this prophetic gift often, as with the woman at the well (John 4:17-19), revealing the secrets of her heart (compare 1 Cor. 14:24-25). (For an entire lesson on the gift of prophecy, see the *Faith & Action* book: *1 and 2 Corinthians,* Lesson 24.) Through supernatural gifts, like prophecy, the Holy Spirit's power and presence edify and encourage believers and unbelievers. We need spiritual gifts today, so let us encourage the fire of the Spirit in our midst.

Q 146 *What is the biblical solution for prophecies that go astray?*

- Paul's **third** command is: *"Test everything"* (1 Thess. 5:21). Paul does not want believers to reject all prophecies. But neither does he say we must approve every message someone claims is from the Lord. Paul encourages believers to seek to prophesy (1 Cor. 14). Yet while prophecy is welcome, it must always be subject to testing. For example, all prophecies must be in harmony with Scripture. In 2 Thessalonians 2:2, it appears that there was a prophecy claiming that Paul said the Day of the Lord was past. Paul rejects this message as a deception, explaining that it does not pass the test of his gospel teachings (2 Thess. 2:1-5).

Q 147 *If believers will not allow their prophecies to be tested, what should they do?*

Some believers who prophesy may feel threatened if we *test* what they say. But the truth can bear examination. If believers are not willing for their *prophecies* to be examined, then let them remain silent. Still, let us keep in mind that a healthy church is not necessarily one that is free from any misuse or mistakes with spiritual gifts. Rather, a healthy church is one that has enough love, tolerance, and truth to examine, receive, or correct the use of spiritual gifts.

Q 148 *If a prophecy falls short, does that mean the person who gave it had a bad motive? Explain.*

Some who misuse spiritual gifts have bad character and bad motives, like *Jezebel,* who claimed to be a prophetess, but led God's servants into sexual sins (Rev. 2:20). This type of person must be disciplined by the church. In contrast, some believers are sincere, but like the Corinthian believers, need to grow in their understanding of using spiritual gifts (1 Cor. 12–14). Blessed is the church that invites and delights in spiritual gifts, and encourages believers to grow in this ministry; but demands godly character in those who minister the gifts, and tests everything by Scripture.

- Paul's *last two* commands in this group of five summarize the results of testing prophecies. [21] "... *Hold on to the good.* [22] *Avoid every kind of evil*" (1 Thess. 5:21-22). With fish we eat the meat and throw away the bones. With wheat we keep the kernel and discard the chaff. With prophecies, we hold on to the good ones and reject those out of order or out of line with Scripture. *Test everything* is a biblical command for prophecies, and also sermons, teachings, songs, customs, and choices. Whatever is unscriptural or unprofitable we avoid. Whatever agrees with Scripture, edifies the Church, and glorifies God, we cling to those things. In this way we keep in step with the Spirit (Gal. 5:25), walk in the Spirit, and enjoy the gifts of the Spirit. We live in a dry and dying world that very much needs the refreshing flow of the Spirit's presence in our lives and churches. May the church be ever thirsty for the moving of the Spirit in our midst and the living waters God intends to flow through us (John 7:38).

John Wesley, founder of the Methodist Church, recorded over 200 divine healings in his revival meetings. He said that spiritual gifts were lost to the Church through unbelief, but we can regain them by faith.[32]

I. Allow God to make you holy—in body, soul, and spirit (1 Thess. 5:23).

[23] *May God himself, the God of peace, sanctify you through and through. May your whole spirit, soul and body be kept blameless at the coming of our Lord Jesus Christ.* [24] *The one who calls you is faithful and he will do it* (1 Thess. 5:23-24).

Holiness is not just for a part of us. God wants to make us holy through and through—body, soul, and spirit. He wants us to be holy in our position, our actions, and our nature. God is holy, so He wants us to be like Him—holy in all we are and in all we do (1 Pet. 1:15-16).

Examine yourself. Are there areas of your life that are unholy? Are you holy and pure in your attitudes, your secret thoughts, your actions, and your habits? If there are areas in which you need to be more pure, come to Jesus with your arms and your heart open. Holiness is His plan for us in this life. As we spend time in His presence, He will sanctify us through and through. Holiness is not just dutiful, it is beautiful. As we are holy and walk in the light of His Word and Spirit, we can fellowship with God, in whom there is no darkness at all (1 John 1:5).

As a boy, D. L. Moody heard a pastor preach, "The world has not yet seen what God can do by His Holy Spirit in and through one man who consecrates his life to Him." Hearing that statement, Moody said to himself, "With God's help I will be that man!"[33] As a result of his holy life, Moody led thousands of sinners to Christ, and discipled them to follow the Master. What about you? Will you be that holy man or woman—body, soul, and spirit?

Q 149 *What is the relationship of 1 Thessalonians 5:21-22 to 1 Thessalonians 5:20?*

Q 150 *What should we test besides prophecies?*

Q 151 *What types of ministry should we reject because they fail two tests?*

Q 152 *What does it mean to be holy in body, soul, and spirit?*

Q 153 *Do you accept the challenge to grow and walk in holiness?*

Test Yourself: Circle the letter by the *best* completion to each question or statement.

1. Why did Paul write 1 Thessalonians?
a) To give guidelines on spiritual gifts
b) To clarify the coming of the Antichrist
c) To encourage new believers in their trials
d) To assure that grace covers our sins

2. The theme of 1 and 2 Thessalonians is:
a) eschatology.
b) the second coming of Christ.
c) godly living.
d) spiritual gifts.

3. Which is TRUE of believers in Thessalonica?
a) They suffered great persecution.
b) They were very poor.
c) They misunderstood spiritual gifts.
d) They were very legalistic.

4. In 1 Thessalonians to Titus, "gospel" includes
a) from the cross to the empty tomb.
b) from the incarnation to the ascension.
c) from the First Coming to the Second Coming.
d) from before creation through forever.

5. Fruitful ministry depends on
a) loving the lost more than anyone else.
b) the love of God flowing through us.
c) avoiding suffering through faith in Christ.
d) a daring commitment to defy the law.

6. What is the scope of biblical holiness?
a) Our position in Christ
b) Our standing and our actions
c) Our position, actions, and condition
d) Our actions, attitudes, and condition

7. Why does Paul want us to grow in responsibility?
a) To win the respect of unbelievers
b) To win the favor of God
c) To provide for the needs of others
d) To grow up in Christ

8. At the second coming of Christ, the sequence is:
a) The living in Christ rise first.
b) The dead in Christ rise first.
c) The living and dead rise at the same time.
d) The living rise, then the dead, then the lukewarm.

9. The "Day of the Lord"
a) has only 24 hours.
b) began when Jesus died on the cross.
c) brings judgment to the disobedient.
d) is for sinners, not saints.

10. Paul's teaching on prophecy in 1 Thessalonians 5 is based on
a) 5 commands.
b) 5 promises.
c) 5 warnings.
d) 5 illustrations.

Essay Test Topics: Write 50-100 words on each of these goals that you studied in this chapter (5 points each). Try to complete your writing in two hours.

- Summarize Paul's ministry to the Thessalonians—its beginning, interruption, and continuation.
- Explain 5 reasons why Paul wrote to Thessalonian believers.
- Define *eschatology*, and summarize its emphasis in the Thessalonian Epistles.
- Summarize the challenges that believers in Thessalonica faced.
- Identify and apply 3 ways Paul encouraged Thessalonian believers.
- Explain what Paul means by *the gospel*.
- Explain and illustrate how fruitful ministry depends on daring commitment (1 Thess. 2:1-16).
- Analyze and illustrate the role of loving commitment in fruitful ministry (1 Thess. 2:1-16).
- Examine the relationship of fruitful ministry to the hearers' response (1 Thess. 2:1-16). Illustrate this.
- Summarize and illustrate the importance of endurance for fruitful servants.
- Explain and illustrate that fruitful service depends on God's love flowing through us.
- Explain and illustrate 3 aspects of growing in holiness.
- Summarize how our cooperation with the Holy Spirit is God's plan for holy living.
- Contrast the love of a young believer and a mature believer.
- Identify and illustrate 2 reasons why Paul wants all believers to grow in personal responsibility.
- Summarize the Thessalonian question and Paul's answer on the Lord's return (1 Thess. 4:13-18).
- Explain what Paul means by *the Day of the Lord*. Include at least 4 key biblical references.
- Contrast the sad and glad aspects of the Day of the Lord.
- Illustrate and practice each of the 15 principles in 1 Thessalonians 5:12-28.
- Explain the 5 commands about spiritual gifts in 1 Thessalonians 5:19-22.

Chapter 2:
Be Steadfast as You Wait for the Lord's Return
(2 Thess. 1–3)

Much of 2 Thessalonians is about the Day of the Lord, which includes the comings of Christ and the Antichrist. In addition to powers, signs, and false wonders, Paul mentions that the Antichrist uses *"every sort of evil that deceives those who are perishing"* (2 Thess. 2:10).

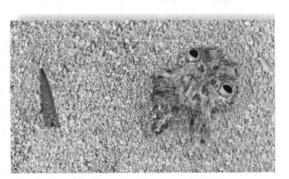

Figure 2.1   The sidewinder snake buries most of its body in the sand, except for its eyes and its tail—which sticks out of the sand like a blade of grass. As the snake wiggles its tail, it attracts ants. Soon, the ants attract a lizard or gecko, and the snake has a delicious dinner.[1]

Sabio warns: "Do not buy everything that wiggles."

Like fool's gold, Satan, the world, and the Antichrist lead the masses astray with the deceitfulness of sin (Heb. 3:13). The pages of history contain the names of millions of people whom Satan has **deceived** with *"every sort of evil"* (2 Thess. 2:10). The devil deceived Adam and Eve into trading paradise for a bite of fruit! He lured Achan to trade his life and his entire family for a bag of treasure he could not keep (Josh. 7). He used the deceitfulness of power and riches to lead a wise king like Solomon into idolatry. And Satan seduced the world's strongest man to trade his strength, reputation, eyes, and life for a few days with Delilah (Judg. 16). Satan uses every sort of evil to deceive—including the misuse of power, position, privilege, money, drugs, and sex. Those who bargain with the devil lose every time. Those who exchange the truth of God for a lie regret it forever (Rom. 1:25). Sabio warns: "Everything that glitters is not gold."

Figure 2.2   There is a mineral called iron pyrite that looks like gold—but its value is very low compared to true gold. People refer to it as *fool's gold*, because it has deceived many.

<u>Paul emphasizes that our destiny depends on our response to truth.</u>   There is safety and security for those who embrace the truth. But there is certain destruction for those who refuse to love truth.

Lessons:

Make the Most of Your Suffering (2 Thess. 1)

Goal A: *Review how we encourage others by affirming their spiritual progress.*
Goal B: *Summarize how the justice of God reveals itself in reward and punishment.*
Goal C: *Contrast the desires of Satan and God for our success.*

The Comings of Christ and Antichrist—Part 1 (2 Thess. 2:1-8)

Goal A: *Summarize the scope, events, and valleys of the "Day of the Lord."*
Goal B: *Identify and illustrate 2 characteristics of the Antichrist (2 Thess. 2).*

The Comings of Christ and Antichrist—Part 2 (2 Thess. 2:9–3:8)

Goal A: *Analyze the rise of the Antichrist to power, and the length of his rule (2 Thess. 2).*
Goal B: *Explain how danger and safety relate to our response to truth (2 Thess. 2).*
Goal C: *Summarize Paul's words of encouragement and rebuke (2 Thess. 3).*

retribution—God's judgment and punishment of the wicked

apostasy—a turning away from the faith, after believing

Sovereign—God; the supreme, permanent ruler over the kingdoms of men and the entire universe

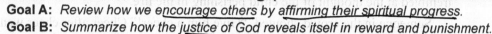

Lesson 9

Make the Most of Your Suffering (2 Thess. 1)

Goal A: *Review how we encourage others by affirming their spiritual progress.*
Goal B: *Summarize how the justice of God reveals itself in reward and punishment.*
Goal C: *Contrast the desires of Satan and God for our success.*

Like many believers, those at Thessalonica had a faith refined by fire. Paul left these new believers within a month after they began to follow Christ. They *"turned to God from idols to serve the true and living God"* (1 Thess. 1:9). At once, former friends began to persecute them since they no longer attended the local feasts to pagan gods. Likewise, unbelieving Jews added them to the list of Christians to persecute. Following Jesus cost them such things as family ties, friends, jobs, acceptance in society, and protection by the local government.

Q 1 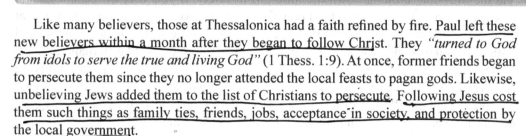 *What types of persecution resulted when new believers refused to attend local feasts to idols?*

A great leader once said, "This is a terrible war, but it is the only one we have. So let's win it!" Likewise, the sufferings of young believers at Thessalonica were fierce. But Paul urged them to make the most of their trials. As one person said, "Don't waste your sufferings?" Let us look at three ways to survive suffering and help others in the fiery trial of faith.

A. Encourage those who suffer by affirming their spiritual progress (1 Thess. 1:2-10; 2 Thess. 1:3-5).

Review verses from 1 Thessalonians 1 that follow. Underline the good things that Paul says to these suffering believers.

²We always thank God for all of you, mentioning you in our prayers. ³We continually remember before our God and Father your work produced by faith, your labor prompted by love, and your endurance inspired by hope in our Lord Jesus Christ. ⁴For we know, brothers loved by God, that he has chosen you, ⁵because our gospel came to you not simply with words, but also with power, with the Holy Spirit and with deep conviction. You know how we lived among you for your sake (1 Thess. 1:2-5).

Q 2 *Underline Paul's words of praise to encourage the Thessalonians (1 Thess. 1).*

³We ought always to thank God for you, brothers, and rightly so, because your faith is growing more and more, and the love every one of you has for each other is increasing. ⁴Therefore, among God's churches we boast about your perseverance and faith in all the persecutions and trials you are enduring. ⁵All this is evidence that God's judgment is right, and as a result you will be counted worthy of the kingdom of God, for which you are suffering (2 Thess. 1:3-5).

Q 3 *Underline 4 reasons why Paul boasted about the Thessalonians (2 Thess. 1:3-5).*

Explanation. Encouragement brings out the best in all of us. People will walk a mile to hear a compliment. Children love to hear their parents brag on them. And all of us appreciate it when someone praises the good things we do. Jesus said that the offering Mary gave would be credited to her wherever the gospel is preached (Matt. 26:13). His words were a great reward for her. Every person on earth likes to be appreciated. We like to hear "Thank you" when we do good deeds for others. We like someone to notice when

Q 4 *How do you feel when someone brags on your progress?*

we do the right things. All of us stand a little bit taller when someone nods their head at us in approval, or praises us for spiritual fruit and progress.

How much does it cost to give someone a compliment, a pat on the back, or a word of encouragement? It costs us nothing. But what is the value of the kind words we share? The cost is low, but the value is high!

Q 5 *What strengthened the fireman to rescue the child who was perishing? Apply this.*

A child came to the window as the flames around her house climbed higher. "Help me," she cried in a loud voice. A fireman started up the ladder to rescue the child from destruction. The wind blew the flames near his face. It got so hot that he wavered, and looked down, as if he would return without the girl. Hundreds looked up. Their hearts trembled at the thought of the child perishing in the fire.

Someone in the crowd shouted, "Give him a cheer!" Cheer after cheer went up, and as the man heard them he gained fresh courage. Up he went into the midst of the smoke and the fire—and brought down the little girl to safety. If you yourself cannot go and rescue the perishing, you can at least pray for those who do, and cheer them on. Do what you can to encourage others, and the Lord will bless your efforts. Do not grumble and criticize; it takes neither heart nor brains to do that.[2] Rather, be like Barnabas, whose name means "Son of Encouragement"—because he was always inspiring, edifying or cheering for someone who needed it. Be a *spiritual cheerleader* for others. Your encouragement can be the difference in success or failure in those you meet. Leave people more encouraged than they were when you met them.

Q 6 *How can you find someone to encourage? Give an example.*

The Thessalonians were growing in faith and increasing in love. They did not remain babies for long. Like all healthy children, they grew day by day. Their faith and love produced endurance and perseverance in their suffering. All of this spiritual growth was evidence that they were *"worthy of the kingdom of God,"* (2 Thess. 1:5) because they were truly children of faith and love—true children of God.

God uses sufferings to perfect, mature, and refine His children (James 1:2-4). Jesus was made perfect and complete as our High Priest through His sufferings (Heb. 2:10). Likewise, sufferings in our life are evidence that God is developing our character, and transforming us into the image of Christ (Rom. 5:3; 8:29). Paul often writes about the role of suffering in our lives. And at the beginning of this letter, the apostle takes time to encourage these young believers with words of praise for their progress.

B. When suffering, remember that God is just (2 Thess. 1:6-10).

Since God is just, He must reward the obedient and punish the disobedient. Believers suffer now, but enjoy forever. In contrast, sinners may celebrate now, but will suffer forever.

Q 7 *In what sense will many things be reversed in the next life? Illustrate.*

For many, things will be reversed in the next life. In this life, the righteous may lack many things. But at the coming of Christ, God will shake the earth. Many on the top will fall to the bottom, and multitudes on the bottom will rise to the top. Recall the story Jesus told about Lazarus and the rich man (Luke 16:19-31).

[19] *"There was a rich man who was dressed in purple and fine linen and lived in luxury every day.* [20] *At his gate was laid a beggar named Lazarus, covered with sores* [21] *and longing to eat what fell from the rich man's table. Even the dogs came and licked his sores.* [22] *The time came when the beggar died and the angels carried him to Abraham's side. The rich man also died and was buried.* [23] *In hell, where he was in torment, he looked up and saw Abraham far away, with Lazarus by his side.* [24] *So he called to him, 'Father Abraham, have pity on me and send Lazarus to dip the tip of his finger in water and cool my tongue, because I am in agony in this fire.'* [25] *But Abraham replied, 'Son, remember that in your lifetime you received your good things, while Lazarus received bad things, but now he is comforted here and you are in agony"* (Luke 16:19-25).

Let us examine two things God's justice brings when Jesus returns.

1. God will give relief and the Kingdom to believers. Relief comes when Jesus comes.

> [6]*God is just: He will pay back trouble to those who trouble you* [7]*and give relief to you who are troubled, and to us as well.* **This will happen when the Lord Jesus is revealed from heaven in blazing fire with his powerful angels** (2 Thess. 1:6-7).

Q 8 ➤ *When does God promise He will give relief to suffering believers?*

The patience of God is costly. *"He is patient ..., not wanting anyone to perish, but everyone to come to repentance"* (2 Pet. 3:9). Yet as long as God is patient with sinners, many insult Him, blaspheme His name, and abuse His grace. Likewise, while God is patient with the disobedient, believers suffer. When Cain is free, Abel gets killed. While the unrighteous prosper, the prophets are murdered. When evil men rule, they grow fat on the wages they steal from the poor (James 5:1-6). Every year that God is patient with sinners, they martyr about 160,000 believers.[3] When the fifth seal was opened in Revelation 6:9, John saw a vision of souls who had been slain for their testimony about Christ and righteousness. He heard them ask, *"How long, Sovereign Lord, holy and true, until you judge the inhabitants of the earth and avenge our blood?"* And God's answer was, *"until the number of their fellow servants and brothers who were to be killed as they had been was completed"* (Rev. 6:10-11). God's patience is expensive. Delayed relief means continued suffering. Nevertheless, we are certain that relief will come when Jesus returns (2 Thess. 1:7). So when suffering for Christ, let us encourage ourselves with the assurance that relief is coming. *"Weeping may remain for a night, but rejoicing comes in the morning"* (Ps. 30:5).

Q 9 ↖ *Complete Figure 2.3 on what will happen when God rewards the righteous.*

Reference	Your Summaries
Luke 12:32	
Rom. 8:18	
2 Cor. 4:16-18	

Figure 2.3 Practice summarizing verses about future rewards for the righteous.

"Fear not, little flock; for it is your Father's good pleasure to give you the kingdom" (Luke 12:32).

[18]*I consider that our present sufferings are not worth comparing with the glory that will be revealed in us* (Rom. 8:18).

[16]*Therefore we do not lose heart. Though outwardly we are wasting away, yet inwardly we are being renewed day by day.* [17]*For our light and momentary troubles are achieving for us an eternal glory that far outweighs them all.* [18]*So we fix our eyes not on what is seen, but on what is unseen. For what is seen is temporary, but what is unseen is eternal* (2 Cor. 4:16-18).

The future of God's suffering children is as bright as the sun at noon. But the future of rebels is as dark as midnight in a storm.

2. God will decree everlasting destruction to those who trouble believers.

Q 10 ↖ *Complete Figure 2.4 on verses related to future punishment of God's enemies.*

Reference	Your Summaries
Matt. 13:41	
2 Cor. 5:11	
2 Thess. 1:8-10	
Heb. 10:31	
2 Pet. 2:13	

Figure 2.4 Practice summarizing verses related to the future punishment of the unrighteous.

[6]*God is just: He will pay back trouble to those who trouble you* [7]*and give relief to you who are troubled, and to us as well. This will happen when the Lord Jesus is revealed from heaven in blazing fire with his powerful angels.* [8]*He will punish those who do not know God and do not obey the gospel of our Lord Jesus.* [9]*They*

will be punished with everlasting destruction and shut out from the presence of the Lord and from the majesty of his power [10] *on the day he comes to be glorified in his holy people and to be marveled at among all those who have believed. This includes you, because you believed our testimony to you* (2 Thess. 1:6-10).

Q 11 ↖ How do believers feel about the future punishment of the disobedient?

The time is coming when God will pay the disobedient with the wages they have earned. This doctrine of judgment for the wicked is called *retribution.* God is just. He must punish evil (2 Pet. 2:13). When Christ returns, God will pour out His wrath on all *"who do not know [Him] and do not obey the gospel of our Lord Jesus.* [10] *They will be punished with everlasting destruction and shut out from the presence of the Lord and from the majesty of his power"* (2 Thess. 1:8-9). This terrible truth brings great sorrow to our hearts, and tears to our eyes. All of us have suffered trouble. Some have been excluded, mocked, cheated, betrayed, slandered, beaten, robbed, and even martyred. Yet on our worst day, we do not desire for even our worst enemy to suffer eternal destruction. We believers do not want our enemies to suffer the eternal fire of hell. And God does not desire it. He has no pleasure in the death of the wicked (Ezek. 33:11). Half the world is missing heaven *without* the opportunity to hear and obey the gospel. Many will go to hell, not just because of their sin (for all have sinned), but rather, they will go to hell because, to the end, they rejected the open arms of our loving Savior.

Q 12 ↖ Why is it necessary for God to punish the wicked?

Retribution, the punishment of the wicked, is a terrible but necessary doctrine. Our biblical song of hope must include a verse about judgment.[4] For peace and holiness to fill the earth, God must separate out of His kingdom everything that causes sin and all that offends (Matt. 13:41). A little leaven spreads through the whole. There cannot be peace among the sheep while wolves are attacking. And God's kingdom cannot come in its fullness until He judges the wicked and separates them from the righteous.[5] So, knowing the terror of the Lord, we try to persuade people to turn from their sin to the Savior (2 Cor. 5:11). It is a fearful thing for the disobedient *"to fall into the hands of the living God"* (Heb. 10:31).

Julian, an emperor of Rome, was once a Christian. But he returned to serve Satan. His love for sin filled him with hate for the godly. So he spent the rest of his life trying to wipe out Christianity from the Roman kingdom. One Roman soldier mocked a Christian and asked: "Where is your carpenter now?" Sadly the Christian replied, "He is making a coffin for your emperor."[6] Justice may be delayed, but it is as certain as death. What we sow, we must reap—unless we accept God's gracious plan of forgiveness.

C. Remember that God desires our spiritual success—whatever we face (2 Thess. 1:11-12).

[11] *With this in mind, we constantly pray for you, that our God may count you worthy of his calling, and that by his power he may fulfill every good purpose of yours and every act prompted by your faith.* [12] *We pray this so that the name of our Lord Jesus may be glorified in you, and you in him, according to the grace of our God and the Lord Jesus Christ* (2 Thess. 1:11-12).

Q 13 ↗ Does God want us to succeed or fail? Explain.

As early as Eden, we see God encouraging sinners to change directions. When Cain's offering was not accepted, God tried to encourage him, saying:

"Why are you angry? Why is your face downcast? [7] *If you do what is right, will you not be accepted? But if you do not do what is right, sin is crouching at your door; it desires to have you, but you must master it"* (Gen. 4:6-7).

Q 14 ↖ Give any 2 examples that show God wants us to succeed.

God is always cheering for us, even when we get it wrong the first time. With God, the next time is always more important than the last time. He is always more concerned about our future than our past.

As the prophet told King Asa, God is always on our side when we are on His side (2 Chron. 15:2; 16:9). He is always with us when we are seeking His will and Kingdom.

Some people are jealous or angry when others succeed. Cain murdered Abel because his own actions were evil and his brother's were righteous (1 John 3:11-12). King Saul hated David because of his success and popularity (1 Sam. 18:6-9). The Pharisees envied Jesus because He was more popular than they were (Matt. 27:18). And Satan would like to see every believer fail. In contrast, God wants us to succeed in every godly and noble goal (2 Thess. 1:11). He is always cheering for us to succeed in the desires He gives us, and He is eager to give us victory through Jesus Christ (1 Cor. 15:57). God wants us to be spiritual winners so that He is glorified. He desires us to bear much fruit for His kingdom (John 15:1-8). So no matter how rocky your path is or how steep the mountain is you are climbing, remember that **God is on your side.** When you are seeking to please God, you are never alone. *"If God is for us, who can be against us"* (Rom. 8:31)?

The prophet Jeremiah wrote to Israelites from Judah who became captives in Babylon. The last 75 years of the Southern Kingdom the people practiced idolatry and disobedience to God. Evil kings, such as Manasseh who reigned 55 years, had a terrible influence on the nation. God sent various prophets, like Jeremiah, calling the people to repent and return to Him. But the people refused. Finally, the day of judgment came and Nebuchadnezzar conquered the Southern Kingdom of Judah. Still, even in the midst of 70 years of judgment, God desired their spiritual success. Recall the beautiful promise God sent to encourage the people He was disciplining:

He wants us to desire for our [handwritten margin note]

Q 15 *What helps you understand how much God wants you to succeed?*

This is what the LORD says: "When seventy years are completed for Babylon, I will come to you and fulfill my gracious promise to bring you back to this place. [11] *For I know the plans I have for you," declares the LORD, "plans to prosper you and not to harm you, plans to give you hope and a future.* [12] *Then you will call upon me and come and pray to me, and I will listen to you.* [13] *You will seek me and find me when you seek me with all your heart"* (Jer. 29:10-13).

Figure 2.5 Captives from the Southern Kingdom going to Babylon

Even when God must discipline His people for sin, He is always looking ahead to the days He can bless and prosper us, when we turn our hearts toward Him.

Lesson 10 — The Comings of Christ and Antichrist—Part 1 (2 Thess. 2:1-8)

Goal A: *Summarize the scope, events, and valleys of the "Day of the Lord."*
Goal B: *Identify and illustrate 2 characteristics of the Antichrist (2 Thess. 2).*

Overview of confusion at Thessalonica, and the Day of the Lord. Most preachers repeat and review biblical teachings for their members. And for young believers like the Thessalonians who turn from idols to Christ, it is necessary to review teachings many times. When Paul was with these new converts in Thessalonica for 3 to 4 weeks, he covered the same teachings often (2 Thess. 2:5). Still, there was confusion, especially about eschatology. Sometimes we think we understand a subject, until new questions arise. It seems that some believers at Thessalonica had died. This raised a new question about the dead in Christ: "Will they miss the Day of the Lord?" Paul wrote about this question in 1 Thessalonians 4:13-18. Likewise, in that first letter to the Thessalonians, Paul wrote about the suddenness of the Day of the Lord, coming as a thief in the night. He explained that the Day of the Lord will bring surprise and shock upon the unrighteous, but joy and salvation to those who are alert and self-controlled (1 Thess. 5:1-11). Still, personal circumstances we experience cause us to re-visit and re-examine previous teachings.

Q 16 *In Thessalonica, what probably raised a new question about eschatology?*

Some believers at Thessalonica died. [handwritten margin note]

Q 17 ⊼ *Why is it difficult to makes sense out of what the young believers at Thessalonica were thinking?*

Paul's *first letter* answered the Thessalonian question about the dead in Christ. But questions and confusion continued at Thessalonica. Some may have misinterpreted Paul, thinking he claimed *"the day of the Lord* had *already come"* (2 Thess. 2:2). Or perhaps there was a **fake letter, or an errant word of prophecy—claiming Christ had already returned and left.** Studies in eschatology have often been a source of disagreement. It is not clear what the new believers at Thessalonica thought. These young believers were in a panic. They seemed to fear that the Second Coming was past, and they themselves had missed it (2 Thess. 2:1-2). But how could they believe this, since Paul himself was still on earth? Did they think Jesus had come and the apostle Paul had been left behind? Had listening to some prophecy caused them to push aside what Paul himself wrote or said? Were they failing to obey Paul's words about judging all prophecy (1 Thess. 5:19-22)? We are unsure what was troubling them. **When people are confused, it is hard to understand what they are thinking, because their thoughts are incorrect or illogical.**

Sabio says: "We must always use **the Bible** to judge letters, sermons, revelations, and spiritual gifts."

In Paul's *second letter* to the Thessalonians, he reviews again the whole scope of the Day of the Lord, with more details on what will happen to unbelievers. In 1 Thessalonians 1, Paul wrote that the disobedient *"will not escape"* (1 Thess. 5:3). And he contrasted *those under wrath* with believers appointed to salvation (1 Thess. 5:9). In 2 Thessalonians we find an emphasis about God's justice on the disobedient. Those who do not know God and those who do not obey the gospel will be deceived by the Antichrist. In the end, they will be shut out from the presence of the Lord and punished with everlasting destruction (2 Thess. 1:9).

Q 18 ⊼ *Does 2 Thessalonians 2 introduce the coming of the Lord? Explain.*

As we study this famous chapter (2 Thess. 2), do **not** make the mistake of thinking that 2 Thessalonians 2:1-2 *introduces* the coming of Christ or the Day of the Lord. Recall that Paul's original letters had no chapter numbers. Recognize that 2 Thessalonians 1:6-10 is an overview of the Day of the Lord, summarizing what will happen to sinners and saints. Then, in 2 Thesslonians 2:1-13, Paul reviews details about the Antichrist, his followers, and their fate.

Q 19 ⊼ *What are 4 events related to the coming of the Lord?*

It is important to discern that there are *several events* related to the coming of the Lord, which include the Rapture, judgment of the Antichrist and his followers, Christ's reign on earth, and the Great White Throne judgment. The sequence of these events is a matter of debate. Among Pentecostals and Charismatics, there are good people with differing views. Some believe the Rapture is pre-Tribulation, others think it is mid-Trib, others post-Trib. A large group of evangelical believers agree with the pre-Tribulation view.[7] The most important thing is to keep our eyes on Jesus and live ready for the **event** of His coming. While on earth, Jesus Himself said that only the Father knows the day and the hour (Matt. 24:36), so we should be alert and watchful (Matt. 24:42). Let all of us live ready—as if Jesus is coming back today!

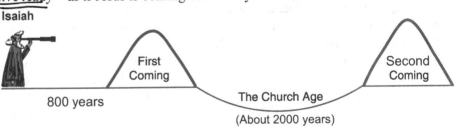

Figure 2.6   Two mountains or events may blend into one if someone is seeing them from a great distance.

Groups of people in the world have different values. In the *Faith & Action* book, *Cross Cultural Communications*, we contrast the values of culture.

Lesson	Values of Culture A Pedro:	Values of Culture B Frank:
28	Pedro is **indirect**—he circles the point.	Frank is **direct**—he goes straight to the point
30	He emphasizes **relationships**.	He emphasizes **rules**.
31	He measures **time** by the **event**.	He measures **time** by the **clock**.
32	He puts the **group** first.	He puts the **individual** first.
33	He focuses on **interaction** (relationships).	He focuses on a **task** (goal).
34	He believes in **status** by position or office.	He believes in **achievement** through work.
35	He minimizes a **crisis** (he ignores it, winks at it, or brushes it aside).	He prepares for a **crisis**.
36	He conceals **vulnerability**.	He reveals **vulnerability**.

Figure 2.7   Contrasts of values in different cultures[8]

Notice that in Figure 2.7 Culture A values the event, but Culture B values time. As we interpret the Bible, it is very important to remember that all of the biblical writers were from Culture A. They focused on an event, like the coming of the Lord, but paid little attention to the time of the event. Therefore, let us be wise interpreters of the end times. It is foolish, and poor hermeneutics to interpret writers from Culture A, using values of Culture B. It's like trying to eat soup with a fork. So let us avoid arguing about the time of the Lord's return, and focus on the event of His Coming. No one knew what time the bridegroom was coming, and he was much later than they expected. But the five wise virgins were ready for the event (Mt. 25:1-13).*Selah (pause and think about this).

Hidden valleys.   Standing at a distance, a man saw the tops of two mountains far away. From where he stood, the 2 mountains blended together as one. Later, when he arrived at the first mountain, he discovered it was a great distance to the next mountain. Likewise, godly men such as the prophet Isaiah saw the coming of Christ. This prophet wrote as if Christ was coming only once. It seems that Isaiah did not see the valley between the First and Second Comings of our Lord (Isa. 11; 53; 65–66). Yet history has revealed that the hidden valley between the comings of Christ is at least 2,000 years wide.

Q 20 Why did Isaiah write as if the Messiah was coming only once?

The apostle John saw two resurrections, with a valley of 1,000 years between them. John wrote:

Q 21 How many years did John see between the judgments of the righteous and the wicked (Rev. 20:4-6)?

⁴*I saw thrones on which were seated those who had been given authority to judge. And I saw the souls of those who had been beheaded because of their testimony for Jesus and because of the word of God. They had not worshiped the beast or his image and had not received his mark on their foreheads or their hands. They came to life and reigned with Christ a thousand years.* ⁵*(**The rest of the dead did not come to life until the thousand years were ended**.) This is the first resurrection.* ⁶*Blessed and holy are those who have part in the first resurrection. The second death has no power over them, but they will be priests of God and of Christ and will reign with him for a thousand years* (Rev. 20:4-6).

John, like all biblical writers, had specific purposes. But unlike any other biblical writer, John wrote an entire book about the victory of Christ over the antichrist, in the last days. John writes about the seven seals, seven trumpets, and seven bowls of wrath that God will pour out on the earth. He tells about Michael and his angels fighting against Satan and his angels, who are defeated and cast out of the heavens. On earth Satan leads his forces against the saints. They overcome by the blood of the Lamb, and by being martyrs on earth (Rev. 12:11). John warns that the beast (antichrist), will make war against the saints, and overcome them (Rev. 13:7); yet the saints must endure persecution and martyrdom. John describes the great harlot, who is drunk from the blood of the saints, who testified for Jesus (Rev. 17:6). Throughout the book of Revelation, John encourages the saints often–rising above the horrors of earth, to describe the joys of heaven. So let us keep in mind that John has unique purposes in Revelation. He describes Christ's victory over Satan. He describes the antichrist overcoming the saints on earth by killing them. Yet John describes the saints, beyond the short years of earth, with new bodies, reigning forever with Christ. And John contrasts these faithful overcomers with sinners who escape the antichrist's wrath on earth, but 1000 years later, they are resurrected, judged and cast into the lake of fire for eternity. In the resurrection of Revelation 20:4, the only people John sees is those beheaded for their testimony about Jesus Christ. Where are all the other saints who died normal deaths, or died in ways other than being beheaded? This is not John's concern. He is writing to encourage the martyrs of the Great Tribulation. So let us remember that John's purposes differ from those of other biblical writers, as we recognize that his description of the resurrections differ from Daniel, Matthew, John's gospel, and Paul's letters.

Q 22 ✎ *Do you think the 1,000 years John saw between the judgments of the righteous and the wicked is hidden in John 5:28-29? Explain.*

John saw a valley of 1,000 years between the resurrections of the righteous and the wicked. Jesus prophesied about the resurrection of both the wicked and the righteous. Recall our Lord's words: *"A time is coming when all who are in their graves will hear his voice* [29] *and come out—those who have done good will rise to live, and those who have done evil will rise to be condemned"* (John 5:28-29).

Is the valley John saw hidden *between* the resurrections in John 5:28-29? Many of us think so.

Q 23 ✎ *Do pre-Millennialists think there is a valley of 1,000 years between 2 Thessalonians 1:6 and 2 Thessalonians 1:7?* yu

Q 24 ✎ *Which is more important to you, the event of God judging the unrighteous, or the timing? Explain.*

Likewise, Paul assured the Thessalonians that when Christ returns, He will punish the wicked and reward the righteous (2 Thess. 1:6-10). But is the valley of 1,000 years that John saw hidden *between* the verses of 2 Thessalonians 1:6 and 2 Thessalonians 1:7? This is our view as *pre-Millennialists. We harmonize John 5:28-29 and Revelation 20:4-6 with 2 Thessalonians 1:6-7 by understanding that neither Jesus nor Paul mentions the hidden valley between the resurrections of the righteous and the wicked.

We are sure that a time is coming when God will raise all the dead who have ever lived on the earth. The Almighty will repay the wicked for their evil deeds. And He will reward the righteous for their faith and obedience. Over the centuries and millennia, prophets and scholars have strained to see events of the last days. But it is difficult to see the hidden valleys between the mountains of time. We are sure that the Bible is true. We are certain that Jesus is coming back to earth. We know that all who have ever lived must stand before our Creator to give account. But passages such as Revelation 20:4-6 cause us to be humble when we speak about the future. If there is a valley of 1,000 years that Paul does not mention in 2 Thessalonians 1:6-10, it should not surprise us that he did not mention a 7-year valley between the Rapture and the judgment of the wicked. Biblical writers were more concerned about events than their timing.

Q 25 ✎ *What is the key to having peace about eschatology?*

> LET US LIVE READY TO MEET THE KING AT ANY MOMENT—LIVING AS HOLY AND OBEDIENT SERVANTS ABOUT OUR MASTER'S BUSINESS.

Let us live ready to meet the King at any moment—living as holy and obedient servants about our Master's business. Let us be ever alert and watchful, knowing that life on earth is but a shadow in eternity. Let us rest in the fact that the times and seasons belong to God, and all is well as we belong to Him.

[38] *For I am convinced that neither death nor life, neither angels nor demons, neither the present nor the future, nor any powers,* [39] *neither height nor depth, nor anything else in all creation, will be able to separate us from the love of God that is in Christ Jesus our Lord* (Rom. 8:38-39).

So let us abide in and keep ourselves *"in God's love"* as we wait for our Lord to return (Jude 1:21). And let us keep the focus on **Jesus**, rather than the time of His coming.

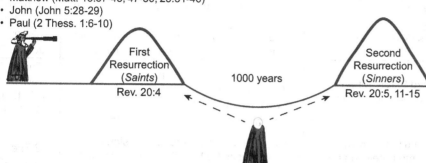

4 views that do not mention the 1000-year valley:
- Daniel (Dan. 12:2)
- Matthew (Matt. 13:37-43, 47-50; 25:31-46)
- John (John 5:28-29)
- Paul (2 Thess. 1:6-10)

First Resurrection (Saints) Rev. 20:4 — 1000 years — Second Resurrection (Sinners) Rev. 20:5, 11-15

John on Patmos

Figure 2.8   Looking from one point of view, Daniel, Matthew, John, and Paul all describe the resurrections of the righteous and the wicked together—without mentioning the 1000-year valley between the resurrections. Looking from a different point of view, the Spirit shows John a valley of 1000 years between the resurrections (Rev. 20:4-6; 11–15).

Gomez and Montigo discussed eschatology with their pastor. Gomez asked, "Pastor, if we will *not* be here in the 7 years of Tribulation, why do the Scriptures warn us about them? The wise pastor responded, "The Bible warns of many things we will *not* experience—such as God's wrath, the judgment of sinners at the Great White Throne, and eternal hell. But knowing about these terrible things motivates us to lead others away from future danger." Montigo nodded and asked, "Pastor, are you *sure* we will not be here during the Tribulation?" Smiling, the pastor replied, "Our belief is in a pre-Tribulation Rapture, although many godly believers do not agree with us. If we are mistaken, we hope the Rapture will occur by mid-Trib. But let us all be prepared, even if the Rapture is post-Trib. Sabio counsels: "When planning for an important event, get ready early, and stay ready as long as necessary."

Q 26 ↗ *Was the pastor's answer to Gomez wise? Explain.*

Q 27 ↖ *Do you agree with Sabio about planning for important events?*

Paul reviews what he had already taught them. Then he urges them to hold firmly to apostolic teaching—the foundation of our faith. Paul wrote: *"So then, brothers, **stand firm and hold to the teachings we passed on to you, whether by word of mouth or by letter** (2 Thess. 2:15).*[9]

Five characteristics of the Antichrist (A–B in this lesson, and C–E in Lesson 11)

We have analyzed the overview and setting of 2 Thessalonians 2. Take time to read the passage below; then we will examine characteristics A and B of the Antichrist. Recall that when Paul speaks of the Coming of the Lord, he refers to the broad scope of this event—which includes rewards for the righteous and judgment for the wicked. Review Paul's overview one more time in 2 Thessalonians 1:6-10. Then read what Paul says **as he continues** to summarize the reward of the righteous and judgment of the wicked.

Q 28 ↗ *What events does the coming of the Lord include?*

[1]Concerning the coming of our Lord Jesus Christ and our being gathered to him, we ask you, brothers, [2]not to become easily unsettled or alarmed by some prophecy, report or letter supposed to have come from us, saying that the day of the Lord has already come. [3]Don't let anyone deceive you in any way, for that day will not come until the rebellion occurs and the man of lawlessness is revealed, the man doomed to destruction. [4]He will oppose and will exalt himself over everything that is called God or is worshiped, so that he sets himself up in God's temple, proclaiming himself to be God. [5]Don't you remember that when I was with you I used to tell you these things? [6]And now you know what is holding him back, so that he may be revealed at the proper time. [7]For the secret power of lawlessness is already at work; but the one who now holds it back will continue to do so till he is taken out of the way. [8]And then the lawless one will be revealed,

whom the Lord Jesus will overthrow with the breath of his mouth and destroy by the splendor of his coming (2 Thess. 2:1-8).

Q 29   *Which spirit is working in you—that of the Antichrist or the Christ? Examine yourself.*

Lessons	Reference	5 Characteristics of the Antichrist	5 Characteristics of Christ	Reference
10	2 Thess. 2:3	**A.** He is known for sin—lawlessness.	He is known for submission to God's will and God's law.	Heb. 10:7; Ps. 40:8
	2 Thess. 2:4	**B.** He opposes God and exalts himself.	He humbled Himself. And He denied Himself, saying, *"Not my will, but yours be done."*	Luke 22:42; John 8:29
11	2 Thess. 2:5-8	**C.** He is allowed to rule for a season, and then he is judged.	He is destined to exaltation and eternal victory over evil. He was, is, and will be.	2 Thess. 2:8; Rev. 1:4-5, 7-8; 12:10; 19:11-16
	2 Thess. 2:3, 9-12; Rev. 12:9; 13:3-4, 8-10, 11-18	**D.** He leads a multitude away from truth—into rebellion and apostasy.	He leads a multitude into submission to God. (He uses truth, self-sacrifice, and the powerful influence of the Holy Spirit.)	2 Thess. 2:10, 13
	2 Thess. 2:13–17	**E.** He cannot deceive those who stand firm in the truth and live for Christ.	He protects those who follow Him.	1 Thess. 5:23-24; 2 Thess. 3:3

Figure 2.9   Contrasts between the Antichrist and Christ (2 Thess. 2:1-12).

A. The Antichrist is known for lawlessness (2 Thess. 2:3).

Q 30   *What is lawlessness in relation to God the King and His kingdom?*

Q 31   *In what sense is the Antichrist lawless?*

Don't let anyone deceive you in any way, for that day will not come until the rebellion occurs and the man of lawlessness is revealed, the man doomed to destruction (2 Thess. 2:3).

Lawlessness defines sin in one word. *Sin is lawlessness*—refusing to submit to God's rule (1 John 3:4). Lawlessness is the creature rebelling against the Creator. The kingdom of God is the realm where God rules. The kingdom of Satan is the kingdom of lawlessness—the place for all who choose rebellion and disobedience to God.

Q 32   *In what ways was Antiochus IV like the Antichrist?*

The Greek King Antiochus IV Epiphanes hated the Jews. He ruled from 175–164 B.C. The Greek name he chose, *Epiphanes,* means "God manifest, or revealed." But the Jews called him *Epimanes,* which means "mad man." Antiochus IV was a type of the Antichrist. His reign was known for unrighteousness, cruelty, and even murder. He was the first person in history to persecute a people just for their religious faith. He caught a big group of Jews in a cave observing the Sabbath. So he sealed the entrance and set fires to suffocate or choke them. Another time Antiochus executed Eliezer for refusing to eat pork. Later, he forced a mother to watch as her seven sons were tortured to death. And when the mother refused to obey his commands against Scripture, he murdered her also. As Antiochus boiled over with hate for the Jews, the Antichrist will erupt with fury toward God and His children. Like Antiochus, the Antichrist will be known for his unfair, unholy, lawless deeds. He will make laws, but they will be laws against God and against those who love God (Rev. 13:12-13, 16-17).[10]

B. The Antichrist opposes God and exalts himself (2 Thess. 2:4).

Q 33   *Will the final Antichrist be a real person?*

Q 34   *How does the final Antichrist seek to replace God?*

He will oppose and will exalt himself over everything that is called God or is worshiped, so that he sets himself up in God's temple, proclaiming himself to be God (2 Thess. 2:4).

The Antichrist opposes the rule of God, and exalts himself as God. Daniel gives us the background of the Antichrist. Near 530 B.C. Daniel wrote about an evil ruler who would defile the temple by setting up an image of himself in it (Dan. 9:24-27). This first occurred in 168 B.C. when the Greek ruler Antiochus Epiphanes IV conquered the Middle East, including Israel. At that time Antiochus set up an altar to the Greek god Zeus on the holy altar of the temple in Jerusalem. Over 5 centuries later, Jesus referred to the abomination of desolation, which Daniel spoke about. Although Antiochus was a forerunner or shadow of the Antichrist, Jesus and Paul referred to the final Antichrist.

John the apostle adds details about the Antichrist. And John emphasizes that this lawless ruler exalts himself as God.

> [11]Then I saw another beast, coming out of the earth. He had two horns like a lamb, but he spoke like a dragon. [12]He exercised all the authority of the first beast on his behalf, and made the earth and its inhabitants **worship the first beast**, whose fatal wound had been healed. [13]And he performed great and miraculous signs, even causing fire to come down from heaven to earth in full view of men. [14]Because of the signs he was given power to do on behalf of the first beast, he deceived the inhabitants of the earth. He ordered them to set up an image in honor of the beast who was wounded by the sword and yet lived. [15]He was given power to give breath to the image of the first beast, so that it could speak and cause all who refused to **worship the image** to be killed. [16]He also forced everyone, small and great, rich and poor, free and slave, to receive a mark on his right hand or on his forehead, [17]so that no one could buy or sell unless he had the mark, which is the name of the beast or the number of his name. [18]This calls for wisdom. If anyone has insight, let him calculate the number of the beast, for it is man's number. His number is 666 (Rev. 13:11-18).

Q 35 What 2 things does the Antichrist require of those living on the earth?

Beware of anyone who exalts himself and draws attention away from the One True God. The word *anti* can mean either "against" or "instead of." One of the characteristics of the **Anti**christ is that he tries to be a substitute for Christ—*instead of* the true Christ. Jesus warned that many false christs would come:

Q 36 What does the word Antichrist mean?

> "Watch out that no one deceives you. [5]For many will come in my name, **claiming, 'I am the Christ,'** and will deceive many" (Matt. 24:4-5).

Evidence is strong that Antiochus IV not only encouraged the worship of Zeus, but he also encouraged the worship of himself. Many of the coins from that day show the Greek god Zeus, made to resemble Antiochus IV Epiphanes. One coin in the British Museum, a silver *tetra*drachm, has the head of Antiochus IV as if he were Zeus, crowned with laurel. The writing on the coin says: "King Antiochus, God Manifest (Epiphanes)."[11] A drachma was an early Greek coin, and a *tetra*drachm was worth four drachma (Matt. 17:24, 27; Luke 15:8-9 [ten drachma]).

Figure 2.10 Ancient coin showing the image of Antiochus IV Epiphanes in the form of the Greek god Zeus

Lesson 11 The **Comings of Christ and Antichrist—Part 2 (2 Thess. 2:9–3:8)**
Goal A: Analyze the rise of the Antichrist to power, and the length of his rule (2 Thess. 2).
Goal B: Explain how danger and safety relate to our response to truth (2 Thess. 2).
Goal C: Summarize Paul's words of encouragement and rebuke (2 Thess. 3).

C. God allows the Antichrist to rule for a season (2 Thess. 2:3-8).

As you read 2 Thessalonians 2:1-8, note that in 2:3 "*that day*" refers back to *the day of the Lord* (in 2:2), rather than the Rapture in 2:1. Recall that *the Day of the Lord* is a period of time that includes a series of events, including such things as the Rapture, the rewarding of the saints, the Tribulation, the rule of the Antichrist, the Second Coming, the Millennium, and the final judgment of Satan and sinners after it. In eschatology, *the Day of the Lord* is a broad topic and a broad period of time.

Q 37 In 2 Thessalonians 2:3, to what does "that day" refer?

Q 38 In 2 Thessalonians 2:2, what are some events "the Day of the Lord" includes?

> [1]Concerning the coming of our Lord Jesus Christ and our being gathered to him, we ask you, brothers, [2]not to become easily unsettled or alarmed by some prophecy, report or letter supposed to have come from us, saying that **the day of the Lord has already come**. [3]Don't let anyone deceive you in any way,

for that day will not come until the rebellion occurs and the man of lawlessness is revealed, the man doomed to destruction. [4]*He will oppose and will exalt himself over everything that is called God or is worshiped, so that he sets himself up in God's temple, proclaiming himself to be God.* [5]*Don't you remember that when I was with you I used to tell you these things?* [6]***And now you know what is holding him back, so that he may be revealed at the proper time.*** [7]*For the secret power of lawlessness is already at work;* **but the one who now holds it back will continue to do so till he is taken out of the way.** [8]*And then the lawless one will be revealed, whom the Lord Jesus will overthrow with the breath of his mouth and destroy by the splendor of his coming* (2 Thess. 2:1-8).

Q 39 ✎ *Why is it difficult to harmonize Paul's teachings on eschatology with John's teachings in Revelation?*

Note that Paul is not giving these young believers a complete teaching on eschatology. Unlike John in the book of Revelation, Paul is just giving some basic teaching to new converts. He wants them to understand that Jesus is coming back to earth, and the dead in Christ (together with living believers) will be caught up to meet Jesus in the air. Paul does not mention the length of time the Antichrist will reign, or the plagues of the Tribulation. He does not mention that Jesus will reign on the earth for 1,000 years. Paul does not mention the judgment of all sinners at the Great White Throne. Rather, the apostle only covers a few highlights of eschatology. He assures his young flock that Jesus will return to reward saints and to judge sinners and the Antichrist. So keep in mind that Paul only gives us a few notes from the chapter of eschatology, due to his purpose of helping young believers in Thessalonica.

Q 40 ➶ *What do we mean by "God is Sovereign"?*

A big purpose of Paul is to emphasize that **God is in control**. God is *Sovereign— He is the supreme, permanent ruler over the kingdoms of men and the entire universe. Recall what Daniel wrote after God revealed King Nebuchadnezzar's dream to Daniel:

Q 41 ✎ *In what sense is the Antichrist just one more king that God raises up and puts down?*

[19]*During the night the mystery was revealed to Daniel in a vision. Then Daniel praised the God of heaven* [20]*and said: "Praise be to the name of God for ever and ever; wisdom and power are his.* [21]*He changes times and seasons;* **he sets up kings and deposes them**" (Dan. 2:19-21). ✴✴✴

God is in control?

God raises kings up, as he raised King Saul and King David to the throne. And He deposes or puts kings down in a single day, as he judged Pharaoh (Exod. 12); and dethroned King Belshazzar, after the handwriting on the wall (Dan. 5). Likewise, God will raise up the Antichrist for a short season, and then cast him into the lake of fire forever (Rev. 19:19-20; 20:10).

God will allow the Antichrist to rule for a short season. As the 10 kings will be allies with the Antichrist for *"one hour"* (which may represent 3½ years, Rev. 17:12). The season of the Antichrist is brief compared to eternity—and the God who was, is, and will be. Yet Paul writes that even the brief rule of the Antichrist is being prevented by *something* and *someone*. Review what Paul wrote in 2 Thessalonians 2:1-8, and then we will look at three possible interpretations.

Q 42 ➶ *Summarize 3 views on how God is preventing the Antichrist from rising to power.*

[6]*And now you know* **what** [Greek: neuter, *it*] *is holding him back, so that he may be revealed at the proper time.* [7]*For the secret power of lawlessness is already at work;* but **the one** *who now holds it back will continue to do so till* **he** [Greek: masculine, *he*] *is taken out of the way* (2 Thess. 2:6-7).

Q 43 ✎ *Which way or ways do you think God is using to hold back the Antichrist?*

Something [Greek: *it*] and someone [Greek: *he*] is preventing the Antichrist from ruling. There are **three main views** on what and who are holding back the rule of the Antichrist (2 Thess. 2:6-7).

- Some think God uses **government** to restrain the coming of the Antichrist (see Rom. 13:1-5). Government may be referred to as a power, or as a person, such as a king. Thus it may be called an it or a he. In Daniel's vision, the head of gold (it) and Nebuchadnezzar (he) were one and the same. In Revelation, the government and the governor (the kingdom and the king) mean the same. When the time comes that there is not government, lawlessness and the Lawless One will rule.

- Some think God is using the **church** to hold back the coming of the Lawless One. This is a powerful view. The Scriptures refer to believers as the light of the world and the salt of the earth. Wherever there are sin and lawlessness, the church counters it with the gospel, good deeds, protests of abuse, and the cry for righteousness and justice. When the salt is gone, the earth will decay and rot rapidly. At the Rapture of the Church, the moral light on earth will go out in the twinkling of an eye.

- Some think God is delaying the revelation of the Antichrist through the power of **the Holy Spirit**. This view does not teach that the Holy Spirit is taken out of the world during the 7 years of Tribulation; for some are saved during these years, and salvation is only possible through the ministry of the Spirit. Rather, this position recognizes that the Spirit of God keeps evil from ruling the earth. So when the Spirit stops restraining the Antichrist, he will be revealed at once. In the days of Noah, the time came when God stopped protecting the earth and loosed the waters of the flood. Likewise, a day is coming when the Almighty will loose the forces of evil on earth.

All three views **credit God with holding back the Antichrist**—whether through the government, the Church, or the Spirit. John saw an evil rider on a white horse. Many scholars believe this is the Antichrist. *"I looked, and there before me was a white horse! Its rider held a bow, and he was given a crown, and he rode out as a conqueror bent on conquest"* (Rev. 6:2). When God stops holding back the Lawless One and gives him power to rule for a season, he will ride onto the scene to rule the world for a short time.

Q 44 *What do the 3 views have in common?*

A janitor named Jim worked in a Bible school. Jim loved the Lord and often listened as the young men and women debated their views on theology. Jim especially liked to hear two students who had different opinions on eschatology. Day after day, Jim listened to their discussions—as they defended their views. One day, in the middle of a debate, one looked at Jim and asked, "What do you think about all these things about Christ and the Antichrist?' Smiling, Jim said, "Jesus is going to win."

Q 45 *In what way did the janitor show more wisdom than the theology students?*

Sabio says: "The Antichrist and his kingdom will crumble with a cosmic boom—when the command of our King flashes like a two-edged sword, and the heavens shake from its thunder (2 Thess. 2:8; Rev. 1:16). Our God reigns!"

D. The Antichrist leads people away from truth and the true Christ (2 Thess. 2:9-12).

Three factors describe the short success of the Antichrist.

1. A great apostasy prepares the way for the Antichrist.

Don't let anyone deceive you in any way, for that day will not come until the **rebellion** [Greek: *apostasia*] *occurs and the man of lawlessness is revealed, the man doomed to destruction* (2 Thess. 2:3).

Q 46 *What is apostasy?*

Scripture foretells an *apostasy (a turning away from the faith, after believing) *before* the Day of the Lord and the events it includes. In a religious sense, the Greek word *apostasia* means "apostasy—turning away from the faith."[12] Jesus warned that a great apostasy was coming, when many would turn away from the faith they had embraced.

[9] *"Then you will be handed over to be persecuted and put to death, and you will be hated by all nations because of me.* [10]***At that time many will turn away from the*** **faith** *and will betray and hate each other,* [11]*and many false prophets will appear and deceive many people.* [12]***Because of the increase of wickedness, the love of*** ***most will grow cold,*** [13]*but he who stands firm to the end will be saved.* [14]*And this gospel of the kingdom will be preached in the whole world as a testimony to all nations, and then the end will come"* (Matt. 24:9-14).

Q 47 *What warning did Jesus give in Matthew 24:10a?*

Q 48 *Does apostasy begin with the rule of the Antichrist? Explain.*

Q 49 ⟑ *About what did Paul warn in 2 Thessalonians 2:3 and 1 Timothy 4:1-5?*

Likewise, Paul reminded the Thessalonians that *before* the time of the Antichrist, there would be an apostasy (2 Thess. 2:3). Later, Paul explains: *"The Spirit clearly says that in later times **some will abandon the faith** and follow deceiving spirits and things taught by demons"* (1 Tim. 4:1).

Note that both Jesus and Paul relate the *apostasy* to the rise of evil (Matt. 24:12; 2 Thess. 2:3). We see the seeds of evil growing already. Paul describes the values of people in the last days—apart from the faith:

> [1]*But mark this: There will be terrible times in the last days.* [2]*People will be lovers of themselves, lovers of money, boastful, proud, abusive, disobedient to their parents, ungrateful, unholy,* [3]*without love, unforgiving, slanderous, without self-control, brutal, not lovers of the good,* [4]*treacherous, rash, conceited, lovers of pleasure rather than lovers of God—*[5]*having a form of godliness but denying its power* (2 Tim. 3:1-5).

In 2 Thessalonians 2:3, Paul explains that the Antichrist comes at a time of great apostasy. ***Before*** the Antichrist deceives people to follow him, many have ***already*** abandoned the truth and the true Christ. Then the Antichrist will lead these deserters and others further away from truth and down the road of error.

Q 50 ⟑ *What happens to those who follow miracles instead of Christ?*

Q 51 ⟍ *Does it surprise you that the Antichrist can do supernatural signs?*

> SATAN'S POWERS AND SIGNS MAY BE REAL, BUT THEY ARE FOR A *FALSE OR COUNTERFEIT* PURPOSE.

2. The Antichrist deceives people in various ways.

> [9]*The coming of the lawless one will be in accordance with the work of Satan displayed in all kinds of counterfeit miracles, signs and wonders,* [10]*and in every sort of evil that deceives those who are perishing* (2 Thess. 2:9-10).

The Greek text says that Satan enables the Antichrist with all kinds of powers, signs, and false wonders. The powers and signs may be real, but they are for a *false or counterfeit* purpose. Throughout history, servants of Satan have at times shown supernatural power. In Egypt, Aaron threw down the staff of Moses and it became a snake. Pharaoh's sorcerers and magicians did the same thing. But Aaron's staff swallowed theirs (Exod. 7:8-12). And when Moses turned the Nile to blood, the magicians did likewise (Exod. 7:20-22). Witches, wizards, and mediums deceive and manipulate people through various methods and evil powers (1 Sam. 28; Acts 13:10). In Samaria, Simon the Sorcerer amazed people with his magic (Acts 8:11). So it does not surprise us that the Antichrist, by the power of Satan, displays *"all kinds of counterfeit miracles, signs and wonders"* (2 Thess. 2:9). Paul describes the Antichrist from a distance. He speaks in *general terms* of the satanic ministry of the Antichrist (2 Thess. 2:9). In contrast, John, in the Spirit, enters the hidden valley of the Antichrist, and observes this evil ruler up close. He sees the 7 years of Tribulation in great detail, and uses most of 13 chapters to write about it (Rev. 6–18). John mentions two specific signs that the Antichrist uses to deceive people: either he or his kingdom are healed of a deadly wound (Rev. 13:3, 12); and he has authority and military power from Satan to conquer (Rev. 13:1-8). Likewise, John mentions that the false prophet, who represents the Antichrist, deceives people by calling down fire from heaven (Rev. 13:13), and by enabling an image of the Antichrist to speak (Rev. 13:15). Through these satanic powers, signs, and misleading wonders, the Antichrist deceives those who belong to the earth. Sabio says: "Not everyone who does miracles is from God."

Q 52 ⟍ *What types of evil is Satan using to deceive people where you live?*

In addition to powers, signs, and false wonders, Paul mentions that the Antichrist uses *"**every sort of evil that deceives** those who are perishing"* (2 Thess. 2:10). Review Figures 2.1 and 2.2 that open this chapter.

3. The Antichrist deceives those who refuse to love the truth.

Q 53 ⟑ *Why does Paul say people are deceived and perish?*

> ***They perish because they refused to love the truth** and so be saved.* [11]*For this reason God sends them a powerful delusion so that they will believe the lie* [12]*and*

*so that all will be condemned who have not believed the truth **but have delighted in wickedness*** (2 Thess. 2:10-12).

Jesus said no one can serve two masters—we must choose one or the other (Matt. 6:24; Luke 16:13). People can face only one direction at a time. If we turn our *backs* on the truth, we turn our *faces* toward deception. If we turn *away from* light, we turn *toward* darkness. If we turn *away from* following Christ, we turn *toward* following the flesh, the world, and the Antichrist. To delight in wickedness, we must despise righteousness (2 Thess. 2:12).

Q 54 ⬉ What does loving the truth look like in daily living?

Strong delusion has already guided many toward destruction. These believe they travel the road of sin, yet arrive in heaven. But the truth teaches that those led by the flesh will not inherit heaven. As Paul writes, grace teaches us to say NO to sin, and live self-controlled, godly lives as we wait for the return of Christ (Titus 2:9-11).

¹⁹*The acts of the sinful nature [Greek: flesh] are obvious: sexual immorality, impurity and debauchery;* ²⁰*idolatry and witchcraft; hatred, discord, jealousy, fits of rage, selfish ambition, dissensions, factions* ²¹*and envy; drunkenness, orgies, and the like. I warn you, as I did before, that **those who live like this will not inherit the kingdom of God*** (Gal. 5:19-21; see 1 Cor. 6:9-11).

People walk toward truth or away from it one step at a time. Many in sin today once knew God. Growing in truth is line upon line. And descending into apostasy occurs one step at a time.

Q 55 ✎ Explain: People walk toward truth or away from it one step at a time. Illustrate.

²¹*For although they knew God, they neither glorified him as God nor gave thanks to him, but their thinking became futile and their foolish hearts were darkened.* ²²*Although they claimed to be wise, they became fools* ²³*and exchanged the glory of the immortal God for images made to look like mortal man and birds and animals and reptiles.* ²⁴*Therefore God gave them over in the sinful desires of their hearts to sexual impurity for the degrading of their bodies with one another.* ²⁵*They exchanged the truth of God for a lie, and worshiped and served created things rather than the Creator—who is forever praised. Amen.*

²⁶*Because of this, God gave them over to shameful lusts. Even their women exchanged natural relations for unnatural ones.* ²⁷*In the same way the men also abandoned natural relations with women and were inflamed with lust for one another. Men committed indecent acts with other men, and received in themselves the due penalty for their perversion.* ²⁸*Furthermore, since they did not think it worthwhile to retain the knowledge of God, he gave them over to a depraved mind, to do what ought not to be done.* ²⁹*They have become filled with every kind of wickedness, evil, greed and depravity. They are full of envy, murder, strife, deceit and malice. They are gossips,* ³⁰*slanderers, God-haters, insolent, arrogant and boastful; they invent ways of doing evil; they disobey their parents;* ³¹*they are senseless, faithless, heartless, ruthless.* ³²*Although they know God's righteous decree that those who do such things deserve death, they not only continue to do these very things but also approve of those who practice them* (Rom. 1:21-32).

Sabio says: "Beware of the smallest step away from God, for it leads to the next step, and the last step." He who chooses the beginning of a road has chosen the end. Be careful which direction you face, for people eventually arrive at the place they are traveling toward. Walk with your face toward truth and your back toward evil.

Q 56 ✎ Contrast the danger of taking one step into the darkness, and the safety of walking in the light.

E. The Antichrist cannot deceive those who stand firm in the truth—in word and deed (2 Thess. 2:13–3:18).

¹³*But we ought always to thank God for you, brothers loved by the Lord, because from the beginning God chose you to be **saved through the sanctifying work of***

Q 57 ✎ What contrast is there in 2 Thessalonians 2, and 2 Thessalonians 3?

Q 58 ⟍ *What is the best protection from deception?*

the Spirit and through belief in the truth. [14] *He called you to this through our gospel, that you might share in the glory of our Lord Jesus Christ.* [15] ***So then, brothers, stand firm and hold to the teachings we passed on to you, whether by word of mouth or by letter.*** [16] *May our Lord Jesus Christ himself and God our Father, who loved us and by his grace gave us eternal encouragement and good hope,* [17] ***encourage your hearts and strengthen you in every good deed and word*** (2 Thess. 2:13-17).

Q 59 ⟍ Complete Figure 2.11 on verses about protection from deception.

Reference	Your Summaries
Matt. 7:24	
Rom. 12:9	
2 Cor. 13:5	
2 Thess. 3:13	

Figure 2.11   Practice summarizing verses on protection from deception.

The greatest protection from deception is love for the truth.   A vaccination that people receive prevents diseases such as the flu, smallpox, and polio. Likewise receiving and living the truth protects us from error.

> [25] *"Therefore everyone who hears these words of mine and puts them into practice is like a wise man who built his house on the rock.* [25] *The rain came down, the streams rose, and the winds blew and beat against that house; yet it did not fall, because it had its foundation on the rock"* (Matt. 7:24-25).

Befriending the truth results in safety. *"Examine yourselves to see whether you are in the faith; test yourselves"* (2 Cor. 13:5). Embrace the truth. *"Hate what is evil; cling to what is good"* (Rom. 12:9). Stand firmly in the truth; for with truth in our hearts and under our feet, we will survive the greatest storms of earth.

Q 60 ⟍ *How does meditating on the Lord's return inspire and guide us?*

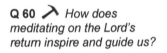

The devil does not want us to grasp the truth of the Lord's return, for nothing wakes up believers as much as a fresh vision of the Coming of Christ. The moment a person takes hold of the truth that Jesus Christ is coming back for his family members, this world loses its grip. Earthly pleasures, pursuits, and possessions fade. The blessed hope of our Lord's return inspires our hearts to live and watch for the return of the King of kings.

Q 61 ⟍ In 2 Thessalonians, what is before and after Paul's section on encouragement?

Teachings About the Day of the Lord and the Antichrist (2 Thess. 1:5–2:12)	Words of Encouragement (2 Thess. 2:13–3:5)	Words of Rebuke and Restoration for the Idle (2 Thess. 3:6-15)

Figure 2.12   Second Thessalonians 2:13–3:5 is an encouragement *between* two tough topics.

The Antichrist has no power over those who live for Christ (2 Thess. 3:1-18).

Q 62 ⟍ *Why were believers at Thessalonica troubled?*

Q 63 ⟍ *How did Paul calm the troubled believers?*

Summary.   The young believers at Thessalonica were troubled by confusion on the comings of Christ and the Antichrist. Some thought the Day of the Lord had already come. Perhaps they thought the Rapture had occurred. Since they were experiencing persecution, maybe they thought this was God's wrath being poured out. They might have thought their faith was in vain. So Paul reminds them that the Day of the Lord is twofold—bringing relief for them and judgment for their enemies. Then Paul reviews what he had already told them in person, about the apostasy and deception related to the reign of the Antichrist (2 Thess. 1:5–2:12). To calm their anxiety, Paul assures the Thessalonians that God is in control. The Almighty will reward believers and punish the wicked at the Coming of Christ.

1. Paul wrote words of encouragement to believers at Thessalonica (2 Thess. 2:13–3:5).

[13] But we ought always to thank God for you, brothers loved by the Lord, because from the beginning God chose you to be saved through the sanctifying work of the Spirit and through belief in the truth. [14] He called you to this through our gospel, that you might share in the glory of our Lord Jesus Christ. [15] So then, brothers, stand firm and hold to the teachings we passed on to you, whether by word of mouth or by letter. [16] May our Lord Jesus Christ himself and God our Father, who loved us and by his grace gave us eternal encouragement and good hope, [17] encourage your hearts and strengthen you in every good deed and word.

[1] Finally, brothers, pray for us that the message of the Lord may spread rapidly and be honored, just as it was with you. [2] And pray that we may be delivered from wicked and evil men, for not everyone has faith. [3] But the Lord is faithful, and he will strengthen and protect you from the evil one. [4] We have confidence in the Lord that you are doing and will continue to do the things we command. [5] May the Lord direct your hearts into God's love and Christ's perseverance (2 Thess. 2:13–3:5).

After the sober topic of the last days, Paul takes time for *words of encouragement.* The apostle reminds the Thessalonians that God chose them **to be saved** through the gospel truth, and the sanctifying work of the Holy Spirit (2 Thess. 2:13). Note that **being saved** includes being born again, *and* the process of cooperating with the Holy Spirit, until we *"share in the glory of our Lord Jesus Christ"* (2 Thess. 2:14). So all believers need to stand firm in the truth (2 Thess. 2:15).

> **Q 64** Does salvation end with being born again? Explain.
>
> *No*

In 2 Thessalonians 3:1-2 Paul expresses faith in God and in the prayers of the Thessalonians for their apostle. God does not just answer the prayers of mature saints. Rather, our Father responds to the prayers of young, growing believers, such as the Thessalonians. So all Christians should pray for their pastors, leaders, and missionaries. Likewise, God will be faithful to protect these young Christians from the evil one; and He will guide their hearts in obedience, the love of God, and the perseverance of Christ (2 Thess. 3:3-5). We can always depend on God to be faithful, as we stand firm in the truth and cooperate with the Spirit.

> **Q 65** Does God hear the prayers of children and young Christians? Explain.
>
> *Yes.*

A missionary to China saw hundreds of families in the Lisu tribe turn to Jesus. He credited the conversions to the prayers of a small group far away. Christians at home can do as much for foreign missions as those who travel to share the good news. In heaven God will reveal how much was done in missionary work by the prayers of faithful believers at home.

2. Paul ~~wrote~~ words of rebuke and restoration for the idle (2 Thess. 3:6-15).

There are always some in the church who would rather talk than work—especially if the topic is eschatology. These run from one new revelation to the next, from one mystery to the next, from one question to the next. It is all right to spend some time studying the end times. All believers should understand the basic truths about the Coming of Christ. But there are always more questions than answers. And there is a balance we must maintain between wondering and working.

> **Q 66** What is the balance between wondering and working?

In every generation, and in every town, there are those who quit working to sit and talk. Some discuss the latest events, as they watch for Jesus to return. Others leave their jobs to wander from house to house talking about spiritual revelations. Athens was famous for this problem. Luke uses *hyperbole to describe this mental illness—this intellectual disease: *"All the Athenians and the foreigners who lived there spent their time doing nothing but talking about and listening to the latest ideas"* (Acts 17:21).

> **Q 67** How were people at Athens and Thessalonica like butterflies?

The academic Athenians were like human butterflies—floating from one idea to the next. Thessalonica had this same problem. In his **first letter** to the Thessalonians, Paul spoke **twice** about this trouble. He gave a gentle nudge or push in the right direction. Recall his words:

> [11] *Make it your ambition to lead a quiet life, to mind your own business and to work with your hands, just as we told you,* [12] *so that your daily life may win the respect of outsiders and so that you will not be dependent on anybody* (1 Thess. 4:11-12).

> *And we urge you, brothers,* **warn those who are idle** *... be patient with everyone* (1 Thess. 5:14).

Q 68 *Why did Paul write so much and use such strong words against idleness?*

But these two admonitions did not correct the situation. So after some words of encouragement, Paul must use a lot of his letter to confront the trouble of idleness. One bad apple or potato spoils the whole bunch. And the virus of idleness soon infects a group of people. So Paul addresses this problem in at least **nine ways**. Read 2 Thessalonians 3:6-15, and see how many of these nine ways you can spot. Then we will discuss them.

Q 69 *Underline the 9 ways Paul comes against the problem of idleness (2 Thess. 3:6-15).*

> [6] *In the name of the Lord Jesus Christ, we command you, brothers, to keep away from every brother who is idle and does not live according to the teaching you received from us.* [7] *For you yourselves know how you ought to follow our example. We were not idle when we were with you,* [8] *nor did we eat anyone's food without paying for it. On the contrary, we worked night and day, laboring and toiling so that we would not be a burden to any of you.* [9] *We did this, not because we do not have the right to such help, but in order to make ourselves a model for you to follow,* [10] *For even when we were with you, we gave you this rule: "If a man will not work, he shall not eat."* [11] *We hear that some among you are idle. They are not busy; they are busybodies.* [12] *Such people we command and urge in the Lord Jesus Christ to settle down and earn the bread they eat.* [13] *And as for you, brothers, never tire of doing what is right.* [14] *If anyone does not obey our instruction in this letter, take special note of him. Do not associate with him, in order that he may feel ashamed.* [15] *Yet do not regard him as an enemy, but warn him as a brother* (2 Thess. 3:6-15).

2 Thess.	Paul's Emphasis	Explanation
3:6	*In the name of the Lord Jesus Christ,*	Paul appeals to the authority of the name above all names.
3:6	*we command you*	Paul uses his authority as God's apostle *to command*—strong language.
3:6	*keep away from every brother who is idle*	Paul insists on isolating the idle, to disciple and correct this bad behavior.
3:7-9	*follow our example*	Paul reminds them that he worked night and day, and paid for his own food, so he would be a good example. He accepted hospitality, but his lifestyle was a model of hard work.
3:10	*we gave you this rule*	Paul cites his own teaching: *"If a man will not work, he shall not eat."* His words are blunt and to the point.
3:11	*We hear that some among you are idle.*	*They are not busy; they are busybodies.* An idle mind is the devil's workshop. A person who does not mind his own business soon meddles in the business of others. But working keeps us away from all kinds of sins.
3:12	*Such people we command and urge in the Lord Jesus Christ*	Paul repeats the command in the name of the Lord Jesus Christ. Believers must put down roots and earn their bread.
3:13	*as for you, brothers*	Paul is concerned that the loafers do not discourage the hard workers. So he exhorts the righteous: *Never tire of doing what is right.*
3:14-15	*If anyone does not obey our instruction in this letter,*	Paul *repeats* the discipline for the idle. *Do not associate with him, in order that he may feel ashamed.* [15] *Yet do not regard him as an enemy, but warn him as a brother.* He calls for tough love, to bring the wayward member back to the flock.

Figure 2.13   In nine ways with strong language, Paul seeks to correct the problem of idleness among believers (2 Thess. 3:6-15).

Paul has written to correct the problem of idleness. The Lord can transform and restore believers who go astray—as the church works together, and the wayward submit to God's Word and Spirit.

Q 70 *Do you enjoy the peace of God that is available to you at all times?*

Paul closes his letter with a prayer for believers to have God's peace, even in the midst of persecution and suffering. And he calls attention to his style of writing, to combat the problem of false letters in his name (2 Thess. 2:1-2).

> [16]*Now may the Lord of peace himself give you peace at all times and in every way. The Lord be with all of you.* [17]*I, Paul, write this greeting in my own hand, which is the distinguishing mark in all my letters. This is how I write.* [18]*The grace of our Lord Jesus Christ be with you all* (2 Thess. 3:1-18).

Before Jesus died and left earth He promised: *"Peace I leave with you; my peace I give you. I do not give to you as the world gives. Do not let your hearts be troubled and do not be afraid"* (John 14:27).

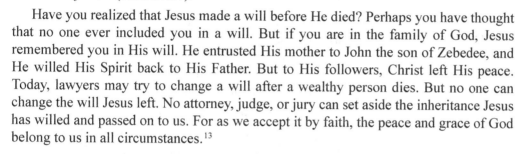

Have you realized that Jesus made a will before He died? Perhaps you have thought that no one ever included you in a will. But if you are in the family of God, Jesus remembered you in His will. He entrusted His mother to John the son of Zebedee, and He willed His Spirit back to His Father. But to His followers, Christ left His peace. Today, lawyers may try to change a will after a wealthy person dies. But no one can change the will Jesus left. No attorney, judge, or jury can set aside the inheritance Jesus has willed and passed on to us. For as we accept it by faith, the peace and grace of God belong to us in all circumstances.[13]

Test Yourself: Circle the letter by the *best* completion to each question or statement.

1. A major way to encourage others is:
a) Quote Scripture to them.
b) Warn them about the world.
c) Praise their progress.
d) Identify their weaknesses.

2. How does God reveal justice?
a) Sending trials to sinners
b) Disciplining His children
c) Rewarding the obedient
d) Avoiding the disobedient

3. When is God on our side?
a) When we are on His side
b) Whenever—no matter what we do
c) When life is going well
d) When times are difficult

4. A probable source of confusion in Thessalonica was
a) a letter from Paul.
b) eschatological differences.
c) false christs.
d) a false prophecy.

5. How many years separate the resurrections of the righteous and the wicked?
a) 2,000
b) 1,000
c) 100
d) 0

6. Sabio says that when planning for an important event, we should:
a) Know the exact time the event begins.
b) Get ready early, and stay prepared.
c) Invite others to go with you.
d) Take a gift for the host.

7. A characteristic of the Antichrist is:
a) He refuses to submit to God's rule.
b) He has lasting power from heaven.
c) He deceives even those who love truth.
d) He is called Epimanes.

8. Which is NOT part of the Day of the Lord?
a) The Incarnation
b) The Rapture
c) The judging of the Antichrist
d) The Great White Throne judgment

9. Whom does the Antichrist deceive?
a) Those who have questions about eschatology
b) Those who are poor or uneducated
c) Those who suffer, and desire relief
d) Those who refuse to love the truth

10. A key to overcoming in the last days is:
a) Know that salvation depends on God, not us.
b) Cooperate with the Holy Spirit.
c) Share with those who will not work.
d) Emphasize that true believers cannot fall.

Essay Test Topics: Write 50-100 words on each of these goals that you studied in this chapter (12 points each and 4 points free). Try to complete your writing in one hour.

- Review how we encourage others by affirming their spiritual progress.
- Summarize how the justice of God reveals itself in reward and punishment.
- Contrast the desires of Satan and God for our success.
- Summarize the scope, events, and valleys of the "Day of the Lord."
- Identify and illustrate 2 characteristics of the Antichrist (2 Thess. 2).
- Analyze the rise of the Antichrist to power, and the length of his rule (2 Thess. 2).
- Explain how danger and safety relate to our response to truth (2 Thess. 2).
- Summarize Paul's words of encouragement and rebuke (2 Thess. 3).

Unit 2:
The Pastoral Letters (1 Timothy)

Paul was Timothy's mentor. They first met in Lystra, in modern Turkey, where Paul healed a cripple—but was stoned when he refused to let the crowd worship him as the Greek god, Hermes. Perhaps Timothy was present when God gave Paul the grace to live and crawl out from under the stones that covered him (Acts 14:8-20).

Timothy began to travel with Paul. The apostle watched Timothy grow from a new convert, to a mature believer, to a young pastor, and finally overseer of the house churches in Ephesus—the biggest and most strategic city in Asia Minor. So much was at stake in Ephesus—such as the purity, reputation, and expansion of the Church.

Timothy was a special leader, who received a spiritual gift as Paul and some elders prayed and laid hands on him. Timothy was gifted, godly, and faithful. But neither Timothy nor most of the other young men Paul mentored had the heart of a lion, as Paul had. Timothy was timid. So as you study the letters to Timothy, notice the ways God encourages this outstanding leader, who was surrounded by false teachers in a strategic center for the gospel.

In Chapter 3, 1 Timothy 1–3, we will enable you to:
* *Summarize the background, setting, date, and purpose of 1 Timothy.*
* *Analyze the problem, result, and methods of false teachers at Ephesus.*
* *Contrast the need for Law among the unrighteous and the righteous.*
* *Define the gospel, and identify topics it spans.*
* *Contrast the penalty and power of sins from which Jesus saves us.*
* *Explain how salvation inspires us to care for our faith—not wreck it.*
* *Explain why Paul wants believers to pray for all people, and how we can have holy hands.*
* *Summarize the context of Ephesian women, and apply Paul's words on dress, teaching, and motherhood.*
* *Explain the meanings and relationships of overseer and deacon, and summarize their qualifications.*

In Chapter 4, 1 Timothy 4–6, you will learn to:
* *Explain a balanced position between eternal insecurity and eternal security.*
* *Identify three ways a leader models good behavior. Give illustrations.*
* *Explain ways a leader can help believers identify and use their spiritual gifts.*
* *Explain four criteria of caring for older widows: relatives, need, godliness, age.*
* *Explain and apply principles to protect your family from sexual sins.*
* *Summarize ways to treat elderly believers as fathers, showing honor without favoritism.*
* *Summarize Paul's attitudes and values for employees and employers.*
* *Summarize the keys to being a faithful minister (1 Tim. 6).*

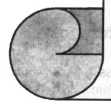

Chapter 3:

Be True and Wise in God's Household

(1 Tim. 1–3)

Q 1 ➤ *What are the 4 groups of Paul's letters?*

We may divide Paul's letters into four groups. The last group of Paul's letters is the *Pastoral Epistles*. They give instructions to pastors for their home life and ministry. Paul wrote these letters to *Timothy and *Titus, two men who had worked closely with him.

Dates of the Pastoral Letters: We know Paul wrote 1 Timothy after the events recorded in Acts 28. Many Bible teachers think Paul was in prison twice

Theme or Characteristic	Letters Paul Wrote
4 letters about salvation (*Soteriological Epistles)	Romans, Galatians, 1 and 2 Corinthians
4 letters from prison (Prison Epistles)	Ephesians, Philippians, Colossians, and Philemon
2 letters about the future (Eschatological Epistles)	1 and 2 Thessalonians
3 letters to pastors (Pastoral Epistles)	1 and 2 Timothy, Titus

Figure 3.1
We may divide Paul's 13 letters into four groups.

in Rome. We think he wrote 1 Timothy and Titus after he was released the first time from a Roman prison (2 Tim. 4:16-17). This was about A.D. 65. Then, he wrote 2 Timothy his second time in a Roman prison (A.D. 67).

Lessons:

False Teachers of the Law (1 Tim. 1:1-11)

Goal A: *Summarize the background, setting, date, and purpose of 1 Timothy.*
Goal B: *Analyze the problem, result, and methods of false teachers at Ephesus.*
Goal C: *Contrast the need for Law among the unrighteous and the righteous.*
Goal D: *Define the gospel. Identify topics the gospel spans in salvation.*

Inspiration: The Worst Sinner Became One of the Best Servants (1 Tim. 1:12-20)

Goal A: *Summarize the first step God took toward Paul, and what God saw in him. Apply this.*
Goal B: *Define "sinners." Give examples of sinners Jesus came to save.*
Goal C: *Contrast the penalty and power of sins from which Jesus saves us.*
Goal D: *Explain how salvation inspires us to care for our faith—not wreck it.*

Objects and Attitudes of Prayer—Part 1 (1 Tim. 2:1-15)

Goal A: *Explain why Paul wants believers to pray for all people.*

Objects and Attitudes of Prayer—Part 2 (1 Tim. 2:1-15)

Goal B: *Analyze the need to lift holy hands in prayer, and explain how this is possible.*
Goal C: *Summarize the context of Ephesian women, and apply Paul's words on dress, teaching, and motherhood.*

Qualifications for Pastors and Deacons—Blameless in Five Ways (1 Tim. 3:1-16; Titus 1:6-9)

Goal A: *Explain the meanings and relationships of overseer and deacon.*
Goal B: *Analyze why Paul forbids drunkenness. Summarize 5 reasons why some abstain from alcohol.*
Goal C: *Explain why church leaders must not be overbearing, quick-tempered, lovers of money, or new converts.*

Qualifications for Pastors and Deacons—Respected for Seven Reasons (1 Tim. 3:1-16; Titus 1:6-9)

Goal A: *Analyze the requirements of a church leader on the topics of marriage, gentleness, and self control.*
Goal B: *Summarize a leader's qualifications on hospitality, righteousness, doctrine, and family life.*
Goal C: *Analyze the form of 1 Timothy 3:16, identifying the 2 parts in each of the six lines.*

Lystra—a city in Asia Minor where Paul was stoned after healing a man during his first missionary journey; Timothy's hometown; in south central present-day Turkey

Ephesus—an important center in Asia Minor. Paul lived there, worked with believers, and organized missionary trips into the regions nearby; Paul left his co-worker, Timothy, to oversee the churches in and around Ephesus

gospel—In the Pastoral Epistles, and all of Paul's writings, the gospel is **not** just good news for lost sinners. Rather, it **is** *the faith*—a fixed body of beliefs to embrace and live by. The beliefs in the gospel include teaching on regeneration, justification, holy living, the kingdom of God, hope, retribution (punishment for the rebellious), and glorification (sharing eternity with our God and King).

ransom—payment on behalf of another; the price paid to free a slave; Jesus gave Himself as the payment for all people to go free.

overseer—one who supervises, like a steward or bishop who watches over God's household; *elder* stresses the spiritual maturity and dignity of an overseer; *pastor* emphasizes one who watches over God's sheep, following the example of the Chief Shepherd.

deacon—one who serves and ministers to help overseers; leaders in the local church

See Appendix A for Key Questions to Answer on the Pastoral Epistles
(Questions based on Gordon D. Fee, *New International Biblical Commentary, 1 and 2 Timothy, Titus*)

Lesson 12

False Teachers of the Law (1 Tim. 1:1-11)

Goal A: *Summarize the background, setting, date, and purpose of 1 Timothy.*
Goal B: *Analyze the problem, result, and methods of false teachers at Ephesus.*
Goal C: *Contrast the need for Law among the unrighteous and the righteous.*
Goal D: *Define the gospel. Identify topics the gospel spans in salvation.*

Background of 1 Timothy

Figure 3.2
Timothy was from Lystra, a small city in Galatia.

Timothy first met Paul in *Lystra. He may have become a Christian during Paul's first missionary trip to Galatia (Acts 14:8-20). On his second missionary trip, Paul invited Timothy to join the team (Acts 16:1-3). The Bible calls Timothy a disciple. Timothy's father was a Greek, but his mother was a Jewess (Acts 16:1, 3). She had taught Timothy the Old Testament Scriptures from the time he was a very small child (2 Tim. 3:14-15). The believers at Lystra and Iconium spoke well of him (Acts 16:2).

In his letters, Paul referred to Timothy a *"my true son in the faith"* (1 Tim. 1:2) and *"my dear son"* (2 Tim. 1:2). Paul had left Timothy in *Ephesus to care for the church. Timothy may not have been Paul's convert. But he *was* Paul's disciple and like a faithful son. Paul wanted the church at Ephesus to see Timothy as the apostle's true son because of his faith.

Timothy traveled with Paul during the rest of his second missionary journey. And he was with Paul during the entire third journey. Later, Paul left Timothy in Ephesus to take care of church problems there (See 1 Tim. 1:3; 3:1-14; 4:6-16).

Q 2 *When and where did Timothy meet Paul?*

Q 3 *What was Timothy's background and reputation?*

Q 4 *What was Timothy's relationship to Paul? When did they travel together?*

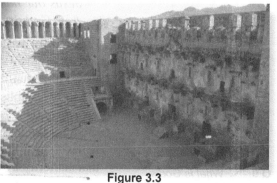

Figure 3.3
Part of an old Roman amphitheater at Ephesus

Q 5 ✗ *Where did Timothy pastor? What does this show us?*

We see from Paul's letters that Timothy was a faithful, hard-working leader. He was close to Paul's heart (Phil. 2:19-20). Paul trusted him with the responsibility of the church at Ephesus. This was a large and important church. So we know that Paul had faith in Timothy's ability and faithfulness.

Q 6 ✎ *How was Timothy like other servants?*

Timothy had spiritual gifts, was faithful, and special (Phil. 2:19-23). Yet at times he needed encouragement from Paul (1 Tim. 4:12-16; 2 Tim. 1:6-7). Paul called him a *"man of God"* (1 Tim. 6:11). He told him to imitate the Lord, *"who while testifying before Pontius Pilate made the good confession"* (1 Tim. 6:13). He urged Timothy: *"Guard what has been entrusted to your care"* (1 Tim. 6:20).

Outline

Theme	1 Tim.
A. Introduction	**1**
Greeting	1:1-2
Warning against false teachers	1:3-11
The Lord's grace to Paul	1:12-17
The purpose of the instructions to Timothy	1:18-20
B. Instructions on Public Worship	**2**
Prayer in public worship	2:1-8
Women in public worship	2:9-15
C. Instructions on Managing the Church	**3**
Qualifications for overseers	3:1-7
Qualifications for deacons	3:8-13
The purpose of the instructions to Timothy	3:14-16
D. Instructions on False Teachings	**4**
False teaching described	4:1-5
Methods of refuting false teaching	4:6-16
E. Instructions on Various People in the Church	**5–6**
The older and younger	5:1-2
Widows	5:3-16
Elders	5:17-25
Slaves	6:1-2
False teachers	6:3-10
The man of God	6:11-16
The rich	6:17-19
Conclusion	6:20-21

Figure 3.4   Outline of 1 Timothy

Q 7 ✗ *Why did Paul emphasize his own authority in the first sentence of his letter to Timothy?*

A. Responsibility: Church leaders must *command* people to stop teaching false doctrines in the church (1 Tim. 1:1-7).

[1]*Paul, an apostle of Christ Jesus by the command of God our Savior and of Christ Jesus our hope,* [2]*To Timothy my true son in the faith: Grace, mercy and peace from God the Father and Christ Jesus our Lord* (1 Tim. 1:1-2).

Purpose of writing. Paul wrote 1 Timothy because the church at Ephesus faced a serious problem. False teachers were leading people away from the truth (1 Tim. 1:3, 6).[1] Paul knew that the church might not accept Timothy's right to correct them. So Paul began by establishing his own authority over Ephesian believers. He wrote, *"Paul, an apostle of Christ Jesus"* (1 Tim. 1:1). Paul normally used this greeting when he wanted to stress the authority that he had, as an apostle, over a church.[2] Here, he reminded believers that he, Paul, had the authority of an apostle over them. He then emphasized that authority by using the word *"command"* (1 Tim. 1:1).

Q 8 ✗ *Why does Paul emphasize the word **command**—a military term?*

Q 9 ✎ *What is God's condition for us to have spiritual authority?*

In 1 Timothy 1, Paul used the word *"command"* four times. Paul mentions that he himself is under the *"command"* of *"God our Savior"* and *"Christ Jesus our hope"*

(1 Tim. 1:1). Paul used a different Greek word, *parangello*, to pass God's command to Timothy and the church. *Parangello* is a military term, which means "to pass commands down through the ranks."[3] Paul used this word in 1 Timothy 1:3, 5, and 18 (translated as *instruction* in some versions, such as the NIV). Paul, under the command of God, commands Timothy and the church. Therefore, the command to them actually comes from God. Before we continue, let us remember an important truth for today. Our authority in the church comes from Jesus. And we have authority over others, only as we ourselves are under His command. Only those under authority have authority.

Q 10 ⚒ *How had some believers at Ephesus wandered away from the gospel? Why? What resulted?*

> [3]*As I urged you when I went into Macedonia, stay there in Ephesus so that you may **command** certain men not to teach false doctrines any longer* [4]*nor to devote themselves to myths and endless genealogies. These promote controversies rather than God's work—which is by faith.* [5]*The goal of this **command** is love, which comes from a pure heart and a good conscience and a sincere faith.* [6]*Some have wandered away from these and turned to meaningless talk.* [7]*They want to be teachers of the law, but they do not know what they are talking about or what they so confidently affirm* (1 Tim. 1:3-7).

Paul had warned the church of Ephesus that false teachers would arise from their *"own number"* (Acts 20:28-31). Later, some in the church (probably church elders), began teaching *"false doctrines"* (1 Tim. 1:3).[4] Their teaching led people away from truth into meaningless talk and conflict (1 Tim. 1:6; 6:20; 2 Tim. 2:16; 3:7).[5] As they grasped for more money, they ruined whole families (Titus 1:11). So, Paul charged Timothy to stop them. He wanted to bring the church back to love for each other. Such love has three sources: *"a pure heart and a good conscience and a sincere faith"* (1 Tim. 1:5). Note that Paul urged Timothy to correct these people even though they were church leaders with friends and influence.

Figure 3.5 **The only Mediator between God and man who gives crowns to faithful believers (Timothy)**
Photo: The main street at Ephesus led to the harbor. Paul left Timothy there to teach the truth (1 Tim. 1:3).

Q 11 ✎ *Why must pastors correct those who wander from the truth?*

False teachers have troubled God's people throughout history. Balaam tried to curse Israel because he wanted money (Num. 22–24). Peter, Jude, and John warned believers of the danger of following *"the way of Balaam"* (2 Pet. 2:15; see also Jude 11; Rev. 2:14). Revelation warns of *"the teaching of the Nicolaitans"* (Rev. 2:15), and a false prophetess named Jezebel (Rev. 2:20). False teachers are spiritual enemies who lead believers into error and bring great harm to true followers of God.

Q 12 ✎ *Why do weak pastors refuse to correct false teachers in the church?*

Paul warned Timothy to stop false teachers. Likewise, today's church leaders must command false teachers to stop. Some do not confront false teachers because of influence or tithes. But God does not show favoritism, and forbids us to practice it (James 2:1-5). Through Jesus, we have the authority and the obligation to stop false teachers.

Wild animals have the ability to recognize danger. Some are so careful and wise that it seems like an angel warns or protects them. Such animals will not eat poison grass, and they avoid their enemies. But some people are less careful than wild animals. They open their doors and their hearts to false prophets who want to destroy them (See 2 Tim. 4:2-4). There is hardly a person in the world so mean that he will lie to another about the right road to the next town. But many teachers mislead others about the right road to heaven![6] Just as shepherds guard their sheep, pastors must protect the eternal souls of those whom God has entrusted to their care.

B. Problem: Many false teachers twist Scriptures (1 Tim. 1:3-7).

Paul's instructions to Timothy	2 Tim.
Fan into flame the gift of God, which is in you…	1:6
Do not be ashamed….But join with me in suffering…	1:8
Keep…the pattern of sound teaching…	1:13
Guard the good deposit that was entrusted to you…	1:14
The things you have heard me say…entrust to reliable men…	2:2
Keep reminding them of these things.	2:14
Do your best to present yourself to God as one approved…	2:15
Flee the evil desires of youth…	2:22
Continue in what you have learned…	3:14
Preach the Word…	4:2

Figure 3.6   Paul's pastoral instructions to Timothy (2 Tim. 1–4)

*³As I urged you when I went into Macedonia, stay there in Ephesus so that you may command certain men not to teach false doctrines any longer ⁴nor to devote themselves to myths and endless **genealogies**. These promote controversies rather than God's work—which is by **faith**. ⁵The goal of this command is love, which comes from a pure heart and a good conscience and a sincere faith. ⁶Some have wandered away from these and turned to meaningless talk. ⁷They want to be teachers of the law, but they do not know what they are talking about or what they **so confidently** affirm* (1 Tim. 1:3-7).

Q 13 *What contrast does Paul make between myths, genealogies, and faith?*

False teachers in Ephesus used Scripture. We do not know exactly what they taught. But we do know they referred to the Old Testament. They wanted *"to be teachers of the law"* (1 Tim. 1:7). All Scripture, including the Old Testament Law, is good because it reflects God's will. But its goodness depends on proper use (1 Tim. 1:8). These teachers were *not* using the Law properly. Instead they used the Law, and especially the genealogies, to teach *myths* (1 Tim. 1:4). *"Myths"* (*muthois*) refers to teachings that people imagine and make up. Human imagination promotes arguments, *"rather than God's work—which is by faith"* (1 Tim. 1:4). Although these teachers did not have a good message, they tried to fool people by speaking with great confidence and loud voices. Sabio says: "He who has a weak message often speaks with a loud voice. An empty cart rattles the loudest!"

Q 14 *Explain the proverb: An empty cart rattles the loudest.*

Q 15 *Why are some more attracted to new stories and teachings that people invent, than to gospel truth?*

Satan attacks the church from the outside through persecution. And he attacks from the inside by using people who appear to be believers, but twist Scripture. Remember how Satan tempted Eve, making small changes in God's Word (Gen. 3:1-5)? Perhaps these false teachers were saying that genealogy had something to do with salvation. Were they saying that some lineages could not be saved? We do not know. One way or another, they were twisting Old Testament Scriptures—causing confusion, division, and arguments in the church at Ephesus. Paul will emphasize that Jesus came to save all sinners—even the worst of them, so our genealogies do not matter (1 Tim. 1:15).

Q 16 *What causes us to think the false teachers were once faithful members at Ephesus?*

Earlier, Paul warned these same believers at Ephesus about false teachers (Acts 20:13-38). He prophesied that false teachers would arise from among their own body and *"distort the truth"* (Acts 20:30). First Timothy reveals the fulfillment of Paul's warning.

Paul told the Ephesian elders, *"Be on your guard!"* (Acts 20:31). Those words apply to us as well. But how do we guard against false teachers who misuse Scripture?

Q 17 *What are 2 ways we can be on our guard against false teachers?*

- We must study the Scriptures ourselves to make sure that our teachers are teaching truth. Let us be like the believers of Berea. They examined the Scriptures *"to see if what Paul said was true"* (Acts 17:11). Let us make sure the message we receive *"conforms"* to the true *gospel (1 Tim. 1:11). A godly teacher *"correctly handles the word of truth"* (2 Tim. 2:15). A false teacher misuses it.

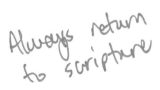

Always return to scripture

- We should examine the fruit of our teachers. Godly teachers lead believers into godly love—teaching with *"a pure heart and a good conscience and a sincere faith"* (1 Tim. 1:5). In contrast, the fruit of false teachers includes *controversies*—arguments, quarrels, and division (1 Tim. 1:4).

Sabio offended some people because he refused to argue in public meetings. If the unbelievers were honest, he showed love and sympathy—doing all he could to help them. But he would not waste time on those who delighted in asking foolish questions. Sabio said, "If a skeptic can puzzle a young Christian with a question such as 'Who was Melchizedek?', the skeptic will laugh as though the believer's faith is invalid, inadequate, and insufficient." So Sabio said that answering the questions of insincere people is like standing on the beach and arguing with the waves of the sea. For if you answer one question, another is always coming after it. Such skeptics want to become a stumbling block to sincere seekers of truth. But no human can answer every question. A scientist, after years of study, cannot answer every question you can ask about the heavens and the earth. Likewise, Christians cannot explain everything in the Bible. So let us avoid foolish quarrels and questions, and spend our time with the sincere, and emphasize the truth we understand in God's Word.[7] As Paul told Timothy, there are some topics we should avoid, because they waste time, create confusion, and stir up arguments (1 Tim. 1:3-7).

Q 18 Have you seen believers led astray by false teachings? Illustrate.

C. Clarification: Law is for the lawless (1 Tim. 1:8-11).

Picture or Comparison	Explanation	2 Tim.
1. As a *son*	he is to be strong and active.	2:1-2
2. As a *soldier*	he is to suffer hardship and please his commander.	2:3-4
3. As an *athlete*	he is to obey the rules of the game.	2:5
4. As a *farmer*	he is to work hard. He should be the first to eat some of the food he grows.	2:6
5. As a *workman*	he is not to be ashamed. Rather, he should correctly handle the Word of God.	2:15
6. As an *instrument*	he is to be holy and useful for the Master.	2:21
7. As a *servant*	he is to be gentle and helpful.	2:24-25

Figure 3.7   Seven comparisons of a pastor in 2 Timothy 2

Since the false teachers were emphasizing Law, Paul takes time to explain that the Law restrains the unrighteous, not the righteous.

[8] *We know that the law is good if one uses it properly.* [9] *We also know that law is made not for the righteous but for lawbreakers and rebels, the ungodly and sinful, the unholy and irreligious; for those who kill their fathers or mothers, for murderers,* [10] *for adulterers and perverts, for slave traders and liars and perjurers—and for whatever else is contrary to the sound doctrine* [11] *that conforms to the glorious gospel of the blessed God, which he entrusted to me* (1 Tim. 1:8-11).

The false teachers misunderstood the Law's purpose.   God did not give the Law for the righteous (1 Tim. 1:9). Law is unnecessary for those who practice what is right.[8] New spiritual life, love for God and others, and the Holy Spirit make the written Law unnecessary for believers.

Q 19 Did Jesus do away with the Law? Is there Law in God's kingdom? Explain.

Q 20 Who is a fitting leader for the disobedient and the lawless?

Some misunderstand God.   They think that God made harsh laws in the Old Testament, then changed to love and grace in the New Testament. But God does not change (James 1:17; Heb. 13:8). Jesus did not come to abolish the Law but to fulfill it (Matt. 5:17). The Law is not *over* us—as a judge or as a savior (Rom. 3:20; 6:14-15). Likewise, the Law is not *under* us or *behind* us. We do not live like rebels, trampling on God's moral law—as though it does not apply to Christians. Lawlessness is the essence of sin (1 John 3:4). At the final judgment, Jesus will say to all workers of *lawlessness*

[Greek: *a-nomian*], *"I never knew you"* (Matt. 7:23). The Antichrist, whom Scripture calls *"the man of lawlessness,"* is a fitting leader for the lawless (2 Thess. 2:3).

Q 21 *What kind of people does the Law restrain? Illustrate.*

So why don't believers need the written Law? Hebrews tells us that we don't need the written Law because the Law is *in us*. Under the new covenant, God writes His laws on our hearts and minds (Jer. 31:31-34; Heb. 8:10; 10:16).

Q 22 *Summarize these verses on why believers do not need written laws to restrain us from evil.*

So, for whom did God make the Law? What kind of person does the Law hold back? Paul lists types of sinners whom the Law restrains (1 Tim. 1:9-10). The first six in this list are general. The others correspond to some of the Ten Commandments (Exod. 20:1-17). Paul was saying that God gave the Law to curb, prevent, or stop sins. He did not give the Law for genealogies, myths, and idle talk.[9]

Reference	Your Summaries on Verses Relating God's Law to Believers Under Grace
Rom. 8:3-4	
Rom. 13:8-10	
Heb. 8:8-10	
Titus 2:11-12	

Figure 3.8   Practice explaining the relationship of believers to God's Law.

The Jews misused the Law when they had Pilate crucify Jesus (John 19:7). The Pharisees misused the Law when they swore by the temple, but not by its gold (Matt. 23:16). The Pharisees misused the Law when they tithed mint, anise, and cumin, but avoided major moral concerns such as judgment, mercy, and faith (Matt. 23:23). The Pharisees also misused the Law when they strained out a gnat, but swallowed a camel (Matt. 23:24). False teachers at Ephesus misused the Law for genealogies, myths, and idle talk (1 Tim. 1:3-5).

D. Solution: The gospel is the source and standard (measure) of all healthy, religious teachings (1 Tim. 1:10-11).

[10]*For adulterers and perverts, for slave traders and liars and perjurers—and for whatever else is contrary to the* **sound doctrine** [11]**that conforms to the glorious gospel of the blessed God**, *which he entrusted to me* (1 Tim. 1:10-11).

The Christians in Ephesus needed a standard to help them recognize the difference between good and bad teaching. Paul gave them, and us, that standard when he wrote that *"sound doctrine"* conforms to the *"gospel"* (1 Tim. 1:10-11). *"Sound doctrine"* is a medical term that means "healthy teaching." The unhealthy teaching of false teachers spreads like a disease (2 Tim. 2:17). In contrast, *"sound doctrine"* is like healthy food for healthy people.[10] Paul emphasized the importance of healthy doctrine throughout the Pastoral Epistles.

Q 23 *Explain what the gospel is not, and what it is. Which topics does the gospel include?*

The gospel is our standard to measure teachings. As we measure an object with a ruler, we measure a teaching with the gospel. Christians can recognize unhealthy teaching by comparing it to Paul's gospel. In the Pastoral Epistles, and all of Paul's writings, the gospel is **not** just good news for lost sinners. Rather, it **is** *the faith*—a fixed body of beliefs to embrace and live by.[11] The beliefs in the gospel include teaching on regeneration, justification, holy living, the kingdom of God, hope, retribution (punishment for the rebellious), and glorification (sharing eternity with our God and King). The gospel is not just an intersection; it is a way of life—a road. To embrace the gospel, we must turn away from ungodly, unholy, sinful, lawless living that God condemns (1 Tim. 1:8-11). Sinful living is contrary (in opposition) to the healthy doctrine of the gospel. The gospel is based on grace. God invites us to come to Him with an empty hand and receive His free offer of salvation. But those He redeems He calls to high standards of ethical and moral living. And through the Holy Spirit of grace, God gives us all the help we need to fulfill His law and please Him (Rom. 8:3-4; Titus 2:11-14).[12]

Q 24 *How can we use the gospel to measure or weigh teachings? Illustrate.*

In the Pastoral Epistles, Paul uses the words *"the gospel"* in a broad way. In these three pastoral letters, **synonyms** of *the gospel* include:

- The faith (1 Tim. 1:11, 19; 3:9; 4:1, 6; 5:8; 6:10, 12; 2 Tim. 3:8; 4:7; Titus 1:13).
- The truth (1 Tim. 2:4, 4:3; 2 Tim. 2:25, 3:7; Titus 1:1).
- The deposit to guard (1 Tim. 6:20; 2 Tim. 1:14).
- Healthy teachings (1 Tim. 1:10, 6:3; 2 Tim. 1:13, 4:3; Titus 1:9; 2:1, 8).
- Our religion (1 Tim. 3:16, 4:7-8, 6:3, 5-6; Titus 1:1).[13]

Q 25 *In the Pastoral Epistles, what are 5 synonyms of "the gospel"?*

Q 26 *Complete Figure 3.9 on ways Paul explains and refers to his gospel in the Pastoral Epistles.*

Reference	In These Passages the Gospel Means "the Faith."
1 Tim. 1:11	
1 Tim. 1:19	
1 Tim. 3:9	
1 Tim. 4:1	
1 Tim. 4:6	
1 Tim. 5:8	
1 Tim. 6:10	
1 Tim. 6:12	
2 Tim. 3:8	
2 Tim. 4:7	
Titus 1:13	

Figure 3.9   Practice summarizing verses in which "the gospel" means "the faith"[14]

Q 27 *Fill in the blanks of the middle column as you search the Scriptures in column 3.*

Aspects of the Gospel	Summary of Gospel Aspects in the Pastoral Epistles	Reference
Sinfulness of humans	Paul defines sin as _____ or _____ against God.	1 Tim. 1:9-10, 13, 15; 2 Tim. 3:2-5; Titus 3:3
Sinfulness: its scope	All humans have the disease of _____, and mankind has produced no cure for it.	1 Tim. 3:13-16; 2 Tim. 1:9; Titus 3:3, 5
Salvation from God	For salvation, God must intervene with _____.	1 Tim. 3:13-16; 2 Tim. 1:9-10; Titus 3:3-7
Ministry of Jesus	He commissions apostles and ministers. He came into the world _____. He is coming back (appearing). He is the source of grace, peace, and life. He calls us to _____. He will judge the _____ and the _____.	1 Tim. 1:1, 12, 15; 4:6; 6:4; 2 Tim. 1:1, 9; 4:1; Titus 1:1, 4; 2:13
Justification	We are justified in the _____, we are justified by grace.	1 Tim. 1:15-16
Scope of salvation	Salvation can reach all _____; it is in ____: can redeem from all _____.	1 Tim. 1:13-16; Titus 2:14
Faith	Contributes to godly _____, can be _____, can be _____.	1 Tim. 1:4, 14; 6:1:1, 2; 2 Tim. 2:18; 3:15
Rebirth and renewal	He saves us through the washing of rebirth and renewal by the _____.	Titus 3:5-6
Holy living and ministry	The Law reveals the need for _____. We should pray for those in authority that we may live peaceful, holy lives. Those who confess the Lord's name must turn away from _____ to _____.	1 Tim. 1:8-11; 2:2; 2 Tim. 2:19-22
Fruit of grace	Grace leads us to _____.	Titus 2:11-12
Eternal life	We lay hold of eternal life. Believers have the _____ of eternal life.	1 Tim. 6:12; Titus 1:2; 3:7
Christ's Second Coming	We look forward to His glorious appearing—the _____ _____.	1 Tim. 6:14; 2 Tim. 4:1; Titus 2:13-14
Judgment	Jesus is _____ of both the _____ and the _____.	2 Tim. 4:1, 8 (2 Thess. 1:6-10)

Figure 3.10   Aspects of the gospel in the Pastoral Epistles[15]

Application. When we refer to the gospel, or share it with others, let us make sure we do not cut off part of it. The gospel does not end with the cross or the Resurrection.

Q 28 *Why is it vital for us to share the full gospel, and not cut off part of it?*

Share the full gospel!!!

And it does not end with justification. In the Pastoral Epistles, *the gospel* refers to the Christian faith—all that we believe, based on the Scriptures. In the Pastoral Epistles, the gospel includes all of the doctrines we study in theology, such as the *16 Fundamental Truths of the Assemblies of God. The gospel teaches about such things as the love of God, the lostness of man, how to be justified, victory over the penalty and power of sin, holy living, divine healing, the Second Coming of Christ, the final judgments—eternal rewards for the obedient, and eternal punishment for the disobedient. So let us share the *full gospel*, and not just a few verses about our need to be born again. For if we cut off the gospel at the new birth, this is like cutting off the road that continues to heaven and eternity. The gospel summarizes the basic teachings of our faith, from A to Z. Shall we teach people the first few letters of the alphabet, and tell them they have learned it all? The gospel includes such things as recognizing our need for a Savior, meeting Jesus, believing in Him, following Him, living in the light of His coming, and enjoying eternity with Him. Would you give someone half of a ticket to an event, and let them find out later that they could not enter with only part of a ticket? Justification without sanctification (holy living) is fiction. And telling people they can be saved without following Jesus is untrue. So let us share the *full gospel*—the whole of the Christian faith—lest some begin on the road to heaven, with only half of the road map to get there.

Inspiration: The Worst Sinner Became One of the Best Servants (1 Tim. 1:12-20)

Lesson 13

Goal A: *Summarize the first step God took toward Paul, and what God saw in him. Apply this.*
Goal B: *Define sinners. Give examples of sinners Jesus came to save.*
Goal C: *Contrast the penalty and power of sins from which Jesus saves us.*
Goal D: *Explain how salvation inspires us to care for our faith—not wreck it.*

Setting

Q 29 *What example did Paul use to show that neither genealogies nor Law save people?*

Paul has just contrasted myths and lawless living to the healthy teachings of the gospel (1 Tim. 1:1-11). God entrusted *"the glorious gospel of the blessed God"* to Paul (1 Tim. 1:11). Now, the apostle continues to contrast the gospel with the teachings of the false teachers. He does this by sharing the gospel in the form of his personal testimony. The preceding passage emphasized the Law. God gave the Law *to restrain* sinners. But Law lacks the power to save those sinners. In contrast, Paul's testimony emphasizes God's grace toward sinners. God's grace brings faith and love with it and offers eternal life.[16] Paul had a good Jewish genealogy, and he tried to live by the Law—but neither of these saved him. Rather, it was through the gospel of Jesus Christ that Paul discovered salvation.

A. Jesus looks beyond our faults and sees faithful servants (1 Tim. 1:12-13).

Q 30 *How was Jesus able to look at Paul as a blasphemer, and see a faithful servant?*

[12]*I thank Christ Jesus our Lord, who has given me strength, that he considered me faithful, appointing me to his service.* [13]*Even though I was once a blasphemer and a persecutor and a violent man, I was shown mercy because I acted in ignorance and unbelief* (1 Tim. 1:12-13).

Paul thanked God when he spoke of the gospel that God *"entrusted"* to him. Paul gave thanks because Jesus considered him *"faithful"* (1 Tim. 1:12). Here, *"faithful"* means *"trustworthy."*[17] Jesus saw a person who was trustworthy enough to call *"to his service"* (1 Tim. 1:12). Remember, Paul did not look like a potential servant. He was a *"blasphemer"* who insulted Jesus and denied His deity. He was a *"persecutor"* who tried to force others to deny Jesus. Paul arrested others until he himself was arrested—by the grace of God (Acts 8:3; 9:1-18).[18] The first Christians could not see a future servant in Paul. They feared him and saw him as their enemy (Acts 9:13-27). But Jesus knew that Paul acted in *"ignorance and unbelief"* (1 Tim. 1:13).

Jesus looked beyond Saul's hatred and saw a faithful servant. The Savior redeemed him, and changed him to Paul. For all of his life, Paul's heart overflowed with gratitude and humility. Paul saw himself as the least of the apostles (1 Cor. 15:9), the least of the saints (Eph. 3:8), and the worst of sinners (1 Tim. 1:15).

When Jesus called Matthew, everyone but Christ saw only a traitor (Matt. 9:9-13). He was a tax collector, a man whom all men hated. A man like Matthew would have been difficult to love, even if you were his mother! Tax collectors served Rome, the nation that conquered the Jews. And traitors like Matthew had a reputation for cheating the Jews—by collecting more taxes than necessary and putting some in their own pockets. But Jesus has power to see past the surface. He sees what a person is, *and* what the person can become. More than all others, Jesus looks beyond our faults and sees our potential. And when Jesus finished transforming Matthew, parents all over the world would want to name their children after him! Only Jesus can look at a traitor and see an apostle. Only our Lord can look at a thief, a liar, a cheat, an addict, a prostitute, a glutton, or any other sinner, and see someone who can be a wonderful member of God's family. Lord, teach us to see sinners through Your eyes.

Q 31 *How was Matthew's reputation changed after he met Jesus?*

B. Jesus always takes the first step toward us, offering grace, faith, and love (1 Tim. 1:13-14).

[13] *Even though I was once a blasphemer and a persecutor and a violent man, I was shown mercy because I acted in ignorance and unbelief.* [14] *The grace of our Lord was poured out on me abundantly, along with the faith and love that are in Christ Jesus* (1 Tim. 1:13-14).

God takes the first step toward us by pouring out grace. Consider Paul's testimony (Acts 9). Paul (Saul) was persecuting Christians. Then Jesus spoke to Paul and sent Ananias to help him (Acts 9:3-18). Jesus took the first step toward Paul, just as He walks toward all sinners. As the Scriptures say, *"While we were still sinners, Christ died for us"* (Rom. 5:8).

Q 32 *In what way did God take the first step toward Paul? Describe it.*

God's grace has no limits. As a farmer pours a whole bucket of water on a young tree, God poured a big measure of grace on Paul (1 Tim. 1:14).[19] A little grace was not enough for a sinner like Paul. But God's supply of grace is never low. God has so much grace, that the amount He needed for Paul was like a cup of water from the ocean. Our Father's grace is always more than enough. If He poured out grace on the whole world, His source of grace would be no less.

Q 33 *Why did Paul need more grace than others?*

Q 34 *Does the worst sinner challenge the amount of grace that God has? Explain.*

And God's grace did not come by itself. It came with *"faith and love"* (1 Tim. 1:14). Faith is how we should respond to God's generous grace (Rom. 3:23-26; Eph. 2:8). When we respond to grace in faith, we walk through the door of salvation. If that faith is real, it will act in love (Gal. 5:6). However, faith and love are found only in one place—*"in Christ Jesus"* (1 Tim. 1:14). We enter a relationship with Jesus only through the door of grace as He calls to us, just as He reached out to Paul. So we see that our relationship with God is not based on our family lineage, our obedience to God's Law, or our good deeds. We become God's children when we accept the grace God offers us, with faith and love in Jesus Christ.

Rembrandt painted a picture of the crucifixion. At the center of this picture we see Christ on the cross when He died as our substitute. Then we notice the many people at Calvary—and their various attitudes and actions. As our eyes drift to the edge of the painting, we see a small man in the shadows. This is Rembrandt himself. He is saying, "My sins nailed the Savior there. He died for me and I believe it." O the love of Jesus, and the blessings of grace![20]

Figure 3.11 Rembrandt's *Descent From the Cross*

Q 35 *How do you daily express thanks for the grace God has given you?.*

C. Jesus came into the world to save sinners (1 Tim. 1:8-10, 15-16).

*15 Here is a trustworthy saying that deserves full acceptance: **Christ Jesus came into the world to save sinners**—of whom I am the worst. 16 But for that very reason I was shown mercy so that in me, the worst of sinners, Christ Jesus might display his unlimited patience as an example for those who would believe on him and receive eternal life* (1 Tim. 1:15-16).

Paul began verse 15 with a statement that he repeats five times in the Pastoral Epistles; *"Here is a trustworthy saying."* Each time, he presents a key teaching of the Christian faith for all believers to accept and trust. Every word of the Scriptures is trustworthy. But to emphasize the truth, speakers and writers use expressions such as: *"I speak the truth in Christ—I am not lying"* (Rom. 9:1); *"Here is a trustworthy saying"* (Figure 3.12); *"Truly, truly"* (John 3:3 KJV and often in John). When Paul says: *"Here is a trustworthy saying,"* this is his way of calling attention to a statement—like underlining it, putting it in *italics*, in **bold**, or all CAPS.

Q 36 *Complete Figure 3.12 summarizing the 5 "trustworthy sayings" in the Pastoral Epistles.*

Reference	Your Summaries of the "Trustworthy Sayings"
1 Tim. 1:15	
1 Tim. 3:1	
1 Tim. 4:9	
2 Tim. 2:11	
Titus 3:8	

Figure 3.12   Practice summarizing five "trustworthy sayings" in the Pastoral Epistles.

A famous grave marker says something like: "Here lies the body of John Newton, who was once an infidel and a rebel—a seller of slaves. Until the mercy of our Lord and Savior Jesus Christ rescued, restored, pardoned, and appointed him—to preach the faith he labored to destroy." John Newton heard Christ's words: "Be forgiven and free! Go and walk in the light of the gospel!" Newton gives his grateful testimony in the hymn he wrote, *Amazing Grace*:

> Amazing grace! How sweet the sound
> That saved a wretch like me!
> I once was lost, but now am found—
> Was blind, but now I see. [21]

Q 37 *What is the first of Paul's trustworthy statements?*

This first of Paul's five *trustworthy statements* is **very important**. It *"deserves full acceptance"* (1 Tim. 1:15). Christians should understand why Jesus came. He came *"to save **sinners**"* (1 Tim. 1:15). Jesus Himself said, *"I have not come to call the righteous, but sinners"* (Matt. 9:13).

Q 38 *Does Jesus turn away from some sinners, because they are worse than others?*

Jesus can save the worst of sinners, like Paul: blasphemers, persecutors, and violent men.   Jesus came to save terrorists, drug dealers, male and female prostitutes, slave traders, sex abusers, homosexuals, traitors, murderers, and more. The worst we can think of, Jesus can save, wash, and free from sin. One advertisement boasts of a soap so powerful that it can remove the worst stains. Even more, the blood of Jesus is so powerful that it can remove the worst sins we can imagine. Let the worst sinner who has ever lived come to Jesus, and this person will become as pure as the most holy saint!

Do we proclaim this boldly? Or do we think Jesus only saves mild sinners? Do we offer abundant grace poured out on the worst of sinners? Or do we think grace is only for the best of sinners? Do we declare with confidence that Jesus offers a white robe to those in the filthiest, vilest, foul-smelling clothes? Do we believe Jesus can transform a garbage dump into a rose garden?[22]

Q 39 ⬉ *Do you and your church boldly offer the gospel to the worst sinners? Give examples.*

Jesus delights to *"display his unlimited patience"* to encourage others to believe. We know this because Paul was the worst of sinners (1 Tim. 1:16). Paul is an advertisement and testimony for the grace of God. When Paul says he is the worst of sinners, we should realize, "I am not as sinful as Paul, so the grace of God is more than enough for me." Jesus showed Paul mercy to *"display his **unlimited patience**."* Artists like to display their work—such as their paintings or sculptures—for customers to see. Likewise, Jesus likes to display His work in the worst sinners. He does this to encourage others to believe (1 Tim. 1:16). Paul's message was this, "Look at me! If God can save me, the worst of sinners, there is hope for all" (1 Tim. 1:15, 16; 2:3-7).[23]

Pastor Choco in Chicago proclaims the full gospel with boldness to all sinners. His church has special dinners for prostitutes. The church gives the prostitutes money to attend a banquet, roses, and the personal and powerful offer of Jesus Christ to forgive their sins and transform their lives. There are over 100 saints in this church who were once prostitutes, until Jesus forgave them, washed them, and recruited them to be children in His family.[24]

> Like the believers at Corinth, these saints sit side by side with former addicts, drunkards, murderers, swindlers, gossips, liars, and the rest of us sinners whom Jesus redeemed. For Jesus loves and saves big sinners and small ones, bad sinners and worse ones. His love knows no bounds and His grace has no limits. And the only conditions He puts on His love and grace are for us to ask receive, and follow Him.[25]

A sinner is anyone who rebels against God's Law (Rom. 3:19-20, 23). Law reveals sin (Rom. 3:20). It shows that sinners are guilty. But Law cannot make a person righteous. Jesus solved this problem. He can save the worst sinners, even sinners like Paul, who was *"a blasphemer and a persecutor and a violent man"* (1 Tim. 1:13). Consider the worst people in our world. Jesus can save them and free them from sin.

Q 40 ⬉ *Which bad sinner will you pray for each week, and share the love of Jesus with him or her often?*

D. Jesus saves sinners from the penalty and the power of sin (1 Tim. 1:15-16).

Q 41 ⬈ *Why did Jesus come to earth?*

¹⁵*Here is a trustworthy saying that deserves full acceptance: **Christ Jesus came into the world to save sinners**—of whom I am the worst.* ¹⁶*But for that very reason I was shown mercy so that in me, the worst of sinners, Christ Jesus might display his unlimited patience as an example for those who would believe on him and receive eternal life* (1 Tim. 1:15-16).

Q 42 ⬉ *What is the difference between the penalty and the power of sin?*

Law informs, condemns, and restrains. But grace redeems and transforms. Jesus saves from the penalty *and* the power of sin—from the stains *and* the chains of sin. He saves from the guilt *and* the grip of sin.

Some have twisted Paul's, I *am "the worst of sinners"* (1 Tim. 1:15-16). These claim that as an old apostle, Paul was still sinning more than anyone else on earth. These blind guides think Paul was sinning more than the unholy and ungodly he mentions (1 Tim. 1:9-10). Such accusations against Paul are worse than the blasphemy of the false teachers Paul warned about (1 Tim. 1:3-7, 18-20). Those who claim Paul was a slave of sin must ignore verses throughout his writings. Do these false teachers think Paul lived on a level below the lifestyle he required for elders and deacons (1 Tim. 3; Titus 1:5-16)? If the apostle Paul was a slave of sin, would he have commanded Timothy to be an example *"in speech, in life, in love, in faith and in purity"* (1 Tim. 4:12)? Paul was not a hypocrite! After he met Jesus, Paul did not continue to be a slave of sin (Rom. 6:1-2,

Q 43 ⬉ *Is it possible to be saved from the penalty of sin, yet still live as a slave under sin's power? Defend your answer.*

15-16; 8:1-17). And he warned that those who serve the flesh have no inheritance in the kingdom of God (1 Cor. 6:9-10; Gal. 5:19-21). Paul was not a slave of sin. Rather, as Dr. Fee notes, Paul always remembered that he was once a sinner whom God redeemed—a sinner saved and transformed by grace into a saint.[26]

Q 44 *What would happen if Jesus did not save us from the power of all sin?*

If God does not deliver us from all sin, there is big trouble ahead! A home owner named Laban wanted to sell his house for $2,000. Jack wanted to buy it, but he could not afford the full price. After much bargaining, Laban agreed to sell the house for half the original price with one condition—Laban would own one small nail sticking out above the front door, inside the house. After several years, Laban wanted the house back, but Jack would not sell. So Laban went out, found the carcass of a dead dog, and hung it from the nail he owned. Soon the house stunk so bad, the family was forced to sell the house to the owner of the nail. The lesson of the parable is, ***If we leave the devil even one small peg in our life, he uses it to hang his rotting garbage.***

E. God's mercy and grace inspire us to honor and glorify Him—now and forever (1 Tim. 1:12, 17).

[12]I thank Christ Jesus our Lord, who has given me strength, that he considered me faithful, appointing me to his service.

[17]Now to the King eternal, immortal, invisible, the only God, be honor and glory for ever and ever. Amen (1 Tim. 1:12, 17).

Q 45 *For which 4 things does Paul praise God in 1 Timothy 1:17?*

Paul began his testimony with thanksgiving. Now, after telling of God's grace, he ends with worship. Paul exalts God for four reasons:

* The God we serve is the *"King eternal."* He rules the universe through all the ages.[27]
* He is *"immortal."* He does not age or grow old with time. He was, is, and will always be.
* He is *"invisible"* to human eyes (Rom. 1:20; Col. 1:15). But eyes of faith will one day behold Him (Matt. 5:8; 1 John 3:2; see Heb. 11:27).
* He is the *only* true *God*.

For these reasons, and a thousand others, let us give God all glory and honor, both now and forever (1 Tim. 1:17; Rev. 4:9-11; 5:12-13; 7:12).

Q 46 *Does Jesus love you more than the Father loves you? Explain.*

One teacher always began his class on theology by saying, "Let us remember that as we discuss God, He is the One who redeemed us, and He hears every word we say. We can talk about some people behind their backs. But God is everywhere—even here in our classroom. So in all of our discussions let us be aware of His mercy and presence— and talk as He listens." If we will keep these truths in mind, we will, like Paul, always seek to honor and glorify God.[28]

F. Jesus wants us to take care of our faith—not shipwreck it (1 Tim. 1:18-20).

Verse 18 sets the tone for the rest of 1 Timothy.

Q 47 *What are the purposes of prophecy? How did prophecies help Timothy?*

*[18]Timothy, my son, I give you this instruction in keeping with **the prophecies once made about you**, so that by following them you may fight the good fight, [19]**holding on to faith and a good conscience**. Some have rejected these and so have **shipwrecked their faith**. [20]Among them are Hymenaeus and Alexander, whom I have handed over to Satan to be taught not to blaspheme (1 Tim. 1:18-20).*

Q 48 *In what sense did Timothy need to fight for the faith in Ephesus?*

When Timothy was ordained as a pastor, there were prophecies about him. Paul reminded Timothy of these prophecies—to help him *"fight the good fight"* (1 Tim. 1:18). Prophecies are to strengthen, encourage, and comfort (1 Cor. 14:3). (For a study on prophecy see the *Faith & Action* course, *1 and 2 Corinthians*, Lesson 24.) Near the beginning of his ministry, some prophesied over Timothy, to strengthen, encourage, and comfort him. These spiritual words of prophecy were to help Timothy fight. *Fight* is a military word. We do not fight physically with people. But we are in spiritual warfare, so we must put on the whole armor of God and pray in the Spirit (Eph. 6:10-19). Paul says that we do not fight *"against flesh and blood, but against the rulers, against the authorities, against the powers of this dark world and against the spiritual forces of evil in the heavenly realms"* (Eph. 6:12). Paul wrote these words to the Ephesians, where Timothy pastored. Timothy was fighting to protect the faith. Behind the false teachers at Ephesus were doctrines of demons. Later in 1 Timothy, Paul warns:

> [1] *The Spirit clearly says that in later times some will **abandon the faith** and follow deceiving spirits and things taught by demons.* [2] *Such teachings come through hypocritical liars, whose **consciences** have been seared as with a hot iron.* [3] *They forbid people to marry and order them to abstain from certain foods, which God created to be received with thanksgiving by those who believe and who know the truth.* [4] *For everything God created is good, and nothing is to be rejected if it is received with thanksgiving,* [5] *because it is consecrated by the word of God and prayer.* [6] ***If you point these things out to the brothers, you will be a good minister of Christ Jesus**, brought up in the truths of the faith and of the good teaching that you have followed.* [7] *Have nothing to do with godless myths and old wives' tales; rather, train yourself to be godly.* [8] *For physical training is of some value, but **godliness has value for all things, holding promise for both the present life and the life to come*** (1 Tim. 4:1-8).

> [3] *For though we live in the world, we do not wage war as the world does.* [4] *The weapons we fight with are not the weapons of the world. On the contrary, they have divine power to demolish strongholds.* [5] *We demolish arguments and every pretension that sets itself up against the knowledge of God, and we take captive every thought to make it obedient to Christ* (2 Cor. 10:3-5).

Q 49 ⟍ What warning does the Spirit give about believers in the last days?

Q 50 ⟍ Illustrate how believers today must fight for, contend for, and defend the faith?

Figure 3.13   When a ship at sea wrecks, this usually results in the loss of many lives.

At Ephesus, Timothy was in a fight for his soul and the souls of those under his care. Some who were once faithful members of the Ephesian church had gone astray. Like *Hymenaeus and Alexander*, they had ignored conscience, embraced unbiblical teachings, and shipwrecked their faith. These deserters were leading others away from the gospel. As Jude said, we must *"contend for the faith that was once for all entrusted to the saints"* (Jude 3). Paul is urging Timothy to fight for the truth—to stand up for it and insist on it. Christians have *responsibilities*. We must cooperate with God to be saved. God expects us to *hold on* to the faith He has given us. Success in our spiritual warfare is by grace. God gives all the grace we need. But we must *use the grace to persevere*. God saves those who cooperate with Him and hold on to the faith. We must hold on to *"faith and a good conscience"* (1 Tim. 1:19).

If Paul were living today, he might compare faith to a car, a bus, or a train. But in Paul's day, people traveled long distances by a ship. So the apostle compares the faith of each person to a ship. Paul knew what it was like to be on a ship that wrecked (Acts 27). He knew we must steer away from things that will destroy our faith. And he knew that two leaders at the church in Ephesus *shipwrecked* their faith—and the faith of others

Q 51 ⟍ What was at stake in Timothy's fight for the faith? What did the winner receive (1 Tim. 4:16)?

Q 52 ⟍ Why did Paul compare faith to a ship?

Q 53 ⟍ What causes a person's faith to be wrecked and ruined?

(1 Tim. 1:19). How? They were careless with faith and conscience. These leaders were once beloved believers. But they neglected their salvation. And they also damaged the faith of others (2 Tim. 2:17). So Paul put them out of the church—and turned them over to Satan (1 Tim. 1:20). By doing so, he protected the church from their influence. And, he disciplined them, hoping they would repent.[29] Scripture does not tell us if they found their way back into the grace of God.

Jehoshaphat's boats were shipwrecked due to his ungodly alliance with Ahaziah (1 Kings 22:48; 2 Chron. 20:35-37). Jonah's boat was almost shipwrecked because of his disobedience to God's will (Jonah 1:4). The ship Paul traveled on to Rome was shipwrecked because the captain refused to heed God's warning. Gentle winds deceived him (Acts 27:9-13.). In modern times the Titanic shipwrecked because its captain was careless and sailed too close to an *iceberg—a mountain of ice in the sea. As we pay attention to the gospel, godly teachers, and conscience, we can avoid shipwrecking our faith.

Q 54 *What are some examples the Bible gives of believers who shipwrecked their faith?*

The Bible tells of many believers who shipwrecked their faith. Esau shipwrecked his faith by selling his birthright (Gen. 25:29-34). The multitude who followed Moses out of Egypt shipwrecked their faith in the desert (Heb. 3:7-19). They rebelled against God, turned loose of their faith in God, and so they died in the wilderness—and never reached the Promised Land of Canaan. Some today shipwreck their faith by rebelling and choosing to sin, after they have received the truth (Heb. 10:26-27). In contrast, let us hold fast to the faith and pay attention to conscience. For *"we have come to share in Christ if we hold firmly till the end the confidence we had at first"* (Heb. 3:14). Jesus warned that in the last days *"the love of most will grow cold"* (Matt. 24:12). So let us not be quitters in whom God has no pleasure (Heb. 10:38-39). Rather, let us, by the grace of God and the help of the Spirit, endure to the end and be among the saved (Matt. 24:13).

Q 55 *Which 2 types of people does history record? Illustrate each.*

God has poured out grace, mercy, and love on us. Let us be careful and diligent—avoiding the examples of Hymenaeus and Alexander. They were once beloved leaders in the church. But somehow they were seduced into false teachings, sin, and the world. History reveals at least two types of people—the careful and the careless. Let us be among those who always value and protect the salvation God has provided.

Q 56 *What are some keys to avoid shipwrecking our faith?*

Q 57 *Summarize the warnings in these verses of Scripture (Figure 3.14).*

Reference	Your Summaries on Verses About Caring for Our Precious Salvation
1 Cor. 10:1-5	
1 Tim. 1:18-20	
Heb. 2:1-4	
Heb. 10:26-31	

Figure 3.14   Practice summarizing the danger of wrecking the faith God gives.

Warning: Danger!		Hebrews
1.	The danger of neglect	2:1-4
2.	The danger of unbelief	3:7-19
3.	The danger of immaturity	5:11–6:12
4.	The danger of not persevering to the end	10:26-31
5.	The danger of letting sin crowd out grace	12:14-29

Figure 3.15   Five warnings in the book of Hebrews

Lesson

14 Objects and Attitudes of Prayer—Part 1 (1 Tim. 2:1-7)
Goal A: *Explain why Paul wants believers to pray for all people.*

Setting

Paul began this letter on the topic of false teachers (1 Tim. 1:1-20). Now, he gives instructions about prayer and worship (1 Tim. 2:1-15). In 1 Timothy 2:1 Paul writes: *"I urge, then"* [Greek: *oun*]. The Greek word *oun* is often translated *"therefore"*, as in Romans 12:1. In 1 Timothy 2:1 *oun* is like a bridge. It connects Paul's concerns about false teachers (1 Tim. 1:1-20) to his call for prayer and worship (1 Tim. 2:1-15).[30] But what is the connection? Verses like 1 Timothy 2:4 emphasize that God wants all people to be saved—even false teachers. Praying for all people helps us discern false teachers, and even transform them. God does not stop loving people because they go astray in actions or in doctrine. The Father's heart longs for all the lost and scattered children of God in every nation to come home to Him—before it is forever too late (Matt. 23:37; Luke 15; John 11:52).

In 1 Timothy 2:1-15, Paul emphasizes three principles, A–C, about prayer and worship. We will study Point A in this lesson, and Points B and C in Lesson 15.

Q 58 ⬈ *How do Paul's teachings on prayer (1 Tim. 2) relate to the false teachers (1 Tim. 1)?*

Figure 3.16 In 1 Timothy 2.1 the Greek word *oun* (which means "therefore" or "so then") is like a bridge that connects chapters 1 and 2 of 1 Timothy.

A. To pray well we should pray for *all*—because God wants *all* to be saved (1 Tim. 2:1-7).

[1]*I urge, **then**, first of all, that requests, prayers, intercession and thanksgiving be made for everyone—*[2]*for kings and all those in authority, that we may live peaceful and quiet lives in all godliness and holiness.* [3]*This is good, and pleases **God our Savior**,* [4]***who wants all men to be saved** and to come to a knowledge of the truth.* [5]*For there is one God and one mediator between God and men, the man Christ Jesus,* [6]*who gave himself as a ransom for all men—the testimony given in its proper time.* [7]*And for this purpose I was appointed a herald and an apostle—I am telling the truth, I am not lying—and a teacher of the true faith to the Gentiles* (1 Tim. 2:1-7).

The main truth of this passage is *"God our Savior... wants **all** men to be saved"* (1 Tim. 2:4). The false teachers emphasized salvation for a few based on genealogies (1 Tim. 1:4). In contrast, Paul gave his personal testimony, showing that God saved the worst of sinners. Paul taught that we should pray for *everyone*, because God wants to save *every person* (1 Tim. 2:1). Jesus gave His life as a ransom for *all* (1 Tim. 2:6). God wants *"all men to be saved"* (1 Tim. 2:4). *"He [God] is patient with you, not wanting anyone to perish, but everyone to come to repentance"* (2 Pet. 3:9).

Go all the way back to the first pair of brothers. Abel's sacrifice pleased God, but Cain's sacrifice was not acceptable. Perhaps Cain should have offered an animal sacrifice. Or maybe it was his attitude or lifestyle that caused God to reject his offering. But an inspiring point of the story is that God was still cheering for Cain, even when his first offering was not acceptable. God encouraged Cain to try again (Gen. 4:6-7). With God, the present and the future is always more important than

Q 59 ⬈ *Why does Paul want us to pray for everyone—from kings to slaves?*

Q 60 ⬈ *What is the main truth of 1 Timothy 2:1-4?*

Q 61 ⬈ *How do God's words to Cain illustrate His desire for all to be saved (Gen. 4:6-7)?*

our past mistakes. God wants all of us to be saved, and enjoy a good relationship with Him. God is always reaching out His arms to hug us, even when we refuse to reach toward Him. But Cain had a stubborn streak as broad as his shoulders. Scripture gives no evidence that he ever humbled himself and repented. He led an entire genealogy away from God toward the flood. God wants every person in the whole world to be saved, but He leaves the choice to each of us.

Q 62 ⌐ *Is Paul emphasizing the types of prayers, or the focus of all prayer? Explain.*

Paul urged that *"requests, prayers, intercession and thanksgiving be made for everyone"* (1 Tim. 2:1). The apostle uses four different words for prayer. But his point is not the kinds of prayer we should offer. Rather, Paul is emphasizing the importance of various prayers for *everyone*.[31] And Paul puts kings and those in authority at the top of the prayer list. Why? Because government enables us to *"live peaceful and quiet lives in all godliness and holiness"* (1 Tim. 2:2). When there is chaos, rebellion in the streets, fighting, and turmoil, it is difficult to meet with people and share the gospel. When Paul wrote these words, the evil emperor Nero was persecuting Christians. Still, Paul urged believers to pray for kings and authorities—*so that* God's people could live peaceful, godly, and holy lives (1 Tim. 2:2).

Q 63 ⌐ *If God wants all to be saved, are all saved? Is God's will done on earth? Explain.*

Although salvation is for all, this does not mean all are saved. Salvation comes through *"knowledge of the truth"* (1 Tim. 2:4). To be saved, people must hear, believe, and live the truth of the gospel (1 Tim. 3:15; 2 Tim. 3:7-8; 4:4; Titus 1:1). Half of the world has not yet heard the clear truth of the gospel. More than 3.5 billion people on earth have never heard the good news that Jesus saves from the guilt and the grip of sin. And many who have heard refuse to believe.

Parts of 1 Timothy 2:5-6	Your Summaries
One God	
One mediator between God and men	
Christ Jesus, who gave himself as a ransom for all men	

Figure 3.17   Practice analyzing and explaining the three parts of 1 Timothy 2:5-6.

Paul gives evidence that God wants all to be saved (1 Tim. 2:5-6). We may examine the evidence in three parts. Notice that the first and second part are necessary steps to the third part—Paul's main point.[32]

- **First:** There is *"one God"* (1 Tim. 2:5) who is over all people. There are not many gods—only one. And this One God is not just the God of the Jews, who are less than one percent of earth's population. Rather, this One God is over all people. And as the rest of the evidence in 1 Timothy 2:5-6 shows, this One God over all has provided salvation for all.

Q 64 ⌐ *What are the meanings of* ransom *and* redeem?

- **Second:** There is *"one mediator between God and men"* (1 Tim. 2:5). Jesus is the one and only mediator, negotiator, and Savior between God and humanity.

- **Third:** Jesus *"gave himself as a ransom for all men"* (1 Tim. 2:6; Matt. 20:28). The Greek noun translated *ransom* is *anti-lutron*. The word *ransom* [Greek: *lutron*] means "payment." In the first century, *lutron* referred to the ransom—the price paid to free a slave.[33] Recall that the prophet Hosea paid a ransom of 15 shekels of silver to redeem (buy back) his adulterous wife, Gomer, who had become a slave (Hos. 3:2). Gomer was an illustration of Israel, and all of us, who have been unfaithful to God. *Lutron* is sometimes used with *anti* (Greek: against, instead of, or on behalf of). For example, Matthew 20:28 says *"the Son of Man did not come to be served, but to give*

Q 65 ⌐ *How did Hosea redeem Gomer?*

Q 66 ⌐ *What ransom did Jesus pay for us?*

his life as a **ransom** [*lutron*] *for* [*anti*] *many"* (See also Mark 10:45). The thought is "payment as substitution." The *payment* of money was a substitute *for* Gomer. She went free when the payment was made. Likewise, *Jesus gave **Himself** as a payment, a **ransom**, so that we could go free.* In this unique passage of 1 Timothy 2:6, Paul joins *lutron* and *anti* together as one word—*anti-lutron* (found in the New Testament only in 1 Timothy 2). Jesus gave Himself as the payment for all people to go free.

Problem.   The penalty of sin is death, spiritual separation from God. We have answered the question: *For whom did Jesus make the payment of his life?* He paid *for* all. He paid enough so that *everyone* could be free. The questions arise: *To whom did Jesus make the payment—and why?* Certainly not to the devil. For Satan has no sense of justice. He is a liar and a thief. The payment of Jesus' death was to God. Like all the sacrifices of the Old Testament, Jesus sacrificed Himself to satisfy God's sense of justice. God is just. He makes laws and decrees to govern the universe. The Almighty Judge decreed that the person who sins must die. Under the Law of the Old Testament, God allowed an animal to be sacrificed for a human, **temporarily**—until Jesus died as the necessary payment to redeem humans.

Q 67 *Why was a ransom needed for each of us?*

Q 68 *To whom did Jesus pay the ransom?*

Problem.   The blood of animals cannot pay for the sin of humans. The writer of Hebrews explains the ransom Jesus paid:

Q 69 *Why was it necessary for Jesus to die for us?*

[1] ***The law is only a shadow*** *of the good things that are coming—not the realities themselves. For this reason it can never, by the same sacrifices repeated endlessly year after year, make perfect those who draw near to worship.* [2]*If it could, would they not have stopped being offered? For the worshipers would have been cleansed once for all, and would no longer have felt guilty for their sins.* [3]*But those sacrifices are an annual reminder of sins,* [4]***because it is impossible for the blood of bulls and goats to take away sins****.* [5]*Therefore, when Christ came into the world, he said: "Sacrifice and offering you did not desire, but a body you prepared for me;* [6]*with burnt offerings and sin offerings you were not pleased.* [7]*Then I said, 'Here I am—it is written about me in the scroll—I have come to do your will, O God.'"* [8]*First he said, "Sacrifices and offerings, burnt offerings and sin offerings you did not desire, nor were you pleased with them" (although the law required them to be made).* [9]*Then he said, "Here I am, I have come to do your will." He sets aside the first to establish the second.* [10]*And by that will, we have been made holy through the sacrifice of the body of Jesus Christ once for all.* [11]*Day after day every priest stands and performs his religious duties; again and again **he offers the same sacrifices, which can never take away sins***.* [12]*But when this priest had offered for all time one sacrifice for sins, he sat down at the right hand of God.* [13]*Since that time he waits for his enemies to be made his footstool,* [14]*because by one sacrifice he has made perfect forever those who are being made holy.* [15]*The Holy Spirit also testifies to us about this. First he says:* [16]*"This is the covenant I will make with them after that time, says the Lord. I will put my laws in their hearts, and I will write them on their minds."* [17]*Then he adds:* ***"Their sins and lawless acts I will remember no more."*** [18]***And where these have been forgiven, there is no longer any sacrifice for sin*** *(Heb. 10:1-18).*

Figure 3.18   The smallest human has more worth in God's eyes than the biggest animal, or all the animals combined, because humans (unlike animals) are created in the image of God.

Q 70 ➹ *What are some cheap payments people try to give for their sins?*

Do not be in a hurry to leave 1 Timothy 2:6. Be sure you understand the full meaning of this short verse. It may be the most important verse in the Bible. If you only learn one Greek word, learn *anti-lutron*—the payment Jesus made for you, me, and everyone in every nation. In some religions, guilty sinners seek to make their own plan to walk into God's presence and pay for their sins. Some bring an offering of money, food, flowers, or a life of service and sacrifice. Shall we lie, cheat, steal, covet, commit adultery, and kill, and then walk into God's presence with a bouquet of flowers, a plate of food, or a bag of money, hoping to pay for our sins? Shall we live in selfishness, ignoring the hungry, the poor, and the abused, and then bring an offering to erase our sins of neglect? Shall we pray five times a day, fast one month of the year, and give offerings, hoping to pay the Judge for our forgiveness? Shall we die in our sins, and hope to be reborn as a cow, a plant, or another person, as a payment for our sins against God and others? Can a good cow atone for a bad human? Never! Neither the death nor the life of an animal can pay for human sin, because the value of an animal is too low—compared to men and women, whom God created in His image (Gen. 1:27). These cheap payments by people do not match the debt of human sin. God is serious about human sin. He has decreed: *"The soul who sins shall die"* (Ezek. 18:4). *"The wages of sin is death"*—spiritual death, separation from God (Rom. 6:23). The justice of God Almighty will not allow cheap offerings as a payment to cancel sin. Shall we offer God a penny to cancel the debt of a million dollars?

Q 71 ➘ *What is the only payment God accepts to forgive human sins? Why?*

Solution.   Our Father Himself made a plan to redeem and forgive everyone. There was one offering, so valuable that it was worth more than all of the humans who would ever live on the earth. Revelation 5 records a drama in heaven as angels searched for someone who was worthy to open the scroll about the future judgments of the earth. Only one person was found, for only One was worthy. John wrote:

> COULD MY ZEAL NO WEAKNESS KNOW;
> COULD MY TEARS FOREVER FLOW;
> THESE FOR SIN COULD NOT ATONE;
> YOU MUST SAVE, AND YOU ALONE.
> NOTHING IN MY HAND I BRING;
> SIMPLY TO YOUR CROSS I CLING.
> TOWARD YOUR JUDGMENT THRONE I FLY;
> SAVE ME JESUS, OR I DIE. [34]

Figure 3.19   Only Jesus can save us from the penalty and power of sin.

⁶Then I saw a Lamb, looking as if it had been slain, standing in the center of the throne, encircled by the four living creatures and the elders... ⁷He came and took the scroll from the right hand of him who sat on the throne. ⁸And when he had taken it, the four living creatures and the twenty-four elders fell down before the Lamb. Each one had a harp and they were holding golden bowls full of incense, which are the prayers of the saints. ⁹And they sang a new song: **"You are worthy to take the scroll and to open its seals, because you were slain, and with your blood you purchased men for God from every tribe and language and people and nation.** *¹⁰You have made them to be a kingdom and priests to serve our God, and they will reign on the earth"* (Rev. 5:6-10)

¹¹For the grace of God that brings salvation has appeared to **all** *men. ¹²It teaches us to say "No" to ungodliness and worldly passions, and to live self-controlled, upright and godly lives in this present age, ¹³while we wait for the blessed hope—the glorious appearing of our great God and Savior, Jesus Christ,* **¹⁴who gave himself for us to redeem us from all wickedness and to purify for himself a people that are his very own, eager to do what is good** (Titus 2:11-14).

Q 72 ➘ *Complete Figure 3.20 on aspects of the salvation that God provides.*

Questions on Aspects of Salvation	Answers on Aspects of Salvation
For whom did Jesus come?	
How did God save us?	
To whom did Jesus make the payment?	(Heb. 9:14)
Why did Jesus save us?	
From what does He save us?	
For whom does He save us?	

Figure 3.20   Practice analyzing aspects of the salvation that God provides for all (1 Tim. 2:6; Titus 2:14).

By **sacrificing** His own life, Jesus **provided for ALL deliverance from** the slavery of sin and **restoration to** God. And as Paul notes in 1 Timothy 4:10, Jesus is *"the Savior of all men, and especially of those who believe."* God does not force anyone to accept His offer of salvation. He paid the price for all to be saved. He opens His arms wide, and promises that whoever comes to Him, He will never cast out (See John 6:37 NIV and NKJV). *"And the one who trusts in him will never be put to shame"* (Rom. 9:33; 10:11; 1 Pet. 2:6; based on Isa. 28:16). Behold the love of the Father, who gave His One and Only Son to save us. Let us give praise, thanksgiving, glory, respect, and honor to this God of love. And let us worship Jesus, who gave Himself as a ransom to redeem us from all evil, and to purify us to be God's children, eager to serve Him!

Q 73 Whose vote determines if a person will be saved? Explain.

Q 74 Complete Figure 3.21 on verses that emphasize God votes for all to be saved.

 Jesus gave His life, voting for all to be saved. The devil votes for all to be lost. The vote of each person determines whether he or she will be saved.

Reference	Your Summaries
Ezek. 18:23; 33:11	
Matt. 18:14	
Luke 13:34; Matt. 23:37	
John 3:16	
John 6:40	
1 Tim. 2:6	
Titus 2:11	
Rom. 10:11-13	
2 Pet. 3:9	
Rev. 22:17	

Figure 3.21   Practice summarizing verses showing that God wants all to be saved.

Because God wants salvation for all, He appointed Paul as a messenger to the Gentiles (1 Tim. 2:7). He commanded Paul to take the salvation message to a sinful world. God still calls and sends pastors, evangelists, missionaries, and witnesses today. God wants all who are separated from Him to come back to Him. He offers salvation to the worst sinners. God invites all slaves of sin to become His free children. As we pray and live godly and holy lives (1 Tim. 2:1-2), sinners can find the way to the Father. Missionaries once brought the gospel to us. We must be missionaries and send missionaries to the perishing of our generation.

Q 75 Why is it vital for messengers to share the gospel with the lost?

Lesson 15 — Objects and Attitudes of Prayer—Part 2 (1 Tim. 2:8-15)

Goal B: *Analyze the need to lift holy hands in prayer, and explain how this is possible.*
Goal C: *Summarize the context of Ephesian women, and apply Paul's words on dress, teaching, and motherhood.*

In Lesson 14, we studied Point A, emphasizing that God wants us to pray for all because He desires for all to be saved. Here in Lesson 15, we study Points B and C, which explain the type of lifestyles that make our prayers fruitful. God does not pay much attention to the prayers of sinners, unless they are praying to repent. In contrast, the prayers of the righteous are powerful (James 5:16). The psalmist and Peter contrasted the prayers of the unrighteous and the prayers of the righteous:

Q 76 What was the main point of 1 Timothy 2:1-4?

Q 77 How does our lifestyle nullify or empower our prayers?

[11] Whoever would love life and see good days must keep his tongue from evil and his lips from deceitful speech. [11] He must turn from evil and do good; he must seek peace and pursue it. [12] For the eyes of the Lord are on the righteous and his ears are attentive to their prayer, but the face of the Lord is against those who do evil (1 Pet. 3:10-12; based on Ps. 34:16).

The words of a prayer are only as powerful as the righteous living in the life of the person who prays. So let us pay close attention to Paul's revelation on how men and women can pray with influence.

B. To pray well, men (and women) must live holy lives (1 Tim. 2:8).

Figure 3.22   Paul urged men to lift up holy hands in prayer.

*I want men everywhere to lift up **holy hands** in prayer, without **anger or disputing*** (1 Tim. 2:8).

At first glance, it appears that Paul is being unfair to women. For he writes the responsibilities of men in one verse, but Paul uses seven verses on guidelines for women to pray well (1 Tim. 2:9-15). Yet as we examine the words *lift up holy hands* we realize that Paul said as much to men—using fewer words.

What does it mean to *"lift up holy hands"*? In Scripture, hands symbolize deeds, actions, and lifestyle—whether holy or unholy. We use our hands for almost everything. Paul wants believers to pray with *"holy hands"* (1 Tim. 2:8). Our hands first become holy when God forgives our sins and washes us. Our hands remain clean and pure as we submit to the Word and the Spirit, and live righteous lives. Consider the choices we make that involve our hands. With our hands we pick up books and magazines to read. With our hands we choose entertainment on the radio, Internet, or television. With our hands we touch others in ways that are godly or sinful. With our hands we can help people or hurt them. We can use our hands to share food, clothes, or money and to do other good deeds. Or we can use our hands to steal, cheat, hit, or send ugly messages. So much of life is connected to what we do with our hands. Men, let us live in ways that please God, so that the hands we lift in prayer may be holy. A pretty prayer means nothing to God if it comes from a man with unholy hands. God watches what we do with our hands throughout the week. So Paul urges men to lift up *"holy hands"* when we pray (1 Tim. 2:8). Then when we pray, God will say, "Look at those clean and holy hands that man is lifting toward heaven as he prays."

Consider this parable about prayer. In a certain town there is a rich and powerful judge who is the father of a large family. A local citizen named Cain makes an appointment to request help from the judge on Friday. On Monday Cain steals from one of the judge's sons. On Tuesday Cain has an immoral relationship with one of the judge's daughters. On Wednesday he gossips about one of the judge's children. And on Thursday he refuses to help one of the judge's children who was in an accident. On Friday, how do you think the judge will respond as Cain reaches out his filthy hands with a request for help?

God welcomes into His presence those with holy hands. David wrote:

[3] Who may ascend the hill of the LORD? Who may stand in his holy place? [4] He who has clean hands and a pure heart, who does not lift up his soul to an idol or swear by what is false (Ps. 24:3-4).

Does God *ever* answer the prayer of a person with unholy hands? Yes, recall the prayer of the sinful tax collector: *"God, have mercy on me, a sinner"* (Luke 18:13). Likewise, Jesus answered the same type of prayer when the thief on the cross prayed (Luke 23:42-43). All believers rejoice that God hears sincere prayers of repentance, before we come to Christ, and even after.

Q 78 *Are Paul's guidelines on prayer less for men than for women? Explain.*

Q 79 *What are some characteristics of holy hands? What do they do and avoid?*

Q 80 *Do you lift holy hands to God in prayer? Examine them.*

Q 81 *How do you think the judge will respond to citizen Cain? Apply this.*

Q 82 *Which prayers of sinners does God answer?*

Jesus washes our sins away when we repent and choose to follow Him.

> [9] *Do you not know that the wicked will not inherit the kingdom of God? Do not be deceived: Neither the sexually immoral nor idolaters nor adulterers nor male prostitutes nor homosexual offenders* [10] *nor thieves nor the greedy nor drunkards nor slanderers nor swindlers will inherit the kingdom of God.* [11] *And that is what some of you were.* **But you were washed, you were sanctified, you were justified in the name of the Lord Jesus Christ and by the Spirit of our God** (1 Cor. 6:9-11).

All who abide in Christ are led by His Spirit and have holy hands.

The Scriptures emphasize our responsibility to keep ourselves clean and holy *after* Jesus washes us.

Q 83 *What are some examples of those who became unclean, after Jesus made them holy?*

Peter compares some to a sow that returns to the mud (2 Pet. 2:22). **James** reminds believers that pure religion to God the Father means keeping *"oneself from being polluted by the world"* (James 1:27). **John** praises the few believers at Sardis *"who have not soiled their clothes"* (Rev. 3:4). **Paul** commands believers to remove all *unholy* actions, such as *sexual immorality, impurity, lust, evil desires and greed...anger, rage, malice, slander, and filthy language, lying, and stealing* (Col. 3:5-10; Eph. 4:25–5:7). He says that among believers *"there must not be even a hint of sexual immorality, or of any kind of impurity, or of greed, because these are improper for God's **holy** people"* (Eph. 5:3). Paul insists that true believers are led by the Spirit, and not by the flesh (Rom. 8:13; Gal. 5:16-25). If we have sinned, we must wash our hands (James 4:8). That is, we must repent, turn from sin, and follow Jesus in the light. The Spirit leads us to walk in the light of Scripture and conscience. As we obey the Word and the Spirit, we remain with clean hearts and clean hands (1 John 1:7). As we submit to the Spirit, God gives us grace and power to overcome the world and to live holy lives.

Q 84 *What enables our hands to remain holy after Jesus washes us?*

> [15] *When you spread out your hands in prayer, I will hide my eyes from you; even if you offer many prayers, I will not listen. Your hands are full of blood;* [16] *wash and make yourselves clean. Take your evil deeds out of my sight! Stop doing wrong,* [17] *learn to do right! Seek justice, encourage the oppressed. Defend the cause of the fatherless, plead the case of the widow.* [18] *"Come now, let us reason together," says the* LORD. *"Though your sins are like scarlet, they shall be as white as snow; though they are red as crimson, they shall be like wool.* [19] *If you are willing and obedient, you will eat the best from the land;* [20] *but if you resist and rebel, you will be devoured by the sword." For the mouth of the* LORD *has spoken* (Isa. 1:15-20).

Q 85 *Why did God refuse to listen to the prayers of many Israelites (Isa. 1:15-20)?*

Holy hands are guided by love—God's standard for our behavior.[35] As we love God and others, we live holy lives, and we can lift up holy hands. Then our prayers are powerful with God.

Q 86 *Summarize the verses in Figure 3.23 as a review.*

Reference	Your Summaries on Our Responsibilities to Keep Our Hands Holy
Isa. 1:15-20	
Rom. 8:12-14	
Gal. 5:16-25	
Col. 3:5-10	
James 1:27	
James 4:8	
1 John 1:7	
1 John 1:9	
Rev. 3:4	

Figure 3.23 **Practice summarizing our responsibility to remain with holy hands after Jesus washes us.**

Q 87 ⟋ *How are holy hands related to healthy relationships? Illustrate.*

Therefore [Greek *oun*], *"I want men everywhere to lift up holy hands in prayer, without anger or disputing"* (1 Tim. 2:8). Paul links holy hands to relationships. As we noted earlier, the false teachers at Ephesus were stirring up controversies and division in the house churches (1 Tim. 1:4). Damaged relationships were one fruit of the false teachers. Bitterness, hatred, lasting anger, fighting, and quarreling—these stain our hands and hinder our prayers. Jesus said to make peace with our brother before we pray to God at an altar (Matt. 5:23-24). Lifting holy hands includes living in right relationships with others.

James reminds us that anger and disputing are the fruit of deeper roots.

Q 88 ⟋ *According to James, what things hinder prayer?*

*¹What causes fights and quarrels among you? Don't they come from your desires that battle within you? ²You want something but don't get it. You kill and covet, but you cannot have what you want. You quarrel and fight. You do not have, because you do not ask God. ³When you **ask**, you do not receive, because you ask with wrong motives, that you may spend what you get on your pleasures. ⁴You adulterous people, don't you know that friendship with the world is hatred toward God? Anyone who chooses to be a friend of the world becomes an enemy of God* (James 4:1-4).

What is the solution to avoiding anger and quarrels? Stand firm on the solid foundation of the gospel. Turn away from twisted teachings that appeal to fleshly desires. And *"wash your hands"* (James 4:8)! Ask God to forgive and cleanse. Draw near to God, and walk close to Jesus. Be led by the Spirit.

To lift up holy hands, men must live holy lives—in private, and in relation to others. God will not listen to the prayers of the unholy (Isa. 1:15). David said, *"If I had cherished sin in my heart, the Lord would not have listened"* (Ps. 66:18). But the prayer of a holy man is powerful and effective (James 5:16; 1 Pet. 3:12).

Q 89 ⟍ *Which 3 men were mighty in prayer because of their righteous living, but lacked the power to save the ungodly nation of Israel (Ezek. 14)?*

Of the seven deadly sins, anger may be the most fun. To lick your wounds, to smack your lips over offenses long past, to retell the bitter things people have done to you, to savor to the last bite the pain you receive and the pain you give back—in many ways anger is a feast fit for a king. But the main problem is that what you are chewing and destroying is yourself. The carcass at the feast is you.³⁶ Sabio says, "He who continues to be angry destroys himself." An old Greek proverb says, "He whom the gods would destroy, they first make angry."

C. To pray and worship well, women (and men) need proper relationships (1 Tim. 2:9-15).

Q 90 ⟍ *What things must believers today avoid and do, to be able to lift up holy hands?*

Figure 3.24 Our horizontal relationships on earth affect our vertical relationship to the God of heaven.

⁹I also want women to dress modestly, with decency and propriety, not with braided hair or gold or pearls or expensive clothes, ¹⁰but with good deeds, appropriate for women who profess to worship God. ¹¹A woman should learn in quietness and full submission. ¹²I do not permit a woman to teach or to have authority over a man; she must be silent. ¹³For Adam was formed first, then Eve. ¹⁴And Adam was not the one deceived; it was the woman who was deceived and became a sinner. ¹⁵But women will be saved through childbearing—if they continue in faith, love and holiness with propriety (1 Tim. 2:9-15).

Setting. The topic of 1 Timothy 2:1-15 is: Instructions on prayer and worship. It is helpful to note that 1 Timothy 2:8-15 is just *one* paragraph in the Greek. Paul's point for men *and* women is that *earthly* relationships affect our *heavenly* relationship. The two great commandments are to love God, and love people. To have power with God in prayer, we must maintain righteous relationships on earth. Poor relationships with people result in useless prayers to God (1 Tim. 2:8-15;1 Pet. 3:7).

Paul instructs men to lift up holy hands, without quarreling (1 Tim. 2:8). But why does he use seven verses to instruct women (1 Tim. 2:9-15)? We find the answer as we understand the context. False teachers at Ephesus were causing problems in the house churches. Two passages in Paul's letters to Timothy shed light on the problem: 1 Timothy 5:3-15 and 2 Timothy 3:5-9. The bad behavior of **a few** in society always affects others.

Problem. Paul links the false teachers to sinful women in Ephesus. False teachers wormed their way into homes, to "⁶*...gain control over weak-willed women, who are loaded down with sins and are swayed by all kinds of evil desires, ⁷always learning but never able to acknowledge the truth*" (2 Tim. 3:6-7).

According to 1 Timothy 5, among these ungodly women are younger widows who:
- Live for pleasure (1 Tim. 5:6);
- Have become *"gossips and busybodies, saying things they ought not to"* (1 Tim. 5:13);
- Were giving the gospel a bad reputation (1 Tim. 5:14);
- Had in some cases *"already turned away to follow Satan"* (1 Tim. 5:15; compare 1 Tim. 2:14 and 4:2).

Solution. Paul's advice for these few, ungodly women is that they should marry (1 Tim. 4:3), have children (1 Tim. 2:15), and take care of their homes (1 Tim. 5:14). With this context in mind, we can understand three things Paul writes about women: concerning their dress, teaching, and motherhood.[37]

1. Dress. Women should dress modestly, not calling attention to themselves. They should clothe themselves with good deeds instead of expensive clothes. This is appropriate for women who claim to worship God (1 Tim. 2:9, 10). Paul emphasizes the inner qualities of women. Likewise, in a parallel passage, Peter stresses that a woman's beauty should be from the inside out.

> ³*Your beauty should not come from outward adornment, such as braided hair and the wearing of gold jewelry and fine clothes. ⁴Instead, it should be that of your inner self, the unfading beauty of a gentle and quiet spirit, which is of great worth* [like gold] *in God's sight* (1 Pet. 3:3-4).

Customs vary from place to place. What looks good to one husband, in his culture, may offend another husband in a different place. Abraham's servant gave Rebekah a gold ring for her nose, and two gold bracelets, with silver jewelry and articles of clothing (Gen. 24:22-30, 53). This was a part of their culture. But Rebekah was already beautiful without the jewelry, just watering camels by the well (Gen. 24:16). Her main beauty shone from a pure heart, and a gentle spirit. In some cultures a Christian husband wants his wife to wear a head scarf. Blessed is the wife who dresses to please her godly husband, and does not attract or seduce the attention of other men in church.

John contrasts the great prostitute (the great city of the Antichrist) and the holy city, the New Jerusalem. The prostitute *"was dressed in purple and scarlet, and was glittering with gold, precious stones and pearls"* (Rev. 17:4). Her gaudy clothes and flashy jewelry flaunted and advertised her vileness. In contrast, the Holy City was coming down from heaven, *"prepared as a bride beautifully dressed for her husband"* (Rev. 21:2). She too wore beautiful clothes and costly stones, but her purity

Q 91 ⟋ *Poor relationships with people result in _____ prayers to God.*

Q 92 ⟍ *Were most women in the church at Ephesus living holy lives?*

Q 93 ⟍ *What are 4 examples of bad behavior by a few ungodly women at Ephesus?*

Q 94 ⟍ *How does Paul see marriage as a solution to some of the problems at Ephesus?*

Q 95 ⟋ *Is it wrong for a woman to dress in ways that please her husband?*

Q 96 ⟍ *What main point does Paul emphasize about a women's dress? Illustrate this.*

Q 97 ⟍ *How might a holy woman's dress vary in rural and urban areas, or from culture to culture?*

Q 98 ⟋ *What should a wife's greatest beauty be?*

and virtue shone like the moon in its glory. It is fitting and proper for a woman to dress in a way that she looks beautiful to her husband. A man should not have to leave his home to see a woman who looks beautiful to him. But a wife's greatest beauty should always be her godliness, as shown in a gentle and quiet spirit.

Isaiah rebuked the haughty women of Israel, and prophesied God's judgment upon them. Note that Isaiah mentions 21 items of exterior fashion.

Q 99 ↗ *Why was Isaiah upset with the haughty women of Israel?*

> [16] *The LORD says, "The women of Zion are haughty, walking along with outstretched necks, flirting with their eyes, tripping along with mincing steps, with ornaments jingling on their ankles. [17] Therefore the Lord will bring sores on the heads of the women of Zion; the LORD will make their scalps bald." [18] In that day the Lord will snatch away their finery: the bangles and headbands and crescent necklaces, [19] the earrings and bracelets and veils, [20] the headdresses and ankle chains and sashes, the perfume bottles and charms, [21] the signet rings and nose rings, [22] the fine robes and the capes and cloaks, the purses [23] and mirrors, and the linen garments and tiaras and shawls. [24] Instead of fragrance there will be a stench; instead of a sash, a rope; instead of well-dressed hair, baldness; instead of fine clothing, sackcloth; instead of beauty, branding. [25] Your men will fall by the sword, your warriors in battle* (Isa. 3:16-25).

Someone has humorously said: "Cosmetics are used by teen-age girls to make them look older sooner, and by their mothers to make them look younger longer." "Cosmetics were used in the Middle Ages; in fact, they're still used in the middle ages." "Cosmetics are a woman's hope of keeping men from reading between the lines."[38]

Q 100 ✎ *How was the older pastor wiser than the younger one?*

"A young pastor preached in the morning against the pride and extremes of fancy dresses, ribbons, ruffles, chains, and jewels. In the afternoon, an old pastor preached on the sinful desires of humans, the separation of the soul from God, and the need for a new heart. Later, as they sat together in private, the young minister asked, 'Sir, why do you not preach against the fashion and dress of the people?' 'O, my son,' replied the wise elder, 'while you trim a few branches of the evil tree, I am seeking to cut the roots—for then the whole tree must die!'"[39]

Q 101 ✎ *What are some biblical examples of women in ministry?*

Q 102 ✎ *In your culture, how do women show submission to their husbands?*

2. Teaching. Women *"should learn in quietness and full submission"* (1 Tim. 2:11). At Ephesus, the false teachers wanted to instruct others, but did not know what they were talking about (1 Tim. 1:7). Likewise there were some women in the same category. These women needed to be learners, not teachers. Elsewhere, as in Crete, Paul encouraged older women to:

> [4] *...train the younger women to love their husbands and children, [5] to be self-controlled and pure, to be busy at home, to be kind, and to be subject to their husbands, so that no one will malign the word of God* (Titus 2:4-5).

Paul was not opposed to women helping in the ministry. Priscilla was the main teacher who helped Apollos understand Pentecost (Acts 18:26). Paul encouraged *all*—men and women—to prophesy (1 Cor. 11:5). But Paul never allowed women to have authority over, or dominate men.

Q 103 ↗ *Who are some women in ministry that Paul commended?*

Q 104 ✎ *Why does Paul emphasize that sin came though Adam in Romans 5:12-20, but through Eve in 1 Timothy 2:13-15?*

To support his teaching about women being quiet and submissive, Paul refers to Genesis 2–3. He states that Adam was formed first. Then Eve was deceived and sinned (1 Tim. 2:13-14). These references fulfill Paul's purpose to protect the house churches at Ephesus. Writing to the Romans for a different purpose, Paul emphasizes that sin and death entered the world *through Adam* (Rom. 5:12-20). Also in his letter to the Romans, Paul praises several women for their leadership roles. So let us remember the context of 1 and 2 Timothy. False teachers at Ephesus were finding a way into the house churches through ungodly women. So Paul needed to emphasize some guidelines to protect the church there.

Husbands who read this should remember Paul's commands to men. The Bible commands husbands to treat their wives as they treat themselves, and not as slaves (Eph. 5:28). Paul commands husbands never to be harsh with their wives (Col. 3:19). Wives, children, employees, and citizens do not resent submission when leaders treat them with love and respect.

> SPURGEON SAID THAT JUST AS THE WOMAN,
>
> BY HER SPIRIT OF ADVENTURE,
>
> STEPPED FIRST INTO SIN—GOD ORDAINED THAT
>
> THE WOMAN ALONE WOULD GIVE BIRTH TO THE
>
> SAVIOR OF MANKIND,
>
> LEST MEN DESPISE HER. [40]

Application. When we interpret Scripture, we must determine if it describes or prescribes. Some Scripture is for a local culture, at a certain time and place. For example, kissing on the cheek and washing feet pertain to some cultures. These verses do not contain a Scriptural principle for all believers, in all places, at all times. In Paul's day, a woman was restricted. She had no part in the synagogue service. She could listen, but not speak or ask questions. A woman could not teach in school—she could not teach even the youngest children. A strict rabbi would not greet a woman on the street. A Jewish man thanked God for three things: that he was not born a Gentile, a slave, or a woman. Even Greek women of high status seldom went to public meetings. [41]

Twenty centuries have passed since Paul wrote. In most nations slaves are no longer the property of masters. Likewise, Christianity has lifted the status of women. In most nations women can vote, own property, and often receive as much or more education than their husbands. In today's world, women often hold positions of leadership in government, business, and in schools. Should women teach in the church today? Should they be ordained for ministry? The answer to this question varies within nations and cultures. But in many churches women are ordained for ministry and are respected teachers. Blessed is the woman who shines the light and love of Christ—in her home, church, and society.

Q 107 *Can a woman be saved without bearing children?*

Q 108 *Why did Paul say that widows who married and bore children would be saved? What contrast was he making?*

3. Motherhood. *"But women will be saved through childbearing—if they continue in faith, love and holiness with propriety"* (1 Tim. 2:15).

To interpret 1 Timothy 2:15, it is helpful to begin with the second half of the verse. For the last half of the verse emphasizes that women, like men, are saved by faith, from start to finish. The first woman, Eve, came into sin, outside of submission to her husband. For Eve surely knew that neither God nor Adam wanted her to eat the forbidden fruit (Gen. 3:3). Even so, we cannot excuse Adam's disobedience. He should have stood firm and refused the fruit Eve offered him. When either spouse is weak, the other should add strength. Paul wants a woman to submit to her husband, have children, and continue in faith, love, and holiness with good judgment. In other words, a woman is saved from deception and transgression as she is a godly wife and mother. This is her role in the home, the church, and in society. She is to be a godly example, known for her good deeds (1 Tim. 2:10)—which include marriage, bearing children, and keeping a good

Q 105 *What word of encouragement did Spurgeon give for women?*

Q 106 *In your culture, what are some roles of women in society and in the church?*

home (1 Tim. 5:11, 14). The reason the text says the woman *"will be saved"* is because the preceding verse said the woman became a sinner.[42]

Q 109 ✎ *From Figure 3.25: What are some contrasts between the godly and ungodly women?*

Reference	Godly Women	Ungodly Women	Reference
1 Tim. 2:9	Dress modestly with decency and good judgment to please their husbands.	Wear braided hair, gold, pearls, and costly clothes to attract attention to themselves.	1 Tim. 2:9
1 Tim. 2:10; 5:9-10	Do good deeds, such as worship God, raise children, be faithful to husbands, show hospitality, wash feet of saints and help those in trouble.	Are malicious talkers, slanderers; have the habit of being idle and going from house to house.	1 Tim. 3:11; 5:13; Titus 2:3
1 Tim. 2:11	Learn in quietness and full submission.	Follow false teachers and sin with them.	2 Tim. 3:5-9
1 Tim. 2:15	Continue in faith, love and holiness.	Are busybodies.	1 Tim. 5:13
1 Tim. 3:11	Are worthy of respect; temperate, trustworthy.	Say things they ought not say.	1 Tim. 5:13
1 Tim. 5:14; Titus 2:5	Give the enemy no opportunity for slander.	Discredit the gospel; some have even turned away to follow Satan.	1 Tim. 5:14-15
Titus 2:3	Are reverent in the way they live.	Some are addicted to much wine.	Titus 2:3

Figure 3.25   The Pastoral Epistles contrast godly and ungodly women.

Qualifications for Pastors and Deacons—Blameless in Five Ways (1 Tim. 3:1-16; Titus 1:6-9)

Lesson 16

Goal A: *Explain the meanings and relationship of overseer and deacon.*
Goal B: *Analyze why Paul forbids drunkenness. Summarize 5 reasons some abstain from alcohol.*
Goal C: *Explain why church leaders must not be overbearing, quick-tempered, lovers of money, or new converts.*

In the Pastoral Epistles, we see two church leadership positions: **overseers* and **deacons*.

Overseer [Greek: *episkopos*] is one who supervises, like a steward or bishop who watches over God's household (1 Tim. 3:2; Titus 1:7; Acts 20:28; Phil. 1:1; 1 Pet. 2:25).

Two other terms in the New Testament refer to overseers.
- *Elder* [Greek: *presbuteros*] emphasizes that overseers were usually older men. *Elder* stresses the spiritual maturity and dignity of an overseer (Titus 1:5; Acts 20:17).
- *Pastor or shepherd* [Greek: *poimen*] emphasizes one who watches over God's sheep (Acts 20:28). Jesus is the Chief Shepherd (John 10; Heb. 13:20; 1 Pet. 2:25). Lesser shepherds should follow the example of the Chief Shepherd, laying down their lives for the sheep (John 10:11).

Q 110 ✎ *Complete Figure 3.26 on aspects of pastoral ministry.*

Acts 20:28 refers to overseers who are elders that shepherd God's flock—which Jesus purchased with His own blood.

Words	Greek Word	Summary of Characteristics or Pastoral Ministry
Overseer		
Elder		
Pastor/shepherd		

Figure 3.26   Practice explaining three aspects of pastoral ministry.

Q 111 ➤ *How is the ministry of a deacon related to an overseer or pastor?*

Q 112 ➤ *How many of the 12 requirements for pastors and deacons relate to ability or talent? What does this tell us?*

Deacon is the second ministry position.   A deacon [Greek: *diakonos*], is *one who serves.* Deacons are ministers who help *overseers.* The first deacons were probably the seven whom the apostles chose to care for believers in Jerusalem (Acts 6:1-6). Deacons were leaders in the church, and their qualifications were much the same as those of overseers.

Mature leaders do not just appear. They must grow and develop. Becoming like Jesus is a process. All of life is a spiritual journey. But there is a level of spiritual maturity to reach *before* becoming an overseer or pastor. Paul insists on certain moral and spiritual standards that qualify a person to oversee the church. Study Figure 3.27. It contains 12 requirements for church leaders (1 Tim. 3:1-7; Titus 1:5-9). Because the qualifications for *overseers* and *deacons* are similar, we will look at them together. Notice that only *one* of the 12 requirements relates to ability or talent! A pastor's character is more important than his ability to speak or organize. A pastor's character is more important than his education. God *is not* searching for ability. He has no problem with a man like Moses who considered himself a slow speaker. Many have the ability to be good speakers. But God calls overseers and pastors on the basis of their character, not their ability to talk. To lead well, pastors must live what they preach. As Paul told Timothy, *"...set an example for the believers in speech, in life, in love, in faith and in purity"* (1 Tim. 4:12).

Q 113 ⟋ *How many qualifications of pastors and deacons are negative? How many are positive?*

1 Tim.	Titus	Qualifications for OVERSEERS	Qualifications for DEACONS	1 Tim.
3:2	1:6-7	**(−) Blameless (Not Guilty) of 5 Accusations:**	Worthy of respect	3:8, 11
			Sincere	3:8
3:3	1:7	1. Not given to drunkenness	Not given to drunkenness	3:8
3:3	1:7	2. Not overbearing or quarrelsome		
3:3	1:7	3. Not quick-tempered; not violent		
3:3	1:7	4. Not a lover of money; not pursuing dishonest gain	Not pursuing dishonest gain	3:8
3:6	—	5. Not a recent convert	Tested	3:10
3:2, 7	1:7	**(+) Respected for 7 Good Reasons:**		
3:2	1:6	1. The husband of one wife	The husband of one wife	3:12
3:3	—	2. Gentle		
3:2	1:8	3. Temperate; self-controlled; disciplined	(Wives) temperate; not malicious talkers	3:11
3:2	1:8	4. Hospitable		
—	1:8	5. One who loves what is good; upright and holy	(Wives) trustworthy in everything	3:11
3:2	1:9	6. Able to teach; holding firmly to sound doctrine	Holding to the deep truths of the faith with a clear conscience	3:9
3:4	1:6	7. A good manager of his own family	A good manager of his family	3:12

Figure 3.27   Qualifications for overseers and deacons (1 Tim. 3; Titus 1)

A pastor or overseer must be blameless and respected—having a good reputation (1 Tim. 3:2; Titus 1:6-7). To be *blameless* means "not guilty of blame." Blame comes, either when a person does bad or neglects good. Paul writes five bad (negative) characteristics to avoid and seven good (positive) characteristics to desire. In Lessons 16 and 17 we will study these 12 characteristics or character traits of a pastor. These 12 qualities explain how a pastor can be blameless and have a good reputation. Let us look first at the five sins for pastors and deacons to avoid (A–E).

A. A church leader must not be given to drunkenness (1 Tim. 3:3, 8; Titus 1:7).

*   *"Not given to drunkenness"* (1 Tim. 3:3)
*   *"Deacons likewise... not indulging in much wine"* (1 Tim. 3:8)
*   *"Not given to drunkenness"* (Titus 1:7)

Scripture warns of the danger of drunkenness (Prov. 20:1; 23:29-35). It records the shame of Lot, who while drunk, committed incest with his daughters. The pagan nations of Moab and Ammon were the result of drunkenness (Gen. 19:30-38). In biblical times, even pagans considered drunkenness a disgrace.[43] How much more should Christian leaders beware of alcohol? Those who get drunk damage the church's reputation, and disqualify themselves from leadership.

Q 114 ⟋ *What is the first sin that all pastors and deacons must avoid?*

Carl reminded his pastor that the first miracle of Jesus was turning water into wine (John 2). Then Carl asked, "So is it all right for me to drink wine today?" The wise pastor thought for a moment, and then replied. "Fill up a pot or a glass with water, and then raise it toward heaven. If Jesus turns it into wine, drink it at once.

Q 115 ⟍ *Do you agree with the advice of Carl's pastor? Explain.*

For the church has no questions about water that Jesus turns into wine. Rather, our problem is with grape juice, that sinners turn into wine."

Application. We agree that Jesus and the apostles drank wine, in Israel about 2,000 years ago. And if the wine of that day was not fermented, then the Scriptures would not warn about drunkenness. In biblical times, wine was a part of many cultures. Water was often impure, and fresh juice did not stay fresh for long. But over the past 2,000 years, societies have improved the water, and marketed many new drinks, including 100 Coke products, various coffees, teas, sodas, many juices, and a host of other beverages. So the question arises, "Would Jesus and the apostles drink wine if they were living on the earth today?" The answer to this question varies from nation to nation, and even within nations. Many national churches in Europe and elsewhere drink wine as a part of their culture. No doubt there are thousands of believers who drink wine, without feeling any sense of guilt or condemnation. We should love and respect believers everywhere. And as Paul says about matters of conscience, believers should not judge each other on disputable matters, outside of the main beliefs of the gospel (Rom. 14:1-13).

Why do people drink alcohol? Answers vary. Some drink for social and cultural reasons. Others drink because they see ads showing beautiful people having fun. Those who make and sell alcohol spend millions of dollars guiding people to think that drinking is cool. Children and youth may try alcohol because they see adults and peers drinking it. Many drink to forget their problems for a few hours. Alcohol is a drug that clouds and depresses the brain. So it offers a quick fix. Yet alcohol creates 10 problems for each one it briefly covers.

While some national churches drink wine, other national churches, such as the Assemblies of God in the United States, have taken the position of abstinence. These believers do not look down on or condemn believers who drink wine. Still millions of believers worldwide give these reasons for refusing alcoholic drinks for pleasure.

Q 116 *Did Jesus and the apostles drink fermented wine?*

Q 117 *What types of drinks are available today that were not present in the days of the apostles?*

Q 118 *Where you live, what are some reasons why people drink alcohol?*

Q 119 *Complete Figure 3.28 summarizing 5 reasons why millions of believers do not drink alcohol.*

Reason	Your Summaries of Reasons Why Millions Do Not Drink Alcohol for Pleasure
1.	
2.	
3.	
4.	
5.	

Figure 3.28   Practice summarizing five reasons why millions of believers abstain from alcoholic drinks.

Reason 1: Some abstain from drinking as a protest to the suffering that results from alcoholic drinks. Half of the fatal accidents on US highways are caused by people under the influence of alcohol. The US government estimated that the problems caused by alcohol cost more than $2.23 billion each year.[44] Problems caused by alcohol included accidents, loss of health, violent crimes, spouse abuse, child abuse, loss of virginity, loss of jobs, loss of reputations, and loss of property by fire. Such terrible fruit guides many to turn from alcohol rather than toward it.

Reason 2: Many choose not to drink alcohol because it is not the *best* decision.

> *⁹And this is my prayer: that your love may abound more and more in knowledge and depth of insight, ¹⁰so that you may be able to discern what is best and may be pure and blameless until the day of Christ, ¹¹filled with the fruit of righteousness that comes through Jesus Christ—to the glory and praise of God* (Phil. 1:9-11).

Reason 3: Others refuse to drink because of the worldliness, sin, and shame linked with liquor, beer, and wine. Drinking alcohol is one of the world's core values. Wherever sinners party, they drink alcohol. Those who make and sell alcoholic drinks use lust, sex, and worldly desires to seduce buyers. In contrast, the Bible guides believers to be separate from the world, and not to be guided by the lust of the flesh [the cravings of sinful man] or the lust of the eyes (1 John 2:16). Is it the Spirit or the flesh that leads people to drink alcohol?

Reason 4: Multitudes avoid alcohol because it is a risk—a bridge to danger. It is a known fact that too much alcohol makes fools out of people. Why play with fire? The person who never drinks will never be drunk, and never be on the long list of alcoholics. Why take the risk? Scripture warns that wine is a mocker. So why take the risk of taking the first drink?

> [29] *Who has woe? Who has sorrow? Who has strife? Who has complaints? Who has needless bruises? Who has bloodshot eyes?* [30] *Those who linger over wine, who go to sample bowls of mixed wine.* [31] *Do not gaze at wine when it is red, when it sparkles in the cup, when it goes down smoothly!* [32] *In the end it bites like a snake and poisons like a viper* (Prov. 23:29-32).

The risk of being bitten by a snake increases if you pick up the snake.

Sabio says, "He who chooses the beginning of a road, has chosen its end." Few who drink alcohol intend to act foolish, get drunk, or become addicts. But alcohol is the master of many slaves.

Reason 5: A number of believers do not drink alcohol so they will not cause weaker believers to stumble. As sheep follow their shepherd, disciples follow their mentors, and children follow their parents. What parents may handle in moderation, their children often use in excess. What big brother steps over, little brother trips over. What big sister can master, enslaves little sister. The weak we have with us always.

> [13] *Therefore let us stop passing judgment on one another. Instead, make up your mind not to put any stumbling block or obstacle in your brother's way. ...* [20] *Do not destroy the work of God for the sake of food* [or anything else].... [21] *It is better not to eat meat or drink wine or to do anything else that will cause your brother to fall* (Rom. 14:13, 20-21).

If only one person is saved from harm or hell by refusing alcohol, it was worth it.

Friedeman Bach, the most gifted son of the great German composer, Johann Sebastian Bach, went to pieces through drink. Michael Haydn, younger brother of Joseph Haydn (Austrian composer), and hardly less gifted, was ruined by drink. Franz Schubert, a famous composer, became addicted to wine and died in his early thirties. The alcoholism of Robert Schumann (another great German composer) led to a nervous breakdown. After the death of his wife, the famous painter Rembrandt, at age 36, became an alcoholic. Sabio says: "Alcohol is one of the greatest traps that life has set for the feet of genius!"[45] If great men like these can become victims of alcohol, so can others if they are not careful.

B. A church leader must not be overbearing or quarrelsome (1 Tim. 3:3, Titus 1:7).

- *"Not quarrelsome"* (1 Tim. 3:3)
- *"Not overbearing"* (Titus 1:7)

An *overbearing* leader is a self-willed person who demands that he always gets his own way. The plain meaning of *overbearing* is "pleasing himself."[46] An *overbearing* person is not willing to accept any way of doing things but his own. It is his way or the highway. This style of leadership, which is common in the world, leads to conflict. So an *overbearing* leader is also a *quarrelsome* leader.

In contrast, God's leader must be a servant. He is overseeing God's household, not his own life. Jesus told His disciples that the leaders of the Gentiles use their authority to rule over people. But followers of Jesus must lead by serving, for Jesus Himself came

Q 120 ⟋ *Why must church leaders not be overbearing?*

Q 121 ⟍ *What does* overbearing *mean? Give an example.*

"to serve, and to give his life as a ransom for many" (Mark 10:45). A pastor must be overseeing without being overbearing.

When Spurgeon was still a young preacher, someone warned him that an overbearing critic was coming to him. Soon the critic whipped him with a scourge of words. Spurgeon smiled and said, "Yes, thank you, I am quite well. I hope you are the same." Later another person attacked him with more hateful words. The young pastor replied, smiling, "Yes, it does look like it might rain. I think I had better be moving on." "Bless the pastor!" said the critic. "He's as deaf as a post. So what is the use of storming at [criticizing] him?"[47] And so the overbearing person left and never complained again.

C. A church leader must not be quick-tempered; not violent (1 Tim. 3:3; Titus 1:7).

- *"Not violent but gentle"* (1 Tim. 3:3)
- *"Not quick-tempered... not violent"* (Titus 1:7)

Q 122 *How can anger hinder great leaders such as Moses?*

Those who are quick to become angry cause great harm to those nearby. Most people are afraid of the bite of a poisonous snake. But the tongue can strike as fast as the hand or the fist. The poison of a striking tongue has hurt many. Jesus warned that anyone who holds onto anger against his brother is in danger of judgment (Matt. 5:22). And James wrote that all should be *"slow to become angry"* (James 1:19). He also wrote,

> [9]*With the tongue we praise our Lord and Father, and with it we curse men, who have been made in God's likeness.* [10]*Out of the same mouth come praise and cursing. My brothers, this should not be.* [11]*Can both fresh water and salt water flow from the same spring?* [12]*My brothers, can a fig tree bear olives, or a grapevine bear figs? Neither can a salt spring produce fresh water* (James 3:9-12).

Q 123 *Why is there little hope for a man who speaks in haste?*

A church leader who fails to control his temper or his tongue can destroy years of good ministry in a moment. Remember how a moment of anger caused a great leader like Moses to fall short of the promises God intended for him (Num. 20:8-12). The wrath of man is not the path to the righteous life God desires (James 1:20). A wise pastor keeps a bridle on his tongue.

Figure 3.29 The skunk earns a bad reputation, so people do not like to be near it.

Sabio says: "When the ink of a pen flows too fast, it writes many mistakes." *"Do you see a man who speaks in haste? There is more hope for a fool than for him"* (Prov. 29:20). As people keep a distance from a skunk for its reputation, they avoid a person who spews words in a moment of anger.

The tongue is the only tool that grows sharper with constant use. So let us be careful, or you will cut yourself and others with it.[48]

D. A church leader must not be a lover of money; not pursuing dishonest gain (1 Tim. 3:3; 1 Tim. 3:8; Titus 1:7).

- *"Not a lover of money"* (1 Tim. 3:3)
- *"Deacons, likewise, are to be men worthy of respect, sincere... not pursuing dishonest gain"* (1 Tim. 3:8).
- *"Not pursuing dishonest gain"* (Titus 1:7)

Q 124 *Why is there no room in a pastor's heart for the love of money?*

Greed was one of the seven deadly sins of the false teachers (1 Tim. 6:5-10). Every New Testament list of qualifications for Christian leaders warns against greed (1 Tim. 3:3-8; Titus 1:7; Acts 20:33). Those who make money the most important thing in life replace the love of God with the love of money.[49] Such love *"is a root of all kinds of evil"* (1 Tim. 6:10). In this passage, Paul mentions just one of the evils that come from loving money. Note that Paul's emphasis is against more than dishonesty. The pastor's heart is for loving God and people—not money.[50]

Sometimes church leaders who lack integrity use the ministry to make money. Further, church leaders handle offerings, pay the church's bills, and distribute money to needy people. It can be tempting to steal or use the church's money selfishly. Those who handle money in the church need to have a spiritual attitude toward money—always remembering that they are stewards who will give account to God.

Dives was an old rich man with a cranky, miserable attitude. He visited Sabio, his neighbor, who lived a simple life. Soon Sabio got an idea for illustrating the bad values of Dives. He took Dives by the hand and led him to his window, saying, "Look out the window and tell me what you see." Looking, Dives replied, "I see men, women, and children." Then Sabio took him by the hand and led him across the room to a mirror. "Now, look and tell me what you see," said Sabio. Dives frowned and said, "I see only myself." "Interesting," said Sabio. "In the window there is glass, and in the mirror there is glass. But the glass of the mirror is covered with a little bit of silver. And as soon as the silver is added, you cease to see others—and see only yourself."[51]

Q 125 *How did Sabio try to help Dives? Explain the parable of the mirror.*

E. A church leader must not be a recent convert (1 Tim. 3:6, 10).

- *"He must not be a recent convert"* (1 Tim. 3:6).
- *"They must first be tested; and then if there is nothing against them, let them serve as deacons"* (1 Tim. 3:10).

Pride and conceit led to the devil's fall (Isa. 14:12-14). Jesus saw him fall from heaven like lightning (Luke 10:18).

Q 126 *Why is it unwise to put much responsibility on a new convert? Illustrate.*

[12] *How you have fallen from heaven, O morning star, son of the dawn! You have been cast down to the earth, you who once laid low the nations!* [13] *You said in your heart, "I will ascend to heaven; I will raise my throne above the stars of God; I will sit enthroned on the mount of assembly, on the utmost heights of the sacred mountain.* [14] *I will ascend above the tops of the clouds; I will make myself like the Most High."* [15] *But you are brought down to the grave, to the depths of the pit* (Isa. 14:12-14).

When a church gives leadership or great responsibility to a new convert, that convert may become proud, like Satan. And his conceit can lead him to the same condemnation that awaits the devil.[52] This danger also applies to older believers who have not been rooted in the faith. So Christian leaders, especially deacons who are new to church leadership, must *"first be tested"* (1 Tim. 3:10). This does not mean that the church must give a written exam like students take in school. It means that those over deacons must examine their life and conduct. New believers should have a place of service. But churches should not put them into leadership positions until they have a godly character, display the fruit of the Spirit, earn a good reputation for faithfulness in service and relationships, and grow in the knowledge of God's Word.

Q 127 *What type of evidence shows a person may serve as a pastor or deacon?*

Some young pastors are like the arrogant woodpecker. He was pecking on a dead tree when lightning struck and shattered the tree into thousands of little pieces. The woodpecker flew away unharmed, but confused. Looking back, the proud bird boasted, "Look what I did! Wow, what a beak!"[53]

**Figure 3.30
Remember
the confused
woodpecker.**

Qualifications for Pastors and Deacons: Respected for Seven Reasons

Lesson

17

(1 Tim. 3:1-16; Titus 1:6-9)

Goal A: *Analyze the requirements of a church leader on the topics of marriage, gentleness, and self control.*

Goal B: *Summarize a leader's qualifications on hospitality, righteousness, doctrine, and family life.*

Goal C: *Analyze the form of 1 Timothy 3:16, identifying the two parts in each of the 6 lines.*

Note: This lesson covers the bottom half of Figure 3.27.

Paul wants the lives of church leaders to be good examples of Christian living. In Lesson 16, we examined five characteristics that Christian leaders must avoid. Now, in this lesson, we will look at seven characteristics Christian leaders should desire. We should not select church leaders simply because they are popular or have money. The fact that a person is likeable or successful in business does not mean that person is spiritually mature. We should choose church leaders by *what* they believe and *how* they live.

A. A church leader must be the husband of one wife (1 Tim. 3:12; Titus 1:6).

- *"A deacon must be the husband of but one wife and must manage his children and his household well"* (1 Tim. 3:12).

- *"An elder must be blameless, the husband of but one wife, a man whose children believe and are not open to the charge of being wild and disobedient"* (Titus 1:6).

Q 128 ↗ *Did Paul mean that a church leader must be married? Explain.*

Q 129 ↖ *Do people qualify to be leaders before they met Christ or after? Explain.*

Paul told Timothy that a church leader must be *"the husband of but one wife"* (1 Tim. 3:12). Here, Paul is not saying that a church leader must be married. Paul himself did not have a wife, and neither did Timothy. However, most leaders are married. Their marriage and home should be good examples for other believers. Paul approached the topic of marriage from a different direction in his letter to Titus. He wrote that a leader must be *"faithful to his wife"* (Titus 1:6). Divorce and unfaithfulness were common in the pagan marriages of Paul's day. And some of the pagan cultures still practiced polygamy—more than one wife at a time. Christian leaders should provide a contrast to worldly practices. In ancient Roman culture, there were records of faithful wives—who married once and were faithful to a husband all their life.[54] Paul wanted Christian leaders to be men with one woman for life. Church leaders should be men who avoid polygamy, divorce, and even the appearance of unfaithfulness—as they follow Christ.

B. A church leader must be gentle (1 Tim. 3:3).

- *"Not given to drunkenness, not violent but gentle, not quarrelsome, not a lover of money"* (1 Tim. 3:3)

Q 130 ↖ *Use the Scripture references of the chart to complete the last column of Figure 3.31, identifying **contrasts** in negative and positive qualifications for overseers. (see Figure 3.27).*

1 Tim.	Titus	Qualifications for Overseers	Qualifications for Overseers
3:2	1:6-7	(−) Blameless of 5 Accusations:	(+) Respected for Good Reasons:
3:3	1:7	1. Not given to drunkenness	
3:2-3	1:7-8	2. Not overbearing or quarrelsome	Gentle; _____; _____; disciplined.
3:2-3	1:7-8	3. Not quick-tempered; not violent	
3:2-3	1:7-8	4. Not a lover of money; not pursuing dishonest gain	One who loves what is _____; _____ and _____
3:6, 9-10, 12	—	5. Not a recent convert	Holding to _____ with a _____; _____; A good _____ of his _____

Figure 3.31   Practice noting contrasts in negative and positive qualifications for overseers.

Paul wants church leaders to be *gentle* and kind—even when they have to correct someone who falls into error (1 Tim. 3:3). Harsh church leaders can cause great harm by using their authority to lash those who fall into sin. Likewise, harsh leaders hurt their reputations and others when they attack those who disagree with them—instead of speaking the truth in love. It is true that we must correct sin and false doctrine. But when we do so, it must be with gentleness and compassion. Remember the example of Jesus when the teachers of the Law brought an adulterous woman to Him (John 8:3-11). He told her to *go and leave her life of sin.* But He did not harm or attack her or her accusers. He was considerate and gentle. We are to speak the truth in love even to the wayward and the legalists (Eph. 4:15).

Q 131 ↖ *How should church leaders correct sinful behavior in the church?*

C. A church leader must be temperate, self-controlled, and disciplined (1 Tim. 3:2, 11; Titus 1:8).

- *"Now the overseer must be above reproach, the husband of but one wife, temperate, self-controlled, respectable, hospitable, able to teach"* (1 Tim. 3:2).

- *"In the same way, their wives are to be women worthy of respect, not malicious talkers but temperate and trustworthy in everything"* (1 Tim. 3:11).

- *"Rather, he must be hospitable, one who loves what is good, who is self-controlled, upright, holy and disciplined"* (Titus 1:8).

Paul told Timothy that the church leader must be *temperate* and *self-controlled* (1 Tim. 3:2, 11). This word *temperate* is often in contrast to *drunk*, but also means "to be free from excess or foolishness."[55] To Titus, Paul used the word *self-controlled* (Titus 1:8). The important truth here is that church leaders must be sober, self-controlled and respectable. This includes what people drink and eat as well as how they behave. Paul is lifting up leaders who rule over their time and desires. The apostle insists on leaders who submit mind and body under the control of the Holy Spirit. Recall Paul's letter to the Galatians; self-control is a fruit of the Spirit (Gal. 5:23). And in his second letter to Timothy, Paul wrote: *"God did not give us a spirit of timidity, but a spirit of power, of love and of self-discipline"* (2 Tim. 1:7).

Q 132 ↖ *What is the key to controlling yourself?*

 In ancient times, the most famous leaders conquered one or more cities. History books give the names of many kings, emperors, and generals who conquered cities by slow siege or sudden force. In contrast, Proverbs exalts an even greater victor. Proverbs declares: *"Better a patient man than a warrior,* [better] *a man who controls his temper than one who takes a city"* (Prov. 16:32). Alexander the Great conquered all the world that he knew. But he could not control himself. At a banquet one evening he became drunk, and in an argument killed his best friend. The God who rules over the whole universe values, honors, and exalts the person who conquers and rules himself—more than someone who conquers an entire city. Those who, by the power of the Spirit, control their own emotions and desires are the greatest of all conquerors.[56] Through self-control, a minister can overcome opposition and set a good example for others to follow.

Q 133 ↗ *Who are the greatest conquerors?*

Wesley once said, "There are some men who preach so well in the pulpit, that it is a shame they ever come out of it. For when they are out of the church, they live so badly that it is a shame they ever enter it."[57]

D. A church leader must be hospitable (1 Tim. 3:2; Titus 1:8).

- *"Now the overseer must be... hospitable"* (1 Tim. 3:2).
- *"Rather he must be hospitable"* (Titus 1:8).

Church leaders must be *hospitable* (1 Tim. 3:2; Titus 1:8). Hospitality in the New Testament is more than entertaining friends or having guests for dinner. The meaning of the Greek word for *hospitality* means "loving strangers."[58] In biblical times, traveling

Q 134 ↖ *Does your family practice hospitality? Why or why not?*

teachers and preachers needed hospitality. There were also many slaves with no homes of their own. So being welcomed into a Christian home was a great blessing. For us, today, hospitality means to welcome visitors—including family, friends, and those less known. Many people have become members of a church because a pastor or deacon invited them for a meal in his home. Remember Hebrews 13:2—*"Do not forget to entertain strangers, for by so doing some people have entertained angels without knowing it."*

Q 135 ⬑ *Illustrate the proverb: He who opens the door to his own home, opens many doors for the church.*

A businessman in the city of Chicago called his wife. He wanted to be sure if he could bring home a foreign guest for dinner that night. The family had four children, so the wife had plenty to do without welcoming a stranger. But she agreed and the meal went well. The foreigner, an important Spanish official, never forgot that meal. Years later, some friends of that family went to Spain as missionaries. They faced a closed door because of some government policies. Then the Spanish official learned that the missionaries were friends of that hospitable couple in Chicago. And he used his influence to open the door they needed to walk through. There is a church today in that province of Spain, due in part to that one meal.[59] Sabio says, "He who opens the door of his home to others, opens doors for the church."

E. A church leader must love what is good—living upright and holy (Titus 1:8).

- *"Rather he must be... one who loves what is good, who is self-controlled, upright, holy and disciplined"* (Titus 1:8).

Q 136 ⬑ *How can people know if a leader loves what is good and lives uprightly?*

In his letter to Titus, Paul warned of false teachers who ruin families for the love of money (Titus 1:11; 1 Tim. 3:3). In contrast, church leaders must love what is good (Titus 1:8). This enables them to live upright, holy lives (Titus 1:8). They treat God and others with respect. Therefore, their friends and neighbors know these leaders are honest and fair in their dealings with other people. They pay their debts, and remember that each person is created in the image of God. Thus they earn the reputation of being separated from sin and dedicated to God.

F. A church leader must be able to teach; holding firmly to sound doctrine (1 Tim. 3:2, 9; Titus 1:9).

Of all the 12 qualifications for overseers and deacons, only this one requires ability or talent. All the other qualifications are about character, godly values, and a blameless reputation.

- *"Now the overseer must be... able to teach"* (1 Tim. 3:2).
- *"They must keep hold of the deep truths of the faith with a clear conscience"* (1 Tim. 3:9).
- *"He must hold firmly to the trustworthy message as it has been taught, so that he can encourage others by sound doctrine and refute those who oppose it"* (Titus 1:9).

Paul told Timothy that church leaders *"must keep hold of the deep truths of the faith with a clear conscience"* (1 Tim. 3:9). They must know the truth—the Word of God. But they need more than head knowledge of the Scriptures. They must live the truth with a clean conscience.

Q 137 ↗ *What is the first rule for teachers?*

A wise man once received a letter stating: "I want to be a teacher. What is the secret of successful teaching?" The wise man replied, "Be what you want your pupils to be. This is the first rule for teachers."[60] People learn more from what we are and do, than what we say. Actions speak louder than words.

Q 138 ⬑ *Which of the seven laws for teachers is: The easiest? The hardest? The most important?*

Besides knowing and living the truth, leaders must also be able to influence others to follow their examples. So, overseers must be able to teach (1 Tim. 3:2). They need the ability to teach truth and refute false doctrine (Titus 1:9).[61]

1. KNOW THE LESSON WELL. STATE THE MAIN TRUTH IN A PRINCIPLE, AND THEN EXPLAIN, ILLUSTRATE, APPLY, AND LIVE IT.
2. AWAKEN INTEREST AND KEEP IT WITH QUESTIONS, ILLUSTRATIONS, AND PARTICIPATION. STUDENTS ONLY BUY SHOES THEY TRY ON.
3. KEEP IT SIMPLE. NEVER USE A DOLLAR WORD WHEN A PENNY WORD WILL DO.
4. RELATE THE NEW TO THE OLD. CONNECT THE FAMILIAR TO THE UNFAMILIAR. WALK FROM EXPERIENCE TO ENCOUNTER.
5. INVOLVE STUDENTS TO EXAMINE, QUESTION, DISCOVER, ILLUSTRATE, ANALYZE, ADMIRE, AND DESIRE. LEAD THEM TO BE PARTICIPATORS, NOT SPECTATORS.
6. LEAD STUDENTS UP THE LEVELS OF LEARNING: REMEMBER → UNDERSTAND → APPLY → ANALYZE → EVALUATE → SYNTHESIZE.
7. MOVE TRUTH FROM THE HEAD TO THE HEART—FROM THE CLASSROOM TO THE LIVING ROOM.

Figure 3.32   Seven laws of a good teacher

As a child, I liked to visit my grandmother—because she made lots of good things to eat, and kept them on a low shelf. Likewise, people want teachers who provide something spiritual to eat, on a shelf that is easy to reach.

G. A church leader must be a good manager of his own family (1 Tim. 3:4, 12; Titus 1:6).

Q 139 ⟩ *What is the pastor's most important sermon?*

- *"He must manage his own family well and see that his children obey him with proper respect"* (1 Tim. 3:4).

- *"A deacon must be the husband of but one wife and must manage his children and his household well"* (1 Tim. 3:12).

- *"An elder must be blameless, the husband of but one wife, a man whose children believe and are not open to the charge of being wild and disobedient"* (Titus 1:6).

A church leader *"must manage his own family well and see that his children obey him with proper respect"* (1 Tim. 3:4). He should have children who are believers, *"and are not open to the charge of being wild and disobedient"* (Titus 1:6). The home is a testing place for leadership in the church. So, a Christian leader must be able to lead and manage his family. How can we expect a man who fails to lead his family to be able to lead the church (1 Tim. 3:5)? Sometimes, Christian leaders think their work is so important that they can ignore their families. But spiritual leadership begins at home. A Christian leader's children must be obedient and behave well—examples for other children to follow. A pastor's most important sermon is the life he and his family live.

Conclusion.   (1 Tim. 3:14-16) Paul has come half way in this letter. He began by charging Timothy to stay in Ephesus and correct false teachers. In chapter 2 the apostle encouraged prayer for all, and emphasized guidelines for living. Most of chapter 3 focused on qualifications for the church's leaders. At the end of 1 Timothy 3, Paul restates his purpose for writing to Timothy. Timothy and the church must hold fast to the gospel, because God has entrusted the Church (**and only the Church**) with the truth. The Church is *"the pillar and foundation of the truth"* (1 Tim. 3:15).

Q 140 ⟩ *What purpose does Paul underline in 1 Timothy 3:14-15?*

[14]Although I hope to come to you soon, I am writing you these instructions so that, [15]if I am delayed, you will know how people ought to conduct themselves in God's household, which is the church of the living God, the pillar and foundation of the truth (1 Tim. 3:14-15).

Paul finishes 1 Timothy 3 quoting an old hymn that emphasizes six truths of the gospel.

Beyond all question, the mystery of godliness is great: He appeared in a body, was vindicated by the Spirit, was seen by angels, was preached among the nations, was believed on in the world, was taken up in glory (1 Tim. 3:16).

Line	Passive Verb	Prepositional Phrase	Explanations
1	*He appeared*	*in a body*	The Incarnation
2	*was vindicated*	*by the Spirit*	The Spirit proved Jesus was divine, enabling Him to cast out demons, heal the sick, and do miracles (Matt. 12:28). Most of all, the Spirit raised Jesus from the dead (Rom. 1:4; 1 Pet. 3:18).
3	*was seen*	*by angels*	At His birth, ministry, resurrection, and ascension (Luke 2:8-15; Matt. 28:2; John 1:51; Acts 1:10)
4	*was preached*	*among the nations*	By the apostles and other believers
5	*was believed on*	*in the world*	By many Jews and Gentiles
6	*was taken up*	*in glory*	The Ascension

Figure 3.33   First Timothy 3:16 is part of an old hymn.
Each of the six lines has two parts (in Greek): a passive verb, and a prepositional phrase.

Opinions vary on the form and relationship of the six lines in 1 Timothy 3:16. Scholars of the NIV think there are three verses in the old hymn: verse 1 (lines 1 and 2); verse 2 (lines 3 and 4); verse 3 (lines 5 and 6). Thus the NIV translators indent lines 2, 4 and 6, showing that each of these completes the line just above it. This view sees the themes of humiliation and exaltation in each of the three verses.

Others think there are two verses.

- Verse 1 (lines 1, 2 and 3), refers to Christ's incarnation.
- Verse 2 (lines 4, 5 and 6), refers to His glorification; with line 6 emphasizing the glory Christ had at His Ascension and afterward.[62]

Q 141 *Do you think Amphilochus was wise or foolish? Explain.*

The point of the old hymn in 1 Timothy 3:16 is to proclaim and celebrate the deity and ministry of Jesus Christ—who came to us from heaven and then ascended to His former glory. During the reign of Theodosius the Great in the fourth century, the Arians attacked the doctrine of the deity of Jesus Christ. The Roman Emperor Theodosius laughed at how the Arians dishonored the Son of God. Yet this emperor honored his own son, Arcadius—elevating him to be a partner on a throne, at a public ceremony. Among the bishops who came to congratulate Theodosius at the ceremony was the famous church leader, Amphilochus—who suffered much persecution from the Arians. Amphilochus approached the emperor, made a short speech, but did not mention the emperor's son. "What!" said the angry emperor. "Do you not mention my son? Do you not know that I have made him a partner with me in the empire? Is this all the respect you pay to a prince whom I have made equal to myself?" Bishop Amphilochus looked into the eyes of the emperor and said, "Sir, do you so highly resent my neglect of your son, because I do not give him equal honor with you? What must the eternal God think of you, who has allowed His Son and co-equal to be shamed in every part of your empire?"[63]

The honor we give to the God the Father, we must also give to the Son of God.

[22]The Father judges no one, but has entrusted all judgment to the Son, [23]that all may honor the Son just as they honor the Father. He who does not honor the Son does not honor the Father, who sent him (John 5:22-23).

Q 142 Complete Figure 3.34.

Line	Passive Verb	Prepositional Phrase
1	He appeared	
2	was vindicated	
3	was seen	
4	was preached	
5	was believed on	
6	was taken up	

Figure 3.34   Practice learning the hymn of 1 Timothy 3:16.

Test Yourself: Circle the letter by the ***best*** completion to each question or statement.

1. Timothy was the overseer of churches in
a) Rome.
b) Philippi.
c) Ephesus.
d) Corinth.

2. Why does Paul say we do not need the Law?
a) We are under grace, not law.
b) There is no law in God's kingdom.
c) Law is behind us, not over us.
d) Law is to restrain the unrighteous.

3. In the Pastoral Epistles, a synonym for *the gospel* is:
a) the cross.
b) the faith.
c) the good news.
d) Jesus.

4. Why did Jesus come into the world?
a) To save sinners like Paul
b) To show us that God loves people
c) To be an example for us
d) To do away with law

5. Which phrase appears 5 times in the Pastoral Epistles?
a) I am the chief of sinners.
b) Jesus Christ is Savior and Lord.
c) The grace of God has appeared.
d) Here is a trustworthy saying.

6. Why does Paul say to take care of our faith?
a) To receive a reward for good works
b) To be a good example to others
c) To avoid shipwrecking it
d) To be careful and diligent

7. Why should we pray for all, including kings and those with authority?
a) God wants all to be saved.
b) Prayer helps us have a right attitude.
c) The prayer of faith has great power.
d) Without prayer, God does not act.

8. How is it possible to pray with holy hands?
a) Be born again.
b) Submit to the Spirit and the Word.
c) Avoid talking to unholy people.
d) Discern between conscience and will.

9. How were a few women causing problems in the churches Timothy oversaw?
a) They were not willing to learn.
b) They were unwilling to marry.
c) They were influenced by false teachers.
d) They were not desiring salvation.

10. How many guidelines does Paul give for overseers and deacons?
a) 6
b) 12
c) 18
d) 22

Essay Test Topics: Write 50-100 words on each of these goals that you studied in this chapter (6 points each). Try to complete your writing in two hours.

- Summarize the background, setting, date, and purpose of 1 Timothy.
- Analyze the problem, result, and methods of false teachers at Ephesus.
- Contrast the need for Law among the unrighteous and the righteous.
- Define the gospel. Identify topics the gospel spans in salvation.
- Summarize the first step God took toward Paul, and what God saw in him. Apply this.
- Define sinners. Give examples of sinners Jesus came to save.
- Contrast the penalty and power of sins from which Jesus saves us.
- Explain how salvation inspires us to care for our faith—not wreck it.
- Explain why Paul wants believers to pray for all people.
- Analyze the need to lift holy hands in prayer, and explain how this is possible.
- Summarize the context of Ephesian women, and apply Paul's words on dress, teaching, and motherhood.
- Explain the meanings and relationships of overseer and deacon.
- Analyze why Paul forbids drunkenness. Summarize 5 reasons why some abstain from alcohol.
- Explain why church leaders must not be overbearing, quick-tempered, lovers of money, or new converts.
- Analyze the requirements of a church leader on the topics of marriage, gentleness, and self control.
- Summarize a leader's qualifications on hospitality, righteousness, doctrine, and family life.
- Analyze the form of 1 Timothy 3:16, identifying the 2 parts in each of the six lines.

Chapter 4:
Be Strong and Faithful Serving the Lord
(1 Tim. 4–6)

First Timothy 3 closes with six lines from an old gospel hymn. In contrast, 1 Timothy 4 begins with a warning about apostasy. The word *apostasy* comes from a Greek word that means "falling away." Bible scholars use apostasy to refer to believers who abandon the truth of the gospel.

Some believe it impossible for a believer to lose salvation. They call this doctrine *eternal security.* Another description of this doctrine is "once saved, always saved." Eternal security claims that if a person has been born again, he or she cannot do anything to lose salvation. But is this teaching true?

The New Testament gives many warnings about falling away from Christ. If it were impossible to fall away, why would God warn us of this danger? The danger of apostasy is a big theme in 1 Timothy 4.

Figure 4.1 The family of God includes young and old, male and female, rich and poor.

Lessons:

The Pastor's Responsibilities in the Family of God (1 Tim. 4:1-16)

Goal A: *Explain a balanced position between eternal insecurity and eternal security.*
Goal B: *Identify 2 false teachings a faithful pastor should warn about where you live.*
Goal C: *Identify 3 ways a leader models good behavior. Give illustrations.*
Goal D: *Explain ways a leader can help believers identify and use their spiritual gifts.*

Relating to Widows in the Family of God (1 Tim. 5:1-16)

Goal A: *Explain 4 criteria of caring for older widows: need, family, age, character (1 Tim. 5).*
Goal B: *Analyze the problem and solution for younger widows at Ephesus. Apply this.*

Relating to the Threat of Sexual Sins
Goal: *Explain and apply each of the 11 principles to protect your family from sexual sins.*

Relating to Elders in the Family of God (1 Tim. 5:17-25)

Goal A: *Summarize ways to treat elderly believers as fathers.*
Goal B: *Explain how and when to show double honor to an elder.*
Goal C: *Summarize guidelines for disciplining an elder who sins.*
Goal D: *Analyze the problem and solution for favoritism.*

Relating to Slaves, False Teachers, Self, and the Rich in the Family of God (1 Tim. 6:1-21)

Goal A: *Summarize Paul's attitudes and values for employees and employers.*
Goal B: *Identify preachers in your region who use religion as a business.*
Goal C: *Summarize the keys to being a faithful minister (1 Tim. 6).*
Goal D: *Relate the wise use of riches in the present world to the next age (1 Tim. 6:17-19).*

apostasy—a turning away from the faith, after believing; abandoning the truth of the gospel

eternal security—a doctrine that claims if a person has been born again, he or she cannot do anything to lose salvation; often called "once saved, always saved"

Lesson 18

The Pastor's Responsibilities in the Family of God (1 Tim. 4:1-16)
Goal A: *Explain a balanced position between eternal insecurity and eternal security.*
Goal B: *Identify 2 false teachings a faithful pastor should warn about where you live.*
Goal C: *Identify 3 ways a leader models good behavior. Give illustrations.*
Goal D: *Explain ways a leader can help believers identify and use their spiritual gifts.*

A. Faithful leaders teach the balance between eternal insecurity and eternal security (1 Tim. 4:1).

The Spirit clearly says that in later times some will abandon the faith and follow deceiving spirits and things taught by demons (1 Tim. 4:1).

1. Eternal *insecurity* is an unbiblical teaching. Some have taught what we might call "eternal *insecurity*"—that we cease to be God's children the moment we commit one sin. No pastor wants to encourage his sheep to sin. Like John, we minister *"so that you* [believers] *will not sin"* (1 John 2:1). But faithful pastors also preach the rest of the verse—*"if anyone sins, we have an Advocate with the Father"* (1 John 2:1 NKJV). God does not disown His children for sinning. Rather, like an earthly father, He disciplines us (Heb. 12:6). And our Father's discipline is proof that we are still His children. The love of God is deep, and the grace of God is wide. The patience of the Lord is long-suffering. His mercies are new every morning. Our Father is slow to anger and quick to pardon (Ps. 103:8). *If we confess our sins* [and turn from them], *he is faithful and just to forgive us our sins, and to cleanse us from all unrighteousness* (1 John 1:9 KJV).

Q 1 *How does our Heavenly Father respond when His children sin?*

2. Eternal security or "once saved, always saved" is also an unbiblical teaching. The New Testament warns more than twenty times about the danger of severing our vital union with Christ (1 Tim. 4:1).

The Spirit clearly says that in later times some will abandon the faith and follow deceiving spirits and things taught by demons (1 Tim. 4:1).

Paul clearly warns against apostasy in his letters to Timothy (1 Tim. 1:5-6, 19; 4:1, 16; 5:15; 6:10-12, 21; 2 Tim. 2:18; 4:2-5) . He refers to those who wander from the faith, abandon the faith, shipwreck it, reject it, and turn away from it. In 1 Timothy 4:1, Paul prophesies that some will *"abandon the faith and follow deceiving spirits"* (1 Tim. 4:1). God's apostle also refers to the possibility of falling away in 1 Corinthians and Colossians (1 Cor. 15:1-2; Col. 1:21-23). John writes how Jesus describes disciples as branches that must bear fruit or be thrown into a fire and be burned (John 15:6). The writer of Hebrews warns us to avoid falling away (Heb. 6:6). And Peter adds that those *"who have escaped the corruption of the world by knowing our Lord and Savior Jesus Christ"* and then fall back into the world's corruption are *"worse off at the end than they were at the beginning"* (2 Pet. 2:20).

Q 2 *What is apostasy? (See the opening paragraphs of this chapter.)*

Q 3 *Have you known some who abandoned the faith they had once embraced? What did they follow?*

Would God give us 20 warnings about a danger that is not real? Would a parent warn a child about crossing a street if traffic was not dangerous? The Scriptures warn of apostasy because the danger of turning away from salvation is real. Faith in Christ leads to righteousness—a living relationship with Christ (Rom. 3:22). And in Christ, *"we have peace with God"* (Rom. 5:1). But we sever that relationship if we refuse to abide in Christ (1 Tim. 4:1). And those who cut their relationship with Christ no longer have peace with God.

One scholar has found 18 examples in the Bible of people who committed apostasy, such as: Saul (1 Sam. 16:14), Solomon (1 Kings 11:9-10), those who believe for a while (Luke 8:13), Demas (2 Tim. 4:10; see 1 John 2:15), the prodigal son (Luke 15:23-24), Judas Iscariot (John 17:12), Simon (Acts 8:13, 18-23), Hymenaeus and Philetus (2 Tim. 2:17-18), unnamed Christians destroyed by false teaching (2 Tim. 2:17-18), many unnamed disciples (John 6:66), some younger Christian widows (1 Tim. 5:11, 14-15; see Rom. 8:5-6), some Christians eager for money (1 Tim. 6:8-10), fruitless Christians (John 15:2, 6), the servant who backslides in Luke 12 (Luke 12:46), the unrepentant lukewarm (Rev. 3:14-16), the unforgiving in heart (Matt. 6:14-15), the weak Christian of 1 Corinthians 8 (1 Cor. 8:10-11), and the recent convert who is potentially a spiritual leader (1 Tim. 3:6).[1]

Q 4 ⬎ *Complete Figure 4.2, by summarizing verses about apostasy in 1 and 2 Timothy.*

Reference	Your Summaries
1 Tim. 1:5-6	
1 Tim. 1:19	
1 Tim. 4:1	
1 Tim. 5:15	
1 Tim. 6:10	
1 Tim. 6:21	
2 Tim. 2:18	
2 Tim. 4:4	

Figure 4.2   Practice summarizing verses about apostasy in the Pastoral Epistles.

For students who want more practice summarizing verses that warn of apostasy, complete Figure 4.3.

Q 5 ⬎ *What is the balance between eternal security and eternal insecurity?*

Q 6 ⬎ *Complete Figure 4.3 on warnings about apostasy.*

Reference	Your Summaries That Warn of Apostasy
Matt. 24:10-12	
John 15:1-6	
Acts 11:21-23	
Acts 14:21-22	
Rom. 6:12-18	We must not let sin reign in our bodies.
Rom. 8:12-17	
1 Cor. 9:27	
1 Cor. 10:12	
1 Cor. 15:1-2	
Gal. 6:7-9	Those who sow to the flesh will reap eternal destruction.
Col. 1:21-23	
1 Tim. 4:1, 16	
1 Tim. 6:10-12	
2 Tim. 4:2-5	
Heb. 2:1-3	
Heb. 3:6,11-14; 4:9, 11	We must avoid falling as Israel fell, and forfeited their promises.
Heb. 6:4-6	
Heb. 10:26-31, 39	
James 5:19-20	
2 Pet. 1:8-11; 3:17-18	We must grow in Christ so we will not fall away.
1 John 2:23-25	

Figure 4.3   Biblical warnings of apostasy—abandoning our faith in Christ

In the physical world, we cannot choose to change fathers. But in the spiritual realm we have the free will to choose who we want as our Father. We were not born children of God, but each believer chose to become a child of God—through a life of faith and obedience. Sadly, some who choose to become God's children abandon the faith, return to their sins, and become slaves of sin and Satan (John 8:42-44; 1 John 3:7-10).

Q 7 *In the spiritual realm, can a person change fathers? Explain.*

B. Faithful leaders warn believers about false teachings (1 Tim. 4:1-11).

¹The Spirit clearly says that in later times some will abandon the faith and follow deceiving spirits and things taught by demons. ²Such teachings come through hypocritical liars, whose consciences have been seared as with a hot iron. ³They forbid people to marry and order them to abstain from certain foods, which God created to be received with thanksgiving by those who believe and who know the truth. ⁴For everything God created is good, and nothing is to be rejected if it is received with thanksgiving, ⁵because it is consecrated by the word of God and prayer (1 Tim. 4:1-5).

Much false teaching is demonic (1 Tim. 4:1), but it comes ***through*** men. Paul gives us some characteristics and examples of false teachers.

Q 8 *Complete Figure 4.4 on characteristics of some false teachers.*

Topic	Your Explanations About Characteristics of False Teachers
Hypocrisy	
Conscience	
Marriage	
Diet	

Figure 4.4   Practice explaining characteristics of some false teachers.

- False teachers are *"hypocritical liars"* (1 Tim. 4:2). Holding a Bible, they preach lies from demons. Acting holy, they lie to people face to face. Such people are hypocrites. What they preach, they do not practice. Therefore, believers must not believe everyone who carries a Bible. The Bible is true, but even Satan quotes Scripture (Matt. 4:6). We must search the Scriptures, and know more about preachers than what they look like or sound like. We know a tree by its fruit, and we can know preachers by their character and their message—whether it is biblical.

- False teachers have *"seared"* consciences (1 Tim. 4:2). Disobedience has damaged their consciences like a hot iron burns flesh. Seared flesh has no feeling. Those with a seared conscience cannot discern the difference between truth and lies.

- False teachers sometimes forbid people to marry (1 Tim. 4:3). Anyone who forbids people to marry is going against the Bible. We believers must separate ourselves from sexual sin. And all sex outside of marriage is sin. But what our Creator creates is *"good"* (1 Tim. 4:4). God created male and female and said it was *"very good"* (Gen. 1:27, 31). Marriage was God's idea from the beginning. And it was God who said it is *"not good"* for man to live alone (Gen. 2:18). Many who forbid marriage live in sin to fulfill the sexual desires of the body God gave us. As Paul said, it is better to marry than to burn with lust (1 Cor. 7:9).

- False teachers ordered people to *"abstain from certain foods"* (1 Tim. 4:3). Some say we cannot eat any meat. Others say we cannot eat pork. But these are foods *"which God created to be received with thanksgiving by those who believe and who know the truth. ⁴For everything God created is good, and nothing is to be rejected if it is received with thanksgiving, ⁵because it is consecrated by the word of God and prayer"* (1 Tim. 4:3b-5).

- Unto the pure, things such as marriage and foods are pure; but the vile find fault with good things God has created for us to enjoy (Titus 1:15).

Paul contrasts false teachers (1 Tim. 4:1-5) with faithful servants (1 Tim. 4:6-10).

Q 9 *In 1 Timothy 4:6, to what does " these things" refer?*

Q 10 *According to 1 Timothy 4:6, how can we recognize a good minister of Jesus Christ?*

[6]***If you point these things out*** [1 Tim. 4:1-5] *to the brothers,* ***you will be a good minister of Christ Jesus,*** *nourished on the truths of the faith and of the good teaching that you have followed.* [7]*Have nothing to do with godless myths and old wives' tales; rather, train yourself to be godly.* [8]*For physical training is of some value, but godliness has value for all things, holding promise for both the present life and the life to come.* [9]*This is a trustworthy saying that deserves full acceptance* [10]*(and for this we labor and strive), that we have put our hope in the living God, who is the Savior of all men, and especially of those who believe* (1 Tim. 4:6-11).

Ministers must be willing to confront anyone who promotes false teaching. For an example, "As an Indian evangelist was preaching, a youth interrupted him. 'You tell about the burden of sin. I feel none. How heavy is it?' The preacher answered, 'If you laid four hundred pounds of weight on a corpse, would it feel the load?' The youth replied, 'No, because it's dead.' The preacher said, 'Likewise, a spirit, too, is dead that feels no load of sin.' "[2]

Q 11 *In your culture, what is the proper way to correct false teachings?*

Application.   Faithful servants warn believers about false teachings (1 Tim. 4:6, 10). Some cultures do not like to confront people face to face. Such cultures are very polite and sensitive with relationships, and the feelings of people. Still, in a manner that matches the culture, pastors must find a way to correct false teachings in the church, for God has given leaders this responsibility. Otherwise, as a wolf destroys sheep, a false teacher will destroy God's flock.

Suppose a child is about to cross a busy street with much traffic. Would a faithful parent warn the child to be careful? Those who teach "once saved, always saved" are like a parent who does not warn a child of danger, but even worse, tells the child that there is nothing to watch out for, because he cannot die.

Q 12 *Where you live, what are some false teachings that are leading believers astray?*

Faithful servants must also take care of themselves spiritually. Paul told Timothy that a good minister is *"nourished on the truths of the faith"* and *"good teaching"* (1 Tim. 4:7). Good ministers of Jesus Christ feed themselves with biblical teachings and pass them on to their sheep.

C. Faithful leaders are good models (1 Tim. 4:12).

Don't let anyone look down on you because you are young, but set an example for the believers in speech, in conduct, in love, in faith and in purity (1 Tim. 4:12).

Paul sent Timothy to lead a church where many of the leaders were older than Timothy. He was part of a culture where people gave greater respect for elders than for young men. How was Timothy to lead in that setting? First, he could not allow the church to look down on him because he was young. And he was to lead by example.

Paul's words to Timothy apply to leaders of any age and every culture. Faithful leaders serve as models for both godly living and ministry. Like Timothy, we should be living examples of the Christian life in five ways.

Q 13 *Complete Figure 4.5, summarizing ways a church leader must be a good example.*

Area	Your Summaries of Ways Leaders Are Good Examples
In speech	What kind of words and joking must all believers avoid (Eph. 5:4)?
In conduct	
In love	
In faith	
In purity	How should a leader relate to women (1 Tim. 5:2; Eph. 5:3)?

Figure 4.5   Practice explaining ways a church leader must be an example.

- *In speech*—Christian leaders must avoid arguments. Their speech must be honest and loving (Eph. 4:14, 4:29, 5:4, 19; Col. 3:16). A leader's words should be pure, wholesome, edifying…

Do not let any unwholesome talk come out of your mouths, but only what is helpful for building others up according to their needs, that it may benefit those who listen (Eph. 4:29).

Nor should there be obscenity, foolish talk or coarse joking, which are out of place, but rather thanksgiving (Eph. 5:4).

Speak to one another with psalms, hymns and spiritual songs (Eph. 5:19a).

Let the word of Christ dwell in you richly as you teach and admonish one another with all wisdom, and as you sing psalms, hymns and spiritual songs with gratitude in your hearts to God (Col. 3:16).

- **In conduct**—Christian leaders live the truth as well as speak it (Titus 1:16). They should allow God's Word and God's Spirit to control their lives.

- **In love**—The false teachers had abandoned love (1 Tim. 1:5-6). Christian leaders should live Jesus' words about love: [30] *"Love the Lord your God with all your heart and with all your soul and with all your mind and with all your strength.* [31] *...Love your neighbor as yourself"* (Mark 12:30-31).

- **In faith**—The false teachers had left the road of faith (1 Tim. 1:6-7). Faithful servants trust God and are faithful to Him.

- **In purity**—Ephesus was a center of sexual impurity. Faithful servants must be models of holiness and purity, not the false purity that came through the strict rules of the false teachers.

D. Faithful leaders encourage believers to use their spiritual gifts (1 Tim. 4:14; 2 Tim. 1:6; Eph. 4:7-11, Rom. 12:3-8, 1 Cor. 12:1-11).

[14] *Do not neglect your gift, which was given you through a prophetic message when the body of elders laid their hands on you* (1 Tim. 4:14).

Paul reminded Timothy not to neglect his spiritual gift. This gift came to Timothy through prophecy and the laying on of hands by the elders. In 2 Timothy 1:6, Paul states that the gift came through his hands, probably as the apostle and elders were praying together for Timothy. Scripture reveals that the Holy Spirit may impart spiritual gifts as believers pray. Jesus prayed for and breathed on His disciples and imparted the new life of the Holy Spirit to them (John 20:22). In Samaria, the apostles prayed for new believers and laid hands on them, and the Holy Spirit filled them (Acts 8:17). Likewise at Ephesus, Paul laid his hands on some disciples and prayed for them, and the Holy Spirit filled them (Acts 19:6). Many examples in the Gospels and Acts show that healings flow through believers by prayers of faith (Mark 6:5; 16:18; Luke 4:40; 13:13; Acts 28:8). James teaches that healings come by faith through church elders as they pray and anoint the sick with oil (James 5:14-15). As God's holy people pray today, filled with the Spirit and faith, God continues to use spiritual gifts to bless His Church, reach the lost, and glorify His name.

In 1 Timothy Paul does not say which gift the Holy Spirit gave to Timothy. And it does not matter to us today what Timothy's spiritual gifts were. Whatever our gifts are, we need to stir them up and fan them into flame. And we need to live filled with the Word and the Spirit, so we can pass on spiritual gifts to others as we pray with faith in the name of Jesus. The spiritual gifts God gives are the key to the spiritual fruit God desires. Paul emphasized that God does not want us to lack any spiritual gifts as we await the Lord's return (1 Cor. 1:7). John Wesley believed that God intended the Church to overflow with spiritual gifts, but they are lost through unbelief. He taught that we can regain these gifts as we seek them by faith. Wesley recorded over 200 healings that occurred as he prayed for the sick, including the healing of his horse, which he depended on for his traveling ministry.[3]

Q 14 *From Acts 20:17-35, in what ways was Paul a good example?*

Q 15 *How did Timothy's spiritual gift come to him?*

Q 16 *What are some keys to God imparting spiritual gifts today?*

Stir up your spiritual gift.

Q 17 How can we stir up our spiritual gifts?

The apostle reminded Timothy to stir up his spiritual gift—as a person fans coals of a fire into flame.

"For this reason I remind you to fan into flame the gift of God" (2 Tim. 1:6). How can we fan our spiritual gifts into flame? We must pay attention to them. We must thank God for our gifts, and pray for the Spirit to help us use them. We fan our gifts into flame as we take little steps to use these gifts, and look for opportunities to serve. Has God given you the gift of showing mercy? Then practice showing mercy to those you meet. Has God given you the gift of teaching? Then blow the dust off your Bible and look for opportunities to teach! When a fire gets low, only coals remain. But the fire can be revived with fanning and kindling. Likewise, our gifts are still in us. But we must fan them and stir them up—putting them into practice so they will burn brightly. So let us get off the couch and into the Lord's work.

Geese fly in the form of a **V**, with one goose at the front. Each goose flapping its wings creates an upward lift for the geese that follow. When each goose does its part, the whole flock can fly 70 percent further than if each bird flew alone.[4] Likewise, as believers use their spiritual gifts, each gift helps other believers.

Application. **Identify your spiritual gift—your way of serving in the church** (Rom. 12:3-8). In his letters, Paul gives four lists of spiritual gifts. None of the lists of Ephesians 4, 1 Corinthians 12, or Romans 12 names every gift (Figure 4.6). (In *The Full Life Study Bible,* see three resources: the chart, *The Gifts of the Holy Spirit;* the article, *Spiritual Gifts for Believers;* and the article, *The Ministry Gifts of the Church.* There are many different kinds of gifts. Wise leaders guide believers to identify and use their gifts.

Romans 12:6-8	1 Corinthians 12:8-11	1 Corinthians 12:27-31	Ephesians 4:11-13
Prophecy	Wisdom	Apostles	Apostles
Service	Knowledge	Prophets	Prophets
Teaching	Faith	Teachers	Evangelists
Encouragement	Healing	Workers of miracles	Pastors
Giving	Miracles	Those with gifts of healing	Teachers
Leadership	Prophecy	Those able to help others	
Mercy	Discernment	Those with gifts of administration	
	Tongues	Those speaking in tongues	
	Interpretation	Those who interpret tongues	

Figure 4.6   Four lists of gifts in the New Testament

Q 18 In Ephesians 4:11-12, what are the 4 or 5 types of people Christ gives as gifts to the Church?

Q 19 How do the four lists of gifts in Ephesians 4, 1 Corinthians 12, and Romans 12 differ? How are they alike?

Q 20 What are your spiritual gifts? How can you stir them up and use them?

Paul told Timothy, *"Do not neglect your gift, which was given you through a prophetic message when the body of elders laid their hands on you"* (1 Tim. 4:14). Here, the word *gift* is a translation of the Greek word *charisma*—often translated *spiritual gift.* Paul's point is that believers must use the spiritual gifts that the Holy Spirit gives. To overcome and be fruitful, we must stir up the spiritual gifts God gives us for ministry.

Paul's writings contain four lists of gifts (Figure 4.6). But each list is from a different point of view. Ephesians 4 lists people—gifts whom Christ gives to the Church (Eph. 4:11-13). First Corinthians 12:8-11 lists manifestations of the Holy Spirit. These nine gifts in 1 Corinthians 12 are not people, and people do not own these gifts. Rather, the Holy Spirit reveals Himself through people He chooses. Likewise 1 Corinthians 12:27-31 lists ways that God uses people, as gifts to serve in the church. And the list in Romans 12 emphasizes seven ways people minister. This list in Romans 12 is broad. Some call the gifts in Romans 12 *motivational gifts,* or gifts that inspire and guide us to serve in certain ways.

An electrician puts wires in a house, so electricity can flow through the wires. We say that a house is "wired" in a certain way. But the wiring is not the electricity. First Corinthians 12 emphasizes the electricity or power of the Spirit that flows through people, rather than the way people are made or "wired." In contrast, Romans 12 emphasizes the way people are wired—the way God made them to respond, as well as the power of the Spirit that flows through them. Except perhaps for the gift of prophecy, the gifts of Romans 7 are woven into a person. So your gifts of Romans 12 are not just what you do, but who you are.

Some Ministries That a Church Can Have	
Community service	Missionettes—girls program
Ministry to the poor (food, clothes)	Royal Rangers—boys program
Home for abused women	College students (campus and church)
Crisis telephone line	Young adult ministry (younger)
Literacy—reading classes for the illiterate	Single adult ministry (older)
Skills (for jobs, marriage, society, and such)	Single mothers ministry (help and fellowship)
Prison ministry	Senior adult ministry
Recovery Through Christ—addictions	Women's Ministry
Deaf culture ministry	Men's Ministry (includes Honor Bound—Men of Promise)
Soul winning—training and practice	Student ministries—evangelism and discipleship
Street evangelism—special events and tracts	Youth Alive—secondary school program
Athletes ministry—outreach and discipleship	Youth discipleship
Adopt-an-Area—praying for and visiting every home	Youth Bible Quiz
Ministry to the handicapped	Youth drama
Ministry to the terminally ill	Youth choir
Hospital visitation ministry	Speed the Light—youth missions fundraising
Comforting Touch ministry (funerals, sickness, and such)	Youth leadership training
Counseling ministry	Master's Commission—1-2 year training program
Widows ministry	Adult choir
Foreign language ministry	Orchestra
Health ministry—Basic health teachings and clinics	Worship team
Sidewalk Sunday School (Saturday outreach)	Evangelistic music—outreach team
Children's meeting or rally—for children outside the church	Adult drama—acting, costumes, and support
Camps for children and youth	Special events/productions—holiday and evangelistic
Sunday School for all ages	Illustrated sermons
Children's Church—for church children	Fine Arts—using art talents to bless others
Children's choir	Art and design for church needs
Junior Bible Quiz (children)	Helping hands ministry for church tasks
Weddings—coordinating	Small groups—home fellowships; Bible studies
Welcome center ministry	Prayer ministries (including prayer chain)
Communion—prepare and clean up	Marriage ministries
Church bookstore	Pre-marriage mentoring to prepare couples for marriage
Greeters and ushers	Leadership School
Visitation—visiting new families and visitors	Financial principles training classes
Deacon Ministry—responsible for assigned members	World Missions—praying, giving, and going

Figure 4.7   Some churches have as many as 200 different ministries that church members are doing![5]

A small child wandered off in the tall grass near an African village. Many people searched in vain to find the child. The next day all the people in the village assembled. Holding hands with each other, they walked through the tall grass together in a long line. Together, they found the lost child. But he was dead. The cold night had been too severe for him. With tears the mother sobbed, "If only we could have held hands sooner."[6] When we all use our gifts together, believers help many people.

Q 21 ↖ *How can you apply 1 Timothy 4:15-16 to your life? (Compare Matthew 5:22.)*

Q 22 ↗ *What are some ways Paul wants Timothy to be diligent?*

warning believers being a good example and using his spiritual gift.

Conclusion (1 Tim. 4:15-16)

[15] Be diligent in these matters; give yourself wholly to them, so that everyone may see your progress. [16] Watch your life and doctrine closely. Persevere in them, because if you do, you will save both yourself and your hearers (1 Tim. 4:15-16).

Paul closed chapter four by telling Timothy to *"be diligent in these matters"* (1 Tim. 4:15). Timothy must work at warning believers, being a good example, and using his spiritual gifts. He must give himself *"wholly"* to these things so that everyone can see his *"progress"* (1 Tim. 4:15). What impresses others must be his growth, not his ability or personality.[7] As he does these things, he must *"watch his life and doctrine"* (1 Tim. 4:16). He must *persevere* **so that** he will save both himself and his hearers (1 Tim. 4:16). This does not mean that Timothy will actually save his hearers. God alone saves. But Christians can be God's tools to enable the salvation of others. Salvation involves perseverance. Timothy's task, as all church leaders, is to model and teach truth in a way that leads others to persevere in faith, love, and salvation.[8]

Lesson 19

Relating to Widows in the Family of God (1 Tim. 5:1-16)

Goal A: *Explain 4 criteria of caring for older widows: need, family, age, character (1 Tim. 5).*
Goal B: *Analyze the problem and solution for younger widows at Ephesus. Apply this.*

Q 23 ↗ *In which 2 areas must every pastor do well?*

Setting: Relationships in the family of God.   In 1 Timothy 1–4, Paul emphasizes the need for right doctrine, right attitudes, and a right reputation. In chapters five and six he focuses on right relationships. Note that 1 Timothy 4:15-16 serves as a transition. We know that church leaders need skill in handling the Scriptures. But they also need skill in relating to people. Right doctrine and right relationships are both important. To be a faithful shepherd, a leader needs to preach well, **and** relate well to people. Paul was aware of this twofold need. So after emphasizing right doctrine (1 Tim. 1–4), he emphasizes right relationships (1 Tim. 5–6).

Paul introduced the theme of family in 1 Timothy 3. He referred to the Church as *"God's household"* (1 Tim. 3:15). Pastors who please God must lead the local church as a family, but never as a business. A business attitude in a pastor's heart is deadly.[9] In 1 Timothy 5–6 Paul continues the theme of *family*.

First Timothy 5:1-2 is a general introduction for what Paul will say about several groups: older widows, younger widows, elders, slaves,[10] and the rich. In lessons 19–22, we will explore principles for these groups of believers in the family of God.

*[1] Do not rebuke an **older man** harshly, but exhort him **as if he were your father**. Treat **younger men as brothers**, [2] older women as mothers, and younger women as sisters, with absolute purity* (1 Tim. 5:1-2).

Q 24 ↗ *How does Paul want Timothy to treat believers?*

Relationships are among the biggest challenges believers face. Paul coaches Timothy to treat church members like family members—fathers, mothers, sisters, and brothers.

Aristotle was a non-Christian teacher of Paul's day. His writings reveal ancient values of Greek families. Aristotle wrote that a person should allow his friends and brothers "freedom of speech" and the "use of common things."[11] That is, people should share ideas and possessions. Do some unbelievers practice more love and respect than Christians practice? We should be examples of God's love—at home, at work, and in the church.

Q 25 ↖ *Do some unbelievers practice more love and respect than some believers you know? Explain.*

Some families do not follow God's plan. In these, children do not respect their parents; or perhaps older *siblings mistreat their younger brothers and sisters. In contrast, God's plan is for family members to show love and respect to each other.

Treating a believer as a family member goes beyond respect and fairness. We have a special love for family members. We care about their needs, their future, and their fruitfulness. We look for ways to encourage and bring out the best in those we love most.

Paul led younger men like Timothy and Titus and modeled for them how to live the Christian life and serve as a leader (Acts 16:1-5; 1 Tim. 1:2; 2 Tim. 1:2; 2 Cor. 8:23; Gal. 2:1; Titus 1:4). He did much the same for John Mark (Acts 15:37-40; 2 Tim. 4:11). Paul did the same for Demas, who later deserted Paul, *"because he loved this world"* (Col. 4:14; 2 Tim. 4:10; Philem. 24). A few, whom we love and nurture, may go astray. Paul also loved and mentored Epaphras, Epaphroditus, Trophimus, and Onesimus, who were all probably younger than him. He treated them as family members—as brothers in the Lord.

Pastor, your success or failure in the ministry depends greatly on how you treat God's family members. As we study Lessons 19–21, open your heart to the Holy Spirit. Ask Him to teach you about relationships. For sadly, we study many books in school, but how many books have you studied on getting along with people? In 1 Timothy 4–6, Paul talks about relating to groups of people: older women, younger women, elders, slaves, false teachers, and the rich.

A. Family principles for older widows (1 Tim. 5:3-10)

After introducing some groups of family members in 1 Timothy 5:1-2, Paul writes about how to relate to older widows.

> [3]*Give proper recognition to those widows who are **really in need**.* [4]*But if a widow has **children or grandchildren**, these should learn first of all to put their religion into practice by caring for their own family and so repaying their parents and grandparents, for this is pleasing to God.* [5]*The widow who is really in need and left all alone puts her **hope in God** and continues night and day to **pray** and to ask God for help.* [6]*But the widow who lives for pleasure is dead even while she lives.* [7]*Give the people these instructions, too, so that no one may be open to blame.* [8]*If anyone does not provide for his **relatives**, and especially for his immediate family, he has denied the faith and is worse than an unbeliever.* [9]*No widow may be put on the list of widows unless she is **over sixty**, has been **faithful to her husband**,* [10]*and is well **known for her good deeds**, such as bringing up children, showing hospitality, washing the feet of the saints, helping those in trouble and devoting herself to all kinds of good deeds* (1 Tim. 5:3-10).

Pastors should be kind to older women as with *mothers* (1 Tim. 5:2). In God's household we are all part of the same family. Paul wrote, *"Give proper recognition to those widows who are really in need"* (1 Tim. 5:3). *Recognition* means "care for."[12] Taking care of widows is a vital concern in the Old and New Testaments (Exod. 22:22; Deut. 24:17, 19-21; Job 29:13; Ps. 68:5; Isa. 1:17; Acts 6:1-4; 9:36, 39, 41; James 1:27). Paul gives four guidelines for helping widows.

1. Need: The church should help only godly widows who *"are really in need"* (1 Tim. 5:3).

> [3]*Give proper recognition to those **widows who are really in need**.* [4]*But if a widow has children or grandchildren, these should learn first of all to put their religion into practice by caring for their own family and so repaying their parents and grandparents, for this is pleasing to God.* [5]*The widow who is really in need and left all alone puts her hope in God and continues night and day to pray and to ask God for help.* [6]*But the*

Q 26 How does love for family members go beyond respect and fairness?

Q 27 How was Paul a good example of relating to younger men?

Q 28 To which group of people does Paul first talk about relating?

Q 29 What are the 4 guidelines for helping older widows? (Use a total of 4 words to identify them.)

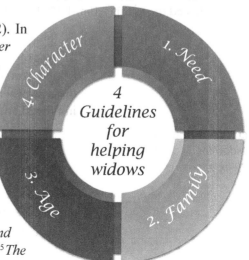

Figure 4.8 Paul gives four guidelines for helping older widows.

widow who lives for pleasure is dead even while she lives. ⁷Give the people these instructions, too, so that no one may be open to blame (1 Tim. 5:3-7).

Q 30 ↗ *In what ways was the life of a widow difficult in Paul's day?*

Widows in need do not have family or other means of support (1 Tim. 5:4-5).[13] Caring for elderly widows in need is one of the ways believers express love in the family of God, and testify to the world.

In this passage, Paul contrasts two kinds of widows. Those who *put their hope in God* (1 Tim. 5:5) and widows who *live for pleasure* (1 Tim. 5:6). Some scholars think that widows who *live for pleasure* were living immorally to support themselves.[14] The life of a widow in Paul and Timothy's day was difficult. The law did not allow widows to own property or get a job. Other scholars think *"lives for pleasure"* refers to widows who gave the flesh whatever it desired.[15] Such a person is *"dead even while she lives"* (1 Tim. 5:6). In contrast, the godly widow *"puts her hope in God"* (1 Tim. 5:5). She prays and asks God for help (1 Tim. 5:5).

Q 31 ↗ *What are 2 reasons why believers care for elderly family members?*

2. Family: The church must care for *godly* widows in need, who are without *relatives* (1 Tim. 5:3, 5-7, 9-10).

⁴But if a widow has children or grandchildren, these should learn first of all to put their religion into practice by caring for their own family and so repaying their parents and grandparents, for this is pleasing to God. ... ⁸If anyone does not provide for his relatives, and especially for his immediate family, he has denied the faith and is worse than an unbeliever (1 Tim. 5:4, 8).

Q 32 ↖ *Why are apostates worse than unbelievers? (Figure 4.9)*

Figure 4.9 Paul recognizes three groups: believers, unbelievers, and apostates [those who were once believers, but have abandoned and denied the faith] (1 Tim. 1:19; 4:1; 5:8).

Children and grandchildren owe a debt to aged parents and grandparents (1 Tim. 5:4, 7-8). Family responsibility is a part of Paul's gospel—our faith. Caring for elderly family members is one of the ways we show love and obey God's commandment to honor fathers and mothers. And caring for the elderly is also a way that believers let their light shine in the world (Matt. 5:14-16; Phil. 2:15). Those who call themselves Christians, but do not care for their children and aged parents, have committed apostasy. They have denied the faith and are *worse* than unbelievers. Why are they called worse than infidels? Because they are hypocrites—claiming to love God and people, yet giving the church a bad name. Those lacking love outside the church do not hurt the church's reputation. But selfish, loveless people in the church are a stumbling block near the gospel. Jesus rebuked religious people who did not care for their elderly parents (Matt. 15:4-7a).

3. Age: The church should help widows who are over the age of *sixty* (1 Tim. 5:9). Church resources were reserved for older widows who were unlikely to remarry. Today, the age of widows to help might be 70 or more in some nations, since healthcare has improved and people live longer.

Q 33 ↖ *How does a godly widow today differ from a godly widow in Paul's day?*

4. Character: The church should help widows who are *godly* (1 Tim. 5:9-10).

*⁹No widow may be put on the list of widows unless she is over sixty, **has been faithful to her husband**, ¹⁰and is well known for her good deeds, such as bringing up children, showing hospitality, washing the feet of the saints, helping those in trouble and devoting herself to all kinds of good deeds* (1 Tim. 5:9-10).

A widow shows her godliness through her life. She was *"faithful to her husband"* while he lived (1 Tim. 5:9). She is known for *"good deeds"* (1 Tim. 5:10). These deeds include *"bringing up children,"* which may include caring for orphans. She has a reputation for hospitality and humble service (1 Tim. 5:10).

There are many women in the Bible with good characteristics. Figure 4.10 lists a few of the many outstanding women of the New Testament.

Q 34 ↖ *Complete Figure 4.10.*

Women	Reference	Characteristics for Which These Women Were Known
Mary, mother of Jesus	Matt. 1:18, 23 Luke 1:26-35, 46-48	
Anna	Luke 2:36-38	She trusted in God for years as a widow; prayed, and prophesied about the Messiah.
Woman of Samaria	John 4:1-42	After she discovered Jesus, she was the key to reaching a whole city.
Mary Magdalene	John 19-20	
Woman of Canaan	Matt. 15:21-28	
Mary of Bethany	Luke 10:39, 42; John 12:1-8	
Martha of Bethany	Luke 10:38-42; John 11:20-27	The sisters were known for service, faith, and devotion.
Dorcas	Acts 9:36-39	
Lydia	Acts 16:13-15	
Priscilla	Acts 18; Rom. 16:3	
Phoebe	Rom. 16:1-2	
Persis	Rom. 16:12	
Mother of Rufus	Rom. 16:13	

Figure 4.10   Practice identifying the characteristics of faithful women of the New Testament.

Application.   The Bible relates good deeds to widows (1 Tim. 5:3-10), orphans (James 1:27), brothers in need (James 2:15, 1 John 3:17), and all believers, as opportunity and resources permit (Gal. 6:10). But remember Paul's rules: Those unwilling to work should not eat (2 Thess. 3:10); we should care for believers in need in the family of God *before* we care for unbelievers (Gal. 6:10). Compare Matthew 25:31-46, that also emphasizes pastoral care to the family of God.

Q 35 ↖ *Fill in the blanks in Figure 4.11.*

Topic	Your Explanations
1. Need	
2. Family	
3. Age	
4. Character	

Figure 4.11   Practice identifying Paul's four guidelines for helping widows.

B. Family principles for younger widows (1 Tim. 5:11-16)

In 1 Timothy 5:11, Paul shifts to the second group of members in God's family— younger widows. Recall that earlier, Paul emphasized that a pastor must treat younger women as sisters—*"with absolute purity"* (1 Tim. 5:2). Pastors face great danger in relating to younger women. In Lesson 20, we will study 11 principles to protect your marriage, sexual purity, and ministry. For now, let us study the problems and solutions related to younger widows at the church in Ephesus under Timothy's care.

Q 36 ↗ *Which 2 groups of family members does Paul discuss first in 1 Timothy 5?*

Problems (1 Tim. 5:11-16)

[11]*As for younger widows, do not put them on such a list. For when their sensual desires overcome their dedication to Christ, they want to marry.* [12]*Thus they bring judgment on themselves, because they have broken their first pledge.* [13]*Besides, they get into the habit of being idle and going about from house to house. And not only do they become idlers, but also gossips and busybodies, saying things they ought not to* (1 Tim. 5:11-13).

Q 37 ⭢ *What problems in life cause a married woman to become a widow?*

Paul does not tell us how the younger women became widows. Even in the family of God, tragedy strikes. Some husbands die from disease or accidents. For these or other reasons, there were younger widows in the church at Ephesus.

Some husbands and wives do not work at and pray enough to learn to live together. So those whom God has joined together are torn apart. And in some cases, spouses abandon their spouse and children, following their sinful lusts.

In the beginning, God said that it was not good for man to live alone (Gen. 2:18). That is one side of the coin. The other half of this truth is that it is not good for woman to live alone. God's plan is for a man and woman to live life in marriage, enjoying each other's company, and sharing the burdens and the joys together.

Q 38 ⭠ *In what way did younger widows break a pledge? Why?*

Paul writes that the younger widows break *"their first pledge"* (1 Tim. 5:12). The meaning of this is unclear. Perhaps some widows pledged to remain single, and to serve like Anna (Luke 2). But as time went by, they found that living alone was too difficult for them. As Jesus said, living alone does not work for most (Matt. 19:11). Also, living alone is lonely—for men or for women. Because of loneliness, the younger widows looked for others to talk with. Too much idleness and talking, among men or women, leads to gossip. So we see that the widows in the Ephesian church were not doing well living alone. They had chosen marriage instead of living alone, but their husbands were dead or deserted. So Paul gives these family members his advice.

Q 39 ⭢ *What is Paul's solution for younger widows?*

Q 40 ⭠ *What biblical condition comes with marriage?*

Solution.   Paul urges younger widows to remarry a believer (1 Tim. 5:14).

> [14]*So I counsel younger widows to marry, to have children, to manage their homes and to give the enemy no opportunity for slander.* [15]*Some have in fact already turned away to follow Satan.* [16]*If any woman who is a believer has widows in her family, she should help them and not let the church be burdened with them, so that the church can help those widows who are really in need* (1 Tim. 5:14-16).

Paul does not want younger widows to be put on the list of women that the church is responsible for their care. Rather, the apostle says remarriage is the answer. Marriage is God's beautiful solution to solve many problems, and to create a home full of joy and fulfilment. Elsewhere Paul emphasizes that remarriage must be *in the Lord* or *in the faith—to a believer* (1 Cor. 7:39). As the younger widows remarry in the faith, have children, and oversee their homes, life will return to God's plan (1 Tim. 5:14). Married women or men stay busy with family duties. This keeps the enemy from slandering their character or the gospel (1 Tim. 5:14).

Application.   As Ruth remarried to Boaz, younger widows today should welcome the opportunity to remarry in the Lord.

Likewise, *"if any woman* [whether she is a widow or not] *who is a believer has widows in her family, she should help them and not let the church be burdened with them, so that the church can help those widows who are really in need* (1 Tim. 5:16). In other words, believers who can work should help those who are too old to work, or who for various reasons cannot find employment.

Paul told Timothy to treat the younger women *"as sisters, with absolute purity"* (1 Tim. 5:2). Brothers and sisters have a unique relationship, without a hint of sexual impurity. This ought to be true about all relationships between Christian men and women. And it is especially important for leaders in the church.

Jim Elliott gave the following advice about the way Christian men should view women, both in and out of the church. He said, "It is true that a man cannot ignore women—but he can think of them as he ought, as sisters, not objects of lust."[16]

Q 41 ⭠ *How should a leader treat a woman he finds attractive?*

Consider the honor and trust God places in a pastor. Church leaders often stand on a stage at the front of the church—which may even be at a higher level than the people. A leader has the honor of speaking, while others focus all their attention on him. Women may admire and be attracted to a pastor, as he receives such honor. How should a pastor treat a woman who admires him, shows an interest in him, or even flirts with him?

Q 42 *How should a leader respond to a woman who admires him?*

Relating to the Threat of Sexual Sins

Goal: *Explain and apply each of the 11 principles to protect your family from sexual sins.*

Nothing destroys a family faster than adultery. In this lesson we will study 11 principles to protect you and your family from this family killer.[17]

Figure 4.12   Satan, like a roaring lion, seeks to destroy people. He continues to destroy many through sexual sins (1 Pet. 5:8).

A. Recognize the problem and the danger of sexual sins.

Sexual sins are spreading in every society. Many husbands and wives are not faithful to each other. Some have sexual affairs with other spouses. Some view pornography in magazines or videos or on the Internet. We are living in the last days, and sin is increasing (Matt. 24:12-13). So all believers need to beware. *"Your enemy the devil prowls around like a roaring lion looking for someone to devour"* (1 Pet. 5:8).

The Bible records that people who knew God—men like Samson, the strongest man; David, a man after God's own heart; and Solomon, one of the wisest men—all committed sexual sins. *"So, if you think you are standing firm, be careful that you don't fall!"* (1 Cor. 10:12).

Q 43 *Which types of sexual sins are the greatest problem in your culture? Explain.*

B. Understand the process from temptation to sin.

[12]*Blessed is the man who perseveres under trial, because when he has stood the test, he will receive the crown of life that God has promised to those who love him.* [13]*When tempted, no one should say, "God is tempting me." For God cannot be tempted by evil, nor does he tempt anyone;* [14]*but each one is tempted when, by his own evil desire, he is dragged away and enticed.* [15]*Then, after desire has conceived, it gives birth to sin; and sin, when it is full-grown, gives birth to death* (James 1:12-15).

Notice that James mentions four steps that lead from temptation to sin.

- *First,* a person is tempted. As a fisherman uses bait to tempt a fish, the devil and the world use bait to tempt a human. Temptation knocks at every door. All people are tempted. Even Jesus was tempted to sin (Heb. 4:15). Temptation is not a sin, but it is a sign that tells us that danger is near. People pay attention when a dog growls. Likewise, we should beware when temptation comes. Blessed is the man who perseveres when trials and temptations come. He stands the test and will receive a crown of life (James 1:12). This person in James 1:12 responds to temptation through the Spirit (Rom. 8:4-14; Gal. 5:16-25). He says "no" to temptation. He treats temptation like an evil bird to scare away. He knows that you cannot prevent a bird from flying over your head, but you can prevent it from building a nest in your hair!

Q 44 *What are the 4 steps that lead from temptation to sin?*

temptation
desire
sin
death

Q 45 *Is it a sin to be tempted by an evil thought? Explain.*

- *Second,* evil desires (not a demon) within a person respond to a temptation. Unlike the person in James 1:12, the person described in James 1:14 does not stand the test. This person is not led by the Spirit. Rather, his flesh leads him to say "yes" to the temptation. He welcomes temptation into his life and takes the devil's bait.
- *Third,* as a child is conceived in a woman, sin is conceived in a person. The evil desires within a person unite with temptation to conceive sin. Then, sin begins to grow in a person's thoughts, and finally, is born in a person's actions.
- *Fourth,* as a child grows into an adult, sin grows from a small thing into a big one. In the end, sin brings forth spiritual death—eternal separation from God.

C. Walk in the Spirit and you will win the battle over temptation.

Q 46 *How does God expect us to have victory over temptation?*

Those who understand the process from temptation to sin stop the process at Step 1. By the power of the Holy Spirit, they learn to stand firm in the time of temptation (James 1:12). Like Joseph, they run *away from* temptation instead of *toward* it. They depend on the Spirit and cooperate with Him. They say "yes" to things that please the Spirit, and "no" to things that grieve Him. Those led by the flesh produce fruit such as sexual sins (Gal. 5:19-21). In contrast, those led by the Spirit produce fruit such as patience, kindness, gentleness, and self-control (Gal. 5:22-23).

> [6] *The mind of sinful man is death, but the mind controlled by the Spirit is life and peace;* [7] *the sinful mind is hostile to God. It does not submit to God's law, nor can it do so.* [8] *Those controlled by the sinful nature* [the †flesh] *cannot please God.* [9] *You, however, are controlled not by the sinful nature* [the flesh] *but by the Spirit, if the Spirit of God lives in you* (Rom. 8:6-9).

> *So I say, live by the Spirit, and you will not gratify the desires of the sinful nature* [the flesh] (Gal. 5:16).

Those who walk in the Spirit recognize that temptation is common. But they allow the Spirit to help them stand firm in times of temptation.

> *No temptation has seized you except what is common to man. And God is faithful; he will not let you be tempted beyond what you can bear. But when you are tempted, he will also provide a way out so that you can stand up under it* (1 Cor. 10:13).

D. Pay attention to outward warning signs in others.

Q 47 *What are some outward signs to warn you that sexual danger is near?*

Here are some <u>outward</u> signs to warn you that sexual danger is near if you are working with or counseling a person of the opposite sex.

- The person spends a lot of time with you.
- The person begins to depend on you.
- The person begins to affirm and praise you.
- The person begins to complain about feeling lonely.
- The person talks often about personal matters.
- The person tries to attract you in sexual ways.
- The person begins to touch your body. This may begin with a handshake, a hand on the shoulder, or a hug of thanks. But it soon rises to much more.
- Your spouse begins to feel bad about your relationship with this person.

Figure 4.13   Beware when you see <u>outward</u> signs that warn of sexual danger.

E. Pay attention to inward warning signs in you.

Q 48 *What are some inward warning signs that you need to repent—change directions?*

Here are some <u>inward</u> signs to warn you that sexual danger is near if you are working with or counseling a person of the opposite sex.[18] <u>Discern this:</u> A relationship can be going the wrong direction *long* before it becomes sexual.

---

† In the Greek language, the word is *sarx*, which means "flesh" or "fleshly desires."

- You dress in a way to please the person.
- You are disappointed if you do not see the person; excited when you meet the person.
- You spend a lot of time with the person; you look forward to seeing him or her.
- You think the person understands you better than your spouse understands you.
- You enjoy being with this person more than being with your spouse.
- You imagine what it would be like if this person were your spouse.
- You share private and personal matters with this person, such as problems in your marriage.
- You develop feelings of romantic love for this person.
- You try to hide your feelings for and meetings with this person.
- You ignore warnings from others and pretend that this person is only a friend.
- You look for ways to be with this person in secret, even if you must deceive others.
- You become angry if your spouse wants more attention or is jealous.
- You imagine a sexual relationship with this person and do not reject these thoughts.
- You and the other person focus on each other's needs.
- You commit sexual sins after ignoring all of these inward signs.

Figure 4.14   Beware when you see <u>inward</u> signs that warn of sexual danger.

Dr. James Dobson, a wise family counselor, describes how people often become adulterers.[19] The affair usually begins as a friendship, through such things as a lunch that lasts too long or a touch. This first step is enjoyed, so the action is repeated. The next day, or perhaps the next week, the touch or lunch goes further with more pleasant feelings. The two people begin to meet more often, and their attraction to each other grows. Before long, the romantic feelings overcome fears, and the two people commit sexual sin.

Q 49 *Do you think most people plan to be unfaithful sexually? Explain.*

F. Guard your heart.

"Above all else, guard your heart, for it is the wellspring of life" (Prov. 4:23). Your heart is the center of your desires and emotions. Jesus should rule as king over all of our desires. But as weeds grow in a garden, evil desires can take root in the heart. This is why daily devotions, prayer, Bible study, and attending church are so important. People guard their money, their homes, and their reputations. But the most important thing to guard is your heart.

Q 50 *How can you guard your heart?*

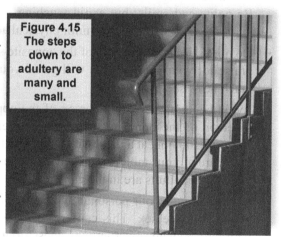

Figure 4.15 The steps down to adultery are many and small.

G. Guard your mind.

The apostle Paul said, *"We take captive every thought to make it obedient to Christ"* (2 Cor. 10:5). Thoughts are like grains of sand—alone, they weigh almost nothing, but together, they can bury a person. So if your thoughts are your enemies, they will drag you down to destruction. But if your thoughts are your friends, they will escort you into the presence of God.

How can you practice thinking good thoughts—making good thoughts a habit?

- **First,** be aware of your thoughts—like a mother hen is aware of her chicks. Be as watchful as a business owner in his store. Do not be mentally lazy or sleepy. Roll up the shirtsleeves of your mind. *"Prepare your minds for action; be self-controlled"* (1 Pet. 1:13). Be alert, and keep your thoughts out in front of you, like food on your table.

A RELATIONSHIP CAN BE GOING THE WRONG DIRECTION *LONG* BEFORE IT BECOMES SEXUAL.

Q 51 *What are 4 keys to guarding our minds?*

Q 52 ✎ *Is it right to hate what is wrong? Explain.*

- *Second,* love what is right, and hate what is wrong (Rom. 12:9; Heb. 1:9). Rule over your thoughts—like a judge rules in a courtroom. Love what God loves, and hate what He hates. *"How can a young man keep his way pure? By living according to your word"* (Ps. 119:9). Choose to honor God with your secret thoughts, and He will honor you.

Q 53 ✎ *How can a person guide his thoughts?*

- *Third,* do not allow your thoughts to travel wherever the flesh and the world lead them. Rather, guide your thoughts as a rider steers a bicycle. Say "no" to fleshly desires and "yes" to the Holy Spirit (Gal. 5:16). Pray so that you do not enter into temptation (Matt. 26:41). Refuse to look at any form of pornography. Make a covenant with your eyes (Job 31:1). Block out evil from your telephone, television, or computer by using filters or other methods.

Q 54 ✎ *Can a person think two opposite thoughts at the same time? Explain and apply.*

- *Fourth,* replace bad thoughts with good ones. You will become tired if you spend your energy trying to chase away bad thoughts. But remember, your mind can only think on one thought at a time. So when an evil thought knocks at the door of your mind, turn away from it, and welcome a good thought. *"Whatever is true, whatever is noble, whatever is right, whatever is pure, whatever is lovely, whatever is admirable—if anything is excellent or praiseworthy—think about such things"* (Phil. 4:8).

H. Guard your marriage.

Loving your mate is the best protection against sexual sins.

Q 55 ✎ *Summarize 6 keys to guarding your marriage.*

- A married couple should fulfill each other's needs. God commands them to be faithful. They have vowed to forsake all other lovers and give themselves only to each other. *"Drink water from your own cistern, running water from your own well"* (Prov. 5:15).

- Avoid touching, shaking hands with, or hugging a person of the opposite sex. Be polite and smile, but avoid touching. This is a good boundary to protect your marriage. You will never commit physical adultery with a person you do not touch!

- Do not praise how a person of the opposite sex dresses or looks. Save your words of praise for your spouse. This will guard your marriage. Tell your spouse often how much he or she pleases you.

- Avoid being alone with a person of the opposite sex. For example, if you counsel a person of the opposite sex, require an elder or some other adult to be present. Likewise, do not eat a meal with a person of the opposite sex unless other adults you know are at your table. And do not ride in a car with a person of the opposite sex unless other adults are in the car.

- Do not discuss your personal matters or problems in your marriage with a person of the opposite sex. This can create an emotional bond. Keep your relationships with the opposite sex strictly business-oriented. In contrast, it is wise for a husband to discuss a personal problem with an older man, or for a wife to discuss a marital problem with an older Christian woman whom she trusts and respects.

- Guard your non-verbal actions. Without speaking, people give signals of sexual interest. These signals change from culture to culture, but they must stop when you are married. These signals lead to wrong thinking and plant seeds of trouble. Give attention to your spouse, not someone else.

Q 56 ✎ *Why should a husband and wife seek to understand each other's needs?*

The needs of men and women are not the same! Husbands and wives should continue to learn about each other. A husband and wife should become best friends. Friendship grows deeper and stronger as spouses learn about each other. A wise person practices seeing things through the eyes of another. Compare the needs of husbands and wives (Figure 4.16).[20]

Five Needs of Men	Five Needs of Women
Unconditional love and acceptance	Unconditional love and acceptance
Intimacy: sex	Intimacy: talk and friendship
Admiration, respect, esteem, approval	Affection (love, kindness, tenderness)
Support and praise at home	Security: family commitment, financial support
Friendship	Honesty and openness

Figure 4.16   Five needs of most men and women.
How well do you know your spouse's needs?

It is very important to discern that needs and wants are not the same. For example, there may be times when a husband wants sex but the wife is sick or too tired. In such cases, he should realize that although sex is a basic need, he can be patient. He does not have to have sex immediately every time he wants it.

Some say, "But my wife (or husband) is not meeting my sexual needs, so I must seek sex outside of marriage." God will not accept any reason for committing adultery.

> [13]*Another thing you do: You flood the LORD's altar with tears. You weep and wail because he no longer pays attention to your offerings or accepts them with pleasure from your hands.* [14]*You ask, "Why?" It is because the LORD is acting as the witness between you and the wife of your youth, because you have broken faith with her, though she is your partner, the wife of your marriage covenant.* [15]*Has not the LORD made them one? In flesh and spirit they are his. And why one? Because he was seeking godly offspring. So guard yourself in your spirit, and do not break faith with the wife of your youth.* [16]*"I hate divorce," says the LORD God of Israel, ... So guard yourself in your spirit, and do not break faith* (Mal. 2:13-16).

All the wealth you need is in the field of your marriage. If you are not satisfied, dig a little. Discuss the problems with your spouse and find solutions. Get some counsel from a pastor or a wise elder if necessary. Do not turn away from your marriage because it is not all you want it to be. Hoe the field you have already bought, and it will produce more.

> [15]*Drink water from your own cistern, running water from your own well.* [16]*Should your springs overflow in the streets, your streams of water in the public squares?* [17]*Let them be yours alone, never to be shared with strangers.* [18]*May your fountain be blessed, and may you rejoice in the wife of your youth.* [19]*A loving doe, a graceful deer—may her breasts satisfy you always, may you ever be captivated by her love.* [20]*Why be captivated, my son, by an adulteress? Why embrace the bosom of another man's wife?* [21]*For a man's ways are in full view of the LORD, and he examines all his paths.* [22]*The evil deeds of a wicked man ensnare him; the cords of his sin hold him fast.* [23]*He will die for lack of discipline, led astray by his own great folly* (Prov. 5:15-23).

I.   Consider the cost of adultery so that you will not agree to pay it.

A wise preacher once said that **sin will take you further than you want to go, keep you longer than you want to stay, and cost you more than you want to pay.** Delilah cost Samson his relationship with God and both eyes (Judges 16). For an hour of adultery with Bathsheba, David paid the rest of his life. His payments included the death of his child, a guilty conscience, a sword that never left his house, and a reputation of shame for the whole world to read about (2 Sam. 11). Likewise, sexual sins cost Solomon the kingdom, his reputation, and perhaps his soul. When Satan sells sin, he never mentions the price. There was no price written on the forbidden fruit in the Garden of Eden. And there was no price written on Bathsheba. But do not be deceived;

> IF THE GRASS ON THE OTHER SIDE OF THE FENCE LOOKS GREENER, THERE IS OFTEN A SEWER NEARBY!

Q 57   Did David pay too much for Bathsheba? Explain.

God is not mocked. Whoever commits adultery will spend a lifetime paying the price for those few minutes of sin. The fruit that is sweet in your mouth will become bitter in your stomach.

Q 58 *What costs of sexual sin do you think are the most expensive? Explain.*

One man made a list of what sexual sin would cost him. He said, "From time to time I remind myself that for one sexual sin, here are some ways I will pay:

- I will grieve the Lord, who gave His life to redeem me.
- Like David, I will drag the name and reputation of the Lord through the mud.
- I will cause others to stumble and sin. Some may go to hell following my example.
- I will lose—for the rest of my life—the respect and honor of my name. As Scripture says, *"his shame will never be wiped away"* in this life (Prov. 6:33).
- I will lose the trust of my beloved wife.
- I will bring shame and sorrow on my parents, family, and friends.
- I will exchange my self-respect for guilt, tears, bad memories, and shame.
- I may get many sexual diseases, such as gonorrhea, syphilis, herpes, or AIDS; also, I may pass these diseases on to my innocent spouse.
- I will lose the chance to witness to those who know me.
- I will harm or destroy the life and family of the person with whom I commit adultery.
- I will bring shame on my church—and all believers who know me—and hinder their witness.
- I may cause pregnancy, thus bringing an unwanted child into the world—a lifelong reminder of my sin."[21]

When we think about the cost of adultery, we realize that it is too expensive. This causes us to turn from sexual sins and think about something good and positive! Sin loses its appeal when we look at the price tag.

J. Guard your health.

Q 59 *How can a person guard his health to prevent sexual sin?*

Temptations are the strongest when we are the weakest. Satan knew this, so he tempted Jesus when the Lord was the weakest—after fasting for 40 days (Matt. 4:1-11). Likewise, Elijah was tempted the most when he was the weakest. After his ministry on Mount Carmel—and running all the way to town—Elijah was tired. In this weak condition, he was tempted to despair (1 Kings 19). Also, John the Baptist was tempted to doubt when he became weak in the prison (Matt. 11:1-6).

So, as believers, it is wise for us to guard our health. Sometimes we feel the pressure to work too hard so that we can succeed. But over a period of time, working too hard makes a person weak—either physically, emotionally, mentally, or spiritually. So we must learn to do a day's work and leave the rest for tomorrow, for others, or for God. If you begin to feel hungry, angry, lonely, or tired, it is time to rest. These feelings are signs that God has given us to guard our health. They are like red lights telling us to stop.

K. Be accountable to others.

Q 60 *Do you give account of yourself to a friend? If not, choose one and build that relationship.*

Sin grows in the dark, but dies in the light. So plan your life in a way that others know what you are doing and thinking. Each day in prayer, invite the Holy Spirit to search your heart and mind. Respond to any changes He speaks to you about. Also, be a member of a church or group that requires you to give an account of yourself. Talk with your spouse from time to time about your thoughts, temptations, and struggles. Choose a friend or elder to hold you accountable. Invite this person to ask you about your thoughts and actions each week or month. Request this person to ask you questions about your private life and inspect it. Getting temptations into the light makes them weaker and us stronger. So do not fight the battle alone—be open with others who can help you.

"Though one may be overpowered, two can defend themselves. A cord of three strands is not quickly broken" (Eccles. 4:12).

Note: If you have a computer, there are excellent programs like *Covenant Eyes* that can help you be accountable for your thoughts and actions.

Conclusion

Sexual sins kill families. To overcome this threat, we do not need a new revelation. Those who obey the 11 principles in this lesson will never commit sexual sins. Ephesians 5:3 tells us, *"But among you there must not be even a hint of sexual immorality, or of any kind of impurity."*

Lesson 21

Relating to Elders in the Family of God (1 Tim. 5:17-25)

Goal A: *Summarize ways to treat elderly believers as fathers.*
Goal B: *Explain how and when to show double honor to an elder.*
Goal C: *Summarize guidelines for disciplining an elder who sins.*
Goal D: *Analyze the problem and solution for favoritism.*

A. Honor elderly men with the *respect fathers deserve* (1 Tim. 5:1).

One of the challenges Timothy faced at Ephesus was older believers. Some honored the old and looked down on the younger. So Paul gave Timothy and the church special instructions about their relationship with each other. *First,* he told Timothy to make sure that no one despised his youthful age (1 Tim. 4:12). *Then,* in contrast, Paul told Timothy to treat older men (and women) with respect.

We have already seen that in God's household, a leader should treat people as his own family members. This is very important when the leader needs to rebuke an older man.

It is always hard to rebuke people. And it is even more difficult when the person we rebuke is older than we are. At such times, the leader must be careful not to rebuke the older man *"harshly"* (1 Tim. 5:1). Do not seize an older man by the shoulders and shake him! [22] Instead, *"exhort him as if he were your father"* (1 Tim. 5:1). Another word for *exhort* is *urge,* [23] which means "to encourage." [24] The leader must correct older men gently, encouraging them to do what is right. If a young pastor must correct an elder, it would be wise to seek counsel from an older pastor or trusted elder. Some problems in the early years of ministry are too difficult to solve without the wisdom learned from many years of experience in relationships.

Sabio reminds: "Because young King Rehoboam did not follow the advice of the elders, he lost most of the kingdom on one decision (1 Kings 12:8). Boom! The kingdom was there one minute and gone the next! In contrast, it is easy to see far ahead, by standing on the shoulders of a wise elder."

Application. A common error of young pastors is failing to listen well to the older men and women of a church. Treating older men as fathers, and older women as mothers means more than just caring for them in their old age. Young Nabal became the pastor of an old church. He had no idea about who built the church, or who the faithful members were that paid the bills. He did not understand the views and values of members who had worshiped in the church for more than 40 years. He did not appreciate the history and roots of families who were saved in the church, and had seen their children and grandchildren saved in the church. But young Pastor Nabal was full of new ideas he had just learned in Bible school. He led the church in songs that the older people did not know. He seldom asked the elders any questions, but he was often eager to share his own ideas. Church seemed more about what he liked, than the sheep he was called to pastor

Q 61 ✎ *How would you correct an elderly believer who was accused of drunkenness?*

Q 62 ✎ *How could Pastor Nabal have shown true respect for the elders of the church?*

and serve. He felt so full of faith and vision. One year after he came, Pastor Nabal was surprised that half of the people no longer attended. He was discouraged when the tithes were not enough to pay his bills. And he was shocked when the few remaining members voted for him to leave the church. Nabal was young. Perhaps in time he would learn what it meant to honor older men as fathers, and older women as mothers.

Q 63 ⟍ *What lesson did Pastor Gordon learn by listening with humility?*

Pastor Gordon was going to preach, and travel with a friend who was much older. As they walked down the street, the name of a common friend came up. Gordon said something unkind about that person. His comment was sarcastic. The older friend stopped, and turned until he was face to face with Gordon. With deep, slow words he said, "Gordon, since we love God, let us not speak unkind words about a friend." These words were gentle, although they caused Gordon some private pain and embarrassment. But for the rest of his ministry, Pastor Gordon was thankful he respected the counsel of an elder, as if the man were his father.[25] Sabio reminds: "Wounds from a sincere friend are better than kisses from an enemy" (Prov. 27:6 NLT).

B. Give double honor to elders who lead in the church (1 Tim. 5:17-18).

Q 64 ⤴ *What does double honor mean? Why are some worthy of double honor?*

[17]*The elders who direct the affairs of the church well are worthy of double honor, especially those whose work is preaching and teaching.* [18]*For the Scripture says, "Do not muzzle the ox while it is treading out the grain," and "The worker deserves his wages"* (1 Tim. 5:17-18).

All Elders

Preaching and Teaching Elders

Figure 4.17   Preaching and teaching elders are worthy of double honor.

In 1 Timothy 5:1, Paul used the Greek word *presbuteroi* to refer to older men in the church. Later, in 1 Timothy 5:17, he uses the same Greek word (*presbuteroi*) to refer to leaders. Paul says three things about these elders who lead the church.[26] *First,* they *"direct the affairs of the church"* (1 Tim. 5:17). These leaders oversee or manage the church. *Second,* some of them are *"preaching and teaching"* (1 Tim. 5:17). These ministries require more time and work. *Third,* those who do their task *"well"* are worthy of *"double honor"* (1 Tim. 5:17). Double honor refers to respect and financial help (1 Tim. 5:2, 18).[27] Those who lead the church well should receive some pay from the church. And to many, kind words of thanks and recognition are worth more than money. For others, some financial help enables them to buy books, study, pray, and plan sermons and lessons. Some deserve double honor because they do double the work.

Q 65 ⤴ *Which 2 illustrations support Paul's standard of double honor?*

Paul uses two biblical illustrations to support paying elders who minister. *First,* he refers to Deuteronomy 25:4. *"Do not muzzle the ox while it is treading out grain"* (1 Tim. 5:18). If God commanded men to allow the ox to eat some of the grain it was grinding, how much more does the minister who labors in the church deserve payment for his labor? *Second,* Paul quoted Luke 10:7, *"The worker deserves his wages"* (1 Tim. 5:18). When we faithfully work hard for our employer, we deserve to receive our salary. When pastors are faithful in leading the people, the church ought to be faithful to pay them well. The other side of the coin is this: Pastors must never do ministry just to earn money (1 Tim. 3:3).[28] Likewise, Paul told the Corinthians, *"The Lord has commanded that those who preach the gospel should receive their living from the gospel"* (1 Cor. 9:14).

Figure 4.18
In biblical times, people used an oxen to grind grain. The ox walked in a circle, causing a large mill stone to grind grain. God said that the ox deserved some food to eat, in exchange for the hard work he did for others.

Jesus taught that our heart follows our treasure. Believers who give tithes and offerings into a church discover that they enjoy church. In contrast, stingy believers who refuse to support the church with their finances soon discover that their heart is not in the church. When you hear people criticizing and complaining about a pastor, you often find that they do not support the church with finances, prayers, or faithfully attending. Wise believers learn that they get out of a church what they put into it. As they invest finances in a local church, their hearts overflow with love for the church and the family of God in it.

Q 66 ⟋ *How does funding church leaders help those who give?*

C. Do not consider an accusation against a church elder without two or three witnesses (1 Tim. 5:19).

Q 67 ⟋ *What is the main thought of 1 Timothy 5:19?*

Paul wrote, *"Do not entertain an accusation against an elder unless it is brought by two or three witnesses"* (1 Tim. 5:19). God first gave this principle to Moses as part of the Old Testament Law (Deut. 19:15). Paul mentioned it in his second letter to the Corinthians (2 Cor. 13:1). The key thought is this: Those who hear an accusation must make sure of the facts before they bring any charges. This protects elders from angry or malicious people who want revenge or are looking for a way to attack the church.

An old minister served 5 years in his first pastorate and 41 at the second church. He left his first pastorate, scared away by criticism. Afterward he learned that one person was the source of all the complaints. So he shares the insight that one sour person in a church or community may, with a loud voice, create the impression that everyone is unhappy, and demanding a change. So young pastors should keep in mind the amount of noise that one, old barking dog can make.

Application. The standard of two witnesses is good for all church members (1 Tim. 5:19). But accusations about sexual abuse deserve careful investigation—and notes kept in a church file, even when two or three witnesses are not available. In some nations, laws require an investigation of accusations of sexual misconduct. Before a believer is placed in ministry, the pastor and elders must examine this person's reputation—getting references from his background. In 1 Timothy 3 we studied 12 tests that elders or deacons must pass to enter ministry. Likewise, it is wise to check the background and character references of any believers *before* allowing them to work with children or youth. For one sexual sin in a church damages believers, shames the name of God, and hurts a church's reputation in the community for many years.

Q 68 ⟍ *Why do sexual accusations require special attention?*

D. Discipline church elders who sin, so others will fear sinning (1 Tim. 5:20).

Q 69 ⟍ *If an elder sins, should a pastor discipline him in public or in private? Explain.*

When an accusation against a church leader is true, the pastor must expose this sin. A holy church cannot tolerate sin. Rather, the discipline of that elder must be public *"so that others may take warning"* (1 Tim. 5:20). Public discipline provides a strong warning to the other elders and to the church as a whole.[29] Elders who lead well receive double honor. But great responsibility comes with that honor. We teach by example as much as we teach by words. So, as double honor comes to elders who serve well, double shame comes to elders who fall into sin. How do you know when to discipline publicly? The general rule is to deal with public sins publicly; and deal with private sins privately. It is less necessary to expose a guilty person in public for a sin others do not know about—if the accused repents and resigns from leadership, unless the sin was sexual.

Peter confronted Simon the sorcerer, when he offered money for the power to bestow the Spirit, so others would learn never to do this (Acts 8:18-23). Paul confronted Peter when he refused to fellowship with Gentile believers, so that others would avoid this sin (Gal. 2:11-14).

[18] *"To the angel of the church in Thyatira write: These are the words of the Son of God, whose eyes are like blazing fire and whose feet are like burnished bronze.* [19]*I know your deeds, your love and faith, your service and perseverance, and that you are now doing more than you did at first.* [20]*Nevertheless, I have this*

Q 70 ⟋ *Why did Jesus warn that He would discipline believers at Thyatira?*

*against you: You **tolerate** that woman Jezebel, who calls herself a prophetess. By her teaching she misleads my servants into sexual immorality and the eating of food sacrificed to idols. ²¹I have given her time to repent of her immorality, but she is unwilling. ²²So I will cast her on a bed of suffering, and I will make those who commit adultery with her suffer intensely, unless they repent of her ways. ²³I will strike her children dead. Then all the churches will know that I am he who searches hearts and minds, and I will repay each of you according to your deeds* (Rev. 2:18-23).

E. Caution, Pastor: Do not show favoritism to elders (1 Tim. 5:21-25).

Q 71 ➤ *What words show us that Paul is roaring like a lion?*

In this passage Paul roars like a lion!

²¹ *I charge you, in the sight of God and Christ Jesus and the elect angels, to keep these instructions **without partiality, and to do nothing out of favoritism**. ²²Do not be hasty in the laying on of hands, and do not share in the sins of others. Keep yourself pure. ²³Stop drinking only water, and use a little wine because of your stomach and your frequent illnesses. ²⁴The sins of some men are obvious, reaching the place of judgment ahead of them; the sins of others trail behind them. ²⁵In the same way, good deeds are obvious, and even those that are not cannot be hidden* (1 Tim. 5:21-25).

Q 72 ➤ *What factors can tempt a pastor to show favoritism?*

Explanation. Favoritism is a sin in itself, and it involves us in the sins of others. So Paul warns against favoritism. Every church leader, sooner or later, is tempted to show favoritism. There are always some deacons or elders in the church who have influence and/or money. Sometimes these elders follow strange teachings, or live in sin—and thus fall short of the biblical qualifications for church elders. When pastors are low

> FAVORITISM IS A SIN IN ITSELF!

on money and powerful people, they may be tempted to compromise biblical standards, and thus show favoritism. Likewise, fleshly church members with bad doctrine or a sinful reputation may use money or influence—trying to manipulate a pastor.

Q 73 ➤ *Why must a pastor avoid favoritism?*

Against favoritism, Paul rises up to his full height, filled with the Spirit of God, and speaks to Timothy in a loud voice with his authority as an apostle. With this charge against favoritism, Paul calls the Father, the Son, and the angels as witnesses! The command to avoid favoritism is as loud, powerful, and forceful as Paul can make it. For if a pastor lowers the standards that God gives for His family, the souls of people will be lost, the reputation of the church will be ruined—and the blood of Christ will have been shed in vain. So Paul insists on the **same qualifications** for all elders and deacons (1 Tim. 3). He does not allow any possible leader to bypass the process of testing. He will not allow Timothy to wink at sin in order to get or keep a wealthy or prominent believer on the board—and certainly not a recent convert (1 Tim. 3:6). God's apostle insists on the same standards for helping all widows (1 Tim. 5:3-16). And the apostle commands the same guidelines for all elders who deserve double honor or double shame (1 Tim. 5:17-20). One God, One mediator, one Church, one gospel, and one standard— for Jews and Gentiles, for men and women, for rich and the poor.

By holding firmly to one standard, church leaders *"do not share in the sins of others"* (1 Tim. 5:22). In contrast, those who compromise God's guidelines share in the sins they allow, and bring judgment on themselves.

Under the old covenant, the Israelites shared in the sins of their kings—because the common people did not stand up for righteousness and speak out against sin (1 Kings 21:22; 22:52; 2 Kings 23:15). They also shared in the sins of the false prophets (Jer. 23:32; Micah 3:5). And the Jewish Christians in Galatia shared in Peter's sin against the Gentile Christians there (Gal. 2:11-13). Sometimes to avoid sin, we have to find new groups. If you have to do wrong to stay in a group, you are in the wrong group.

Q 74 ⤡ *How did the Israelites share in the sins of their leaders?*

Those who lower God's standards to gain friendship, money, or influence will be exposed. We know the truth about people—sooner or later. So better to find out the truth, and build on it sooner, and keep the church pure (1 Tim. 5:24-25).

Q 75 ⤢ *What warning does Paul give against favoritism?*

> [24]*The sins of some men are obvious, reaching the place of judgment ahead of them; the sins of others trail behind them.* [25]*In the same way, good deeds are obvious, and even those that are not cannot be hidden* (1 Tim. 5:24-25).

Church leader, stay pure in appointing deacons, honoring or disciplining elders, and helping widows. Avoid favoritism. Use the same standards for all. Otherwise, *"be sure that your sin will find you out"* (Num. 32:23).

Perkins was a slave of sin while he was a student in Bible school. He had no idea that others knew about his bad habits. Walking along a street in town, he overheard a woman say to her rebellious child, "Bridle your tongue, or I will give you to that drunk, Perkins, passing by." This led Perkins to repent and become a follower of Jesus. People know more about us than we think.[30]

Spurgeon observed that one cannot hide coals of fire for long under a beautiful coat. For soon they will reveal themselves with smoke and flames. Likewise, we cannot hide for long our favorite sins under a fake profession of Christianity. Sooner or later such sins will reveal themselves and burn ugly holes in a person's reputation. Some who try to get rid of sin are like the person who swept away the spiders' web without destroying the spider.[31] But sin needs to be washed away by the Saviour's blood—not hidden under the cloak of religion.[32]

First Timothy 5:23 is tucked in the middle of a paragraph about pastoral work. Paul inserts a word of encouragement for Timothy *to take care of himself*, as he is taking care of the church. From this verse we see that Timothy's health was not the best. Paul's concern is not only for the church, but for the leaders such as Timothy. Is it okay to use medicine with alcohol in it to help cure a sickness? We eat food when we are hungry. We wear clothes to prevent being cold. We build houses to shelter us from rain and sun. So let us seek the medicine God provides to help us overcome sickness. Every good gift comes from the our Father above (James 1:17). Paul told Timothy to take care of himself. Even though Timothy did not drink wine, Paul encouraged him to use a little wine in water, for medical reasons.

Q 76 ⤢ *Did Timothy drink wine? Is alcohol permissible in medicines?*

Lesson 22

Relating to Slaves, False Teachers, Self, and the Rich in the Family of God (1 Tim. 6:1-21)

Goal A: *Summarize Paul's attitudes and values for employees and employers.*
Goal B: *Identify preachers in your region who use religion as a business.*
Goal C: *Summarize the keys to being a faithful minister (1 Tim. 6).*
Goal D: *Relate the wise use of riches in the present world to the next age (1 Tim. 6:17-19).*

A. Slaves and employees: Live as ambassadors for Christ (1 Tim. 6:1-2).

Q 77 ⤡ *Why did God want slaves to show respect to their masters?*

> [1]*All who are under the yoke of slavery should consider their masters worthy of full respect, **so that** God's name and our teaching may not be slandered.* [2]*Those who have believing masters are not to show less respect for them because they are brothers. Instead, they are to serve them even better, because those who benefit from their service are believers, and dear to them. These are the things you are to teach and urge on them* (1 Tim. 6:1-2).

Outsiders evaluate God and the gospel on the basis of Christian behavior (1 Tim. 6:1; Titus 2:9-10; Eph. 6:5).

*Liberation theology teaches that violence is acceptable, *if* the goal is freedom from oppression. Paul had a different theology. He did not tell slaves to fight for freedom. He did not say much about the evils of slavery. Instead, he told Christian slaves to submit to and honor their owners. Paul's letter to Timothy shows more concern about a slave's attitude than a slave's freedom. Paul showed the same concern in Ephesians 6:5. There, he told slaves to obey their masters with respect, fear, and sincerity, just as they would obey Christ.

Q 78 *Why was slavery a hot topic in Paul's day?*

> FOR US TO UNDERSTAND PAUL'S WORDS, WE NEED TO RECOGNIZE THE REALITY PAUL FACED.

For us to understand Paul's words, we need to recognize the reality Paul faced. Some say there were 60 million slaves in the Roman Empire. Masters saw slaves as potential enemies. If Paul had tried to correct the evil of slavery at that time, he might have caused a civil war. And, he would have discredited the gospel of Christ.[33] Paul's concern for the gospel of eternity was his main priority. He wrote that slaves should honor their masters *"so that God's name and our teaching may not be slandered"* (1 Tim. 6:1).

Q 79 *How do those who disregard the laws of culture and society sometimes smear the gospel?*

In Titus, Paul taught the same truth from the positive side. He told slaves to submit to their masters to *"make the teaching about God our Savior attractive"* (Titus 2:9-10). And in a similar way, Peter told wives to win their husbands to the truth of the gospel through the purity and reverence of their lives (1 Pet. 3:1-3). These verses give us a principle that applies to all relationships between believers and non-Christians. Through our behavior, we can adorn the gospel or slander the gospel. We can make the gospel attractive or repulsive. The main way that non-Christians evaluate God and the gospel is by watching Christian behavior. Imagine, in a nation like Rome with millions of slaves, if slaves who became Christians rebelled against their masters. If this happened, most of the society would reject Christianity, because of the behavior of the slaves. God calls us to be light and salt in a world that is dark and decaying. John reminds us that the world is under the influence of Satan (1 John 5:19). Paul reminds us that the Antichrist will deceive the world and rule it (2 Thess. 2). Both John and Paul emphasize that the world is passing away (1 John 2:17; 1 Cor. 7:29-31). Our time on earth is short, but eternity is forever. So let us apply our hearts to wisdom. Let us live on earth as visitors here, preparing for eternity, and influencing others to make peace with God now.

Q 80 *Do you know anyone like Charles? Explain.*

Application.   Charles was driving when he came upon an accident. A bus filled with passengers had crashed, and was lying on its side. Climbing on top of the bus, Charles tried to open the door—but it would not open. Others arrived and began pulling people out of the bus through the windows. Then Charles saw one man climb on top of the bus. He reached down, turned the handle, and opened the door. Suddenly, Charles realized that the reason the door had not opened earlier was because he was standing on it. Likewise, sometimes those who want to lead others to Christ become the biggest problem to their salvation.[34] Today, most churches do not face the relationship between masters and slaves. But we have similar relationships—between bosses and employees. What if a Christian worker has an unsaved boss or co-worker? Or what if a Christian boss has unsaved employees? Let us live in a way that honors Jesus Christ, and attracts others to the one we call Savior, Lord, and God. The first light of the gospel that some sinners will hear is the light that shines through our daily living.

An important value of the gospel is that there should be respect in the household of faith. All believers are God's children, and co-heirs of salvation. There is just *"one Lord, one faith, one baptism; [6]one God and Father of all, who is over all and through all and in all"* (Eph. 4:5-6). Paul taught, *"There is neither Jew nor Greek, slave nor free, male nor female, for you are all one in Christ Jesus"* (Gal. 3:28). Yet freedom in

Christ brought difficulties—especially to Christian slaves who had Christian owners. It would be easy for the slave to think, "My owner is a brother, so I don't have to work hard for him" (1 Tim. 6:2). Such an attitude would harm their relationship, cause division in the church, and give the gospel a bad name. Instead, Paul says that Christian slaves should work even harder *"because they [masters] are brothers"* (1 Tim. 6:2). The slave's brother, whom he (or she) loves, is the one who will benefit from the slave's work.

In 1 Timothy Paul does not give any instructions to slave owners. But Philemon is a letter from Paul to a slave owner. One of Philemon's slaves, Onesimus, had escaped. Onesimus met Paul and became a Christian. Paul sent Onesimus back to Philemon, and asked Philemon to receive this runaway slave as a *"dear brother"* (Philem. 12-16).

Q 81 *What is the balance between being true to the gospel and wise in society?*

In Ephesians, Paul speaks to both slaves and slave owners. He tells slaves to obey their masters as they would obey Christ (Eph. 6:5). And he tells the owners to treat their slaves fairly, without threat (Eph. 6:9). Paul reminds owners and slaves that they both have the same Master in heaven (Eph. 6:9).

A young woman left a secular job to work for a Christian company. Within a month, she complained to her pastor about her Christian boss. Her pastor advised, "Work harder and show him real respect. Just because all of you in the office are Christians does not mean you can do less than your best." She did as her pastor advised and her problems soon decreased.

B. False teachers: They had many faults, but their main goal was money (1 Tim. 6:3-10).

Recall that the false teachers at Ephesus were *in the church*. It appears that some of them were church leaders, or had been. Note that *more than half* of this passage is about money. These false teachers in the family of God were among those who, **because they were "eager for money,"** had *"wandered from the faith and **pierced themselves with many griefs"*** (1 Tim. 6:10). Some piercing of the body is controversial. But all piercing of one's one soul is foolishness. Paul condemns their unhealthy interest in controversies and arguments. He says they were the source of *"constant friction"*—the opposite of Paul's gospel of peace (Eph. 6:15), and the wisdom that comes from above (James 3:13-18). But Paul's emphasis on money causes us to think that finances was the greatest concern of the false teachers. The false teachers at Ephesus had many bad characteristics. But love of money, instead of loving people, seems to be their worst quality.

Q 82 *Which characteristic of false teachers does Paul emphasize most in 1 Timothy 6:3-10?*

*³If anyone teaches false doctrines and does not agree to the sound instruction of our Lord Jesus Christ and to godly teaching, ⁴he is **conceited** and **understands nothing**. He has an unhealthy interest in **controversies** and **quarrels** about words that result in **envy, strife, malicious talk, evil suspicions** ⁵**and constant friction** between men of corrupt mind, who have been **robbed of the truth** and who think that godliness is a means to **financial gain*** (1 Tim. 6:3-5).

Money is the goal of greedy preachers (1 Tim. 6:5-10). It is ironic that those robbing believers of their money have themselves been robbed of the truth (1 Tim. 6:5). Many false teachers use religion and godliness as a banner to attract people. But their real goal is the offering. Like the false teachers Peter rebukes, those at Ephesus were experts in greed who had *"left the straight way and wandered off to follow the way of Balaam son of Beor, who loved the wages of wickedness"* (2 Pet. 2:15). Like Gehazi, Elisha's servant, their lust for money led them astray. These false teachers were ruining whole households—*"for the sake of dishonest gain"* (Titus 1:11). In contrast, Paul worked hard with his own hands, making tents, to avoid the appearance of being greedy for money (1 Thess. 2:9; 2 Thess. 3:8; Acts 20:34; 1 Cor. 4:12).

Q 83 *Do you know any preachers whose main goal is money? Explain.*

Q 84 ➤ *What are 2 ways that following Jesus raises the financial standards of believers?*

Q 85 ➤ *Does God promise that believers will be wealthy? Explain.*

Christianity is not a road to earthly riches. The first believers, like many today, lost their houses, lands, jobs, families, reputations, and even their lives following Jesus (Heb. 10). The first readers of James worked for wages day by day, but their rich employers stole much of their wages (James 5:4-6). As we see in the church at Ephesus, some believers were rich (1 Tim. 6:17-19). But they did not gain money because they followed Christ. Following Jesus is not a guarantee for wealth. It is true that God meets the needs of His children. And there are many testimonies from believers that God is faithful to His children. Following Christian principles helps people not to waste their money on drugs, sexual sins, and other foolish ways of spending. Cooperating with God's laws of giving results in a better harvest. But wealth is never a test of spirituality. Some of the most fleshly people in the church are the most wealthy, like believers at Laodicea (Rev. 3:14-18). And some of the most spiritual believers in the church are the poorest, like believers at Smyrna (Rev. 2:8-10). How much money a person has often depends on factors such as circumstances, inheritance, the national economy, and personal abilities.

Q 86 ➤ *What is the balance between contentment and wanting more?*

Paul contrasts earthly wealth with eternal wealth. He writes: *"But godliness with contentment is great gain"* (1 Tim. 6:6). Paul reminded himself and others that life on earth is temporary. *"For we brought nothing into the world, and we can take nothing out of it"* (1 Tim. 6:7). There are no pockets on a newborn baby, or on a corpse.

"But if we have food and clothing, we will be content with that" (1 Tim. 6:8). Paul had learned the secret of being content with what he had—whether much or little. From prison the apostle wrote:

Q 87 ➤ *To what does Isaiah 56:11 compare some people?*

[11b]I have learned to be content whatever the circumstances. [12]I know what it is to be in need, and I know what it is to have plenty. I have learned the secret of being content in any and every situation, whether well fed or hungry, whether living in plenty or in want. [13]I can do everything through him who gives me strength (Phil. 4:11b-13).

Isaiah said some people are like greedy dogs (Isa. 56:11). There is an old story about a dog with a bone in his mouth, standing beside a lake. As he looked into the water, the dog saw his reflection. It looked to him like there was another dog with a bone. Greedy, the dog opened his mouth and jumped into the water to get the other dog's bone. As a result, he lost the bone he had. Jesus warned us to beware of greed and covetousness (Luke 12:15). And Hebrews counsels us: *"Be content with what you have"* (Heb. 13:5). Enjoy your own wife, and refuse to lust after the wife of someone else. Enjoy the money you earn honestly, and turn away from greed. Remember the story of the greedy dog.

Paul warns that the desire for riches is a temptation and a trap—an invitation to ruin and destruction.

[9]People who want to get rich fall into temptation and a trap and into many foolish and harmful desires that plunge men into ruin and destruction. [10]For the love of money is a root of all kinds of evil. Some people, eager for money, have wandered from the faith and pierced themselves with many griefs (1 Tim. 6:9-10).

Figure 4.19   Don't be like a greedy dog.

Money is a blessed servant, but a poor master. Jesus warned that we cannot serve God and money—we must choose one or the other (Matt. 6:24). The love of money is a root of many evils, such as lying, stealing, murder, greed, and covetousness. Ask people such as Balaam, Achan, Gehazi, Ananias and Sapphira, or Demas about the fruit that comes from the root of loving money.

Q 88 ➤ *Who are some biblical examples of those who loved money?*

Sabio agrees: "Contentment makes much of little; but greed makes little of much.

Contentment is the poor man's riches; but greed is the rich man's poverty."[35]

"To many people money is like a shoe: if the money they have is too small, it pinches and irritates; but if their money is too large, it causes them to stumble and fall.[36]

Steps to Heaven:

1. Repent of sins.
2. Believe in Christ through the healthy gospel.
3. Serve with a clear conscience (2 Tim. 1:3).
4. Continue to study the Scriptures (2 Tim. 2:15).
5. Persevere in holy living and right doctrine (1 Tim. 4:16).
6. Fight the good fight of faith (1 Tim. 6:12).

Steps to apostasy:

7. Stir up controversies.
8. Meditate on temptation.
9. Fall into temptation.
10. Be robbed of truth.
11. Pierce self with many sorrows.
12. Reap ruin and destruction.

Figure 4.20   Steps to apostasy and spiritual suicide

Some at Ephesus began well. When they heard Paul's gospel, they repented, believed, and began to follow Jesus. As they grew in grace they became elders and served the church. Later, they turned from the healthy gospel, and developed an unhealthy interest in teaching controversies. At some point they were tempted by greed and began to desire riches. Following these *"foolish and harmful desires,"* they fell deeply into temptation, piercing their own souls with many sorrows. In the end, unless they heeded Timothy's warnings (1 Tim. 1:3), they would be lost forever in *"ruin and destruction"* (1 Tim. 6:9).

"What good will it be for a man if he gains the whole world, yet forfeits his soul?" (Matt. 16:26).

C. Man of God, run from what is wrong, and toward what is right (1 Tim. 6:11-16).

Note the contrast Paul wants between the false teachers and Timothy.

[11]***But you***, *man of God,* ***flee*** *from all this, and* ***pursue*** *righteousness, godliness, faith, love, endurance and gentleness.* [12]*Fight the good fight of the faith. Take hold of the eternal life to which you were called when you made your good confession in the presence of many witnesses.* [13]*In the sight of God, who gives life to everything, and of Christ Jesus, who while testifying before Pontius Pilate made the good confession, I charge you* [14]*to keep this command without spot or blame until the appearing of our Lord Jesus Christ,* [15]*which God will bring about in his own time—God, the blessed and only Ruler, the King of kings and Lord of lords,* [16]*who alone is immortal and who lives in unapproachable light, whom no one has seen or can see. To him be honor and might forever. Amen* (1 Tim. 6:11-16).

The key to spiritual victory is in the direction we face. Paul wants Timothy's back toward evil, and his face toward God. Victory is sure as we face the right direction. We win or lose by the direction we choose. This truth is not difficult. A child in the first grade can understand it. But our great need is not for more knowledge. What we need is the grace, a will fixed on pleasing God, righteous desires, and discipline to do what we already know is right. If we just keep going in the right direction, we will arrive at the place we are facing. To reach heaven, we must practice rejecting what God hates, and embracing what He loves.

Q 89 *Do you know any who followed Jesus for a time, but later turned away? Explain.*

Q 90 *With whom does Paul contrast those hungry for money?*

Q 91 *Summarize Paul's advice to Timothy in one short sentence (1 Tim. 6:11)*

In his second letter to Timothy Paul emphasizes the same truth: *"Flee the evil desires of youth, and pursue righteousness, faith, love and peace, along with those who call on the Lord out of a pure heart"* (2 Tim. 2:22).

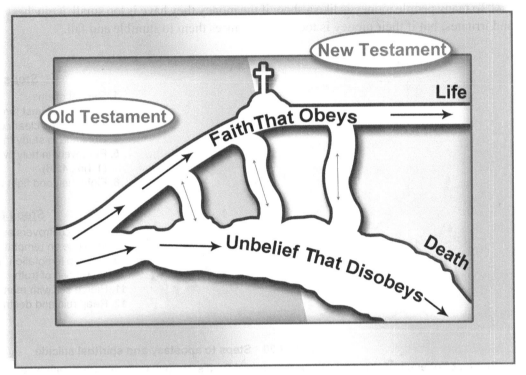

Figure 4.21 Two roads run through both the old covenant and the new covenant. God will bless those whose faith expresses itself in obedience to Him, and He will curse those whose unbelief expresses itself in disobedience to Him (Matt. 7:13-14, 21-23, 24-27).

Winning the spiritual fight depends on two basic things.

Q 92 ⚒ *Who is a good example of one who ran from evil?*

1. Flee from all that is evil. *"But you, man of God, **flee** from all this"* (1 Tim. 6:11). *All this* refers to the characteristics and desires of the false teachers (1 Tim. 6:3-5, 9-10). Paul says to run from evil. In our generation, many believers are not running from evil. Some obey God, and turn their backs toward what they know is wrong. Others tolerate evil, beside them, but do not flee from it. And many these days seek evil entertainment. They watch movies that exalt evil actors and sinful plots. They search the Internet for sinful pictures and videos. They read sinful books. For those who face evil, it is only a matter of time until they begin to accept and practice evil. If we flirt with sin, we will fall into it. Keep your back to sin and you will never walk in the wrong direction. This is half of the key to spiritual success.

Joseph is a good example for us. When Potiphar's wife tried to seduce him into the bed, he did not stand there with his eyes wide, gazing at her beauty. He did not savor the fact that she admired him. He did not pause to wonder how well she could kiss. Rather, he turned away and ran. As a result, Joseph's name is in the hall of fame, not the hall of shame (Gen. 39:12).

There are two types of people in the history books: those who ran from sin, and those whom sin conquered. Evil conquers all who do not flee from it, sooner or later. Flee from sin, as from a poisonous snake.

Before his conversion, Augustine lived with a sinful woman. Then he met Jesus, and began to follow Him. His former lover saw him, and called for him to return. He ran away with all his might, and she ran after him, crying, "Why are you running away? It is I." He answered, "I run away because I am not the man I used to be. I am a new man in Christ."[37]

2. Pursue what is good. We do not have to be the smartest, the fastest, or the strongest to be among the winners of the race in which we run. And we do not need to pursue the right things *forever*. There is a finish line in front of us—the appearing of our Lord Jesus Christ (1 Tim. 6:14). Note that Paul does not attempt to give the date of the Lord's return. He is more concerned about the event than the date. So Paul confidently affirms that God will bring the Lord's Coming to pass **in his own time**. In other words, the timing is God's concern, not something for us to worry about. All we need to do is enjoy the presence of Jesus, use the grace He gives by His Spirit, serve the Lord, and keep going in the right direction. We catch what we run after. Christian, hear the words of the apostle Paul. With all his heart, soul, and authority he urges Timothy and us:

Q 93 ⬉ *What does Paul say is the main key to success in ministry? Being smart, fast, talented?*

> [13]*In the sight of God, who gives life to everything, and of Christ Jesus, who while testifying before Pontius Pilate made the good confession, I charge you* [14]*to keep this command without spot or blame until the appearing of our Lord Jesus Christ,* [15]*which God will bring about in his own time* (1 Tim. 6:13-15).

We can summarize Paul's solemn charge with the words: "Our Father is watching and cheering for you. Jesus Christ was successful, and He will never leave you. Receive strength from the Father and Son to obey what you know is right! Keep going in the right direction—you will see Jesus soon." Everyone who keeps walking in the right direction arrives at where they are going—sooner or later.

Some of the ways we pursue what is good include: prayer, reading and meditating on Scripture, doing good deeds to help those in need, praise and worship, being thankful, counting our blessings, choosing Christian friends, attending spiritual meetings, being accountable, evaluating our progress, making good plans for the future, and making godly decisions.

Q 94 ⬉ *What are some ways we pursue what is good?*

Review the 11 principles in Lesson 20 often. Evaluate yourself daily. Live alert. Do not allow yourself to just drift through a day. Always be aware of what you are thinking and choosing. As you make choices, ask yourself, "Which direction am I facing: — towards good or evil, light or darkness, God or Satan?" Be accountable to a friend with your thoughts, time, and desires. Pay attention to yourself and your progress.

Q 95 ⬉ *Complete Figure 4.22 on pursuing what is good.*

Reference	Your Summaries About Pursuing What Is Good
1 Tim. 4:12	
Heb. 2:1-4	
2 Pet. 1:5-10	

Figure 4.22   Practice summarizing verses that talk about pursuing what is good.

Be an example for others to follow, for many are watching you (1 Tim. 4:12). In several psalms, David refers to his integrity in following the Lord (Ps. 7:8; 25:21; 41:12, and such). Likewise, Daniel was a man of great integrity. The Babylonian officials under King Nebuchadnezzar could find no fault with Daniel except in matters of his religion (Dan. 6:4-5). Our Lord Jesus looked into the eyes of the Pharisees and asked, *"Can any of you prove me guilty of sin"* (John 8:46)? And the apostle Paul followed the Lord so closely that he encouraged others to follow his example as he followed Christ (1 Cor. 11:1; 4:16; Phil 3:17). Church leader, be the type of person that you want others to be. This is godly leadership.

As we leave this point, pay special attention to the *doxology—words of glorious praise to God, often sung in worship (1 Tim. 6:15-16). These verses put everything in 1 Timothy in perspective. For our Great God is sovereign—over Artemis, the goddess of the Ephesians, over the false teachers, and over every person. At the end of our days, we will stand before this Almighty God and give account. Since God is the Beginning and the End, let us be careful how we live in between.

Q 96 ⬈ *What is a doxology?*

Q 97 ⬉ *Which aspects of the doxology do you like the best? Why?*

Q 98 ➘ *Fill in the blanks of Figure 4.23.*

1 Timothy	Seven Statements About God	Explanations and Comments
6:14-15	1. God will bring about the second coming of Jesus Christ in His own time.	God alone sets the limits of _____ on earth. When He decides, Jesus Christ will return to reward the obedient and punish rebels.
6:15	2. God is the blessed and only Ruler	Paul referred to the blessed God in 1 Timothy 1:11. There is no other Ruler in the _____ except God.
6:15	3. God is the King of kings and Lord of lords.	God is the absolute Sovereign over all other _____. These titles are also used of Christ (Rev. 17:17; 19:16).
6:16	4. God alone possesses immortality (NASB).	The Greek word translated immortality (*a-thanasia*) occurs only three times in the New Testament and means "no death." Paul says believers will put on immortality at the _____ (1 Cor. 15:53-54). We will share God's immortality, but only He owns it.[38]
6:16	5. God lives in light that no one dares to approach.	The verse refers to Psalm 104:2. If God reveals Himself in all His glory, He would make the noon day _____ look like a weak flashlight.
6:16	6. God cannot be fully seen by mere humans.	This verse reflects Exodus 33:20. It is not possible for those in human _____ to fully see God and survive the encounter.
6:16	7. God alone deserves honor and might forever. Amen.	God alone deserves our _____ as the Almighty Ruler of eternity. The word *Amen* ends Paul's _____. Compare Romans 11:33-36.

Figure 4.23   Statements about God in the doxology of 1 Timothy 6:15-16[39]

D. The rich should use their wealth wisely (1 Tim. 6:17-19).

Q 99 ➚ *What contrast does Paul use, as he gives commands for the rich?*

The doxology exalts God. It helps us see Him high and lifted up as the only Ruler and King of the universe (1 Tim. 6:15-16). Then Paul surprises us. After he has burst forth with such glorious praise, we do not expect him to return to commands or warnings related to the problems at Ephesus.

But note the connecting phrase *"in this present world"* (1 Tim. 6:17). Paul has just said that God, in His own time, will bring about the appearing of Jesus Christ (1 Tim. 6:15). Thus Paul lifts our eyes from life on earth, to the future *eschaton* or age. And the apostle takes us up even higher to worship the blessed and only Ruler, King of kings and Lord of lords, who alone has immortality, and dwells in the light that no one dares approach (1 Tim. 6:15-16). Then Paul uses this **great contrast** to close his letter. So be aware of this contrast between the future age and the present world as you read Paul's commands for the rich.

*Command those who are rich **in this present world** not to be arrogant nor to put their hope in wealth, which is so uncertain, but to put their hope in God, who richly provides us with everything for our enjoyment* (1 Tim. 6:17).

Q 100 ➚ *To what does Proverbs compare riches?*

Q 101 ➘ *How can riches disappear?*

Paul wants Timothy to warn the rich against pride and false hope. His words about the uncertainty of riches remind us of verses in Proverbs.

[4]*Do not wear yourself out to get rich; have the wisdom to show restraint.* [5]*Cast but a glance at riches, and they are gone, for they will surely sprout wings and fly off to the sky like an eagle* (Prov. 23:4-5).

Wealth is like the morning mist—it can evaporate in a moment. Fire can destroy riches. Thieves can break in and steal our money. Economies crash. Businesses fail. Money can be here today and gone tomorrow. In contrast, those who hope in God are building on the solid rock of certainty.

Instead of strutting about wealth or depending on it, Paul urges:

[18]*Command them to do good, to be rich in good deeds, and to be generous and willing to share.* [19]*In this way they will lay up treasure for themselves as a **firm foundation for the coming age**, so that they may take hold of the life that is truly life* (1 Tim. 6:18-19).

Again, note Paul's contrast between the coming age and the present. So let us be wise stewards over the wealth God entrusts us to manage for Him. For as we are rich in good deeds and generous in sharing, we are sending our treasure ahead *for ourselves,* and building on a firm foundation ***for the coming age*** (1 Tim. 6:18-19).

There is an old story about a rich man and his servant. The wealthy man was a believer, but he spent most of his money on himself. In contrast, the poor servant was faithful to tithe, and generous to share the little he had with those who had less. At the Resurrection, these two believers went to heaven at the same time. An angel escorted them to two mansions—a large one and a small one—saying, "Here are your homes for eternity." Both the rich master and the poor servant were surprised at what happened next. As the poor man started toward the smaller house, the angel stopped him and said, "Excuse me, the larger house is yours, and the smaller one belongs to the brother who was rich on earth. We built each of you all we could with the treasure you sent on ahead, as you invested on earth in God's work and those in need."

Q 102 ⟍ *Why were the rich man and poor servant both surprised in heaven? Explain.*

Conclusion. Guard what God has entrusted to your care—the faith of the church (1 Tim. 6:20-21).

Q 103 ⟍ *Which 2 things does Paul warn against in 1 Timothy 6:17?*

> ²⁰*Timothy, guard what has been entrusted to your care. [How?] Turn away from godless chatter and the opposing ideas of what is falsely called knowledge,* ²¹*which some have professed and in so doing have wandered from the faith. Grace be with you* (1 Tim. 6:20-21).

Q 104 ⟍ *Why is it unwise to trust in wealth?*

In conclusion, Paul commands Timothy to guard the gospel and the sheep God has entrusted to him. In contrast to the Scriptures we see what is *"falsely called knowledge"* (1 Tim. 6:20). The Bible gives us the true knowledge we need for salvation and an eternal relationship with God. In contrast, there are always godless teachers on earth who ridicule our faith, and trust their eternal souls to the teachings of faithless men and women. Earth makes much out of higher education, and in the making of books there is no end. (Studies can be helpful. But Sabio warns: Do not get more education than you can recover from.) Refuse to sit at the feet of infidels, who are like pigs that trample the pearls of your faith in the mud.

Q 105 ⟍ *What is an example of false knowledge?*

Higher education has robbed many of their faith. Some professors delight to ridicule younger students who continue to believe the Word of God. Some professors have learned so much that they no longer believe in the deity of Christ, the resurrection of the dead, heaven, or hell. They stop praying. They quit reading the Bible. Yet we often find these faithless professors teaching in universities and seminaries. Blessed are those who guard the Scriptures that God has entrusted to us, and turn away from the foolishness of teachers who claim to know more than God Almighty. Jesus promised us that even the smallest portions of Scripture will not pass away until all is fulfilled. And in the end, we will see that the Word of God is like an iron anvil, that wears out every hammer that pounds on it. For as Jesus promised, *"Heaven and earth will pass away, but my words will never pass away"* (Matt. 24:35). Guard your faith and your Bible. Put your trust in God and His Word, and you will never be ashamed for all of eternity.

Q 106 ⟍ *How has higher education robbed many of their faith?*

Test Yourself: Circle the letter by the *best* completion to each question or statement.

1. A characteristic of a faithful leader is
a) being known for outstanding preaching.
b) teaching balance between extreme doctrines.
c) having at least three spiritual gifts.
d) being able to win debates with unbelievers.

2. Which areas of character does Paul emphasize for church leaders?
a) Dress and cleanliness
b) Preaching and honesty
c) Speech and purity
d) Faith and administration

3. Paul gives how many lists of spiritual gifts?
a) 1
b) 2
c) 3
d) 4

4. Who has the main responsibility for elderly widows in the church?
a) The church
b) The government
c) Family members
d) Widows themselves

5. A TRUE statement about temptation is:
a) The spiritual are not tempted.
b) Even the most spiritual are tempted.
c) Jesus is the only person who was not tempted.
d) Thinking an evil thought is a sin.

6. The steps down to adultery are
a) few and big.
b) rough and steep.
c) unseen and unknown.
d) many and small.

7. What is a good strategy for correcting an elder who sins?
a) Seek the counsel of an older pastor or elder.
b) Meet with the sinning elder privately.
c) Confront the elder with some other elders.
d) Show the elder Scriptures that shed light.

8. To what does double honor refer?
a) Respect and recognition
b) Respect and financial help
c) Public praise two times
d) Double pay

9. How should a believer work for another believer?
a) Work the same as for an unbeliever
b) Work hardest when being watched
c) Work well and fellowship often
d) Work harder than for an unbeliever

10. What type of contrast does Paul make about money?
a) Eschatological
b) Sociological
c) Educational
d) Occupational

 Essay Test Topics: Write 50-100 words on each of these goals that you studied in this chapter (6 points each plus 10 free). Try to complete your writing in two hours.

- Explain a balanced position between eternal insecurity and eternal security.
- Identify 2 false teachings a faithful pastor should warn about where you live.
- Identify 3 ways a leader models good behavior. Give illustrations.
- Explain ways a leader can help believers identify and use their spiritual gifts.
- Explain 4 criteria of caring for older widows: need, family, age, character (1 Tim. 5).
- Analyze the problem and solution for younger widows at Ephesus. Apply this.
- Explain and apply each of the 11 principles to protect your family from sexual sins.
- Summarize ways to treat elderly believers as fathers.
- Explain how and when to show double honor to an elder.
- Summarize guidelines for disciplining an elder who sins.
- Analyze the problem and solution for favoritism.
- Summarize Paul's attitudes and values for employees and employers.
- Identify preachers in your region who use religion as a business.
- Summarize the keys to being a faithful minister (1 Tim. 6).
- Relate the wise use of riches in the present world to the next age (1 Tim. 6:17-19).

Unit 3:
The Pastoral Letters (Titus and Second Timothy)

Like Timothy, Titus was Paul's son in the faith, and a young man Paul mentored. A part of Paul's calling was to travel as a missionary to new regions, evangelize, and plant new churches. Paul never stayed anywhere for more than a couple of years (Acts 18:11; 19:10). But the churches with new believers needed deacons, house pastors, and overseers—like Titus and Timothy. Indeed, the life and success of young churches depended on overseers such as Crescens, Mark, Trophimus, Titus, and Timothy (2 Tim. 4:9-13).

As you read the letters to Titus and Timothy, think about what life was like for Paul, and these overseers. The apostle had given his life to spread the gospel and plant new churches. He spent many hours mentoring younger men, to help supervise and guide the young churches. As Jesus left everything in the hands of His apostles, Paul left his life's work in the hands of leaders like Titus and Timothy. Keep this in mind as you study the Pastoral Epistles.

In Chapter 5, Titus 1–3, you will discover how to:
* *Explain key words and phrases of the introduction to Titus.*
* *Contrast characteristics of false teachers at Crete, with characteristics of godly leaders.*
* *Explain ways for a pastor to overcome false teaching.*
* *Analyze the relationship of godly behavior to the gospel in Titus 2:1-14.*
* *Summarize how grace brings salvation, and enables holy living.*
* *Analyze the past, present, and future aspects of salvation in Titus.*

In Chapter 6, Second Timothy 1–4, you will study Paul's final letter, and learn to:
* *Analyze the setting of 2 Timothy, including circumstances and challenges.*
* *Explain and illustrate how we encourage ourselves through relationships with believers and the Father, Son, and Spirit.*
* *List advantages of training and involving others in ministry.*
* *Summarize five examples Paul uses in 2 Timothy 2 to motivate believers.*
* *Explain how God is faithful to Himself in dealing with saints and sinners.*
* *Explain the context of two types of vessels in 2 Timothy 2, and contrast these on four topics.*
* *Define inspiration, inerrancy, and infallibility, and explain how belief in these guides us.*
* *Analyze why pastors must preach the Word, and explain four guidelines for preaching it.*
* *Summarize and apply Paul's attitudes toward persecutors, deserters, unmet expectations, and God.*

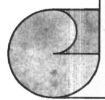

Chapter 5:
Live in the Light of What Grace Teaches
(Titus 1–3)

Figure 5.1 Map showing places where Titus ministered (Jerusalem, Crete, Corinth, Dalmatia)

Theme	Titus
Greeting	1:1-4
A. Instructions About Appointing Elders	1:5-9
B. Instructions About False Teachers	1:10-16
C. Instructions About Various Groups in the Churches	2
Teachings for each group	2:1-10
Lessons from grace	2:11-15
D. Instructions on Godly Living	3
Our relationship with all others	3:1-2
The reason for holy living	3:3-7
Discern between the profitable and unprofitable.	3:8-11
Conclusion	3:12-15

Figure 5.2 Outline of Titus

Q 1 *How many letters did Paul write? Which letters are the Pastoral Epistles?*

Background of Titus.   Review Figure 3.1. Paul called Titus *"my true son in our common faith"* (Titus 1:4). Titus was a Greek, likely from Antioch in Syria. He went with Paul and Barnabas as they traveled from Antioch to Jerusalem—to discuss Paul's ministry to the Gentiles (Gal. 2:1-3).

Titus was a Gentile. He became a follower of Christ without Jewish circumcision. Titus is an example of being saved through faith in Christ, without obeying the ceremonial laws of Moses (Gal. 2:15-16).

Q 2 *What makes us think Titus was tactful and diplomatic?*

Titus is not mentioned by name in the book of Acts. But his name appears 13 times in Paul's letters. He worked closely with Paul. We believe Titus was a man of unusual tact and ability—because Paul sent him to churches where there were big problems.[1] His name appears often in 2 Corinthians (2 Cor. 2:13; 7:6, 13-14; 8:6, 23). Paul was happy when writing 2 Corinthians. Why? Titus had just returned from Corinth with a good report. Titus must have done well in taking care of the problems there (2 Cor. 7:6-10, 13-16). Titus had also checked on the offering that the Corinthians promised to send to Jerusalem believers. His name appears for the last time in 2 Timothy 4:10. There we learn that Titus had gone to *Dalmatia—modern Yugoslavia, Bosnia, Herzegovina, and Croatia. Paul often sent others where he could not go.

Q 3 *Why did Paul want Titus in Crete?*

Purpose of writing to Titus.   After Paul's first release from prison in Rome, it appears that he and Titus went to *Crete (2 Tim. 4:16-17). Crete is the largest island in the Mediterranean Sea, and is straight south of the Aegean Sea. There, they started churches in many towns. Paul continued on to Macedonia by way of Ephesus. He left Titus at Crete to *"straighten out what was left unfinished"* (Titus 1:5). Later, about A.D. 65, Paul wrote for at least three reasons:

- To give Titus apostolic authority and guidance to deal with opposition;
- To give instructions about faith and conduct;
- To give warnings about false teachers (Titus 1:5; 2:1, 7-8, 15; 3:9).

Lessons:

Silence False Teachers (Titus 1:1-16)
Goal A: *Explain key words and phrases of the introduction to Titus.*
Goal B: *Summarize 6 characteristics of the false teachers at Crete.*
Goal C: *Summarize at least 6 characteristics of godly leaders.*
Goal D: *Explain 3 ways for a pastor to overcome false teaching.*

Teach the A, B, C's of Grace (Titus 2:1-15)
Goal A: *Analyze the relationship of godly behavior to the gospel in Titus 2:1-14.*
Goal B: *Contrast man's attempts to please God, and the salvation that only God's grace offers.*
Goal C: *Contrast the lifestyles of those who pass and those who fail under Professor Grace.*

Discern the Past, Present, and Future Aspects of Salvation (Titus 3:1-15)
Goal A: *Analyze whether some deserve God's grace more than others.*
Goal B: *Explain Paul's "so that" aspect of salvation—the present.*
Goal C: *Explain whether the greatest part of salvation is past, present, or future.*

 Key Words

Crete—the largest island in the Mediterranean Sea, straight south of the Aegean Sea. After Paul's first release from prison in Rome, he and Titus started a church in Crete. Paul left Titus to oversee the work there.

grace—the free, kind, and generous ways God relates to people. In Titus 2, Paul does not define grace but compares grace to a teacher from God.

Silence False Teachers (Titus 1:1-16)
Lesson 23

Goal A: *Explain key words and phrases of the introduction to Titus.*
Goal B: *Summarize 6 characteristics of the false teachers at Crete.*
Goal C: *Summarize at least 6 characteristics of godly leaders.*
Goal D: *Explain 2 ways to overcome false teaching.*

Introduction (Titus 1:1-4)

> ¹ ***Paul, a servant of God** and **an apostle of Jesus Christ** for **the faith of God's elect** and the **knowledge of the truth that leads to godliness**—² a faith and knowledge resting on **the hope of eternal life**, which **God, who does not lie, promised before the beginning of time**, ³ and **at his appointed season** he brought his word to light through the preaching entrusted to me **by the command of God our Savior**, ⁴ **To Titus, my true son in our common faith*** (Titus 1:1-4).

As we begin this lesson, let us look at key words and phrases in the introduction of Paul's letter to Titus.

Q 4 ✎ *Complete Figure 5.3 as you read the explanations below it.*

Word or Phrase	Questions to Answer on the Introduction to Titus
Paul, a servant of God and an apostle of Jesus Christ	Why does Paul mention his relationship to God and Christ?
God's elect	How does a person get chosen or elected to God's family?
Truth that leads to godliness	To what does the truth of the gospel lead in daily living?
Hope of eternal life	Do we have eternal life now or later?
God... promised before the beginning of time	When did God plan to save us?
Preaching entrusted... by the command of God	Why does Paul stress his calling and authority from God?
Titus, my true son	Why does Paul refer to Titus as his true son in the faith?

Figure 5.3   Practice explaining key words and phrases in Paul's introduction to Titus (Titus 1:1-4).

"Paul, a servant of God and an apostle of Jesus Christ..." As *a servant* Paul was under the authority of God. And as an *apostle* Paul was *sent* by Jesus Christ to establish the Church. By mentioning his relationship to God and Christ, Paul is underlining the authority he has to guide and manage the Church. As we will see, Paul and Titus must use this authority in the church at Crete.

"For the faith of God's elect..." Paul was a servant and an apostle to impart and strengthen *faith* in God's people—the *elect. Elect* comes from the Greek word *elektos*—which means "chosen." Some twist *election* and claim that God chooses those who <u>can</u> be saved. But God commanded Christians to take the gospel to all people (Matt. 28:19; Mark 16:15-16). God wants all to be saved (1 Tim. 2:4). God offers salvation to everyone. But each person chooses to accept or reject this offer. All who accept Jesus as Savior become part of God's elect, chosen people (1 Pet. 1:1-5).

"For... the knowledge of the truth that leads to godliness." As a servant and apostle, Paul preached and taught the faith—the gospel message. At the heart of our faith is the knowledge of the truth that leads to godliness. Note: Paul uses the words *faith, truth,* and *gospel* as synonyms—words that mean the same thing. The knowledge of truth is not just for the head. Rather, *gospel truth* changes a life from ungodliness to godliness (Titus 1:1; 2:12). Over and over in Titus, Paul will emphasize that following Jesus means turning from wickedness to do good deeds.

"The hope of eternal life..." (Titus 1:2). The hope and goal of our faith, knowledge, and godly living is eternal life. As we accept Jesus as Savior and Lord, <u>a hope is born within us</u>. This hope and firm belief is in eternal life. We begin to share God's eternal life as we become <u>His children.</u> And we <u>will fully inherit eternal life when Jesus returns for us.</u>

"God, who does not lie, promised before the beginning of time..." (Titus 1:2). Our <u>faith, knowledge, and hope rest</u> on a firm foundation—the <u>promise of God Himself.</u> The Cretans were famous for lying, so their word was not trustworthy. In contrast, God *"does not lie"* (Titus 1:2; Num. 23:19; <u>Heb. 6:18</u>). Paul's <u>main point is that the</u> <u>gospel promises that we are receiving were part of God's eternal plan—even before the beginning</u> of earth and time. God <u>planned to save us, even before</u> He created us (See 1 Cor. 2:7-10; 2 Tim. 1:9; Eph. 1:4).[2]

"At his appointed season he brought his word to light through the preaching entrusted to me by the command of God our Savior" (Titus 1:3). God sends His eternal promises to us through the preaching of the gospel. Paul stresses his <u>authority as God's servant and apostle, and that he is under God's command.</u> He is an apostle under authority, with authority to deal with the problems at Crete. Paul is a man under <u>God's command.</u> And in this official letter to Titus, Paul gives Titus commands for guiding the church in Crete.

"To Titus, my true son in our common faith:" (Titus 1:4). This reference Paul uses endorses Titus, and empowers him to minister with the authority of the apostle Paul.

We have looked at key words and phrases in the introduction to Titus. Now let us examine the challenges Titus faced at Crete.

Paul left Titus at Crete to *"straighten out what was left unfinished."* Titus needed to finish the ministry that they had begun by organizing churches and appointing elders, also called pastors (Titus 1:5).[3] Titus faced some big challenges in this task.

A. The Problem: False teachers at Crete were ruining the faith of whole families (Titus 1:10-16).

[10] *For there are many rebellious people, mere talkers and deceivers, especially those of the circumcision group.* [11] *They must be silenced, because they are ruining whole households by teaching things they ought not to teach—and that for the sake of dishonest gain.* [12] *Even one of their own prophets has said, "Cretans are always liars, evil brutes, lazy*

Figure 5.4   Our great God and Savior who gives us grace to be holy
Photo: Knossos Palace on the island of Crete. Paul left Titus at Crete to direct the church (Titus 1:5).

gluttons." [13]*This testimony is true. Therefore rebuke them sharply, so that they will be sound in the faith* [14]*and will pay no attention to Jewish myths or to the merely human commands of those who reject the truth.* [15]*To the pure, all things are pure, but to those who are corrupted and do not believe, nothing is pure. In fact, both their minds and consciences are corrupted.* [16]*They claim to know God, but by their actions they deny him. They are detestable, disobedient and unfit for doing anything good* (Titus 1:10-16).

Do my actions deny Jesus?

Note how Paul describes the character of the false teachers at Crete:

- **Rebellious:** They were rebels who rejected the truth of the gospel (Titus 1:10, 14). They rebelled against the authority of Paul (God's command, and Jesus who sent Paul as an apostle).

- **Deceitful:** They were *"talkers and deceivers"* (Titus 1:10). They had been deceived (2 Tim. 3:13). Then their meaningless talk deceived others.

- **Legalistic/humanistic:** They were Jewish legalists (Titus 1:10, 14). We know that they were Jews because they were *"of the circumcision group"* (Titus 1:10). We know that they were legalists because they taught *Jewish myths* and *mere human commands* (Titus 1:14). They were like those in 1 Timothy (1 Tim. 4:3), who taught that the simple story of Jesus was not enough for salvation. They believed that Christians needed to add the rules and regulations of the Jews (Compare Matt. 15:1-20).

- **Greedy:** Their main goal was dishonest money. *"They are ruining whole households by teaching things they ought not to teach—and that for the sake of dishonest gain"* (Titus 1:11).

- **Corrupt:** Their minds and consciences were corrupt (Titus 1:15). They looked good on the outside, but were dirty on the inside. They taught false doctrine and lived false lives. Their corrupt consciences did not convict them of sin (1 Tim. 4:2).

- **Disobedient:** Although they claimed to know Jesus, their actions denied Him (Titus 1:16). They obeyed human commands, but disobeyed God Himself.

- **Unfit:** They were *"detestable, disobedient, and unfit for doing anything good"* (Titus 1:16). The word *"unfit"* comes from a Greek word *adikimoi*. It describes something that was tested and then rejected. [4]

Q 5 *Complete Figure 5.5, summarizing what Paul says about false teachers at Crete.*

Characteristic	Your Summary	Titus
Rebellious		1:10, 14
Deceptive		1:10
Legalistic		1:10, 14
Greedy		1:11
Corrupt		1:15
Disobedient		1:16
Unfit		1:16

Figure 5.5   Practice describing the false teachers at Crete (Titus 1).

What was the result of these false teachers? Paul said that they were ruining entire families (Titus 1:11). In that day, much of the teaching took places in people's homes. False teachers led *"whole households"* (families) into error. [5] And the main reason was to gain money (Titus 1:11)! False teachers tried to lead believers astray to rob them of their money.

The people of Crete had a reputation for being untruthful and greedy. [6] Paul quoted Epimenides, who was a famous writer from Crete. Epimenides was probably not a Christian, but local people accepted him as some sort of prophet. So referring to Epimenides, Paul wrote: *"Even one of their own prophets has said, 'Cretans are always liars, evil brutes, lazy gluttons'"* (Titus 1:12). Society at Crete was corrupt. And the

Q 6 *What type of reputation did the people of Crete have?*

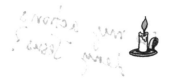

false teachers reflected their society. God's people should reveal their relationship with Him through their behavior. The false teachers claimed to know God, but they denied God through their actions (Titus 1:16).

How can you tell the difference between a live fish and a dead fish? The live fish swims into the current. The dead fish just floats with the current. Likewise, those dead in sin just float along with the values of a corrupt society.

B. The Solutions: Two ways to overcome false teachings (Titus 1:5-16)

1. Appoint godly elders to lead the house churches (Titus 1:5-9).

[5]The reason I left you in Crete was that you might straighten out what was left unfinished and appoint elders in every town, as I directed you. [6]An elder must be blameless, the husband of but one wife, a man whose children believe and are not open to the charge of being wild and disobedient. [7]Since an overseer is entrusted with God's work, he must be blameless—not overbearing, not quick-tempered, not given to drunkenness, not violent, not pursuing dishonest gain. [8]Rather he must be hospitable, one who loves what is good, who is self-controlled, upright, holy and disciplined. [9]He must hold firmly to the trustworthy message as it has been taught, so that he can encourage others by sound doctrine and refute those who oppose it (Titus 1:5-9).

Titus' main task was to appoint godly elders (pastors) to lead the churches. These leaders needed to be men whose lives supported their claims to know God (Titus 1:16). But, how was Titus to recognize a godly leader? Paul's instructions reveal three keys for recognizing those who can help lead the church.

Godly leaders in the church are first good leaders in their homes (Titus 1:6). A man's home life reveals a lot about his character and ability to lead a church.[7] Paul wrote that potential leaders needed to be *"blameless"* in the home (Titus 1:6). *"Blameless"* means "above reproach." Godly leaders are people against whom it is impossible to bring a true charge of doing wrong.[8] Future pastors need to be men who are faithful to their wives (*husband of one wife*). Their lives need to be real enough for their children to follow them in the faith. They need to be *"blameless"* in their homes because they are *"entrusted with God's work,"* (Titus 1:7). If a man cannot lead his own household, how can he care for God's household?[9]

Godly leaders display godly character. Paul gave Timothy a list of five ungodly character traits to avoid (Titus 1:7). He followed with a list of six positive character traits that point to godliness. Those lists are in the two charts that follow this section. We covered these in 1 Timothy 3, and list them here to review.

Q 7 *Examine yourself. Which of the characteristics in Titus 1:7-8 do you fulfill?*

	Characteristics	Explanations
Avoid	*Not overbearing—arrogant or self-willed*	Insists on his (or her) own way.
	Not quick-tempered—not soon angry	Hot-headed leaders destroy churches.
	Not given to drunkenness	Not known for drinking.
	Not violent	Unable to control their emotions or tempers.
	Not pursuing dishonest gain	Not greedy. Church leaders must be honest.
Pursue	*Hospitable*	Godly people care about strangers.
	Loves what is good	Ungodly leaders often value money or position more than people. The godly love those things and characteristics that are truly good.
	Self-controlled—sound-minded	In control of thoughts and desires
	Upright—righteous, just	Godly people act "right" in their relationships with other people.
	Holy.	Godly people live "right" in their relationship with God.
	Disciplined	They keep their bodies and mind under control as they submit to the Holy Spirit (2 Tim. 1:7; Gal. 5:23).

Figure 5.6   Characteristics for leaders to avoid and pursue (Titus 1:7-8)

Godly leaders <u>cling to the truth</u>, even when they face opposition.[10] *They <u>"hold firmly to the trustworthy message"</u>* (Titus 1:9). This enables them to *encourage* those who follow the truth (1 Tim. 4:13; 5:1; 6:2); and *refute* those who oppose the truth (1 Tim. 5:20; 2 Tim. 3:16; 4:2; Titus 1:9).

Pastor Jim was the supervisor for six summers at a camp for students. Under Jim was Benny, leading the youth, who were 13 to 18 years old. Benny had many of the qualities of a leader, but lacked maturity. His greatest weakness was playing jokes on others. Once he put extra salt on the students' food. Many of the students spit out the food and could not eat it. Somehow, Benny thought this was funny.

Pastor Jim asked Benny to come to his office the next day for a little talk. There was a long, awkward silence as the Pastor leaned back in his chair and looked up at the ceiling. There were tears in his eyes. Then he whispered, "Benny," with tenderness. "Benny," he said a second time, when he got control of his emotions and could talk without crying..

> BENNY'S DEFENSES MELTED IN THE PRESENCE OF A LOVING, MATURE MENTOR.

Q 8 *How did Pastor Jim help Benny? Apply this.*

Benny's defenses melted in the presence of a loving, mature mentor. The young leader realized that his foolishness was not a characteristic of a mature leader. His actions did not even pass the test of the Golden Rule. Benny owed the students an apology. Pastor Jim and Benny talked about the need for self-control, being a good example, and showing concern for the students. They talked about the meaning of love in God's family, and the responsibilities that come with leadership. In speaking truth to Benny, Jim was always gracious. His goal was not to tear down but to build up. Just being around Pastor Jim made Benny want to be a leader like him.[11]

2. Emphasize that purity comes through Christ, not by paying attention to myths, or keeping rules (Titus 1:10-16).

[10]*For there are many rebellious people, mere talkers and deceivers, **especially those of the circumcision group**.* [11]*They must be silenced, because they are ruining whole households by teaching things they ought not to teach—and that for the sake of dishonest gain.* [12]*Even one of their own prophets has said, "Cretans are always liars, evil brutes, lazy gluttons."* [13]*This testimony is true. Therefore, rebuke them sharply, so that they will be sound in the faith* [14]*and will pay no attention to **Jewish myths** or to the commands of those who reject the truth.* [15]*To the pure, all things are pure, but to those who are corrupted and do not believe, nothing is pure. In fact, both their minds and consciences are corrupted.* [16]*They claim to know God, but by their actions they deny him. They are detestable, disobedient and unfit for doing anything good* (Titus 1:10-16).

Titus could not ignore the false teachers. They were ruining the faith of entire families (Titus 1:11) So Paul told Titus to rebuke these deceivers (Titus 1:13). Paul compared the false teachers to *"evil brutes"* (Titus 1:12-13). People tie or muzzle fierce dogs to stop them from harming others. These false teachers bullied, damaged, and took advantage of others. Paul told Titus to *"rebuke them sharply"* (Titus 1:13). But as he did so, he needed to remember his purpose. His purpose was to correct them, not to destroy them. He was to correct them so that they would *"be sound in the faith"* (Titus 1:13) and turn away from Jewish myths and the commands of the rebels who rejected the truth (Titus 1:14).

Q 9 *Why must a pastor confront and correct false teachings?*

Paul was correcting false teachers. They taught that the way to spiritual purity was obedience to Jewish food laws. Paul reminded Titus that what people eat cannot make them impure. All food is pure to those who are pure, because faith in Jesus purifies it (1 Tim. 4:3; Col. 2:21; Matt. 15:1-20). In contrast, nothing is pure to corrupt unbelievers.

Q 10 *In your culture, do false teachers say that we are saved by avoiding marriage or certain foods?*

Sinners in Crete could not become pure through obeying rules about food. Their problem was on the inside. Their minds and consciences were corrupt (Titus 1:15). They claimed to be God's people, but denied Him through their actions (Titus 1:16). They obeyed human commands but disobeyed God's laws about holy living. They were useless—like a counterfeit coin that looks good at first glance, but has no real value. When Jesus purifies our hearts, we begin to have a pure outlook on life (Titus 2:14).

Q 11 *What counsel would you give this couple?*

 A man and woman met at church and began an immoral relationship. When the pastor corrected them, they said their behavior was not sin, because Jesus had purified their desires for each other.

Q 12 *Complete Figure 5.7, showing that salvation is from the inside out.*

Reference	Your Summaries About Those Seeking Salvation Through Human Rules Instead of Through Christ
Matt. 15:16-20	
Col. 2:21	
1 Tim. 4:3	

Figure 5.7   Practice showing that salvation is from the inside out, not the outside in.

Figure 5.8a   The vulture saw a dead animal.   Figure 5.8b   The honey bee saw a flower.
Likewise, people see what they look for.

Q 13 *Why did the bee and the vulture see different things?*

A honeybee and a vulture flew over the same field. The vulture saw the rotting body of a dead animal, because that is what he was looking for. But the bee ignored the smelly flesh of dead animals. He saw the flowers that enabled him to make honey. Vultures live on what is dead. Bees live on what is and what can be. Bees and vultures find what they look for, and so do we. If we trust in Jesus Christ for salvation, foods do not look impure to us. But if we hope to be saved by avoiding foods, such as pork, we miss the message of the gospel, and waste time examining foods on the menu.

In Titus 2, Paul will emphasize that we do not save ourselves *by* following human rules. Rather, salvation is seen in living holy, godly lives, *after* Jesus saves us from sin.

Lesson 24   **Teach the A, B, C's of Grace (Titus 2:1-15)**
Goal A: *Analyze the relationship of godly behavior to the gospel in Titus 2:1-14.*
Goal B: *Contrast man's attempts to please God, and the salvation that only God's grace offers.*
Goal C: *Contrast the lifestyles of those who pass and those who fail under Professor Grace.*

Q 14 *Do you think Crete was more ungodly than where you live? Explain.*

Overview: The relationship of godly behavior to the gospel in Titus 2:1-14

Recall that Paul left Pastor Titus on the island of Crete in the Mediterranean Sea. The ministry of Titus was *"to straighten out what was left unfinished, and appoint elders in every town"* (Titus 1:5). The people of Crete did not have a good reputation. They were known for being sinful. *"Even one of their own prophets has said, 'Cretans are always liars, evil brutes, lazy gluttons.' This testimony is true"* (Titus 1:12-13). Some societies are more sinful than others. But without Christ, all of us are slaves of sin. We all need the Savior to free us from sin, and strengthen us to live right. Even on the island of Crete, Jesus, through the gospel of grace, delivered sinners from the stains and chains of sin.

Most of the teachings in Titus 2:1-10 are on the same topics Paul wrote in his first letter to Timothy. For example, Paul tells Titus how to relate to **five groups in the church:** older men, older women, younger women, younger men, and slaves. Paul mentions children in Titus 2:4, and elsewhere the apostle gives guidelines for the group of youth and children (Eph. 6:1-4). **Pastor, remind yourself often that ministry is mostly about relating to people and groups of people.** Paul's instructions to Timothy and Titus are very similar for relating to these five groups. Toward the end of this lesson, we will take a closer look at the instructions Paul gives Titus for these five groups. But here, we want to call attention to one point that Paul emphasizes three times in Titus 2:1-10. You will discover the point as you complete Figure 5.9.

Q 15 ⤴ *What is the main ministry of a pastor? Explain.*

Q 16 ⤴ *To which 5 groups does Paul instruct Titus about relating (Titus 2:1-10)?*

Q 17 ⤵ *What is Paul's main reason for emphasizing godly behavior among five groups of believers?*

Q 18 ⤵ *Complete Figure 5.9, summarizing reasons why Paul commanded godly behavior.*

Titus 2	Groups to Whom Paul Writes Instructions for Godly Behavior	Reason for Godly Behavior	Summaries, in YOUR Words, of Why Paul Commanded Godly Behavior
2:1-5	Older men, older women, younger women	So that	
2:6-8	Younger men	So that	
2:9-10	Slaves	So that	

Figure 5.9   Practice analyzing why Paul commanded godly behavior for five groups in the church.

[1] **You must teach** *what is in accord with sound doctrine.* [2] **Teach** *the **older men** to be temperate, worthy of respect, self-controlled, and sound in faith, in love and in endurance.* [3] *Likewise,* **teach** *the **older women** to be reverent in the way they live, not to be slanderers or addicted to much wine, but to teach what is good.* [4] *Then they can* **train** *the **younger women** to love their husbands and children,* [5] *to be self-controlled and pure, to be busy at home, to be kind, and to be subject to their husbands,* so that no one will malign the word of God *(Titus 2:1-5).*

[6] *Similarly,* **encourage** *the **young men** to be self-controlled.* [7] *In everything* **set them an example by doing what is good. In your teaching** *show integrity, seriousness* [8] *and soundness of speech that cannot be condemned,* so that those who oppose you may be ashamed because they have nothing bad to say about us *(Titus 2:6-8).*

[9] **Teach slaves** *to be subject to their masters in everything, to try to please them, not to talk back to them,* [10] *and not to steal from them, but to show that they can be fully trusted,* so that in every way they will make the teaching about God our Savior attractive *(Titus 2:9-10).*

Faithful believers are like sheep, who follow their shepherd. They seek to obey and practice what their pastor preaches. If he preaches godly standards *above* them, they will seek to improve and become better. But if he preaches standards below them, they will relax and lower their standards. As an old proverb states: "A pastor gets what he preaches." Faithful believers will either live up to or *down to* what their pastor preaches. So Paul begins this chapter with the words: *"**You must teach** what is in accord with sound doctrine"* (Titus 2:1). If a pastor tells believers they are still sinners, they will act like it. But if he teaches, as the Bible says, that we were once sinners, but have been saved from sinning, then his church members will live as God's people. And when the five groups of believers in the church live godly lives, this gives the gospel and the church a good reputation, and an effective witness to the community. The way church members live is the loudest and clearest sermon people in the community will ever hear.

Q 19 ⤵ *Explain: Faithful believers will either live up to or down to what their pastor preaches.*

Q 20 *In what sense do church members preach every day?*

Q 21 *Based on the behavior of believers in your church, what do outsiders think of the gospel?*

Q 22 *Why does Paul begin Titus 2:11 with the word "For"?*

The message of the gospel rises or falls on the behavior of church members. Paul told believers in Corinth that they were **an open letter from Christ to the lost people of Corinth**—a letter from Christ written not on a stone tablet, but written on human hearts:

> [2] *You yourselves are our letter, written on our hearts, known and read by everybody.* [3] *You show that you are a letter from Christ, the result of our ministry, written not with ink but with the Spirit of the living God, not on tablets of stone but on tablets of human hearts* (2 Cor. 3:2-3).

> THE MESSAGE OF THE GOSPEL RISES OR FALLS ON THE BEHAVIOR OF CHURCH MEMBERS.

We have reviewed Paul's instructions to five groups of believers in the church. And we have seen him make one point (so that) three times. A theme in Titus 2:1-10 is that those outside the church evaluate the gospel and the church on the basis of how church members behave.

Transition. *Grace refers to the free, kind, and generous ways God relates to people. The Bible presents the ministry of grace in many ways. In this beautiful chapter, Paul does not define grace. Rather, the apostle speaks of *grace* as if it were a person—a teacher from God. The teachings of Professor Grace in Titus 2:11-14 are the foundation of this chapter. The behavior Paul wants from the five groups, is in response to the grace of God that has appeared and taught us (Titus 2:11-14). Paul begins Titus 2:11 with the word *For*—to show that the appearance and teachings of grace are the basis for the behavior he commands in Titus 2:1-10. Please take time to read Titus 2:11-14 five times. Ask the Holy Spirit to open your heart to these amazing verses.

> [11] *For the grace of God that brings salvation has appeared to all men.* [12] *It teaches us to say "No" to ungodliness and worldly passions, and to live self-controlled, upright and godly lives in this present age,* [13] *while we wait for the blessed hope—the glorious appearing of our great God and Savior, Jesus Christ,* [14] *who gave himself for us to redeem us from all wickedness and to purify for himself a people that are his very own, eager to do what is good* (Titus 2:11-14).

Then we will study the A, B, C's that Professor Grace teaches.

A. Grace alone brings God's offer of salvation to all (Titus 2:11; 3:7).

For the grace of God that brings salvation has appeared to all men (Titus 2:11).

Ponder this beautiful verse of Titus 2:11. What a statement! Paul has urged godly behavior among the five groups because the grace of God that brings salvation has appeared to and for all people. Amazing grace has come. Powerful grace that took us by the hand, forgave our trespasses, and led us away from the foolishness, disobedience, and slavery of sin. In the next chapter, Paul will recall where grace found us, and where grace led us:

Q 23 *What were we like when grace found us?*

> [3] *At one time we too were foolish, disobedient, deceived and enslaved by all kinds of passions and pleasures. We lived in malice and envy, being hated and hating one another.* [4] *But when the kindness and love of God our Savior appeared,* [5] *he saved us, not because of righteous things we had done, but because of his mercy. He saved us through the washing of rebirth and renewal by the Holy Spirit,* [6] *whom he poured out on us generously through Jesus Christ our Savior,* [7] *so that, having been justified by his grace, we might become heirs having the hope of eternal life* (Titus 3:3-7).

Q 24 *What does the Bible say about those who try to save themselves?*

The Problem. Sin separates people from a holy God. Some ignore God and pursue whatever attracts them. But many, all over the world, are aware of their need for God.

They feel a spiritual emptiness inside. They struggle with guilt. So these people try to connect with God. Hindus and Buddhists may torture themselves, or practice forms of self-denial. Some hope to pay for their sins after life on earth, suffering in purgatory, or being reborn (reincarnated) as an animal. Millions of devout Muslims seek to please God through the *five pillars*: *faith* in one God; *praying* five times each day; *fasting*, especially from dawn to dusk in the month of Ramadan; *giving* alms to the poor; and *traveling* to Mecca, at least once in a lifetime. Many, in various religions, seek to make peace with God through sacrifices of money, time, good deeds, animals, or human desires. But the problem is that these humans are trying to please God by their own efforts. We cannot atone for our sins; we cannot save ourselves from our sins. We can never pay for our faults through our good deeds. We cannot build a ladder tall enough to reach heaven. All of our ideas and efforts fall short of salvation. The Bible has bad news for all who hope to be saved by their own efforts. The chances of sinners saving themselves are zero out of eight billion (people).

Q 25 *What are some examples of people trying to save themselves?*

The Solution. God has built the only bridge between heaven and earth. Our Creator saw our problem, loved us, and provided a solution. Since our debt was too big for us to pay, He paid it for us. Through His grace, God offers us forgiveness and deliverance from sin! *Grace* is the undeserved kindness, love, mercy, and favor God extends to us in Christ. God the Father sent His Son, Jesus, *"who gave himself for us to **redeem us from** all wickedness and **to purify for** himself a people that are his very own, eager to do what is good"* (Titus 2:14). Paul emphasizes that it is *"the grace of God that brings salvation"* (Titus 2:11). We are justified—counted righteous—*"by his grace,"* as we receive Jesus by faith as Savior and Lord (Titus 3:7).

Q 26 *What is God's solution by grace for every person?*

Humanity was lost in darkness—*"without hope and without God in the world"* (Eph. 2:12). Then, suddenly, like the dawning of the sun after a stormy night, God's grace appeared.[12] Those who lived in darkness saw a great light (Matt. 4:16). And this gospel light of grace *"appeared to* [or for] *all men"* (Titus 2:11). As the sun shines on all men, God's grace offers freedom and deliverance to *all* people. For *"everyone who calls on the name of the Lord will be saved"* (Rom. 10:13; Acts 2:21). The Lord wants *all* to come to repentance (2 Pet. 3:9).

Paul's personal testimony emphasizes that he was saved by grace:

[12]*I thank Christ Jesus our Lord, who has given me strength, that he considered me faithful, appointing* [even] *me to his service.* [13]*Even though I was once a blasphemer and a persecutor and a violent man, I was shown mercy because I acted in ignorance and unbelief.* [14]***The grace of our Lord was poured out on me abundantly, along with the faith and love that are in Christ Jesus.*** [15]*Here is a trustworthy saying that deserves full acceptance: Christ Jesus came into the world to save sinners—of whom I am the worst.* [16]*But for that very reason I was shown **mercy** so that in me, the worst of sinners, Christ Jesus might display his unlimited **patience** as an example for those who would believe on him and receive eternal life.* [17]*Now to the King eternal, immortal, invisible, the only God, be honor and glory for ever and ever. Amen* (1 Tim. 1:12-17).

Q 27 *According to Paul, was he saved by his works? Explain.*

> SALVATION IS BY GRACE FROM START TO FINISH.

Salvation is by grace from start to finish. It is all by grace or not at all. God sits on a throne of grace (Heb. 4:16). And He offers the gospel of grace (Acts 20:24), through the Spirit of grace (Heb. 10:29; 12:15). We do not deserve God's grace. He did not save us because of anything we have done (2 Tim. 1:9). Yet *"from the fullness of his grace we have all received one blessing after another ... through Jesus Christ"* (John 1:16-17). The obedience and good deeds we do show our response of faith and love to the relationship God freely offers us—as He is our God, and we are His children.

Q 28 *Is salvation by grace + works? Explain.*

Q 29 ➤ *How is the Bible an official invitation from God to meet Him?*

Suppose an official from the government came to you with a letter that had your name and address on it. And the letter invited you to meet the leader of your nation. You would accept it. Likewise, the Bible has come to us through the apostles and prophets, God's official messengers. And the Bible is your invitation to come to Christ. It does not contain your name and address; but it says, *"All,"* which includes you. And the Bible says, *"whoever," "each one," "anyone,"* and *"everyone,"* and all of these include you. What can be surer or freer than an invitation from God, to all who choose to come to Him?"[13]

Q 30 ➤ *Complete Figure 5.10 on the salvation in Christ that God freely offers to all.*

Reference	Your Summaries About the Salvation in Jesus Christ That God Offers by Grace
Matt. 11:28-29	
John 3:18	
Rom. 6:23	
Rom. 10:11	
Rom. 10:13	
Acts 4:12	
1 John 5:12	
Rev. 22:17	

Figure 5.10   Practice summarizing verses that show God offers salvation in Jesus Christ to all by grace.

Q 31 ➤ *How have some misunderstood grace? What is grace like?*

Transition. Grace is wonderful, but many have misunderstood it. Grace is not a blanket we wrap around us, trying in vain to prevent God from seeing our sins. Grace is not a mask we wear to hide who we really are. In Titus 2, Paul likens grace to a teacher (Titus 2:12). If believers are the students, what does Paul say that Professor Grace teaches us?

B. Grace teaches us to say "No" to ungodliness and worldly passions (Titus 2:12).

Q 32 ➤ *What does grace teach those who pass its classes?*

[11]*For the grace of God that brings salvation has appeared to all men.* [12]***It teaches us to say "No" to ungodliness and worldly passions***, *and to live self-controlled, upright and godly lives in this present age,* [13]*while we wait for the blessed hope—the glorious appearing of our great God and Savior, Jesus Christ* (Titus 2:11-13).

The way some describe Professor Grace, we might think this teacher is weak, feeble, fragile, and fearful. Many present Professor Grace as a teacher without backbone, undisciplined, and without a firm will. In contrast to these modern paintings, Professor Grace is bold and powerful—insisting on godly living. Grace is kind, but grace does not tolerate evil. Grace is merciful, but grace requires obedience to God. Grace teaches us to say a loud "NO" to sin—*"No" to ungodliness and worldly passions"* (Titus 2:12)!

Q 33 ➤ *Does Professor Grace teach that believers remain slaves of sin? Explain.*

Some students claim that believers remain slaves of sin on earth. But they have not learned this lesson from Professor Grace. For Professor Grace *"teaches us to say 'No' to ungodliness and worldly passions, and to live self-controlled, upright and godly lives **in this present age**,* [13]*while we wait for the blessed hope—the glorious appearing of our great God and Savior, Jesus Christ"* (Titus 2:12-13).

> PAUL DOES NOT LEAVE US TO GUESS WHAT HE MEANS BY UNGODLINESS AND WORLDLY PASSIONS.

Q 34 ➤ *Complete Figure 5.11 on Paul's explanations of what followers of Jesus overcome and avoid.*

In his letters to the Thessalonians, to Timothy and Titus, and in all his letters, Paul does not leave us to guess what he means by ungodliness and worldly passions. Rather Paul gives specific examples of sins to avoid.

Reference	Your Summaries
1 Thess. 4:3-8	
2 Tim. 2:16	
2 Tim. 3:1-5	
Titus 2:12-13	
1 Cor. 6:9-11	
Gal. 5:19-21	
Eph. 5:5	
Col. 3:5-10	

Figure 5.11   Practice explaining Paul's meaning of *"say 'No' to ungodliness and worldly passions"* (Titus 2:12).

God does not expect students of grace to be perfect. But He expects us to grow in grace. His plan for us is to become like Christ *"more and more"* (1 Thess. 4:1, 10). Paul teaches that we are being changed into the likeness of Christ by the Spirit (2 Cor. 3:18; Eph. 4:24; Rom. 8:29). Adoption into God's family is a gift by grace. But this gift of sonship becomes our assignment and identity. By grace we become God's children. Then, by grace we must behave like God's children.

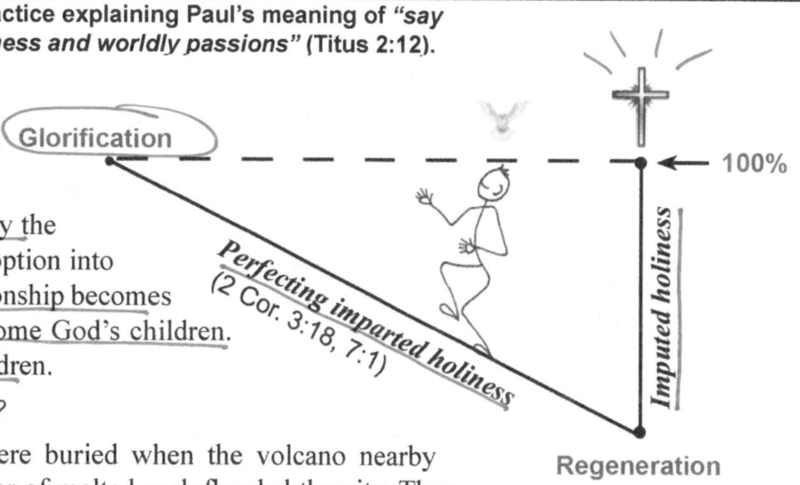

Q 35 How are some like the woman in Pompeii?

The city and people of Pompeii were buried when the volcano nearby exploded. (See Figure 1.26.) A fiery river of melted rock flooded the city. Then the melted rock cooled, and turned into solid rock again, covering the whole city. Years later some people dug in the ruins of Pompeii. They found the petrified body of a woman holding her jewels in her hands. Instead of fleeing from the doomed city to save her life, she tried to gather up some earthly things she valued—thus losing *both* her jewels and her life. Likewise, many today want both the *pleasures* of the world *and* the *treasures* of heaven. But in the end, these double-minded people will lose both.[14]

Figure 5.12   The process of sanctification (holiness) begins at regeneration (the new birth) and reaches its highest level at glorification (the new body). In between the new birth and the new body, we perfect holiness; that is, we mature in our separation from sin and our commitment to God. This growth or perfecting holiness involves our attitudes, choices, and actions, which affect our condition. Right attitudes and actions strengthen and increase holy character.

C. Grace teaches us to say "Yes" to what is good (Titus 2:12-14).

[11] ***For** the grace of God that brings salvation has appeared to all men.* [12] *It teaches us to say "No" to ungodliness and worldly passions, and to live self-controlled, upright and godly lives in this present age,* [13] *while we wait for the blessed hope— the glorious appearing of our great God and Savior, Jesus Christ,* [14] *who gave himself for us to **redeem us from** all wickedness and **to purify for himself a people that are his very own, eager to do what is good*** (Titus 2:11-14).

Q 36 Complete Figure 5.13, by summarizing verses that quote the theme "Doing what is good."

Titus	Your Summaries About the Phrase *"Doing what is good"*
1:16	
2:7	
2:14	
3:1	
3:8	
3:14	

Figure 5.13   Practice. In his letter to Titus, Paul emphasizes that Jesus has saved us *from doing* what is bad, and also washed and renewed us to be God's own people, eager *to do* what is good (Titus 3:3-8). In three chapters, Paul emphasizes six times the words "Doing what is good " (Titus 1:16; 2:7, 14; 3:1, 8, 14).

Q 37 What are some ways an older man or woman can mentor a younger man or woman?

As usual, Paul does not leave us to guess what godly living looks like. He instructs five groups in the church on how to say "Yes" to what is good. He gives each group examples of how to live as God's own people—those God has redeemed and purified by the blood of Christ. Paul told Titus:

- Teach **older men** to live in a way that shows they are *"worthy of respect"* (Titus 2:2). They make the gospel attractive through their character. They must be examples of faith, love, and hope [endurance] (Titus 2:2).

- Teach **older women** *"to be reverent in the way they live"* (Titus 2:3). *Reverent* can mean "holy."[15] Paul calls the older women to "holy" living. Also note that in Titus, unlike his letter to Timothy, Paul introduces the idea that older women are to mentor younger women (Titus 2:4).

- Paul wanted older women to teach the **younger women** how to be good wives and mothers (Titus 2:4-5).

- Teach **young men** *"to be self-controlled"* (Titus 2:6). And for the young men, Paul told Titus to be an example of *"integrity, seriousness and soundness of speech"* (Titus 2:7-8). Also being a living example of life and speech, Titus could make those who opposed him ashamed (Titus 2:8).

- Teach **slaves** *"to be subject to their masters"* (Titus 2:9). In Paul's day it was legal for masters to own slaves. Today, his words apply to workers and bosses—employees and employers. We can *"make the teaching about God our savior attractive"* to our bosses and employers by being completely trustworthy on the job (Titus 2:10).

Q 38 ✎ *Complete Figure 5.14, explaining instructions Paul gave to groups of believers in the church.*

Groups	Your Summaries on How to Live Godly
Elders	
Older women	
Younger women	
Young men	
Leaders, like Titus	
Slaves	

Figure 5.14   Practice explaining what *doing good* looks like in various groups Paul mentions. In Titus, Paul emphasizes that Jesus has saved us *from* doing evil *to* doing good.

Q 39 ✎ *Why did Will succeed, while Willnot failed, in the same class with Professor Grace?*

 Grace is a wonderful teacher, but students vary (Titus 3:14). Will and Willnot were students who sat in the same class with the same teacher. Will studied and learned well. His good attitude and diligence enabled him to pass, and take higher classes the next year. After being a good student for many years, Will became a teacher. In contrast, Willnot would not pay attention in class, and did not complete his homework. After failing some classes, he dropped out of school, and soon forgot the little he had learned. Willnot reminds us of the believers of Hebrews 5:12. After years of school, they should have become teachers. Instead, they still needed someone to teach them the A, B, C's of grace. The fate of the seed depends on the soil (Matt. 13:1-23). And the success of the best teacher depends on the attitudes of the students. Some students receive the grace of God in vain (2 Cor. 6:1). These fail what grace teaches (Heb. 12:15), and fall away from grace (Gal. 5:4). In contrast, other students grow in grace, so that they never fall away (2 Pet. 3:17-18).

Q 40 ✎ *Jesus asked: "Why do you call me, 'Lord, Lord,' and do not do what I say?" (Luke 6:46). Do you think that claiming to be a Christian without obeying Jesus is hypocrisy? Explain.*

What God calls good is beautiful, fresh, fulfilling, and satisfying. The good things to which God guides us make the heart rejoice, and add no sorrow. But what God calls evil turns out to be like a desert that is disappointing—like the fruit that turned bitter when Adam and Eve disobeyed God and tasted it.

Q 41 ✎ *Are good things beautiful, or just dutiful? Explain.*

Goodness is love in action—caring, cooking, cleaning, comforting, helping, and encouraging. Goodness is love carrying something—such as carrying medicine to the sick, water to the thirsty, food to the hungry, and clothes to the poor. Goodness is love reading the Bible to the blind, and explaining the gospel to the prisoner in his cell. Goodness is love teaching the Bible to a class, or helping one disciple of Jesus grow. Goodness is love in action in the neighborhood where you live, or traveling far away to help those in distant places. But whatever path goodness takes, it is *love following in the footsteps of Jesus*, who *"went around **doing good**"* (Acts 10:38).

Summary. Grace inspires us to say "No" to worldly passions and "Yes" to godly living.

The world and the flesh motivate many students to satisfy their selfish desires. In contrast, in Titus 2:11-14, we discern three things that inspire students of grace to be good and to do good.

Q 42 ⬉ *Complete Figure 5.15 on three directions that inspire us to say "No" to evil and "Yes" to doing good.*

We Remember	Your Summaries of What Inspires Us to Say "No" to Worldly Passions and "Yes" to Godly Living
Behind us	
Around us	
Ahead of us	

Figure 5.15   Practice summarizing how looking in three directions inspires us to say "No" to evil, and "Yes" to good.

- We remember the wickedness *behind* us. We know who we were. Jesus *"gave himself for us to redeem us **from** all wickedness"* (Titus 2:14).

  [3] At one time we too were foolish, disobedient, deceived and enslaved by all kinds of passions and pleasures. We lived in malice and envy, being hated and hating one another. [4] But when the kindness and love of God our Savior appeared, [5] he saved us, not because of righteous things we had done, but because of his mercy (Titus 3:3-5).

When we recall the bondage, shame, and danger of our past, we rejoice to be redeemed and released from it.

- We remember the lost are *around* us. We know who we are—the light of the world. Students of the world live for self. But students of grace have a concern for those lost in darkness. At the beginning of this lesson, look at the three times Paul says *so that* (Titus 2:5, 8, 10). Paul urges all groups in the church to live godly lives:

  *"**so that** no one will malign the word of God"* (Titus 2:5);

  *"**so that** those who oppose you may be ashamed because they have nothing bad to say about us"* (Titus 2:8);

  *"**so that** in every way they will make the teaching about God our Savior attractive* (Titus 2:10).

With each *"so that,"* Paul reminds us that the lost are watching us. The future of some depends on how we believers live today. Are we a stumbling block or a stepping stone? If our light shines, some will find their way out of the darkness into God's kingdom of light. For we are the first Bible that many people will read. Students of grace live godly *so* others can be redeemed.

- We remember the glory *ahead* of us. We know whose we are—God's very own people (Titus 2:14). We have an appointment to keep. We are waiting for Someone. We have a *"blessed hope—the glorious appearing of our great God and Savior, Jesus Christ"* (Titus 2:13). So we students of grace are watchful. We keep one eye on the present, and the other eye on the future. Students of the world are like Esau, who was sexually immoral and godless (Heb. 12:16-17). He lived only for the present, and sold his birthright for a single meal. He lived with both eyes on the present. But although we students of grace enjoy the Lord's presence today, we know that tomorrow will be a million times better! For God has promised us a new earth, a new body, and the fulfillment of our destiny—to be fully transformed into His image. We will be like God in holiness and true righteousness (Eph. 4:24). We will shine like the sun forever (Matt. 13:43). And we will live in the glorious presence of our Father and Savior. So the food of earth that fattens people for slaughter does not appeal to us (James 5:5). Our hearts are fixed on things above, not things below (Col. 3:1-2). We are waiting for the Bridegroom, who now sits at the right hand of God the Father. But *"when he appears, we shall be like him"* (1 John 3:2). At that time believers *"will be changed— [52] in a flash, in the twinkling of an eye"* (1 Cor. 15:51-52; see also 1 Thess. 4:16-17).

What a wonderful teacher Professor Grace is—reminding us that wickedness is *behind* us, the lost are *around* us, and glory is *ahead* of us.

Lesson 25

Discern the Past, Present, and Future Aspects of Salvation (Titus 3:1-15)

Goal A: *Analyze whether some deserve God's grace more than others.*

Goal B: *Explain Paul's "so that" aspect of salvation—the present.*

Goal C: *Explain whether the greatest part of salvation is past, present, or future..*

Q 43 *In Figure 5.16 in each row, circle the verses that focus on aspects of salvation in that row. (For example, Titus 3:1 focuses on the present aspect of salvation, so we circled verse 1 in the middle row.)*

Some refer to salvation as though it were entirely a past event. Others refer to salvation as if it is completely in the future. But in this passage, Paul emphasizes the past, present, and future aspects of salvation.

Aspects of Salvation	Verses in Titus 3 That Focus on the Three Aspects of Salvation
Past	1, 2, 3, 4, 5, 6, 7, 8, 9, 10, 11, 12, 13, 14, 15
Present	①, 2, 3, 4, 5, 6, 7, 8, 9, 10, 11, 12, 13, 14, 15
Future	1, 2, 3, 4, 5, 6, 7, 8, 9, 10, 11, 12, 13, 14, 15

Figure 5.16   Practice matching verses in Titus 3 with past, present, and future aspects of salvation.

[1] *Remind the people to be subject to rulers and authorities, to be obedient, to be ready to do whatever is good,* [2] *to slander no one, to be peaceable and considerate, and to show true humility toward all men.* [3] *At one time we too were foolish, disobedient, deceived and enslaved by all kinds of passions and pleasures. We lived in malice and envy, being hated and hating one another.* [4] *But when the kindness and love of God our Savior appeared,* [5] *he saved us, not because of righteous things we had done, but because of his mercy. He saved us through the washing of rebirth and renewal by the Holy Spirit,* [6] *whom he poured out on us generously through Jesus Christ our Savior,* [7] *so that, having been justified by his grace, we might become heirs having the hope of eternal life.* [8] *This is a trustworthy saying. And I want you to stress these things, so that those who have trusted in God may be careful to devote themselves to doing what is good. These things are excellent and profitable for everyone.* [9] *But avoid foolish controversies and genealogies and arguments and quarrels about the law, because these are unprofitable and useless.* [10] *Warn a divisive person once, and then warn him a second time. After that, have nothing to do with him.* [11] *You may be sure that such a man is warped and sinful; he is self-condemned.* [12] *As soon as I send Artemas or Tychicus to you, do your best to come to me at Nicopolis, because I have decided to winter there.* [13] *Do everything you can to help Zenas the lawyer and Apollos on their way and see that they have everything they need.* [14] *Our people must learn to devote themselves to doing what is good, in order that they may provide for daily necessities and not live unproductive lives.* [15] *Everyone with me sends you greetings. Greet those who love us in the faith. Grace be with you all* (Titus 3:1-15).

Morris Plotts was a missionary to Tanganyika. One day he met a movie actor named John Wayne. When Wayne learned that Plotts was a missionary, he asked, "Are you one of those missionaries who goes around doing good?" Plotts replied, "Yes, I am!" If John

Wayne could have asked the apostle Paul that same question, Paul would have given the same answer. *Doing good* is a big theme in Titus. Six times Paul urged his readers to *"do good"* (Figure 5.18). In this lesson, Paul connects doing *good* to past, present, and future aspects of salvation.

A. Past: At one time we were slaves of sin (Titus 3:3).

Q 44 ⬉ *What were we like as slaves of sin?*

³At one time we too were foolish, disobedient, deceived and enslaved by all kinds of passions and pleasures. We lived in malice and envy, being hated and hating one another (Titus 3:3).

To appreciate salvation we need to remember what God saved us *from*. Sometimes, those whom God has forgiven the most love Him the most (Luke 7:36-50). Criminals who accept Jesus may appreciate the grace of God more than *lesser* sinners whom Jesus saves. Those who grow up in church may not realize that they need God's grace and mercy as much as addicts and murderers recognize their need for grace.

Remember, Paul was writing to Titus concerning the people of Crete. One of their own scholars called them *"liars, evil brutes, lazy gluttons"* (Titus 1:12). Cretan believers came from a society that needed God's grace and mercy. In contrast, Paul was a religious man who had tried to please God all his life. He tried to please God and gain salvation by obeying the rules. Yet, here Paul declares that he, and others like him, are just as guilty as the pagans of Crete.

Q 45 ⬈ *Did some of us need salvation less than others? Explain.*

Look at Titus 3:3. Paul writes, *"**We** too were foolish."* **We** lived in darkness without spiritual understanding. **We** were *"disobedient"* to God and *"deceived"* by Satan. **We** knew truth, but we followed lies. Our desires *"enslaved"* **us**. **Our** lives were full of *"malice, envy"* and hatred. **We** were not all guilty of the same sins, but **we** all lived in rebellion toward God. **We** were all disobedient to His Word. Each of **us** needed the grace of God to save **us** from the penalty and power of sin. **The worst sinners and the best sinners need forgiveness and deliverance from sin.**

All types of sinners need forgiveness, but this fact provides no excuse for living in sin. However, those who grow up in the church and give their hearts to Jesus early in life have fewer regrets when they become adults.

Application. Whatever we choose for security and happiness outside the will of God enslaves us. We speak of drug addicts and alcoholics. But what about "power addicts, food addicts, sports addicts, pleasure addicts, and money addicts"? There are also those addicted to work, laziness, and self. There are many forms of slavery to sin.

B. Present: Now, God saved us to do what is good (Titus 3:4-8).

Titus 3:4-7 shows us the goal of salvation.

*⁴But when the kindness and love of God our Savior appeared, ⁵**he saved us**, [Why?] not because of righteous things we had done, but because of his mercy. **He saved us** [How?] through the washing of rebirth and renewal by the Holy Spirit, ⁶whom he poured out on us generously through Jesus Christ our Savior, ⁷[Why?] **so that**, having been justified by his grace, we might become heirs having the hope of eternal life* (Titus 3:4-7).

Like dawn after a stormy night, *"the kindness and love of God our Savior appeared"* (Titus 3:4). Like everyone else, we were wandering in darkness and enslaved by sin. We had no hope, until God revealed His kindness to us. Instead of punishing us, He saved us.

In Greek, Titus 3:4-7 is one sentence. The first part of that sentence gives us the main subject and verb. It tells us what God did when His love and kindness appeared: **He saved us.** The rest of the sentence tells us about the salvation God provided. It tells us *what* God did when He saved us, *why* He saved us, *how* He saved us, and *what* His goal was.[16]

Q 46 ↖ *Complete Figure 5.17 on aspects of salvation.*

Titus	Aspects of Salvation	Your Summaries of Aspects of Salvation
3:4-5	What God did	He saved us, *"when the kindness and love of God our Savior appeared."*
3:5	Why God saved us	
3:5-6	How God saved us	
3:7	What God's goal was in saving us	

Figure 5.17   Practice analyzing aspects of salvation in Titus 3:4-7.

- *God gave us mercy we did not deserve* (Titus 3:5). We cannot earn salvation by obeying the right rules or doing *righteous deeds* (Titus 3:5). Instead, God showed us mercy. To understand mercy, we need to understand the relationship between mercy and justice. Justice would be getting what we deserve. And *mercy* is not getting what we deserve.[17] When an evil harms, the righteous cry out for justice. Justice demands our punishment, but God's mercy gives us salvation.

- *God washed and renewed us when he saved us.* He saved us through *"the washing of rebirth and renewal"* (Titus 3:5). *Rebirth* comes from a Greek word that means "to regenerate or make new."[18] The meaning of *renewal* is similar to rebirth. To *renew* is "to restore, revive, revitalize, recondition—to make new." *"If anyone is in Christ, he is a new creation"* (2 Cor. 5:17).

Q 47 ↗ *What does "justified" mean? What is the twofold basis of our justification?*

- *God justified us when He saved us.* We have been *"justified by his grace"* (Titus 3:7). *Justified* is a legal term that declares a person is free from guilt.[19] God justifies those in Christ. He declares us "not guilty" based on two events. *First,* we admit our guilt. *Second,* we accept the payment Jesus made for us on the cross, as we receive Him as Savior and Lord.

  Some people have misused the word *justified,* saying that once we are saved, it is just as if we had never sinned. But this explanation is not true, because it denies the past. Rather, the truth is that although we were sinful, God washed us and made us clean. Two children played in the dirt, and became very dirty. Afterward, they took a bath and became clean again. If we say they looked like they had never been dirty, we ignore the power of the soap and water. It is good for us to always remember that we were dirty, but Jesus washed us and made us clean.

- *God saved us through the Holy Spirit.* *"He saved us through the washing of rebirth and renewal by the Holy Spirit"* (Titus 3:5). Re-creation is through the ministry of the Holy Spirit. The Spirit brings rebirth and renewal—the presence of God into our lives. In Genesis, the Spirit of God hovered over the darkness, and enabled creation (Gen. 1:2). At salvation, that same Spirit of God hovers over our darkness, and brings light, life, and order into us.

Q 48 ↗ *What aspect of salvation does Paul emphasize for the present (Titus 3:4-8)? Give examples.*

God did not save us *only* to *avoid* punishment for our sin. True, through salvation we *escape* the penalty of sin. But this is not the *only* benefit of salvation. And God did not save us *only* to *receive* good things. Yes, through salvation, we *receive many blessings.* But blessings are just one of the benefits of salvation. God also saved us *to be a blessing to others.* Earlier in this letter, Paul told young women to live pure lives *"so that no one will malign the word of God"* (Titus 2:5). He told Titus to *"set them an example by doing what is good"*... *"so that"* those in opposition would have *"nothing bad to say about us"* (Titus 2:7-8). And he told slaves to behave in a way *"that* [makes] *the teaching about God our Savior attractive"* (Titus 2:10). Now, he comes back to the theme of *"doing good."* He told Titus to *"stress these things, so that those who have trusted in God may be careful to devote themselves to doing what is good"* (Titus 3:8). Paul wanted Titus to stress these truths so people will *do good.* For Paul, *doing good* was more than religious activities at church. For Paul, *doing good* includes submission to government authority, serving in the community, and helping unsaved neighbors. When we *do good,* we affect people in a positive way. We attract them to the truth of the gospel. God is good, but the only way many lost people will see His goodness is through us.

Q 49 ⬋ *Complete Figure 5.18, by summarizing verses that illustrate the theme: "Doing what is good."*

Titus	Your Summaries of Verses That Emphasize *"Doing what is good"*
1:1	
1:6-9	
1:16	
2:1-2	
2:3-5	
2:6-7	
2:8	
2:9-10	
2:11-13	
3:1, 2	
3:13-14	

Figure 5.18   Practice. In his letter to Titus, Paul emphasizes that Jesus has saved us *from doing what is bad,* and has washed and renewed us *to do what is good,* now.

C. Future: The best is yet to come (Titus 3:7).

> SALVATION IS NOT JUST ABOUT THE PAST—IT AFFECTS THE PRESENT AND THE FUTURE.

Salvation is not just about the past—it affects the present and the future. Because God justified us, we have *"become heirs"* (Titus 3:7). Even as our children are our heirs, we are heirs of the living God. As heirs of God, we have access to some of His riches today. We receive His grace. He answers our prayers. He gives us the Holy Spirit. But consider the difference between an earthly and a heavenly inheritance. Earthly children receive their full inheritance on earth when their parents die. In contrast, God's children receive the Spirit, the deposit or down payment of our inherence, at the new birth (Eph. 1:14). But we will receive our full inheritance when we die or when Jesus returns for us. The greatest part of our salvation is ahead of us! *"Do not be afraid, little flock, for your Father has been pleased to give you the kingdom"* (Luke 12:32).

An unbeliever took a Christian to a window of his home to show how much land he owned. Waving his hand across a field, the unbeliever said, "There, that is all mine." The Christians smiled, and waved his hand across the heavens, saying, "In Jesus Christ, I am an heir to all this and more."

Conclusion (Titus 3:9-15)

⁹*But avoid foolish controversies and genealogies and arguments and quarrels about the law, because these are unprofitable and useless.* ¹⁰*Warn a divisive person once, and then warn him a second time. After that, have nothing to do with him.* ¹¹*You may be sure that such a man is warped and sinful; he is self-condemned.* ¹²*As soon as I send Artemas or Tychicus to you, do your best to come to me at Nicopolis, because I have decided to winter there.* ¹³*Do everything you can to help Zenas the lawyer and Apollos on their way and see that they have everything they need.* ¹⁴*Our people must learn to devote themselves to doing what is good, in order that they may provide for daily necessities and not live unproductive lives.* ¹⁵*Everyone with me sends you greetings. Greet those who love us in the faith. Grace be with you all* (Titus 3:9-15).

Q 50 ⬈ *In Titus, what does Paul emphasize six times?*

Paul closes his letter to Titus with final words of instruction:

- Paul says to avoid foolish arguments (Titus 3:9). In this case, the problem was with legalistic Jews who had accepted Christ. They insisted that all Christians should agree with their emphasis on obeying Old Testament Laws. But Paul's instructions apply to believers of all ages. Avoid foolish arguments—because such arguments are *"unprofitable and useless"* (Titus 3:9).

- Paul says to warn a divisive person twice. Then if such a person continues to bring division and cause useless arguments, have *"nothing to do with him"* (Titus 3:10). It is wise to avoid being a friend of those who cause trouble.

- Paul, for the **sixth time**, says believers must *"devote themselves to doing what is good"* (Titus 3:14). Doing good includes working to provide for the *"daily necessities"* of one's family and others in need. Faithful Christians are good citizens, good family members, and good neighbors to others.

I'm caught up in your presence
I just want

Test Yourself: Circle the letter by the **best** completion to each question or statement.

1. In Titus 1, why does Paul emphasize his relationship to God and Christ?
a) To stress that he is a believer
b) To emphasize his authority
c) To connect with believers in Crete
d) To honor the family of God

2. What is TRUE about false teachers at Crete?
a) They were greedy, legalistic, and deceitful.
b) They were rebellious, corrupt, and educated.
c) They were unfit, weak believers, and corrupt.
d) They were unfit and rejected genealogies.

3. The Bible says godly leaders must be
a) gentle and reserved.
b) honest and successful.
c) kind and practical.
d) hospitable and disciplined.

4. How can a pastor overcome false teaching?
a) Keep a tight reign on all matters.
b) Do most of the teaching himself.
c) Appoint godly leaders of house churches.
d) Stress the value of obeying rules.

5. Ministry is mostly about
a) preaching the Word to people.
b) praying for people in need.
c) relating to people.
d) teaching people biblical doctrines.

6. How does God offer us salvation?
a) Through grace alone
b) Through grace and good works
c) Through prayer and godly living
d) Through repentance and sacrifice

7. What does Professor Grace teach?
a) Believers remain slaves of sin.
b) Grace prevents God from seeing sin.
c) Believers say "No" to ungodliness.
d) Grace increases as we mature.

8. What is TRUE about grace?
a) Some deserve grace more than others.
b) Some need grace more than others.
c) All need the grace God offers.
d) Once in grace, always in grace.

9. The main way we attract people to Jesus is
a) preaching and teaching the gospel.
b) witnessing to those we know.
c) worshiping spiritually in church.
d) doing what is good in the world.

10. The greatest part of salvation is
a) past.
b) present.
c) future.
d) unknown.

 Essay Test Topics: Write 50-100 words on each of these goals that you studied in this chapter (10 points each). Try to complete your writing in one and a half hours.

• Explain key words and phrases of the introduction to Titus.

• Summarize 6 characteristics of the false teachers at Crete.

• Summarize at least 6 characteristics of godly leaders.

• Explain 3 ways for a pastor to overcome false teaching.

• Analyze the relationship of godly behavior to the gospel in Titus 2:1-14.

• Contrast man's attempts to please God, and the salvation that only God's grace offers.

• Contrast the lifestyles of those who pass and those who fail under Professor Grace.

• Analyze whether some deserve God's grace more than others.

• Explain Paul's *"so that"* aspect of salvation—the present.

• Explain whether the greatest part of salvation is past, present, or future?

Chapter 6:
Be Faithful and Fruitful as You Finish the Race
(2 Tim. 1–4)

This is Paul's final letter. Nero, the Roman emperor, was persecuting believers in Rome. He was trying to stop the spread of Christianity. For the second time, Paul was Nero's prisoner (2 Tim. 1:16). All of Paul's co-workers, except Luke, had deserted him or were far away (2 Tim. 1:15; 4:11-12). Paul knew that his ministry was over. He had run and won his race. Death was near (2 Tim. 4:6-8, 18).

Figure 6.1
Nero declared in public that he was number one among God's chief enemies.[8] He cut off Paul's head and crucified Peter.

Timothy was dear to Paul. The apostle called him *"my dear son"* and *"my fellow worker"* (2 Tim. 1:2; Rom. 16:21). Timothy had helped deliver six of Paul's letters. He was with Paul the first time the apostle was in the Roman prison (Phil. 1:1; Col. 1:1; Philem. 1). Paul wrote two personal letters to Timothy. So as the great apostle faced death, he wanted to see his son one more time. Twice in 2 Timothy, Paul requests that Timothy come to the prison (2 Tim. 4:9, 21). We do not know if Timothy arrived before Nero executed Paul.

Lessons:

Encouraging Yourself in Hard Times—Part 1 (2 Tim. 1:1–2:13)

Goal A: *Analyze the setting of 2 Timothy, including circumstances and challenges.*
Goal B: *Explain and illustrate how we encourage ourselves through relationships with others.*
Goal C: *Summarize how we strengthen ourselves through our relationship with the Father and Son.*

Encouraging Yourself in Hard Times—Part 2 (2 Tim. 1:1–2:13)

Goal D: *Explain ways believers edify themselves through their relationship with the Holy Spirit.*
Goal E: *List some advantages of training and involving others in ministry.*
Goal F: *Summarize 5 examples Paul uses in 2 Timothy 2 to motivate believers.*
Goal G: *Explain how God is faithful to Himself in dealing with saints and sinners.*

Choosing to Be a Vessel of Honor in the Last Days (2 Tim. 2:14–3:9)

Goal A: *Explain the context of 2 types of vessels in 2 Timothy 2.*
Goal B: *Contrast the choices of honorable and dishonorable vessels on 4 topics.*

Finishing the Race Well—Part 1 (2 Tim. 3:10-17)

Goal A: *Explain the need to continue walking in the light of Scriptures and those who taught us.*
Goal B: *Define inspiration, inerrancy, and infallibility, and explain how belief in these guides us.*

Finishing the Race Well—Part 2 (2 Tim. 4:1-22)

Goal C: *Analyze why pastors must preach the Word, and explain 4 guidelines for preaching it.*
Goal D: *Summarize and apply Paul's attitudes toward persecutors, deserters, unmet expectations, and God.*

 Key Words

eschatological—refers to the last days of humans on earth, and final matters such as the Return of Christ, judgments, punishment and rewards, heaven and hell

inspiration—the process by which God breathed His message into the writers of Scripture, and carried them along by the Holy Spirit—so that they wrote what He intended, free from error

inerrant—truthful and free from error

infallible—absolutely trustworthy and sure; not capable of erring, deceiving, or leading people astray

vessel of honor—a believer who has cleansed himself of what is unfit, has been sanctified by the Holy Spirit, and is useful to the Master for every good work

Last Days—a period of time that stretches from the First Coming of Jesus to His Second Coming; the perilous time near the Lord's return

---

Lesson 26

Encouraging Yourself in Hard Times—Part 1 (2 Tim. 1:1–2:13)

Goal A: *Analyze the setting of 2 Timothy, including circumstances and challenges.*
Goal B: *Explain and illustrate how we encourage ourselves through relationships with others.*
Goal C: *Summarize how we strengthen ourselves through our relationship with the Father and Son.*

The Setting and Problems. Paul sits in a Roman prison awaiting martyrdom for his faith. He writes for the last time to Timothy, his son in the faith. The old apostle has finished his race on earth and is leaving the world. False teachers are ruining the faith of many believers. Some false teachers have shipwrecked their own faith (1 Tim. 1:19-20). They are misusing the Law of Moses and stirring up controversies and doubts among believers. They are being led astray by doctrines from demons (1 Tim. 4:1-4). They are teaching that godliness is a path to riches, and thus plunging themselves and others into ruin (1 Tim. 6:9-10). These false teachers are ruining the faith of entire families as they teach in home groups (Titus 1:11). And the Spirit assured Paul that false teachers would go from bad to worse (2 Tim. 3:13). At the same time, most of Paul's co-workers have left him (2 Tim. 1:15). Paul feels abandoned by those closest to him. As the apostles scattered away from Jesus near His crucifixion, those closest to Paul did not want to be nearby when the sword hissed. Likewise, Timothy is still timid. As an old, scarred apostle, Paul is chained alone, in a cold, damp, dark prison cell in Rome. Winter is coming, and he does not even have a coat to keep him warm (2 Tim. 4:13, 21). If there was ever a time for a man to be discouraged and look down at the floor, this was that time for the apostle Paul.

Q.1 *What types of problems was Paul facing as he wrote his final letter?*

Encouragement of Relationships

Ancestors, Mentors & Teachers, Family & Friends

Father, Son, Holy Spirit

Figure 6.2 Paul encourages Timothy through our relationships with people and with God.

Solution. Jesus and the apostles warned that all believers will face times of suffering, trials, and tribulations. Because lawlessness will increase in the last days, most will fall away (Matt. 24:12). But victory is as certain as suffering, for those who remain steadfast in the faith.

Q 2 *Have you faced times, such as Paul and Timothy did, when you needed to encourage yourself? Explain.*

Often, we receive encouragement and strength from other believers. But there are times when overcoming depends on encouraging ourselves. In Lessons 26 and 27 we will examine seven ways (A–G) for us believers to edify ourselves on the rocky road to heaven.

Q 3 *How many ways to encourage yourself will we explore in Lessons 25 and 26? What is the first way?*

A. Look behind and around; encourage yourself through your RELATIONSHIPS with others—spiritual ancestors, mentors and teachers, family members and friends (2 Tim. 1:3-7).

*³I thank God, whom I serve, **as my forefathers did, with a clear conscience, as night and day I constantly remember you in my prayers.** ⁴Recalling your tears, I long to see you, so that I may be filled with joy. ⁵I have been reminded of **your sincere faith, which first lived in your grandmother Lois and in your mother Eunice and, I am persuaded, now lives in you also.** ⁶For this reason I remind you to fan into flame the gift of God, which is in you through the laying on of my hands. ⁷For God did not give us a spirit of timidity, but a spirit of power, of love and of self-discipline* (2 Tim. 1:3-7).

Q 4 *How did David encourage himself, when no one else strengthened him?*

As a lion seeks the separated calf, discouragement looks for the lonely. Alone, Elijah was discouraged under the juniper tree. Elijah found encouragement through the fact that 7,000 others were still faithful (1 Kings 19:18). Likewise, David was surrounded by black clouds at Ziklag. His soldiers had wept until they could weep no more, because enemies had captured their families. Then

> DISCOURAGEMENT LOOKS FOR THE LONELY.

they accused David of being the problem, and were getting ready to stone him. *"But David encouraged himself in the LORD his God"* (1 Sam. 30:6 KJV). Perhaps he thought about past victories over the lion, the bear, and Goliath. Maybe he sang some of his favorite psalms. And he might have recalled the great and mighty deliverances God brought through his ancestors, such as Moses.

Q 5 *How did Paul encourage himself when life was the darkest?*

Alone, Paul encouraged himself by remembering his spiritual forefathers—his spiritual ancestors (2 Tim. 1:3). For we cease to be alone in the battle when we use precious memories to recall the victories of those who have gone before us. As the writer of Hebrews said, after recalling the heroes of the faith in Hebrews 11, we are never alone; rather, *"we are surrounded by such a great cloud of witnesses"* who have already run and won the race (Heb. 12:1). As we unite ourselves with those who have gone before us, we find ourselves surrounded by a stadium of faithful people cheering for us to keep the faith and finish the race. Paul was not really alone. He was not the only person serving God. He strengthened himself by recalling that he was part of a long line of faithful servants—a line that stretched through the centuries—way back to Noah and Abraham. Likewise, Timothy could encourage himself by remembering that he was part of a mighty army who lived and died by faith in God. The faith in Timothy lived in his mother, Eunice—and even his grandmother, Lois.

Q 6 *How can we encourage ourselves when we feel alone and sorrowful?*

Application. Christian, encourage yourself in the Lord by thinking about your spiritual ancestors. For when we accepted Jesus as Savior, we became part of a huge family tree (Rom. 11:11-24). Our spiritual forefathers include Abraham, Moses, David, Samuel, and the prophets. They are like a cloud of unseen witnesses who cheer us on as we *"run with perseverance the race marked out for us"* (Heb. 12:1). We can encourage ourselves by remembering that we are surrounded by a host of faithful brothers and sisters of the past. What can you do when discouragement tries to pound you into the ground, making you feel like you are alone? Remind yourself that you are part of a multitude that no man can number, from every tribe and nation of the earth (Rev. 7:9-11). You are one among millions of God's children who, under both the old and new covenants, have overcome the world by faith in God.

Some Christians are like a flock of geese that lived by a barn. Every seventh day they paraded to a corner of the yard. Their best gander stretched to his full height, flapped his wings, and trumpeted about the wonders of geese. He told of the great deeds of their feathered forefathers—who dared to rise on wings and fly thousands of miles through the sky. He praised the Creator, who had given geese wings and the ability to fly. This deeply impressed the other geese, who nodded their heads and honked "Amen." The geese paraded, listened to stories about geese that flew, and thanked God that He created them to fly. But they never did one thing. They did not fly. Instead, at the end of the meeting each Sunday, they waddled back to their dinners. They did not fly— for the corn was good and the barnyard was safe. So the farmer ate several geese each year. In contrast, we must *imitate* our spiritual forefathers, not just admire and praise what they did. As they served the Lord in their generation, we must serve the Lord in ours.

When the saints of all the ages gather in heaven and recount their successes, we need to be able to share victories that God did through us. So brothers and sisters, let us fly with the spiritual wings God has given us. Let us stir up the gifts in us and use them for God's glory. Rise up men and women of God! Families are being lost. False teachers are destroying the faith of many. Let us fan our gifts into flame. There are battles to fight, and victories to win. The lives of many depend on our spiritual ministry. *"For God did not give us a spirit of timidity, but a spirit of power, of love and of self-discipline"* (2 Tim. 1:7).

Paul encouraged himself by remembering his friendship with Timothy. He remembered Timothy's tears at their separation. Timothy may have shed those tears when Paul was arrested. Timothy's tears revealed his deep love for Paul. Not only did Paul remember the past, he also looked forward to the future. He looked ahead to the joy of reuniting with Timothy. So we see that Paul encouraged himself and Timothy at the same time. He encouraged Timothy by reminding Timothy of their relationship, their ancestors, and their family members—and the love that Paul and his son in the faith felt for each other. Paul encouraged Timothy that whenever he prayed, he included Timothy in his prayers (2 Tim. 1:3).[1] No matter how hot the battle, Timothy could receive encouragement from knowing Paul's love for him and the assurance that Paul was praying for him.

Dr. Steve Eutsler, a co-author of this course, writes: "One of the first times I experienced God's love was when I was 9 years old, visiting my grandparent's home. I walked into the living room and found my grandma with her knees on the floor and her elbows on the sofa, calling my name in prayer. She prayed, "O God, help little Stevie." I don't know why she was praying for me that day. I don't recall misbehaving. I think Grandma was praying for me because my mother, her daughter, had died a year earlier in a car accident. I think Grandma wondered what would become of me. Quietly, I tiptoed out of the room. I don't think Grandma ever knew I heard her praying for me. But I remember thinking at the time: 'Grandma must really love me.' And I have often encouraged myself with the fact that she prayed for me."[2] Follower of Christ, *encourage yourself by remembering someone who prayed for you.*

Ben traveled far from home to accept a job. By chance, a man visiting from Ben's hometown met him and was shocked to discover that Ben had quit following Jesus. Returning home, the man told Ben's godly parents about the sinful life of their son. They said little, so the next day, the man called the parents again, and repeated what he had told them. The father replied, "We understood you yesterday. My wife and I spent a sleepless night on our knees—praying for our son. About dawn we received the assurance from God that Ben will leave his life of sin and return to follow Jesus at once."

Figure 6.3
Geese are a common sight on many farms.

Q 7 *What lesson should we learn from the geese?*

Q 8 *How can loving relationships encourage us in tough times?*

Q 9 *How can the past prayers of others continue to encourage us?*

Two weeks after, Ben returned home—with his face reflecting his love for his Lord. "How long since this change took place in you?" asked his joyful parents. Ben replied that two weeks earlier, a sense of guilt came over him, and he was unable to sleep. As a result, he spent the night in tears of repentance and prayer for pardon. The parents had not spoken one word to him. But while they were praying for him, God moved him to pray for himself.[3] Let us encourage others with our prayers, and encourage ourselves with the prayers others have prayed for us.

Q 10 Who in your life has been like a star or a person in the balcony cheering for you?

A woman reports, "As a child I heard a man tell a shocking statement from a man digging a well. He said say that in daylight, when he was in the bottom of the well, he looked up and saw the stars. I did not think this man was telling the truth, for I told myself, 'There are no stars in the daytime.' But later in life I learned that the stars are always shining. But we need darkness around us to reveal stars to our eyes. Likewise, when life is the darkest, there is light shining around us, if we look with eyes of faith to see it.[4]

Look up instead of down! Rejoice for one star in the darkness. Think of someone in the balcony, rather than someone in the basement. Many were moving away from Paul, just as the disciples scattered from Jesus when He was about to be crucified. Paul summarized all of these deserters in one short sentence: *"You know that everyone in the province of Asia has deserted me, including Phygelus and Hermogenes"* (2 Tim. 1:15). Then he used four sentences to focus on one friend, Onesiphorus, who remained faithful:

> [16] *May the Lord show mercy to the household of Onesiphorus, because he often refreshed me and was not ashamed of my chains.* [17] *On the contrary, when he was in Rome, he searched hard for me until he found me.* [18] *May the Lord grant that he will find mercy from the Lord on that day! You know very well in how many ways he helped me in Ephesus* (2 Tim. 1:16-18).

Q 11 Why was Timothy tempted to be ashamed of Paul?

B. Look up; encourage yourself through your RELATIONSHIP with God our Father (2 Tim. 1:8-12).

[8] *So do not be ashamed to testify about our Lord, or ashamed of me his prisoner. But join with me in suffering for the gospel, by the power of **God**, [9] **who has saved us and called us to a holy life—not because of anything we have done but because of his own purpose and grace**. This grace was given us in Christ Jesus before the beginning of time, [10] but it has now been revealed through the appearing of our Savior, Christ Jesus, who has destroyed death and has brought life and immortality to light through the gospel. [11] And of this gospel **I was appointed a herald and an apostle and a teacher**. [12] That is why I am suffering as I am. Yet I am not ashamed, **because I know whom I have believed, and am convinced that he is able to guard what I have entrusted to him for that day*** (2 Tim. 1:8-12).

The Problems.   Timothy was not as bold as Paul, who seemed to be part lion. Timothy was more timid and tame—like most people. The false teachers were bold, forward, and loud. They spoke with great confidence about things they did not even understand (1 Tim. 1:7). Likewise, the Roman government was flexing its muscles. Under the orders of Emperor Nero, soldiers seized Paul and put him in prison. Days of great persecution and suffering were at hand and ahead. In a short time, Nero will behead Paul. A wind of fear will blow across the land. So Paul, in his final letter, is seeking to encourage Timothy, Paul's son in the faith who is the overseer of the church at Ephesus. He has exhorted Timothy to encourage himself through inspiring relationships—with ancestors of faith, spiritual mentors like Paul, family members like Eunice and Lois, and friends, like Onesiphorus, who probably brought Paul a report from Ephesus. Then, Paul continues to exhort Timothy to buff up—to be strong and bold.

As the apostle sat in prison, false teachers made jokes about him, laughed at him, and mocked him. And the government was about to execute him. So there was the temptation to be ashamed of Paul, the faith, and the gospel. In the face of these temptations, Paul urges Timothy to come out of the shadows and stand tall and firm. To encourage Timothy, Paul reminds him of his relationship with the Father and the Son. Let us look at each of these emphases, which are woven together.

Q 12 *Complete Figure 6.4, explaining why our relationship with God encourages us on each topic.*

Topic	Your Explanations Why Our Relationship With God Gives Us Courage
Earthly life	
Spiritual life	
Calling	
Knowledge of God	

Figure 6.4   Practice explaining how our relationship with God brings courage.

Paul gives several reasons why Timothy and we should *"not be ashamed to testify for our Lord"* or believers, like Paul, who are in prison (2 Tim. 1:8).

- Earlier, Paul reminded Timothy that life is a gift from God the Father—*"who gives life to everything"* (1 Tim. 6:13). The reason we have a life to serve God is because He gave us that life.

- We were once dead in our sins—headed for eternal punishment. But God was gracious to us. He *"saved us and called us to a holy life—not because of anything we have done but because of his own purpose and grace"* (2 Tim. 1:9).

- God calls His people to serve Him. He appointed Paul to be *"a herald and an apostle and a teacher"* (2 Tim. 1:11). God called Timothy to be an overseer of the church at Ephesus. And He calls each of us to serve Him with the gifts He gives us. Sometimes our calling involves suffering.

- Besides the facts that God gave us life, saved us, and called us to serve Him, Paul adds one great and final, **eschatological* reason why we are not ashamed to suffer for God. We know God! We have a relationship with Him. We believe His promises about the future. God is worthy for us to entrust to Him the life and everlasting soul He has given us. So we do not fear suffering and dying for Him. When our time comes to die, like Jesus we can say, *"Father, into your hands I commit my spirit"* (Luke 23:46). So, like Paul, we can say, *"I am not ashamed, **because I know whom I have believed, and am convinced that he is able to guard what I have entrusted to him for that day"*** (2 Tim. 1:12). Paul lived life on earth for *that day—the day when every person will stand before the Creator and give account for life on earth.*

Sabio says, "Those who know God, and live for *tomorrow,* are not ashamed to stand up for Christ, suffer, and die *today*."

As we meditate on the love, grace, and plans of God for us, these encourage us to stand firm, minister with courage, and accept suffering if necessary.

Q 13 *How is your commitment like or different from Joel's commitment to Christ?*

After much consideration, a young man named Joel came into a pastor's office and said, "I will accept Jesus Christ as my Lord and Savior." He went home and told his wife, who had not yet discovered new life in Christ. Joel said that he had made up his mind to serve Christ, and he added, "After dinner tonight I am going to invite our guests to participate as our family prays and worships Jesus for the first time." "Well," said his wife, "you know some of our visitors coming to dinner are skeptics, and they are older than you are. Perhaps you should wait until they have gone; or you might go with the children into the kitchen to have your first prayer with them." Joel thought for a few moments, and responded, "I have asked Jesus Christ into my home for the first time—and I shall honor Him in the dining room, not just in the kitchen." So later that evening Joel invited his friends to join in family worship. There was a little sneering, but he read and prayed. Years later, Joel became an important judge in his nation. Never be ashamed to stand up for the God who saved you, and before whom you will stand after this life on earth. [5]

C. Look back; encourage yourself through your RELATIONSHIP with Jesus Christ our Savior (2 Tim. 1:8-12).

*[8]So do not be ashamed to testify about our Lord, or ashamed of me his prisoner. But join with me in suffering for the gospel, by the power of **God,** [9]**who has saved us and called us to a holy life—not because of anything we have done but because of his own purpose and grace.** This grace was given us in Christ Jesus before the beginning of time, [10]but it has now been revealed through the appearing of our Savior, Christ Jesus, who has destroyed death and has brought life and immortality to light through the gospel. [11]And of this gospel **I was appointed a herald and an apostle and a teacher.** [12]That is why I am suffering as I am. Yet I am not ashamed, **because I know whom I have believed, and am convinced that he is able to guard what I have entrusted to him for that day*** (2 Tim. 1:8-12).

Paul encouraged Timothy by reminding him of his relationship with Jesus. God planned salvation in Christ before the beginning of creation. Then God revealed His plan through Jesus—His birth, life, death, resurrection, ascension, intercession in heaven, Second Coming, and relationship with us forever. Jesus destroyed the power that death has over us. He brought us life and immortality, which He shares with us as we accept and live by the gospel. Because He lives, we will live also. His gospel and Spirit bring us new life, faith, and hope.

Paul suffered and faced death because Jesus appointed him as *"a herald and an apostle and a teacher"* of the gospel (2 Tim. 1:11). But he was not ashamed because he knew whom he believed (2 Tim. 1:12). As Paul had more than head knowledge of the Father, he likewise knew and trusted Jesus Christ the Son. Paul had a personal relationship with Christ. His faith in Christ was a faith of experience. Salvation begins with a step of faith—repenting and believing the message of Christ, the cross, the empty tomb, and the Second Coming. But the faith that begins as a seed, grows over a lifetime of experience. Paul got to *know* Jesus better through the sunshine and rain of walking with Jesus. The apostle knew Jesus better after Lystra—where unbelievers stoned him and left him for dead. But Jesus raised Paul up. Paul knew Jesus better after the outpouring of signs and wonders in Ephesus. Paul learned to know Jesus one step at a time, one trial at a time, one provision at a time. Finally, at the end of his life as he faces death, he is able to state with assurance: *"I am not ashamed, **because I know whom I have believed, and am convinced that he is able to guard what I have entrusted to him for that day"*** (2 Tim. 1:12).

Today we protect our wealth by depositing our money in a bank. But in Paul's day there were no banks. So when a person traveled, he would entrust his money with his closest friend. That friend would guard the wealth until the day the traveler returned. Likewise, Paul entrusted himself, his life, and his soul to Christ. And he was confident, free from fear, and absolutely sure he was in good hands—because he *knew* from experience that Jesus Christ is trustworthy.

The memory of a very old Christian woman began to weaken. She had once known much of the Bible by memory. And in the last days of her life, she often quoted one verse: *"I am not ashamed, because I know whom I have believed, and am convinced that he is able to guard what I have entrusted to him for that day"* (2 Tim. 1:12). By and by her memory lost its hold, and she would quietly repeat, "That which I have committed unto him." At last, as she came to the border between this world and the next, her family members noticed her lips moving. Bending down close, they heard her softly whisper one word from her favorite verse: "Him, Him, Him". She had lost her grip on the Bible, except for one word. Still, she had the whole Bible in that one word—*Him.* [6]

Q 14 *How sure are you about your future after death? Why?*

Q 15 *How did a relationship with Christ strengthen a dying grandmother?*

Polycarp was a disciple of the apostle John, and pastor of the church at Smyrna. On a feast day unbelieving Jews accused Polycarp of being disloyal to Caesar. They brought the elderly pastor to the Roman governor, where he refused to say that Caesar is Lord. The governor urged the old shepherd to deny Jesus Christ. But Polycarp answered, "Eighty and six years have I served Him and He never did me harm. How then can I blaspheme my King and Savior? I am a Christian!" Later the governor threatened, "I have wild beasts nearby. I will throw you to these if you do not change." As the trial continued, the governor warned, "I will burn you with fire if you are not afraid of the wild beasts!" Polycarp answered, "You threaten me with fire that burns for an hour and becomes cold. Yet you ignore the fire of coming judgment and eternal punishment awaiting the ungodly. But why are you waiting to kill me? Bring what you want!" Then the Jews who rejected Jesus broke their own Sabbath to gather wood for the fire.[7] In the flames, Polycarp gave thanks that he was worthy to be a martyr for Christ. Pastor Polycarp was the twelfth martyr for Christ in Smyrna.[8]

Q 16 ✎ *Will you be faithful unto death, just as Jesus, Polycarp, Stephen, the apostles, and others were faithful? Explain.*

Jesus Christ made a good confession before His death when testifying before Pontius Pilate (1 Tim. 6:13). Apostles like Paul and John remained strong in the faith as they suffered to the end. Pastor Polycarp died with peace in his heart, in the presence of Jesus, as the angels came to usher him into the glory of the age to come. Stephen was a deacon that unbelievers stoned, while his face was shining in glory as he saw Jesus standing at the right hand of the Father, welcoming him home (Acts 7). Likewise let us die faithfully facing our Father and our Savior, as we finish our race, and receive the reward we have looked forward to year after year.

Lesson 27 — Encouraging Yourself in Hard Times—Part 2 (2 Tim. 1:1–2:13)

Goal D: *Explain ways believers edify themselves through their relationship with the Holy Spirit.*
Goal E: *List some advantages of training and involving others in ministry.*
Goal F: *Summarize 5 examples Paul uses in 2 Timothy 2 to motivate believers.*
Goal G: *Explain how God is faithful to Himself in dealing with saints and sinners.*

We are looking at two lessons on <u>ways to encourage ourselves in hard times</u> (2 Tim. 1:1–2:13). In the previous lesson we focused on three sources of encouragement: A) Our relationship with others (such as spiritual ancestors, mentors and teachers, family and friends); B) our relationship with the Father; and C) our relationship with Jesus Christ the Son. In this lesson we will study several more ways to encourage ourselves when we experience the fiery trial of our faith.

D. Look within; encourage yourself through your RELATIONSHIP with the Holy Spirit (2 Tim. 1:7-8, 14).

Q 17 ✎ *In contrast to a spirit of timidity, Who did God give us (2 Tim. 1:7)?*

*6 Fan into flame **the gift of God, which is in you** through the laying on of my hands. 7 **For God did not give us a spirit of timidity, but a Spirit of power, of love and of self-discipline**. 8 So do not be ashamed to testify about our Lord, or ashamed of me his prisoner. But join with me in suffering for the gospel, **by the power of God**... 14 Guard the good deposit that was entrusted to you—guard it **with the help of the Holy Spirit who lives in us** (2 Tim. 1:6-8, 14).*

Notice that we have capitalized the word *Spirit* in the phrase *"Spirit of power"* (2 Tim. 1:7). For in 2 Timothy 1:6-8, Paul contrasts a human *spirit* or an attitude (spirit of timidity) with a Spirit of power (**the Holy Spirit**). Consider four proofs by an outstanding scholar showing that 2 Timothy 1:7 refers to the Holy Spirit.[9]

Q 18 ✎ *In 2 Timothy 1:7, which of the 4 proofs for capitalizing Spirit is strongest? Defend your answer.*

- Paul uses the word *"for"* to connect 2 Timothy 1:6 and 1:7. As Paul laid hands on Timothy, the *"gift of God"* came into Timothy through the Holy Spirit. In Paul's writings, there is always a close relationship between *gift* (Greek: *charisma*) and the Holy Spirit. Whatever ministry gift Timothy received, the Holy Spirit was the source. Spiritual ministry requires supernatural power. For work in the *kingdoms of man*, human abilities and skills may be enough. But ministry in the *kingdom of God* requires the *Spirit of God.*

"But we have this treasure in clay jars, so that it may be made clear that this extraordinary power belongs to God and does not come from us" (2 Cor. 4:7 NRSV).

- Paul often connects the words *power* and *love* to the Holy Spirit.
- There is a close connection between 2 Timothy 1:6-8 and 1 Timothy 4:14 where the *gift* is imparted by the Holy Spirit, through prophecy and prayer.

  "Do not neglect the gift that is in you, which was given to you through prophecy with the laying on of hands by the council of elders" (1 Tim. 4:14 NRSV).

- In 2 Timothy 1:7, the contrast between the clauses with *not* and *but* emphasize the Holy Spirit. This is especially clear when we compare 2 Timothy 1:7 with parallel Pauline verses in Romans 8:15 and 1 Corinthians 2:12 (Figure 6.5).

Reference	*Not* Clauses	*But* Clauses
Rom. 8:15	*For you did **not** receive a spirit that makes you a slave again unto fear,*	***but** you received the Spirit of sonship. And by him we cry Abba, Father.*
1 Cor. 2:12	*We have **not** received the spirit of the world*	***but** the Spirit who is from God.*
2 Tim. 1:7	*God did **not** give us a spirit of timidity*	***but** a <u>Spirit</u> of power, of love and of self-discipline.*

Figure 6.5   Paul often contrasts the human spirit with the divine Spirit.

In 2 Timothy 1:7 some translations do not capitalize *Spirit*. The difficulty in the three *"not"* parts of Figure 6.5 is their negative contrast. These phrases: *"a spirit that makes you a slave"* (Rom. 8:15), *"the spirit of the world"* (1 Cor. 2:12), and *"a spirit of timidity"* (2 Tim. 1:7) do not describe the Holy Spirit. But it is very clear that the second half of each of these verses refers to the Holy Spirit!

Q 19 ✎ *How does the Holy Spirit help us stand firm in every situation?*

Paul's main point in 2 Timothy 1:6-8 and 1:14 is that through His Spirit, God gives us everything we need to be strong, steadfast, and fruitful. The Holy Spirit is our source *"of power, of love and of self-discipline"* (2 Tim. 1:7). The Spirit's presence is the opposite of fear—the cure for cowardice, the source of courage. Our wellspring of ministry is a person, the Holy Spirit. He enables and gifts us to do what God calls us to do. The Holy Spirit is the source of supernatural gifts, and spiritual gifts are a manifestation of the Spirit Himself. To put it another way, all spiritual gifts from God are made possible through the presence of the Spirit. Some err by talking about spiritual gifts as if they were possible without the Spirit's presence. Let us never separate spiritual gifts from the presence of the Holy Spirit. For wherever there is anointing or supernatural gifts from God, the Spirit is present, making the supernatural possible. Without the Holy Spirit, we can only offer what humans have to give. For all aspects of ministry, we must depend on our holy relationship with the Holy Spirit.

The fire is not the firelight, and the fire is not the fire's heat. But the fire is the source of both. Neither firelight nor fire heat exist without the fire. Electricity is neither light nor heat, but it is the source of power for both. Likewise, the Spirit is not the gift, but He is the source of all ministry gifts.

In the Old Testament, the Holy Spirit anointed a craftsman, Bezalel, to make furnishings for the Tabernacle (Exod. 31:1-3). When power in battle was needed, God anointed men such as Gideon and Samson with the Spirit. The Spirit empowered God's prophets and some leaders, such as David. In the New Testament, the Spirit enabled fishermen to influence crowds. He anointed deacons like Stephen to do miracles and deliver powerful messages (Acts 7). God anointed women such as Priscilla and Phoebe to help many (Acts 18; Rom. 16). By the Spirit, God transforms human abilities into supernatural ministry. The Spirit empowers common people to heal the sick, cast out demons, work miracles, and provide anointed teaching or preaching. Throughout the Bible, the source and power of ministry is the Holy Spirit. Paul reminds Timothy to encourage himself through his relationship with the Holy Spirit. Timothy can depend on the Spirit to help him *"guard the good deposit"* that was entrusted to him—which includes the gospel, and Timothy's ministry (2 Tim. 1:14). As Timothy is faithful, the Spirit will make him fruitful and successful as a minister of God.

Application. The Holy Spirit will do His part as we do our part. We must study, meditate on God's Word, pray, obey, and live in the Spirit (2 Tim. 2:15; Gal. 5:16). We must overcome hindrances of hatred, bitterness, unforgiveness, anger, pride, and lust—for these quench the Spirit's presence in our lives. Even as we do our part, we depend on the Spirit, submit to the Spirit, and respond to the Spirit who helps us. As we do our little part, He does His big part. Let us encourage ourselves by our relationship with the Holy Spirit (2 Tim. 1:7-8). He is *God in us.*

Q 20 ↖ *What are ways we enable the Spirit to minister to and through us?*

E. Look in front; encourage yourself by sharing the work of the ministry.

Q 21 ↗ *How does sharing ministry with others encourage us?*

¹*You then, my son, be strong in the grace that is in Christ Jesus.* ²*And the things you have heard me say in the presence of many witnesses entrust to reliable men who will also be qualified to teach others* (2 Tim. 2:1-2).

Don't be a one man band (Figure 6.6). Do not try to do everything yourself. Don't take yourself too seriously. Avoid the pride of feeling as if you are an eagle sitting on a sparrow's nest. God's plan is not for the pastor to do all the ministry. His plan is for believers to share the work of teaching others. Many hands make light work. Multiply the workers. The harvest is great; the laborers are few. So recruit more laborers. *Entrust reliable, qualified men and women to teach others.* This is the 2 Timothy 2:2 principle. *Equip others* (Eph. 4:11-12).

Figure 6.6 Don't be a one-man band, trying to do everything yourself. Instead, obey what Paul told Timothy. Encourage yourself by teaching faithful believers so they can disciple and train others.

Pastor, instead of trying to do everything yourself, entrust part of the ministry to others (2 Tim. 2:1-2). Recruit musicians, deacons, teachers, ushers, greeters, helpers to visit visitors, elders who can help pray for the sick, helpers to clean and cook. Help the faithful members of your church develop and use the gifts God has given them. In this way, the work will not feel too heavy on your shoulders, and the Spirit can bear fruit through the whole body of Christ.

God saw that it was not good for Adam to live alone. So He created Eve to help him. Together they shared the load, enjoyed each other, and strengthened each other. There is power in numbers. *"Though one may be overpowered, two can defend themselves. A cord of three strands is not quickly broken"* (Eccles. 4:12).

Q 22 ↖ *Complete Figure 6.7 by summarizing verses that illustrate the power of teamwork.*

Reference	Your Summaries About the Power of Teamwork, When God Is With Us
Lev. 26:8	
Deut. 32:20	
Josh. 23:10	

Figure 6.7 Practice illustrating that when God is with us, we multiply fruitfulness when we work together.

Q 23 *Why did the father-in-law of Moses counsel him to share his responsibilities with others?*

Moses was tired and grumpy. He was wearing himself out in the ministry, until Jethro, his father-in-law, came to him with wisdom.

> ¹³*The next day Moses took his seat to serve as judge for the people, and they stood around him from morning till evening.* ¹⁴*When his father-in-law saw all that Moses was doing for the people, he said, "What is this you are doing for the people? Why do you alone sit as judge, while all these people stand around you from morning till evening?"* ¹⁵*Moses answered him, "Because the people come to me to seek God's will.* ¹⁶*Whenever they have a dispute, it is brought to me, and I decide between the parties and inform them of God's decrees and laws."* ¹⁷*Moses' father-in-law replied, "What you are doing is not good.* ¹⁸*You and these people who come to you will only wear yourselves out. The work is too heavy for you; you cannot handle it alone.* ¹⁹*Listen now to me and I will give you some advice, and may God be with you. You must be the people's representative before God and bring their disputes to him.* ²⁰*Teach them the decrees and laws, and show them the way to live and the duties they are to perform.* ²¹*But select capable men from all the people—men who fear God, trustworthy men who hate dishonest gain—and appoint them as officials over thousands, hundreds, fifties and tens.* ²²*Have them serve as judges for the people at all times, but have them bring every difficult case to you; the simple cases they can decide themselves. That will make your load lighter, because they will share it with you.* ²³*If you do this and God so commands, you will be able to stand the strain, and all these people will go home satisfied."* ²⁴*Moses listened to his father-in-law and did everything he said.* ²⁵*He chose capable men from all Israel and made them leaders of the people, officials over thousands, hundreds, fifties and tens.* ²⁶*They served as judges for the people at all times. The difficult cases they brought to Moses, but the simple ones they decided themselves* (Exod. 18:13-24).

Later on, there was still too much work for Moses to do by himself. He was so tired he could hardly walk another step. Once again he pleaded with God:

> ¹⁴*I cannot carry all these people by myself; the burden is too heavy for me.* ¹⁵*If this is how you are going to treat me, put me to death right now—if I have found favor in your eyes—and do not let me face my own ruin."* ¹⁶*The LORD said to Moses: "Bring me seventy of Israel's elders who are known to you as leaders and officials among the people. Have them come to the Tent of Meeting, that they may stand there with you.* ¹⁷*I will come down and speak with you there, and I will take of the Spirit that is on you and put the Spirit on them. They will help you carry the burden of the people so that you will not have to carry it alone...* ²⁵*Then the LORD came down in the cloud and spoke with him, and he took of the Spirit that was on him and put the Spirit on the seventy elders. When the Spirit rested on them, they prophesied, but they did not do so again.* ²⁶*However, two men, whose names were Eldad and Medad, had remained in the camp. They were listed among the elders, but did not go out to the Tent. Yet the Spirit also rested on them, and they prophesied in the camp.* ²⁷*A young man ran and told Moses, "Eldad and Medad are prophesying in the camp."* ²⁸*Joshua son of Nun, who had been Moses' aide since youth, spoke up and said, "Moses, my lord, stop them!"* ²⁹*But Moses replied, "Are you jealous for my sake? I wish that all the LORD's people were prophets and that the LORD would put his Spirit on them!"* (Num. 11:14-17, 25-29).

Q 24 *What happens when we try to carry too many responsibilities on our shoulders?*

> PASTOR, THERE IS ENOUGH OF GOD'S SPIRIT TO EQUIP **ALL** BELIEVERS FOR MINISTRY.

Q 25 *Why does God give spiritual gifts to all believers in the Church? Give examples.*

Pastor, there is enough of God's Spirit to equip ALL believers for ministry. God did not give your church members hands so they could put them in their pockets. He did not give them feet so they could just sit in church. He did not give them ears to only hear you preach and teach. He did not give them eyes just to watch you do all the ministry. God created your church members to share the ministry. The Church is a body of believers. Put your people to work. Train them. They will earn eternal rewards for their labors. They will take some of the strain of ministry off your shoulders. Many will be blessed by the gifts God gives through your faithful believers. Some will be called into full time ministry, and become pastors, evangelists, teachers, and missionaries. Even Jesus, the Son of God, did not try to do all the ministry by Himself. He trained 12 apostles to share the load. He equipped 70 disciples to help with the harvest, and sent them out two by two. Likewise, Paul did not try to do all the ministry by himself. He shared ministry with many others such as Timothy, Titus, Trophimus, Demas, Luke, Priscilla and Aquilla, and Apollos. And at Ephesus, where Timothy pastored, Paul taught in the school of Tyrannus for 2 years, training many others. And as those Paul trained taught others, Ephesus became a center of expansion—so that all Asia heard the gospel (Acts 19:10). Likewise today, the Church is expanding more than ever before as faithful believers filled with the Spirit share in the ministry. These believers minister in Bible classes, home groups, mentoring disciples, night schools, Sunday schools, children's ministry, extension schools, and Bible Schools in local churches.

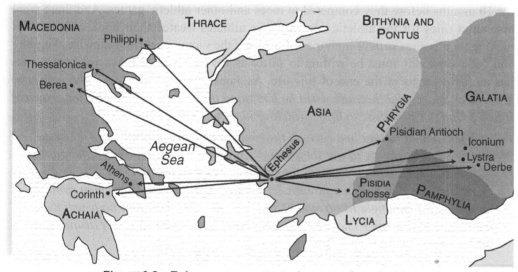

Figure 6.8 Ephesus was a strategic center for missions.

Sabio says: "Pastors who try to do all the work soon wear out. Wise pastors share ministry with faithful believers whom they train."

F. Look ahead; encourage yourself by remembering that your commitment and endurance result in an eternal reward (2 Tim. 2:3-10).

In this section Paul uses five illustrations to encourage Timothy and us as we face hard times. All five of these illustrations emphasize commitment and endurance related to future reward. As you read and examine these five illustrations, practice summarizing them in Figure 6.9.

> [3] *Endure hardship with us **like a good soldier** of Christ Jesus.* [4] *No one serving as a soldier gets involved in civilian affairs—he wants to please his commanding officer.* [5] *Similarly, if anyone competes **as an athlete**, he does not receive the victor's crown unless he competes according to the rules.* [6] *The **hardworking farmer** should be the first to receive a share of the crops.* [7] *Reflect on what I am saying, for the Lord will give you insight into all this.* [8] *Remember **Jesus Christ**, raised from the dead, descended from David. This is my gospel,* [9] *for which **I am suffering** even to the point of being chained like a criminal. But God's word is not chained.* [10] *Therefore I endure everything for the sake of the elect, that they too may obtain the salvation that is in Christ Jesus, with eternal glory* (2 Tim. 2:3-10).

Q 26 ✎ *Complete Figure 6.9 by summarizing verses that illustrate the relationship of commitment and endurance to reward.*

2 Timothy	Illustration	Your Summary of the Lesson Paul Is Illustrating
2:3-4	Soldier	
2:5	Athlete	
2:6-7	Farmer	
2:8	Jesus	
2:9-10	Paul	

Figure 6.9   Practice summarizing five illustrations showing that commitment and endurance lead to reward.

1. Soldier (2 Tim. 2:3-4).   Paul often used illustrations about warfare and soldiers (2 Cor. 10:3-5; Eph. 6:10-18; Philem. 2). Soldiers must endure hardship, suffering, and even death. They must remain loyal to the officer who commands them. Likewise, Timothy must be willing to suffer. He must not look back, but remain committed to Jesus, his Divine Commander. He must avoid defecting and looking for an easier path.

2. Athlete (2 Tim. 2:5).   Athletes of Paul's day endured strict discipline and training for 10 months before they competed in races and other athletic games. And there were also strict rules for the athletic contests. The athletes treated their bodies like slaves, making their bodies suffer—in hopes of winning the victor's crown. Likewise, Timothy and believers today must be willing to suffer as we follow Christ. For we know Jesus has a crown for us at the end of this life. As James wrote, *"Blessed is the man who perseveres under trial, because when he has stood the test, he will receive the crown of life that God has promised to those who love him"* (James 1:12).

Q 27 ✎ *Complete Figure 6.10 by summarizing verses about crowns, for those who endure.*

²⁴Do you not know that in a race all the runners run, but only one gets the prize? Run in such a way as to get the prize. ²⁵Everyone who competes in the games goes into strict training. They do it to get a crown that will not last; but we do it to get a crown that will last forever. ²⁶Therefore I do not run like a man running aimlessly; I do not fight like a man beating the air. ²⁷No, I beat my body and make it my slave so that after I have preached to others, I myself will not be disqualified for the prize (1 Cor. 9:24-27).

Reference	Your Summaries About the Crowns God Promises to Those Who Endure to the End
1 Cor. 9:24-25	
2 Tim. 4:8	
James 1:12	
Rev. 2:10	

Figure 6.10   Practice summarizing the need for commitment and endurance to receive an eternal crown.

3. Farmer (2 Tim. 2:6-7).   Paul reminds Timothy that *"the hardworking farmer should be the first to receive a share of the crops."* Earlier, Paul uses passages about the ox and the worker to illustrate that those who preach and teach should be paid (1 Tim. 5:17-18). But here Paul's point is different, for he is referring to our eternal reward at the end of this life. All of these five illustrations are eschatological—as Paul emphasizes having courage and endurance because *our eternal reward is ahead.*

4. Jesus (2 Tim. 2:8).   Jesus is our great example. He suffered unto death, and then triumphed over the grave. He is our leader. Therefore Paul reminds us *"Remember Jesus Christ, raised from the dead"* (2 Tim. 2:8). Jesus Christ our Lord overcame the world and the grave (John 16:33). So let us remember to follow His example, as we keep our eyes on Him. As the author of Hebrews exhorts:

¹...Let us run with perseverance the race marked out for us. ²Let us fix our eyes on Jesus, the author and perfecter of our faith, who for the joy set before him endured the cross, scorning its shame, and sat down at the right hand of the throne of God. [3]Consider him who endured such opposition from sinful men, so that you will not grow weary and lose heart (Heb. 12:1b-3).

5. Paul (2 Tim. 2:9-10).   Paul modeled how believers should suffer for Christ's sake. Locked in a Roman prison, the old apostles was *"**suffering** even to the point of being chained like a criminal"* (2 Tim. 2:9). Paul endured suffering, to complete his own race and win the crown that Jesus had for him. Yet he also endured suffering to be a good example for others. He endured *"everything **for the sake of the elect, that they too may obtain the salvation that is in Christ Jesus, with eternal glory"*** (2 Tim. 2:10). Though he, God's messenger, was chained, the message was not chained (2 Tim. 2:9). For the Word of God is living and powerful, and supernatural. So, the elderly apostle resolved, *"I press on toward the goal to win the prize for which God has called me heavenward in Christ Jesus"* (Phil. 3:14).

Conclusion of the five illustrations: Beyond a soldier's warfare is victory; beyond an athlete's training and competing by the rules is a victor's crown; beyond a farmer's hard work and patience is a harvest.[10] Jesus overcame the world and conquered death. Paul endured to the end. He ran and won the race God had for him—to receive his crown. Likewise, beyond each believer's commitment, obedience, suffering, and endurance is an eternal reward.

G. Look up again; encourage yourself because God is faithful (2 Tim. 2:11-13).

In this lesson we have studied several ways that Paul encouraged Timothy (and all believers) to remain loyal and steadfast in hard times. We can encourage ourselves through our relationship with spiritual ancestors who have completed the race and are in God's presence. We can inspire ourselves with the relationships of spiritual mentors, teachers, family members, and friends. Even when we feel lonely, we are never really alone. For we are surrounded by a host of other faithful believers—in the past and in the present. Likewise we can lift ourselves out of discouragement as we meditate on our relationship with the Father, the Son, and the Spirit. And we can strengthen ourselves through the five illustrations Paul gave of those who endured hardship as they looked forward to rewards. We can follow the examples of soldiers, athletes, farmers, Jesus, and Paul.

For his final encouragement, Paul gives us part of an ancient hymn or poem. These verses *encourage* endurance, warn against apostasy, and close on the high point of God's faithfulness.

[11]*Here is a trustworthy saying: If we died with him, we will also live with him;* [12]*if we endure, we will also reign with him. If we disown him, he will also disown us;* [13]*if we are faithless, he will remain faithful, for he cannot disown himself* (2 Tim. 2:11-13).

Q 28 ✎ *Complete Figure 6.11 on the four "if–then" statements in 2 Timothy 2:11-13.*

2 Timothy	If Clause (Greek: *Protasis*): Our Actions	Then Clause (Greek:*Apodosis*): The Results in Our Relationship to Christ
2:11	If we died with him, (At conversion, going down into the waters of baptism, which symbolized dying with Christ and dying to sin.)	
2:12	If we endure, (Persevering through trials)	
2:12	If we disown him, (Turning away from faith and obedience)	
2:13	If we are faithless, (Refusing to continue trusting God)	

Figure 6.11   Paul uses four "if–then" statements to summarize our relationship to Christ (2 Tim. 2:11-13).

God is faithful to fulfill both His promises and His warnings. God's faithfulness is a comfort to those who remain loyal. But God's faithfulness is a warning to those who depart from the faith. God must remain faithful to His Word and Himself. Let us consider two ways in which God is faithful.

Q 29 ⟩ *How is God faithful to those who persevere in faith?*

First, God is faithful to reward those who persevere in faith. Deserters cannot prevent God from remaining true to Himself, His promises, and His followers. Unlike people, God never changes. With Him there is no variance or shadow of turning away. He is as faithful as the heavenly lights (James 1:17). God is always faithful to the remnant that remains faithful to Him (Rom. 3:1-8; 11:1-6). He is committed to save those who endure to the end (Matt. 24:13; Heb. 10:35-39; Rev. 2:10-11; 12:11).

Q 30 ⟩ *How is God faithful to those who reject or abandon the faith?*

Second, God is faithful to Himself and His Word, so He must disown deserters (review Figure 4.3, Biblical warnings of apostasy).

When Paul speaks of those who abandon or deny the faith (as in 1 Timothy 4:1 and here in 2 Timothy 2:12), he is not referring to those like Peter, who fail in a moment, and then immediately repent and return to Christ. Rather, Paul has in mind those like Judas, who walk away step by step, following a plan they made and meditated on over a period of time. Like other biblical authors, Paul is referring to deserters such as Israel in the wilderness—who continued to worship idols for 40 years of wanderings, even while God fed them and their children with manna from heaven (Acts 7:42-43; See also Matt. 10:32-33; Mark 8:38; 1 Cor. 10:1-13; Heb. 3:7-19; 10:35-39; 12:25-28).

Q 31 ⟨ *Why is your theology about suffering very important?*

It is okay to discuss and debate the time of the Rapture whether pre-trib, mid-trib, or post-trib. But the result of these debates does not matter much—for those who walk with Christ will rise to meet Him, *whenever* He returns for His own. In **contrast**, it is VERY important to have a proper *theology of suffering*. Paul stood firm in the faith, in a dingy, cold dungeon. He remained steadfast, because he knew whom he had believed, and was persuaded that God would bring him safely into the kingdom—through the dungeon and death. History records that Nero beheaded Paul. But the apostle's faith was not hurt when his head was cut off. Likewise, this year there will be 160,000 or more martyrs for Christ. Like Paul, and those in Smyrna, God enables believers to remain faithful through prison, death, and great suffering (Rev. 2:10). If we deny Him, He will deny us. So let us make up our minds that we will be faithful to the Lamb, and be faithful even to the point of death so we will gain the crown of life (2 Tim. 1:8-10; Rev. 2:10-11; 12:11).

Lesson 28 **Choosing to Be a Vessel of Honor in the Last Days (2 Tim. 2:14–3:9)**
Goal A: *Explain the context of 2 types of vessels in 2 Timothy 2.*
Goal B: *Contrast the choices of honorable and dishonorable vessels on 4 topics.*

Figure 6.12   **Two kinds of vessels—one for honor and one for dishonor; one type of vessel for noble purposes—the other type of vessel for garbage and waste**[11]

[20] In a large house there are articles not only of gold and silver, but also of wood and clay; some are for noble purposes and some for ignoble. [21] If a man cleanses himself from the latter, he will be an instrument for noble purposes, made holy, useful to the Master and prepared to do any good work (2 Tim. 2:20-21).

The context of 2 Timothy 2:14–3:9 is the problems the false teachers are causing in the house churches of Ephesus. Paul sees **a great contrast** between a godly leader, such as Timothy, and the ungodly false teachers. Paul illustrates this contrast with **two types of vessels**. In a large house, where the wealthy live, there are vessels of gold and silver for honorable purposes—such as vases to beautify the home and pots or dishes for meals. In the same large house were vessels of wood and clay for dishonorable purposes—such as collecting garbage and bodily waste. Recall that houses of Paul's day lacked modern plumbing. So people often had to collect human waste in *dishonorable* pots, to empty far from the house. In a large house, there were also vessels that were more neutral and could be used for various purposes. But Paul focuses his illustration on two types of vessels—those for honor and those for dishonor.

Q 32 In Timothy's time, what were examples of vessels of honor and dishonor? Whom did these vessels represent?

As we study this section, we want to answer the two main questions of hermeneutics. *First*, what did these verses of Scripture mean to Timothy, the first reader? We want to understand the contrast Paul was making between Timothy and the false teachers. *Second*, what do these verses of 2 Timothy 2:14–3:9 mean to believers today? As we answer this second question, we will identify four timeless principles (A–D) to guide believers today to be vessels of honor, rather than vessels of dishonor. *Paul emphasizes a sobering principle:* **Our choices determine whether God will use us as a *vessel of honor.** So in this lesson we will look closely at choices that qualify us to be vessels of honor (See A–D, Figure 6.13).

Q 33 What determines whether we are vessels of honor or dishonor?

2 Timothy	Principles That Guide Us to Be Vessels of Honor	Contrasting Behavior of Those Who Are Vessels of Dishonor
2:14-18	**A.** We stay focused on the A, B, C's of the faith—the spiritual essentials.	They delight in worthless, fringe discussions, unbiblical teachings, and the newest topics.
2:16, 19, 21-22	**B.** We turn from evil desires—and pursue righteousness, faith, love, and peace.	They become more and more ungodly. They mix and unite with other vessels of dishonor. They are unholy and worthless to God for any good work.
2:23-26	**C.** We avoid quarreling—and teach in a gentle manner.	They love word battles, have lost their senses, and are captured alive to do the devil's will.
3:1-9	**D.** We choose friends and relationships wisely.	They are *"lovers of themselves, lovers of money, boastful, proud, abusive, disobedient to their parents, ungrateful, unholy, ³without love, unforgiving, slanderous, without self-control, brutal, not lovers of the good, ⁴treacherous, rash, conceited, lovers of pleasure rather than lovers of God—⁵having a form of godliness but denying its power"* (2 Tim. 3:2-5).

Figure 6.13   Paul contrasts vessels of honor and vessels of dishonor (2 Tim. 2:14–3:9).

A. To be a vessel of honor, stay focused on the A, B, C's of the faith (2 Tim. 2:14-18).

¹⁴*Keep reminding **them** of these things. Warn **them** before God against quarreling about words; it is of no value, and only ruins those who listen.* ¹⁵*Do your best to present yourself to God as one approved, a workman who does not need to be ashamed and who correctly handles the word of truth.* ¹⁶*Avoid godless chatter, because those who indulge in it will become more and more ungodly.* ¹⁷*Their teaching will spread like gangrene. Among them are Hymenaeus and Philetus,* ¹⁸*who have wandered away from the truth. They say that the resurrection has already taken place, and they destroy the faith of some* (2 Tim. 2:14-18).

Q 34 To whom does "them" refer in 2 Timothy 2:14?

Q 35 To what does "these things" refer in 2 Timothy 2:14?

Paul does not expect false teaching to disappear. Rather, he warns that it will spread like *gangrene—a condition that infects the body, causing flesh to die and rot, and often resulting in death. Gangrene is a common condition that occurs when soldiers are wounded and not treated in time. Paul compares gangrene to false teaching, which infects and spreads through the body of Christ, killing the faith of many believers. Because of this great danger, Paul tells Pastor Timothy to *"keep reminding **them*** [believers in Ephesus]

Q 36 What is gangrene? To what does Paul compare it?

of *these things"*—the gospel and teachings Paul has already written in 1 Timothy and Titus, and is writing in this final letter to his son in the faith (Review Titus 3:3-10).

Paul commands Timothy to warn his sheep *"before God against quarreling about words; it is of no value, and only ruins those who listen"* (2 Tim. 2:14). Paul has already written about the way the false teachers like to quarrel, argue, and stir up controversy. Review some of Paul's passages as you complete Figure 6.14.

Q 37 *Complete Figure 6.14 on avoiding arguments and word battles.*

Reference	Your Summaries About Avoiding Arguments, Quarrels, and Controversy
1 Tim. 1:3b-4	Certain men teach
1 Tim. 1:6-7	
1 Tim. 2:8	
1 Tim. 6:3-4	
Titus 3:9	
Titus 3:10	
2 Tim. 2:16-18	

Figure 6.14   Practice summarizing passages about avoiding quarrels, arguments, controversy, and division.

Two believers, a tall one and a short one, were attending a big church meeting. Both of these pastors were angry, and they argued while others watched. The tall preacher's face was red, and his words were loud. He was rebuking the shorter pastor for his beliefs on the timing of the Lord's return. "You are wrong," yelled the tall pastor. "And when I say you are wrong, you are wrong!" If the apostle Paul had been present, he would have urged them not to quarrel and argue. And he would have reminded them that God will bring about the Coming of Christ in His own time (1 Tim. 6:14-15). The A, B, C's of the faith include the fact that Jesus is coming back for us. But God is not pleased when believers quarrel, argue, and speculate about the timing of the Blessed Hope. Instead of arguing about the timing of Christ's return, let us rejoice together in worship for this glorious event of the faith! Jesus is preparing a place for us to live with Him forever, and He is coming back for us. If it were not true, He would have told us (John 14:2-3).

The main things are the plain things. Paul wants Timothy and us to focus on the gospel—the A, B, C's of the faith. Titus 3:3-10 contrasts some **basic truths** *that are profitable* with **foolish controversies** *that are unprofitable.* Paul reminds us of who we used to be, and who we have become, because of the love and grace of God—and how we should live:

Q 38 *In Titus 3:8-10, what does Paul contrast with basic truths of the faith?*

foolish controversies

Q 39 *What basic truths of the faith does Titus 3:3-8 summarize?*

*[1]Remind the people to be subject to rulers and authorities, to be obedient, to be ready to do whatever is good, [2]to slander no one, to be peaceable and considerate, and to show true humility toward all men. [3]At one time we too were foolish, disobedient, deceived and enslaved by all kinds of passions and pleasures. We lived in malice and envy, being hated and hating one another. [4]But when the kindness and love of God our Savior appeared, [5]he saved us, not because of righteous things we had done, but because of his mercy. He saved us through the washing of rebirth and renewal by the Holy Spirit, [6]whom he poured out on us generously through Jesus Christ our Savior, [7]so that, having been justified by his grace, we might become heirs having the hope of eternal life. [8]This is a trustworthy saying. And I want you to stress these things, so that those who have trusted in God may be careful to devote themselves to doing what is good. These things are **excellent and profitable** for everyone. [9]But avoid foolish controversies and genealogies and arguments and quarrels about the law, because these are **unprofitable and useless**. [10]Warn a divisive person once, and then warn him a second time. After that, have nothing to do with him. [11]You may be sure that such a man is warped and sinful; he is self-condemned* (Titus 3:1-11).

Focusing on the A, B, C's of the faith requires studying the Bible. As we study Scriptures, we focus on the topics God wants us to learn, discuss, and meditate upon—instead of arguing about controversies. Bible study is God's solution for steering away from foolish debates. So Paul told Timothy:

> *Do your best to present yourself to God as one approved, a workman who does not need to be ashamed and who correctly handles the word of truth* (2 Tim. 2:15).

Some believers waste time and words, arguing about the location of Noah's ark, the clothes in which Jesus was buried, the phases of the moon, or the latest stories of a traveling preacher. In contrast, students like you, who study the Bible and biblical courses such as those in the *Faith & Action Series*, are obeying 2 Timothy 2:15. This is a positive, edifying way to avoid arguments and focus on the essentials of the faith. So thank you for your obedient and diligent study of the Scriptures. God will honor you as a vessel of honor, as you honor Him and His Word.

Q 40 *What is God's solution to avoid useless arguments?*

Q 41 *What are some unprofitable topics about which you have heard believers argue?*

B. To be a vessel of honor, turn from evil desires, and pursue righteousness, faith, love, and peace (2 Tim. 2:19-22).

> [19]*Nevertheless, God's solid foundation stands firm, sealed with this inscription: "The Lord knows those who are his," and,* **"Everyone who confesses the name of the Lord must turn away from wickedness."** [20]*In a large house there are articles not only of gold and silver, but also of wood and clay; some are for noble purposes and some for ignoble.* [21]*If a man cleanses himself from the latter, he will be an instrument for noble purposes, made holy, useful to the Master and prepared to do any good work.* [22]*Flee the evil desires of youth, and pursue righteousness, faith, love and peace, along with those who call on the Lord out of a pure heart* (2 Tim. 2:19-22).

THE ROAD OF OBEDIENCE TO GOD LEADS TO BLESSING. BUT THE ROAD OF DISOBEDIENCE LEADS TO BEING CURSED.

Some false teachers today claim that the grace of God covers those who continue to practice sin day after day. But nothing could be further from Paul's gospel. As we emphasize in Hermeneutics 2, two roads run through both covenants. The road of obedience to God leads to blessing. But the road of disobedience leads to being cursed. How can Paul say it any plainer than: **"Everyone who confesses the name of the Lord must turn away from wickedness"** (2 Tim. 2:19)? **To be a vessel of honor, we must turn away from evil and cleanse ourselves from choosing ignoble, dishonorable, sinful purposes.** Read 2 Timothy 2:19-22 until you see this truth clearly. Grace does not hide the sin we practice. Rather, grace teaches us to say "No" to sin and "Yes" to holy living (Titus 2:12). **Vessels of honor** turn away from what is wrong, and by the power of the Holy Spirit turn toward and practice doing what is good. Recall that Paul repeats one theme six times in three chapters: *Doing what is good* (Titus 1:16; 2:7, 14; 3:1, 8, 14). Did he repeat it enough for us to see the truth?

Q 42 *Which 2 roads run through both the old and new covenants? Explain.*

Paul urges Timothy to flee the evil desires of youth. These evil desires include sexual passions. Elsewhere Paul makes it clear that no immoral person has any inheritance in the kingdom of God (Eph. 5:5; 1 Cor. 6:9). But youth may also be led astray by seeking the approval of peers. Also, youth may have foolish desires for knowledge about new philosophies. A young sheep can be led astray and lost by its desire to chase a butterfly or to see what is over the next hill. The desire to learn is good, but not all learning is profitable. The false teachers at Ephesus (and other places) led many away from the faith under the banner of *knowledge*. In time, some of these errors related to the desire for knowledge became known as *Gnosticism* (based on the Greek word *gnosis*, which

Q 43 *What are some examples of evil desires of youth?*

means "knowledge"). As believers mature, they get older and wiser—and realize that *"all the treasures of wisdom and knowledge are hidden in Christ"* (Col. 2:3). And the new ideas, controversies, and philosophies of wandering teachers are not worth wasting one's time on them. As Adam and Eve traded paradise for a fruit of no value, thousands of youth have traded their faith for hollow philosophies of man that cannot satisfy the soul or restore us to a relationship with our Creator. There is much knowledge that wise people walk away from. Paul wanted believers to be wise about the good, and unknowing about the evil (Rom. 16:19). *"Timothy, guard what has been entrusted to your care. Turn away from godless chatter and the opposing ideas of what is **falsely called knowledge**"* (1 Tim. 6:20). **In contrast, Paul emphasizes thinking on good things** (Phil. 4:8).

Sabio says: "Blessed are those who hunger and thirst for righteousness—rather than the newest ideas the world is peddling."

¹I want you to know how much I am struggling for you and for those at Laodicea, and for all who have not met me personally. ²My purpose is that they may be encouraged in heart and united in love, so that they may have the full riches of complete understanding, in order that they may know the mystery of God, namely, Christ, ³in whom are hidden all the treasures of wisdom and knowledge. ⁴I tell you this so that no one may deceive you by fine-sounding arguments (Col. 2:1-4).

> TO BE A VESSEL OF HONOR WE MUST HONOR GOD WITH OUR WORDS AND ACTIONS.

Q 44 *What choices caused Eli and his household to become vessels of dishonor?*

To be a vessel of honor we must honor God with our words and actions. God promises to honor those who honor Him. And He promises to dishonor and disdain those who despise and disobey Him. Take a moment to review the story of Eli the priest, and his rebellious sons, Hophni and Phineas. God's plan was to honor the household of Eli forever. But Eli and his sons refused to honor God. They stole the best offerings the Israelites brought for God, and committed adultery with some of the women who came to worship. Eli knew about these evils, but did not remove his sons from being priests. So instead of inheriting honor, Eli is known for shame, reproach, and being cursed. **Like the false teachers, Eli and his sons abandoned the A, B, C's of the faith—which include obeying God, and doing good instead of doing bad** (1 Sam. 2:27-36).

*²⁷Now a man of God came to Eli and said to him, "This is what the LORD says: 'Did I not clearly reveal myself to your father's house when they were in Egypt under Pharaoh? ²⁸I chose your father out of all the tribes of Israel to be my priest, to go up to my altar, to burn incense, and to wear an ephod in my presence. I also gave your father's house all the offerings made with fire by the Israelites. ²⁹Why do you scorn my sacrifice and offering that I prescribed for my dwelling? Why do you honor your sons more than me by fattening yourselves on the choice parts of every offering made by my people Israel?' ³⁰Therefore the LORD, the God of Israel, declares: 'I promised that your house and your father's house would minister before me forever.' But now the LORD declares: 'Far be it from me! **Those who honor me I will honor, but those who despise me will be disdained.** ³¹The time is coming when I will cut short your strength and the strength of your father's house, so that there will not be an old man in your family line ³²and you will see distress in my dwelling. Although good will be done to Israel, in your family line there will never be an old man. ³³Every one of you that I do not cut off from my altar will be spared only to blind your eyes with tears and to grieve your heart, and all your descendants will die in the prime of life. ³⁴And what happens to your two sons, Hophni and Phinehas, will be a sign to you—they will both die on the same day.*

³⁵I will raise up for myself a faithful priest, who will do according to what is in my heart and mind. I will firmly establish his house, and he will minister before my anointed one always. ³⁶Then everyone left in your family line will come and bow down before him for a piece of silver and a crust of bread and plead, "Appoint me to some priestly office so I can have food to eat" ' " (1 Sam. 2:27-36).

C. To be a vessel of honor, avoid quarreling—and teach in a gentle manner (2 Tim. 2:23-26).

²³Don't have anything to do with foolish and stupid arguments, because you know they produce quarrels. ²⁴And the Lord's servant must not quarrel; instead, he must be kind to everyone, able to teach, not resentful. ²⁵Those who oppose him he must gently instruct, in the hope that God will grant them repentance leading them to a knowledge of the truth, ²⁶and that they will come to their senses and escape from the trap of the devil, who has taken them captive to do his will (2 Tim. 2:23-26).

In the Greek, the phrase *"has taken them captive"* means literally "has captured them alive."[12] Seducing spirits and doctrines of demons deceive people (1 Tim. 4:1). These victims are captured alive by the devil and are doing his will, even while they believe they are doing God's will. Yet through anointed, gentle teaching, God may grant these prisoners insight into the truth—that they may *"come to their senses and escape from the trap of the devil"* (2 Tim. 2:26). Harsh words will alienate these captives. Paul's only hope is in gentle persuasion.

When I was attending my doctoral studies, one of my professors shocked me. He was expressing his gratitude for what he learned from a book about theology, which was written by an unbeliever. I knew that this author did not believe in the deity of Christ, the resurrection, heaven, or hell. I shook my head in unbelief and said rudely, "I suppose it is possible to find a biscuit, even if you look in a trash can." This made the professor very angry, and I will not repeat what he said! After class, I apologized for being rude, and tried to express my shock in a more polite, gentle manner. The professor said that it was good to have strong convictions about the Bible and our faith—but we should never knock people down with what we believe. Of all the lessons in my doctoral studies, this one truth was the most helpful to me. Some of us with strong convictions tend to forget that *"the Lord's servant must not quarrel; instead, he must be kind to everyone, able to teach, not resentful. ²⁵Those who oppose him he must gently instruct"* (2 Tim. 2:24-25). Some of the people who make us angry are the people who need our help the most. But when we quarrel, or are rude and unkind, people do not remember the truth we tried to tell them. They only recall our rudeness.

Q 47 ⟋ *Which 2 examples illustrate the gentleness of Jesus (Matt. 12:20)? Explain each.*

Jesus is our great example of being kind and gentle. There was a time or two when He cleansed the temple or scathed the Pharisees, as in Matthew 23. But in such times, He was probably just pushing His enemies toward crucifying Him, so He could save them and us. Almost always we see Jesus being gentle. Our Savior was so gentle that He would not break a reed that was already bent. And He would not snuff out a candle that was already smoking.

*¹⁸"Here is my servant whom I have chosen, the one I love, in whom I delight; I will put my Spirit on him, and he will proclaim justice to the nations. ¹⁹He will **not quarrel or cry out**; no one will hear his voice in the streets. ²⁰A bruised reed he will not break, and a smoldering wick he will not snuff out, till he leads justice to victory. ²¹In his name the nations will put their hope"* (Matt. 12:18-21).

Truly Jesus gave us an example that we might follow in His steps.

Q 45 ⟍ *Which A, B, C's of the faith does Paul emphasize in Titus 2:11-14?*

Q 46 ⟍ *Is rudeness necessary for expressing strong convictions? Explain.*

Q 48 ⟍ *How would you describe and illustrate a gentle person?*

22 "He committed no sin, and no deceit was found in his mouth." 23 When they hurled their insults at him, he did not retaliate; when he suffered, he made no threats. Instead, he entrusted himself to him who judges justly (1 Pet. 2:22-23).

Sabio says: "Some preach as if they are looking down a gun barrel or through a rifle scope!" But God does not call us to quarrel and fight. Most of the people we will influence for Jesus are those who feel the love and kindness of God as we talk to them, work beside them, or live near them.

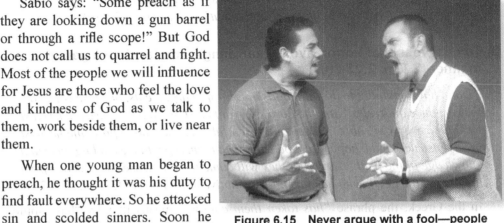

Figure 6.15   Never argue with a fool—people might not notice the difference.

Q 49 ➤ *What mistake did the young preacher make?*

When one young man began to preach, he thought it was his duty to find fault everywhere. So he attacked sin and scolded sinners. Soon he became known as the preacher who ate sour grapes three times a day. One listener compared him to Ishmael, whose hand was against everyone (Gen. 16:12). But as the young pastor matured, he stopped criticizing people and began to preach Christ, who loved us so much that He died on a cross to save us from the penalty and power of sin. So people looked forward to hearing his sermons about the love, grace, goodness, and faithfulness of God. And when he did speak about things such as sin, judgment, and hell, there were tears in his voice, as well as his eyes.

Augustine wrote, "In essentials, unity; in non-essentials, liberty; in all things, charity."[13]

D. To be a vessel of honor, choose friends and relationships wisely (2 Tim. 3:1-9).

Q 50 ➤ *Whose responsibility is it to prevent false teachers from spreading in the church?*

As overseer of the house churches at Ephesus, Timothy has the responsibility of shepherding God's sheep. He must not allow false teachings to spread like a deadly disease among his people. Timothy must not allow the false teachers to mingle with his members, as a wolf enters a fold of sheep to destroy them. He must take a firm stand against these false teachers, put them out of the church, and have nothing to do with them. They are rejected from the faith, because they have rejected it (2 Tim. 3:8). In the same way that Jannes and Jambres, the magicians of Pharaoh, opposed Moses, these false teachers oppose the work of God (Exod. 7:8-13, 22; 8:7). (Note that although these magicians are not named in the Old Testament, over the centuries tradition gives names to the unnamed. By 150 B.C., the memory of Pharaoh's magicians was represented by two, referred to as Jannes and Jambres.[14] A similar example in tradition is naming the rich man Dives in Luke 16:19-31.)

Q 51 ➤ *When do the last days occur?*

As we look at 2 Timothy 3:1-9, notice the phrase *"in the last days"* (2 Tim. 3:1). **The *last days are a period of time that stretches from the First Coming of Jesus to His Second Coming.**

1 But mark this: There will be terrible times in the last days. 2 People will be lovers of themselves, lovers of money, boastful, proud, abusive, disobedient to their parents, ungrateful, unholy, 3 without love, unforgiving, slanderous, without self-control, brutal, not lovers of the good, 4 treacherous, rash, conceited, lovers of pleasure rather than lovers of God—5 having a form of godliness but denying its power. Have nothing to do with them. 6 They are the kind who worm their way into homes and gain control over weak-willed women, who are loaded down with sins and are swayed by all kinds of evil desires, ⁷always learning but never able to acknowledge the truth. ⁸Just as Jannes and Jambres opposed Moses, so also these men oppose the truth—men of depraved minds, who, as far as the faith is concerned, are rejected. ⁹But they will not get very far because, as in the case of those men, their folly will be clear to everyone (2 Tim. 3:1-9).

Recall that the Day of Pentecost occurred **in the last days.**

¹⁶*"...This is what was spoken by the prophet Joel:* ¹⁷*'**In the last days**, God says, I will pour out my Spirit on all people. Your sons and daughters will prophesy, your young men will see visions, your old men will dream dreams. ¹⁸Even on my servants, both men and women, I will pour out my Spirit in those days, and they will prophesy. ¹⁹I will show wonders in the heaven above and signs on the earth below, blood and fire and billows of smoke. ²⁰The sun will be turned to darkness and the moon to blood before the coming of the great and glorious day of the Lord' "* (Acts 2:16-20).

Of course there will be the final days of earth—the last of the last days. But it is important to realize that we are living in a unique period of history—**the last days** of the history of man on earth. The time of animal sacrifices under the old covenant is past. Christ has come to earth, died, resurrected, and ascended to heaven. We live under the new and final covenant that God has made with mankind. It is true that sin will yet increase on the earth. And false teachers will go from bad to worse (2 Tim. 3:13). But Paul's characteristics of people in the last days were present while the ink was still wet on the last letter he wrote to Timothy. All of the 18 evil characteristics of **people** in the last days were present in Ephesus when Paul wrote. This is clear as we read 2 Timothy 3:5b: *"**Have nothing to do with them.**"* Note that **them** includes the false teachers Timothy was battling at Ephesus.

Furthermore, what Paul says about the false teachers in 2 Timothy 3:6-7 helps us interpret what Paul has written about women and younger widows. The false teachers were *worming* their way into the homes of some women to gain control over them. The false teachers were offering teaching and knowledge, and some women were *"always learning but never able to acknowledge the truth"* (2 Tim. 3:7). False teachers were taking advantage of women's sincere desire to learn about God. But the false teachers deceived and manipulated women and men, ruining whole families by leading them astray with false knowledge. What the false teachers were doing through a few women at Ephesus caused Paul to lay down strict rules to protect other women and families. No wonder Paul did not allow women to teach in some cases. When we understand the methods of the false teachers, it helps us interpret Paul's guidelines for those days.

Q 52 ⟋ *How does understanding the methods of false teachers help us interpret what Paul wrote about younger widows?*

As you look at Paul's list of 18 sins of people in the last days, the first sin on the list is lovers of self. Loving self instead of God is the source, the polluted fountain, of the other sins (2 Tim. 2:4). Christianity affirms love of self in the proper relationship to neighbors and God, and does not exclude pleasure, within God's plan. So often sin is the result of desire out of balance or out of bounds.

Q 53 ⟋ *What were 6 main sins of the false teachers at Ephesus?*

Paul has already called attention to some of the 18 sins of the false teachers. They love money, are boastful and proud, and are unholy. But most of all they have a form of godliness, yet deny its power to transform lives. For the wisdom from heaven does not result in arguing and sinful living—but in doing good, bringing peace and a righteous harvest (James 3:13-18). To be vessels of honor, we must avoid close relationships with those who love evil—and choose friends who love God and live to do good.

Second Samuel 13 contains the sad story of Amnon, who was in love with Tamar. In the end, Amnon lost his life because he listened to the advice of an ungodly friend. History would be better if Amnon had chosen a better friend.

Q 54 ⟋ *What bad advice did Amnon receive from his "friend," Jonadab? Apply this.*

Q 55 ✎ *Does 2 Timothy 3:5 teach us to avoid all sinners? Explain.*

On the surface, *"have nothing to do with them"* may seem to conflict with Jesus, who was a friend of sinners. But Jesus Himself told us not to fellowship with those who cause trouble among believers, and refuse to repent (Matt. 18:17). Paul wrote this same command for those in the church who had rejected truth and discipline.

⁹*I have written you in my letter not to associate with sexually immoral people—*¹⁰*not at all meaning the people of this world who are immoral, or the greedy and swindlers, or idolaters. In that case you would have to leave this world.* ¹¹*But now I am writing you that you must not associate with anyone who calls himself a brother but is sexually immoral or greedy, an idolater or a slanderer, a drunkard or a swindler. With such a man do not even eat.* ¹²*What business is it of mine to judge those outside the church? Are you not to judge those inside?* ¹³*God will judge those outside. "Expel the wicked man **from among you**"* (1 Cor. 5:9-13).

To be vessels of honor, we need to form wise relationships with godly people, and avoid friendships with those who disobey God. What fellowship has light with darkness?

Figure 6.16   In the beginning, God made Adam from the ground. God sees each person as clay He desires to shape into a vessel of honor by the hands of the Divine Potter. God welcomes all to come to Him and yield themselves to His plan. But He leaves the choice with each of us.

Conclusion to being a vessel of honor: God leaves the choice to us, but He remains faithful to reward the righteous, and punish the unrighteous. If you are living as a vessel of honor, continue to make wise choices, knowing that God has promised: *"Those who honor me I will honor, but those who despise me will be disdained"* (1 Sam. 2:30). To those who have lived as a dishonorable vessel, God invites tears of repentance, faith in Jesus Christ as Savior and Lord, and a new beginning. As the potter reshaped the clay, God offers to transform dishonorable vessels into vessels of honor. This is the good news, and God's will for all of us who have sinned. As we close this lesson, listen to the Word of the Lord that came to the prophet Jeremiah— showing the two choices God offers each person:

Q 56 ↗ *What 2 choices did Jeremiah show the people? Does each person have similar choices today?*

Q 57 ✎ *How did the Israelites respond to God's prophet?*

¹*This is the word that came to Jeremiah from the LORD:* ²*"Go down to the potter's house, and there I will give you my message."* ³*So I went down to the potter's house, and I saw him working at the wheel.* ⁴*But the pot he was shaping from the clay was marred in his hands; so the potter formed it into another pot, shaping it as seemed best to him.* ⁵*Then the word of the LORD came to me:* ⁶*"O house of Israel, can I not do with you as this potter does?" declares the LORD. "Like clay in the hand of the potter, so are you in my hand, O house of Israel.* ⁷*If at any time I announce that a nation or kingdom is to be uprooted, torn down and destroyed,* ⁸*and **if that nation I warned repents of its evil**, then I will relent and not inflict on it the disaster I had planned.* ⁹*And if at another time I announce that a nation or kingdom is to be built up and planted,* ¹⁰*and **if it does evil in my sight and does not obey me**, then I will reconsider the good I had intended to do for it.* ¹¹*Now therefore say to the people of Judah and those living in Jerusalem, 'This is what the LORD says: Look! I am preparing a disaster for you and devising a plan against you. So turn from your evil ways, each one of you, and reform your ways and your actions.'* ¹²*But they will reply, 'It's no use. We will continue with our own plans; each of us will follow the stubbornness of his evil heart.'"* ¹³*Therefore this is what the LORD says: "Inquire among the nations: Who has ever heard anything like this? A most horrible thing has been done by Virgin Israel.* ¹⁴*Does the snow of Lebanon ever vanish from its rocky slopes? Do its cool waters from distant sources ever cease to flow?* ¹⁵*Yet my people have forgotten*

me; they burn incense to worthless idols, which made them stumble in their ways and in the ancient paths. They made them walk in bypaths and on roads not built up. ¹⁶*Their land will be laid waste, an object of lasting scorn; all who pass by will be appalled and will shake their heads.* ¹⁷*Like a wind from the east, I will scatter them before their enemies; I will show them my back and not my face in the day of their disaster."* ¹⁸*They said, "Come, let's make plans against Jeremiah; for the teaching of the law by the priest will not be lost, nor will counsel from the wise, nor the word from the prophets. So come, let's attack him with our tongues and pay no attention to anything he says"* (Jer. 18:1-18).

Lesson 29 — Finishing the Race Well—Part 1 (2 Tim. 3:10-17)

Goal A: *Explain the need to continue walking in the light of Scriptures and those who taught us.*

Goal B: *Define* inspiration, inerrancy, *and* infallibility, *and explain how belief in these guides us.*

Q 58 *What truth does Pastor John's race illustrate for us?*

Pastor John Palmer tells the story of a race he ran at the age of 13. In those early years, like many youth, John was a bit clumsy. His body was growing faster than his coordination. Many parents had come to the school to watch their kids race. About 12 boys lined up for John's race—eager to run, and excited that their parents were watching. The race began with the sound of a loud clap, as someone yelled "Go!" All of the boys began running except one. For as he started, John had tripped over the shoe of another boy, and was lying on the ground. He got up, although his knee was bleeding, and his ankle was hurting. By this time all of the other boys were more than 50 meters ahead of him. Still, John began running. With every step he was embarrassed. It seemed that he could feel the eyes of everyone staring at him, and even imagined some laughing and pointing at him. Because his ankle was hurting, he could not run his best, so the other boys were getting further and further ahead. As he ran around one curve, he saw an open gate. Suddenly, the temptation came over him to leave the race and run away from the crowd, through the gate. But just then he thought of his father and mother, whom he knew would still be cheering for him to finish the race—even if he was not

Figure 6.17 Paul compares the Christian life to a race that ends in heaven or hell.

the fastest runner. His parents had always emphasized, "Never be a quitter." So with new courage, John continued running on the track, and did not turn aside through the temptation of the open gate. When he finally finished the race, far behind all the others, he was amazed to hear a whole crowd of people cheering for him. And the best part of all was when his parents hugged him and said, "Thank you, John, for representing our family and finishing the race well. We are so proud of you!" Throughout the race from earth to heaven, many of us may stumble and fall a time or two. Still, we get up and keep running. And there are some temptations for us to quit the race. Yet as we think about others who have finished the race, we find inspiration and new strength to run well ourselves—following in the footsteps of heroes of the faith, and being a good example to those who are running behind us. Paul's only command in 2 Timothy 3:10-18 is: *"But as for you,* **continue in what you have learned and have become convinced of***, because you know those from whom you learned it"* (2 Tim. 3:14).

In Paul's day, people liked to watch athletes run races. The athletes trained for at least 9 months. Thousands of people gathered in stadiums, as they do at today's Olympic races. Paul compares our life on earth to a race. The prize at the end of the long race is eternal life with God in heaven (1 Cor. 9:25; Phil. 3:12-14; Heb. 12:1). To be winners in the race, we do not have to be the fastest—but we must please God and remain faithful to the end of the race. In Lessons 29 and 30, we will study three principles (A–C) to help us finish the race well.

A. To finish the race well, we must continue to live in the light of Scripture and the Godly who taught us (2 Tim. 3:10-17).

In this section, Paul turns from the characteristics of the false teachers to face Timothy, his son in the faith. In the eight verses of 2 Timothy 3:10-17, Paul refers to six themes about which he has already written in 2 Timothy 1:3–2:13 (Figure 6.18).

Q 59 *What is the one command in the six themes to which Paul refers in 2 Timothy 3:10-17?*

Second Timothy 3:10-18	Themes From Second Timothy 1:3–2:13	Second Timothy 1:3–2:13
3:10-11, 14	1. Timothy's long relationship with Paul	1:4, 6, 13
3:10-11	2. Paul, the model of loyalty to Christ	1:8, 11-13; 2:9-10
3:11-12	3. The call to suffering	1:8, 16; 2:3-6, 11-12
3:14	4. The **command** to continue following Christ, as Paul and others have followed Him	1:6, 13-14
3:15	5. The faith of Timothy's ancestors	1:5
3:15	6. The focus on salvation	2:10-13

Figure 6.18   As Paul comes to the third section of 2 Timothy, he summarizes six themes he has already emphasized. Paul summarizes these six themes in light of what he has just said about the false teachers in 2 Timothy 2:14–3:9.

Q 60 *What is the main verse of 2 Timothy 3:10-18? How does it relate to the rest of the paragraph?*

But in all these verses of 2 Timothy 3:10-17, there is only one command, which is Paul's main point: ***"Continue in what you have learned and have become convinced of"*** (2 Tim. 3:14).[15] Keep this command in mind as you read this paragraph:

> [10]*You, however, know all about my teaching, my way of life, my purpose, faith, patience, love, endurance,* [11]*persecutions, sufferings—what kinds of things happened to me in Antioch, Iconium and Lystra, the persecutions I endured. Yet the Lord rescued me from all of them.* [12]*In fact, everyone who wants to live a godly life in Christ Jesus will be persecuted,* [13]*while evil men and impostors will go from bad to worse, deceiving and being deceived.* [14]*But as for you, **continue in what you have learned and have become convinced of, because you know those from whom you learned it,*** [15]*and how from infancy you have known the holy Scriptures, which are able to make you wise for salvation through faith in Christ Jesus.* [16]*All Scripture is God-breathed and is useful for teaching, rebuking, correcting and training in righteousness,* [17]*so that the man of God may be thoroughly equipped for every good work* (2 Tim. 3:10-17).

A top leader in a big business told the story of how he had risen to a place of honor and influence. He began as a young man, doing small tasks in the office. Then one day the president of the business called him aside and said, "I want you to come into my office and be with me each day." The young man replied, "But what could I do to help you, sir? I don't know much about finances." The president replied, "That does not matter, you will learn what I want to teach you if you *just stay by my side* with your eyes and ears open!" Years later, the young man had risen to a top position in the business. He testified: "Being with that president day by day helped me be like him. I began to do things the way he did, and that is the reason I am who I am today."[16]

Q 61 *Have you noticed that as years pass, some become worse and others better? Give examples.*

No one stays the same throughout life. The bad become worse. Following the flesh is like walking down stairs—it is easier than walking up stairs—but each step takes us lower into depravity and destruction. In contrast, the good become better (2 Tim. 3:13). Persecution and suffering refine and perfect us. At the beginning of his ministry, Timothy was with Paul at Lystra. He was there when they dragged Paul out from under a pile of stones (Acts 14:8-20). Timothy knew from the first that persecution is a part of following Jesus. Time after time he had watched Paul persevere through trials. Year after year he had seen illustrations of the fact: *"everyone who wants to live a godly life in*

Christ Jesus will be persecuted" (2 Tim. 3:12). Walking with Paul, and following in his footsteps, Timothy grew from a boy to a man, and from a minister's helper to a minister who supervised others.

Sabio reminds us: [18] *"The path of the righteous is like the first gleam of dawn, shining ever brighter till the full light of day.* [19] *But the way of the wicked is like deep darkness; they do not know what makes them stumble"* (Prov. 4:18-19).

Q 62 Why do you think studying the Scriptures helps us finish well?

Studying and obeying the Scriptures is a major key to finishing our race well. As we love and honor God's Word, we are following in the footsteps of godly examples. Earlier Paul urged Timothy:

[1] *Do your best to present yourself to God as one approved, a workman who does not need to be ashamed and who correctly handles the word of truth* (2 Tim. 2:15)

Here again Paul reminds Timothy:

[14] *But as for you,* **continue** *in what you have learned and have become convinced of, because you know those from whom you learned it,* [15] *and how* **from infancy you have known the holy Scriptures**, *which are able to make you wise for salvation through faith in Christ Jesus.* [16] **All Scripture is God-breathed** *and is useful for teaching, rebuking, correcting and training in righteousness,* [17] *so that the man of God may be thoroughly equipped for every good work* (2 Tim. 3:14-17).

Q 63 Summarize Timothy's great heritage.

Q 64 How will you help children learn about God?

Timothy had a great heritage. His mother and grandmother had taught him the Bible from his earliest years. Children are able to learn hundreds of Bible stories before they are 5 years old. Our daughter, Cheryti McGhee, could recognize 50 Bible characters, and answer questions about them by the time she was 2 years old. We taught her from a children's Bible story book that had pictures. Blessed is the child, like Timothy, whom parents and grandparents teach the Bible from infancy. Children who learn the Scriptures at an early age develop godly character. As they walk in the light of God's Word they avoid many temptations and sins of the world. Such children grow up to be a great blessing in the church, serving as strong believers in the community, faithful church members, bold witnesses, responsible parents, teachers, deacons, pastors, evangelists, and missionaries. And blessed are the parents who take time each day to teach their children the Scriptures. For teaching God's Word bears fruit in the children's lives, year after year. Also, every church should teach children in Sunday school, children's church, and through programs such as *Missionettes, *Royal Rangers, and *Bible Quiz—a program that helps children and youth memorize and understand entire books of the New Testament. (For more information on how to teach children, see the *Faith & Action* course, *Children's Ministry*.)

Q 65 Complete Figure 6.19 on key terms about Scripture.

Term	Your Definitions
Inspiration	
Inerrant	
Infallible	

Figure 6.19 Practice defining key terms about Scripture.

Only through Scripture can we learn how to be saved (2 Tim. 3:15). Paul emphasizes that all Scripture is breathed by God. So we say the Bible is *inspired.* *Inspiration* is the process by which God breathed His message into the writers of Scripture, and carried them along by the Holy Spirit—so that they wrote what He intended, free from error. Since God breathed Scripture, and carried the writers along by the Spirit, we affirm that God's Word is *inerrant*, truthful and free from error; it is also *infallible*— trustworthy, not capable of erring, deceiving, or leading people astray. Note that inerrant and infallible are very close in meaning, and almost synonyms. [17]

Q 66 ✎ *Complete Figure 6.20 on the origin and nature of Scripture.*

Reference	Your Summaries
1 Thess. 2:13	
2 Tim. 3:16	
2 Pet. 1:21	

Figure 6.20   Practice summarizing verses about the origin and nature of Scripture.

Q 67 ✎ *How does believing that the Scriptures are inspired, inerrant, and infallible affect our behavior?*

Q 68 ✎ *Would you believe the Bible if it said Jonah swallowed a whale? Explain.*

For us to confess that Scripture is inspired, inerrant, and infallible is to bind ourselves to obey, harmonize, and integrate all that Scripture declares. Without exception, I must believe that Scripture is from God, however little I may like it. I must seek to live by Scripture, letting it shape my beliefs, ways, and commitments.[18]

Q 69 ✎ *Explain this saying: "Let the Bible read you."*

Let the Bible read you (2 Tim. 3:16-17).

There are two ways you can study the Bible: The <u>wrong</u> way is to study the Bible with your mind made up. The right way is to study the Bible to make up your mind.[19] Which way do you study the Bible?

Q 70 ↗ *What point does the illustration about Willie teach?*

THE BIBLE IS LIKE A MIRROR THAT REVEALS TO US OUR TRUE CONDITION.

The Bible is like a mirror that reveals to us our true condition. Pastor Moody told his family one morning: "I will come home early and take you to the park to see the bears." As soon as the pastor left, the youngest boy, Willie, asked his mother to help him get ready. She washed him and put clean clothes on him—so he was ready to go. Then the small boy went outside to play, and got very dirty. When the pastor came home he saw mud on the boy's face and clothes. Willie said, "Daddy, take me to see the bears; I am ready." But Pastor Moody replied, "Willie, I cannot take you in this condition. You must be washed first." "No, I am clean," said Willie. Pastor Moody answered, "No, you are not clean; you are very dirty." The little fellow began to cry, because he thought he was already clean. The dad thought the quickest way to help his son was to let him see himself. So he showed him his dirty face in the mirror. That stopped his crying at once. Willie was shocked to see how dirty he had become. He never said again that his face was clean after he saw himself. Soon, the boy was washed clean by the water, and ready to go with his father.[20]

[22]*Do not merely listen to the word, and so deceive yourselves. Do what it says.* [23]*Anyone who listens to the word but does not do what it says is like a man who looks at his face in a mirror* [24]*and, after looking at himself, goes away and immediately forgets what he looks like.* [25]*But the man who looks intently into the perfect law that gives freedom, and continues to do this, not forgetting what he has heard, but doing it—he will be blessed in what he does* (James 1:22-25).

[16]***All Scripture is God-breathed*** *and is useful for teaching, rebuking, correcting and training in righteousness,* [17]*so that the man of God may be thoroughly equipped for every good work* (2 Tim. 3:16-17).

As pastors preach the Word and believers study it, Scripture shows us how we look to God. The Spirit guides us to submit to the Word, walk in its light, and be cleansed from all sin, living pure and blameless (1 Thess. 5:23; Titus 2:11-14; 2 Tim. 2:19). Then we are able to enjoy fellowship with our Father.

Lesson 30 | **Finishing the Race Well—Part 2 (2 Tim. 4:1-22)**
Goal C: *Analyze why pastors must preach the Word, and explain 4 guidelines for preaching it.*
Goal D: *Summarize and apply Paul's attitudes toward persecutors, deserters, unmet expectations, and God.*

B. To finish the race well, God's servants must emphasize the Word (2 Tim. 4:1-8).

Earlier, in 2 Timothy 3:16, Paul wrote that the Word is profitable for teaching, rebuking, correcting, and training. Here in his final letter, Paul commands Timothy: *"Preach the word!"* The power of Paul's charge echoes like thunder through the centuries.

> [1] *In the presence of God and of Christ Jesus, who will judge the living and the dead, and in view of his appearing and his kingdom, I give you this charge:* [2] ***Preach the Word****; be prepared in season and out of season; correct, rebuke and encourage—with great patience and careful instruction* (2 Tim. 4:1-2).

Preach the Word, no matter what comes. Preach to rebuke, warn, and exhort, with all patience. The Word of God is what God has promised to bless. Our authority is not in our position, imagination, personality, or loudness—but only in the Word of God! Let us examine *four truths* about preaching the Word (2 Tim. 4:1-8).[21]

Q 71 ↖ *What are some reasons why we should preach, teach, and share the Word of God?*

Q 72 ↖ *Complete Figure 6.21 about Paul's commands on preaching the Word.*

2 Timothy	Paul's Commands on Preaching	Your Explanations on How to Fulfill Paul's Commands
4:2	1. Preach the Word in a prepared manner.	
4:2	2. Preach the Word in a relevant manner.	
2:23-26; 4:2	3. Preach the Word with great patience.	
4:3-8	4. Preach the Word with endurance—to the end of the race.	

Figure 6.21   Practice summarizing what Paul commanded Timothy about preaching the Word.

1. Preach the Word in a prepared manner (2 Tim. 4:2).

*Preach the Word; **be prepared in season and out of season*** (2 Tim. 4:2).

Good preaching requires the habits of daily devotions, Bible study, research, prayer, and meditation. As the preacher feeds himself, he finds spiritual food to share with others.

One of the best ways to prepare is preaching a series of messages. There are two types of series: topical and expository. Examples of a topical series are: *16 Bible Doctrines* (Figure 6.22); *Marriage & Family; Heroes of the Bible;* common problems people face (See the Faith & Action book *Biblical Counseling* for a list of problems people face). Every pastor should preach some series on topics that will help his sheep. Likewise, your sheep will eat well spiritually as you preach a series of messages through an entire book of the Bible—expository preaching. Using the *Faith & Action Series*, you can plan groups of sermons on every book of the Bible. Use the *Faith & Action* book *The Life & Teachings of Christ* to plan a series of sermons from Matthew, Mark, or Luke. Use the *Faith & Action* course *Acts of the Holy Spirit* to prepare up to 40 messages on the book of Acts. Planning your messages in a group or series has many

---

16 Basic Doctrines of the Bible

1. The Inspiration of Scripture
2. The One True God
3. The Deity of the Lord Jesus Christ
4. The Fall of Man
5. The Salvation of Man
6. The Ordinances of the Church
7. The Baptism in the Holy Spirit
8. The Evidence of the Baptism in the Holy Spirit
9. Sanctification
10. The Church and Its Mission
11. The Ministry
12. Divine Healing
13. The Blessed Hope
14. The Millennial Reign of Christ
15. The Final Judgment
16. The New Heavens and the New Earth

Figure 6.22   Pastors should preach a topical series on 16 basic truths of the Bible.

Q 73 *Which 2 of the 7 benefits appeal most to you? Why? (Figure 6.23)*

benefits. To review seven advantages of preaching a series of sermons, see the *Faith & Action* course *Homiletics 1*, Lesson 22, points B and C.

Seven Benefits of Preaching a Series of Expository Sermons From a Biblical Book
1. When we plan, we are like God.
2. Planning a series helps a pastor stay longer at a church. People tire of eating beans and rice every day.
3. Planning a biblical series helps people learn the Bible. They can study through a book as you preach it.
4. Planning a series enables you to listen better to the Holy Spirit—rather than being under pressure on what to preach.
5. Planning a series gives you more time to pray—instead of worrying about what you will preach.
6. Planning a series makes it easier to find illustrations—since you can meditate and pray about your messages for several weeks ahead of time.
7. Planning a series enables you to cover sensitive topics. For example, if you preach through Philippians, those who are fighting will not blame you for talking about getting along with each other when you cover Philippians 2 or 4. You are just preaching what is in the book of Philippians.

Figure 6.23   Seven benefits of preaching a series of expository sermons

A wise old believer attended church on a Sunday morning. The preacher's message lacked spiritual food, so he shouted a lot and pounded the pulpit—trying to cover his lack of preparation. After the service someone asked the wise elder what he thought of the preacher's message. Thinking for a moment, the elder summarized his opinion in six words: "High wind. Big thunder. No rain."[22]

2. Preach the Word in a relevant manner (2 Tim. 4:2).

*Preach the Word; be prepared in season and out of season; **correct, rebuke and encourage—with great patience and careful instruction*** (2 Tim. 4:2).

Q 74 *How does stating your main points as principles insure they are relevant?*

Q 75 *What moves truth from the head to the heart?*

As you study Faith & Action courses, notice that we state our main points as *biblical principles* (A, B, C), and then we explain them. Biblical principles are true and relevant—anywhere, anytime, for anyone. Also we illustrate and apply each principle, to make it clear, and to move truth from the head to the heart. Likewise, when you plan your preaching, state your main points as biblical principles—in this way you will be sure they are relevant. Then, illustrate and apply your principles. This enables truth to move from the head, and soak deep into the hearts of your people.

Jesus was the great Master of relevant teaching and preaching. He liked to state truth as a principle, in one short sentence, such as *"Love your neighbor as yourself"* (Matt. 19:19; 22:39; Mark 12:31, 33; Luke 10:27). In the parable of the Good Samaritan, Jesus illustrated and applied this one truth about being a good neighbor. His preaching was clear, easy to remember, powerful, and relevant for every generation in every nation. In Luke 15, Jesus stated a truth in one sentence, and then illustrated it with a coin, a sheep, and a son.

Q 76 *In Luke 15, what principle did Jesus illustrate 3 times? Did the final illustration apply the principle?*

3. Preach the Word with great patience—lest correction and rebuke be harsh (2 Tim. 2:23-26; 4:2).

*Preach the Word; be prepared in season and out of season; correct, rebuke and encourage—**with great patience and careful instruction*** (2 Tim. 4:2).

Recall that patience is a fruit of the Holy Spirit. Do not depend on yourself for patience, but pray and lean on God to help you love people and be patient with them—lest your harshness prevent them from saying "Yes" to the Savior who loves them.

In Burma, Missionary Adoniram Judson preached and taught for 6 years before his first convert to Christ. Then, in 1819, Judson baptized the first believer, Moung Nau. Judson wrote in his journal: "Oh, may it prove to be the beginning of a series of baptisms in the Burman empire which shall continue in uninterrupted success to the end of the age." Converts came slowly—a second, then three, then six, and on to eighteen. Then came persecution. Judson was accused as a spy and spent 21 months in prison. Finally, through prayer and the pleading of his wife with officials, they released Judson. In 1850, at the age of 62, Judson died, after spending 38 years in Burma. Although he waited patiently for 6 years to see his first convert, a government survey after his death recorded 210,000 Christians, one out of every fifty-eight Burmans![23] People seldom change in a hurry. But as we preach with great patience, the love of God can open the hearts of many.

Q 77 ⬉ *What truth does the life of Adoniram Judson illustrate?*

4. Preach the Word with endurance—to the end of the race (2 Tim. 4:3-8).

Preach the Word, even when it is not popular. Tell people the truth, even if they do not like it. Preach like Jeremiah, who prophesied that the Babylonians were coming to conquer Judah. Even though the Jews called him a liar and put him in a dungeon, he stood firm for the truth from God (Jer. 37). Be as faithful to the Word as John the Baptist, who was beheaded because he told Herod that adultery was wrong (Matt. 14:1-12). Preach the Word like Paul did at Lystra. After he healed a man crippled from birth, the local people said Paul and Barnabas were Greek gods, come down to earth. But Paul rejected their praise and insisted that he and Barnabas were only men, preaching the good news about Jesus. As a result the love of the crowd turned to hate, and they stoned Paul. But he later crawled out from under the stones and continued preaching the Word (Acts 14:8-20). Preach the Word like Jesus, who stood for the truth from the beginning of His ministry through His words to Pilate (1 Tim. 6:13). Depend on the Spirit to give you the balance of boldness, wisdom, and love—so that you speak the truth in love, with tears (Eph. 3:14-19; Acts 20:19, 31; Phil. 3:18).

Q 78 ⬈ *Who are 4 men who preached the truth to the end of the race?*

[3]For the time will come when men will not put up with sound doctrine. Instead, to suit their own desires, they will gather around them a great number of teachers to say what their itching ears want to hear. [4]They will turn their ears away from the truth and turn aside to myths. [5]But you, keep your head in all situations, endure hardship, do the work of an evangelist, discharge all the duties of your ministry. [6]For I am already being poured out like a drink offering, and the time has come for my departure. [7]I have fought the good fight, I have finished the race, I have kept the faith. [8]Now there is in store for me the crown of righteousness, which the Lord, the righteous Judge, will award to me on that day—and not only to me, but also to all who have longed for his appearing (2 Tim. 4:3-8).

Q 79 ⬈ *What did Paul warn that people would substitute for biblical teachings?*

The time has come when many people will not put up with the truth. Instead they like teachings that match their own desires and behavior. So they turn away from the truth to myths—false teachings that please those who live by the desires of the flesh, instead of the Spirit. Figure 6.24 contrasts **myths** people like to hear with the **truth** of the gospel:

Q 80 ⬉ *Complete Figure 6.24, adding local myths you have heard, and Scriptures that refute these.*

Reference	Myths Fleshly People Prefer	Truths Spiritual People Discern	Reference
1 Tim. 6:5	Godliness is a path to wealth.	*Some people, eager for money, have wandered from the faith.*	1 Tim. 6:10
x	Grace covers sins we commit. Once in grace, always in grace.	All who follow Christ must turn away from sin. Grace teaches us to say "No" to sin.	2 Tim. 2:20-22; Titus 2:11-14
x	There are many paths to heaven.	*[5]...there is one God and one mediator between God and men, the man Christ Jesus, [6]who gave himself as a ransom for all men.*	1 Tim. 2:5-6; Gal. 1:6-10
x			
x			

Figure 6.24   Practice contrasting myths with healthy biblical teachings.

The Bible is the main book to read in devotions. It is the Word of God to us. His Word is a lamp for our feet and a light to our paths (Ps. 119:105). His Word helps us not to sin against Him. God's Word enables us to understand what He is like. It teaches us what He expects from us. Consider the words of John Wesley that follow:

> To *candid, reasonable men, I am not afraid to lay open what have been the inmost thoughts of my heart. I have thought, I am a creature of a day, passing through life as an arrow through the air. I am a spirit come from God, and returning to God: just hovering over the great gulf; until, a few moments hence, I am no more seen; I drop into an unchangeable eternity! I want to know one thing—the way to heaven; how to land safe on that happy shore. God Himself has *condescended to teach the way; for this very end He came from heaven. He hath written it down in a book. O give me that book! At any price, give me the book of God! I have it: He is knowledge enough for me. Let me be *homo unius libri* [Latin for *a man of one book*]. Here then I am, far from the busy ways of men. I sit down alone: only God is here. In His presence I open, I read His book; for this end, to find the way to heaven. Is there a doubt concerning the meaning of what I read? Does anything appear dark or intricate? I lift up my heart to the Father of Lights: "Lord, is it not Thy word, 'If any man lack wisdom, let him ask of God'? … Thou has said, 'If any be willing to do Thy will, he shall know.' I am willing to do, let me know, Thy will." I then search after and consider parallel passages of Scripture, "comparing spiritual things with spiritual." I meditate thereon with all the attention and earnestness of which my mind is capable. If any doubt still remains, I consult those who are experienced in the things of God; and then the writings whereby, being dead, they yet speak. And what I thus learn, that I teach.[24]

Wesley was a man of one book. That is, the Bible was the main book he studied. No wonder he led more than 250,000 sinners to follow Christ!

There are many other spiritual books that are good to read with the Bible. We discuss this some in chapter 2 of our *Faith & Action Series* course on *Pastoral Ministry*. But the Bible is the Book of books! The time we spend reading the Bible should be more than the total time we spend reading all other books.

C. To finish the race well, guard your attitude when others hurt you (2 Tim. 4:9-22).

In his final days, Paul faced some of the greatest discouragements of his life. His closest friends would not come forward to testify for him. Enemies lied about his ministry. Some of his hopes and dreams did not come true. False teachers increased in strategic cities such as Ephesus, where Paul had a great revival. It was cold and lonely in the Roman dungeon where he was chained as a criminal. His execution was at hand. Yet despite the heartache and tears of these final days, we find Paul standing tall, and rejoicing. How was his cheerful and godly attitude possible? In this last lesson from Paul's life, we will examine four keys to maintaining a godly attitude in any circumstances.

1. Leave vengeance to God, when sinners hurt you (2 Tim. 4:14-15).

[14] Alexander the metalworker did me a great deal of harm. The Lord will repay him for what he has done. [15] You too should be on your guard against him, because he strongly opposed our message (2 Tim. 4:14-15).

It is best to leave vengeance to God. Those who blow out the candle of another, blow out their own.

A wasp lit on a snake's head and tormented it by stinging. The snake became mad with pain. Yet it could not find a way to get revenge. Finally, the snake saw a car coming and sought revenge by putting its head under the wheel—so that they both died together.[25]

Q 81 ⟋ *Instead of vengeance, how did Paul respond to the harm Alexander did to him?*

Q 82 ⟍ *Explain the proverb: "Those who blow out the candle of another, blow out their own."*

Figure 6.25 The snake was mad because the wasp was stinging his head.

[17] Do not repay anyone evil for evil. Be careful to do what is right in the eyes of everybody. [18] If it is possible, as far as it depends on you, live at peace with everyone. [19] Do not take revenge, my friends, but leave room for God's wrath, for it is written: "It is mine to avenge; I will repay," says the Lord. [20] On the contrary: "If your enemy is hungry, feed him; if he is thirsty, give him something to drink. In doing this, you will heap burning coals on his head." [21] Do not be overcome by evil, but overcome evil with good (Rom. 12:17-21).

2. Forgive those who fail you in your greatest hour of need (2 Tim. 4:16).

At my first defense, no one came to my support, but everyone deserted me. May it not be held against them (2 Tim. 4:16).

Jesus says: *"Forgive us our debts, as we also have forgiven our debtors"* (Matt. 6:12).

 Sabio says: "He who forgives releases a prisoner, only to discover he has freed himself."

Joseph forgave his brothers for selling him as a slave (Gen. 45:3-5). Stephen forgave those who stoned him to death (Acts 7:59-60). Jesus forgave those who crucified Him (Luke 23:34).

Archbishop Cranmer was almost alone, as a leader and friend of truth in evil times. Some men made a plan to kill him, creating some false letters. But God caused a friend to discover these false letters, and identify the two authors who wrote them. One of the traitors was in the family of Bishop Cranmer, and the other was a friend whom Cranmer had greatly served. The loving Bishop pulled these two men aside in his palace, and told them that some men he trusted were planning to kill him. The two traitors loudly condemned such a sin. They said the traitors deserved to die. One of them even volunteered to direct the execution. Cranmer was amazed at their dishonesty. He prayed and cried about the corruption of mankind. And he thanked God for protecting his life. Then the Bishop produced their letters, and asked if they knew who wrote them. The traitors fell on their knees, confessed their crimes, and begged for forgiveness. Cranmer summarized their evil conduct, forgave them, and never again mentioned their betrayal. His forgiveness of sins was so well known, that others said, "Sin against Bishop Cranmer, and he will become your friend forever."[26]

3. Do not let unmet expectations blur your vision for ministry (2 Tim. 4:16-17).[27]

[16] At my first defense, no one came to my support, but everyone deserted me. May it not be held against them. [17] But the Lord stood at my side and gave me strength, so that through me the message might be fully proclaimed and all the Gentiles might hear it. And I was delivered from the lion's mouth (2 Tim. 4:16-17).

Hurt feelings did not blur Paul's focus on fulfilling his calling. This was Paul's Gethsemane.[28] But as Jesus remained faithful to the end, Paul continued to preach to the Gentiles, awaiting his appointment with death.

Application. *Some* leaders become bitter, discouraged, or quit when others criticize, slander, abandon, betray, or falsely accuse them. *Others*, like Paul, move closer to Jesus, and find the grace to remain steadfast, loving, and fruitful to the end of their race. Paul's friends hurt him deeply, and they fled in fear for their lives. Still, Paul knew that others would suffer more if he did not share the gospel with them. So he did not allow his own tears to blur his vision and commitment to those God called him to help. In his most difficult hour, Paul, like Jesus, thought more of others than himself. May God help us to follow in the footprints of Jesus and the apostle Paul. Let us not quit helping others when our feelings get hurt. For surely the eternal souls of the lost are more important than the temporary pain of our hurt feelings.

Q 83 *What was Paul's attitude toward close friends who deserted him?*

Q 84 *What is the lesson of Matthew 18:21-35?*

Q 85 *Who are 3 biblical examples of people who forgave?*

Q 86 *Have you ever known anyone as loving as Cranmer? Explain.*

Q 87 *What was Paul's response when his friends deserted him? How was this possible?*

Q 88 *Have you ever been hurt, but found grace to keep on loving those needing your help? Explain.*

4. Do not let disappointments in relationships shake your confidence in God (2 Tim. 4:18). [29]

The Lord will rescue me from every evil attack and will bring me safely to his heavenly kingdom. To him be glory for ever and ever. Amen (2 Tim. 4:18).

Although humans deserted Paul, he still believed God would complete the salvation He had begun. He trusted the Lord to deliver him—whether from death or through it (2 Tim. 3:10-11; 4:18) Paul knew that God delivers in various ways. At Damascus, God delivered Paul through a basket that disciples let down over the city wall (Acts 9:19b-25). But in Lystra, God delivered Paul through stoning (Acts 14:8-20). Both Damascus and Lystra are examples of deliverance. Paul was *certain* that the Lord would walk with him through every trial on the road from earth to heaven (2 Tim. 1:12, Rom. 8:28, 35-39). No disappointments shook Paul's faith in God. He knew whom he had believed (2 Tim. 1:12)!

Q 89 *Who was near Paul in his last days?*

Broken friendships are among the most painful experiences in life. Sometimes when we lose a friend, we die a little.[30] Timothy was not with Paul at the Roman prison (2 Tim. 4:9). Demas had forsaken him (2 Tim. 4:10). Crescens and Titus had left for other countries (2 Tim. 4:10). So Paul sent word for Mark to come and assist him one last time (2 Tim. 4:11). Paul had sent Tychicus on a mission to Ephesus (2 Tim. 4:12). Luke was the only co-worker with Paul in Rome (2 Tim. 4:11), along with some local believers named Eubulus, Pudens, Linus, and Claudia, with other unnamed brothers (2 Tim. 4:21). Paul was not completely alone. He could have a few visitors, so he requested Timothy to come (2 Tim. 4:9). Access to Paul in prison was limited. But God was with the apostle all the time. Human friends may let us down, but God will never leave or forsake us. He is with us, even to the end of the age (Matt. 28:20; Heb. 13:5).

Q 90 *Why might some of us wish 2 Timothy 4:20 were not in the Bible?*

Q 91 *How did Paul respond to prayers that seemed unanswered? Apply this.*

Paul left Trophimus sick in Miletus (2 Tim. 4:20). Some of us may wish this verse were not in the Bible. Another one like it is Paul's counsel for Timothy to take a little wine for his frequent sicknesses (1 Tim. 5:23). Even the greatest apostles like Paul did not receive all they expected in prayer. As we reflect on Paul's life, we recall so many outstanding answers to his prayers. His powerful prayer blinded Elymas, the sorcerer at Cyprus, when he hindered the salvation of the proconsul (Acts. 13:11-12). In Iconium, God confirmed Paul's prayers and message with miraculous signs and wonders (Acts 14:3). In Lystra, Paul, who prayed in tongues more than his followers, healed a man who was a cripple from birth (Acts 14:8-10; 1 Cor. 14:18). At the council in Jerusalem, Paul and Barnabas told about the many signs and wonders God had done through them among the Gentiles (Acts 15:12). In Philippi, after being beaten, Paul and Silas were praying and singing hymns when an earthquake shook the foundations of the prison, unlocked the prison doors, and caused the chains to fall off every prisoner (Acts 16:25-26)! In Ephesus, a dozen men were instantly filled with the Spirit and prophesied when Paul laid his hands on them and prayed (Acts 19:1-7). Also, in this great city of Ephesus, where Timothy later pastored, God did extra-ordinary miracles through Paul, so that even handkerchiefs and aprons that had

Figure 6.26   Paul and Silas prayed and sang in prison at Philippi.

touched him cured the sick and sent demons looking for new homes (Acts 19:11-12). Later, Paul said goodbye to Trophimus and others at Macedonia, and traveled on to Troas, where his prayers raised Eutychus when he fell out a window in the third story of a house, after Paul had taught all night (Acts 20:7-12). On the way to Rome, Paul's prayers and communion with God saved the lives of 276 people when a great storm wrecked the ship they were on (Acts 27:27-44). And on the island of Malta, this apostle, whose life was soaked with prayer, shook off a viper into the fire, healed the father of Publius, the chief official of the island, and healed all the sick on the island (Acts 28:1-10). So why was it that this spiritual giant could not pray the prayer of faith to bring healing to Trophimus or Timothy? We do not know. With Paul, we must leave our unmet expectations with God. Let us rejoice that our names are written in heaven. Let us give thanks for the prayers our Father has answered. And let us continue worshiping Him who is altogether faithful, good, and worthy of our trust.

Test Yourself: Circle the letter by the ***best*** completion to each question or statement.

1. How many letters did Paul write after 2 Timothy?
a) 0
b) 1
c) 2
d) 4

2. The main way we encourage ourselves is through
a) the Scriptures.
b) praying.
c) worshiping.
d) relationships.

3. Paul's strategy for ministry was
a) doing almost everything himself.
b) training others to help.
c) preaching, but having others teach.
d) teaching, but having others preach.

4. Which illustration did Paul use to encourage Timothy?
a) Job
b) A steward
c) A farmer
d) Moses

5. Which is TRUE about God's faithfulness?
a) He will honor all who emphasize grace.
b) He will overlook the sins of believers.
c) He will deny those who deny Him.
d) He will love with no conditions.

6. In 2 Timothy 2, a principle for vessels of honor is:
a) In everything give thanks.
b) Avoid arguments.
c) Face the future, not the past.
d) Rejoice always.

7. Which command is in 2 Timothy 3:10-17?
a) Continue in what you have learned.
b) Press toward the mark of your calling.
c) Be an example for others to follow.
d) Leave vengeance to God.

8. Which word emphasizes that the Bible cannot deceive us?
a) Inspired
b) Inerrant
c) Infallible
d) Plenary

9. What did Paul emphasize about preaching?
a) Be anointed.
b) Be comprehensive.
c) Be consistent.
d) Be prepared.

10. Which did we study on finishing the race?
a) Roll up the shirt sleeves of your mind.
b) Avoid stumbling over unmet expectations.
c) Let the past be the past.
d) Give thanks in all situations.

Essay Test Topics: Write 50-100 words on each of these goals that you studied in this chapter (9 points each and 1 point free). Try to complete your writing in one and a half hours.

- Analyze the setting of 2 Timothy, including circumstances and challenges.
- Explain and illustrate how we encourage ourselves through relationships with others.
- Summarize how we strengthen ourselves through our relationship with the Father, Son, and Spirit.
- List some advantages of training and involving others in ministry.
- Summarize 5 examples Paul uses in 2 Timothy 2 to motivate believers.
- Explain how God is faithful to Himself, in dealing with saints and sinners.
- Explain the context of two types of vessels in 2 Timothy 2, and contrast these on 4 topics.
- Explain the need to continue walking in the light of Scriptures and those who taught us.
- Define *inspiration, inerrancy,* and *infallibility,* and explain how belief in these guides us.
- Analyze why pastors must preach the Word, and explain 4 guidelines for preaching it.
- Summarize and apply Paul's attitudes toward persecutors, deserters, unmet expectations, and God.

Appendix A

Key Questions to Answer on 1 & 2 Timothy

Questions based on Gordon D. Fee, *New International Biblical Commentary, 1 and 2 Timothy, Titus,* (Peabody, Massachusetts: Hendrickson Publishers, 1988).

Reference	Question	Fee
1 Tim. 1:1, 3; 4:11; 6:17	In what sense is the word *command* a two-edged sword in the Pastoral Epistles?	35
1 Tim. 1:2	Was Timothy, Paul's *"son in the faith,"* Paul's convert? Explain.	36-37
1 Tim. 1:3-11	How were the wayward elders at Ephesus misusing the Law?	39-48
1 Tim. 1:8-11; Rom. 8:4; 13:8 Gal. 5:22-25	Why is the written Law made for sinners, but unnecessary for God's children?	
1 Tim. 1:8-11;	What are some synonyms of the word *gospel* in the Pastoral Epistles?	15-17, 47
1 Tim. 1:6-7; 12-20	What contrast is there between the way false teachers at Ephesus were using the Law and Paul's personal testimony of salvation?	
1 Tim. 1:15-16	Did Paul's gospel proclaim that believers continue to be slaves of sin? Does Jesus save us now from the penalty and the power of sin? Explain.	42-44
1 Tim. 1:19-20	What does *"shipwrecked their faith"* mean?	58-59
1 Tim. 2:1-7	What is the main reason why Paul urges prayer for everyone?	61-69
1 Tim. 2:1-7	On the theme of salvation, what contrast is there in 1 Timothy 2:1-7 with the narrow, Jewish elitist view of the false teachers in Ephesus?	61-69
1 Tim. 2:8-15	In this passage, why does Paul say so little to men, and so much to women?	70-71
1 Tim. 2:8	What are some things to do and to avoid today in order to lift up holy hands in prayer?	
1 Tim. 2:9-11; 5:6, 11-15	What contrast is there between godly and ungodly women in 1 Timothy?	72-73
1 Tim. 2:15; 4:3; 5:10, 14	What contrast is there in God's plan for the family and false teachings at Ephesus?	75, 99
1 Tim. 3:1-7	If there were already elders at Ephesus, why does Paul send Timothy the list of qualifications?	
1 Tim. 3:1-13	What do the qualifications for elders and deacons emphasize?	
1 Tim. 3:15	Which two metaphors does Paul mix, as he did in Ephesians 2:19-22?	92
1 Tim. 3:14-16	What is the main purpose of 1 Timothy? Why is this purpose so important?	91-92
1 Tim. 3:16	How are the six lines of the hymn in 3:16 alike in form? What are some key words and phrases in this hymn? (Interpret these.)	92-95
1 Tim. 1:4; 3:15-16; 2:8; 4:1; 6:4-5	Believers have a common, unified confession about the faith—the truth, the gospel. How do the Pastoral Epistles contrast unity in the faith with the false teachings at Ephesus?	
1 Tim. 5:1	What family principles does Paul give for older men? (Compare Swindoll, *New Testament Insights, 1 & 2 Timothy, and Titus.*)	
1 Tim. 5:1-10	What family principles does Paul give for older men and women?	
1 Tim. 5:1-2, 11-16	What family principles does Paul give for younger men and women?	
1 Tim. 6:1-2	What family principles does Paul give for slaves and the rich?	
1 Tim. 5:17-20	What family principles does Paul give for pastors?	
1 Tim. 6:1	How was slavery in New Testament times different than today? (Swindoll, p. 121)	136-138
1 Tim. 6:1	What truth helps believers live victoriously in slavery or other difficult situations?	138
1 Tim. 6:1	Why is it important for Christian slaves/employees to respect those they serve?	138

Figure 7.1   Key questions to answer on the letter to 1 & 2 Timothy

Appendix B

Key Questions to Answer on Titus

Questions based on Gordon D. Fee, *New International Biblical Commentary, 1 and 2 Timothy, Titus,*
(Peabody, Massachusetts: Hendrickson Publishers, 1988).

Titus	Question	Fee
1:1, 3	In his letter to Titus, why was it important for Paul to refer to himself as an *apostle,* under a command?	167
1:1	What is a synonym for *truth*?	167
1:1	Who are *God's elect*?	168
	How can we discern if someone has received the true gospel?	
1:2, 10, 12	What contrast does Paul paint between the truthfulness of God and the false teachers at Crete?	
1:2	What is Paul's meaning and point in the phrase *"before the beginning of time"*?	169
1:4	In what sense was Titus a *true son* of Paul?	170
1:5, 10	How does the source of the problem at Crete differ from the source at Ephesus?	171
1:5-9	Whom does Paul expect to correct the false teaching at Crete? How does this apply today?	171
1:5	Was there just one assembly in Crete? Explain.	172
1:5-6	How would you describe the first elders of churches Paul founded?	173
1:10	What does the word *for* emphasize in Titus 1:10?	177
1:10-16	What were some characteristics of the false teachers from the *circumcision group* at Crete? How were the Cretan false teachers like those at Ephesus (1 Tim. 4:3)?	177
1:12-13	Were all Cretans liars? Are there exceptions to *proverbs*?	179
1:11	What was the major motivation of false teachers at Crete and Ephesus? What was the result? How would appointing elders help protect believing families?	178-179
1:12-13	What funny history is behind the proverb *"Cretans are always liars"*?	179
1:14	What are some examples of commands we should ignore? (See Matt. 15:9.)	180
1:15	To what type of purity was Paul referring in Titus 1:15? Explain and apply a principle based on this verse.	180-181
1:16	What contrast is there in Titus 1:16 and the theme of Titus?	182
2:1-15	What reputation is Paul's main concern in Titus 2?	184
2:1-3	What age were elders, older men, and older women?	185
	Did Paul expect older believers to live by the same standards as elders and deacons? Explain.	185-186
2:3	What did it mean for an older woman to *"act like a priestess"*?	186
2:3	What does this mean: Healthy doctrine is best taught by the way we live"? [behavioral, not just mental]	185-188
2:5, 8, 10	What is the significance of Paul's threefold use of *"so that"*? Is the letter to Titus more concerned about the relationship of believers to each other, or to the world? Explain.	
	How is Paul's advice to groups of believers related to the highest expectations of culture and society? Give examples.	
	In Paul's day, what are some ways believers could avoid being stumbling blocks to the lost, and make the gospel attractive? Apply these to believers today.	
2:11	What does Dr. Fee mean when he says the nature of the letter to Titus is *prophylactic*? Explain.	193
2:11-14	In what sense is Titus 2:11-14 the theological basis for the instructions of Titus 1:10 to 2:10?	193
2:11-14	How do Titus 2:11-14, 3:4-7, and 3:14 reflect Paul's chief concern for writing to Titus?	193
2:13	What is the appositive of Jesus Christ?	196

Figure 7.2   Key questions to answer on the letter to Titus

Definitions

The right-hand column lists the chapter in the textbook in which the word is used.

	Chapter
16 Fundamental Truths—basic teachings of faith that all Assemblies of God churches believe; Four of these—salvation, the baptism in the Holy Spirit, divine healing, and the Second Coming of Christ—are considered major doctrines—essential to the Church's mission of reaching the world for Christ.	3
apodosis—the clause expressing the consequence in a conditional sentence, often beginning with *then*— "If you will help, <u>then</u> I will..."	6
apostasy—a turning away from the faith, after believing; abandoning the truth of the gospel	2, 4
archangel—chief angel; an angel who seems to be the leader of other angels	1
Bible Quiz—a game that reviews what children learned in previous Bible lessons; a game in which children answer questions about Bible stories, doctrines, or memory verses they have studied; <u>Junior Bible Quiz</u> (JBQ) is an Assemblies of God program for elementary children. It uses 576 questions and answers. The children race to see who can answer a question first. They memorize more than 100 Bible verses, learn the order of the Bible, and about Bible stories, doctrines, theology terms, the Church, and the role of believers. <u>Teen Bible Quiz</u> is a discipleship ministry geared for youth, working from simpler for the younger students to harder for older students. Each year a different book or books of the New Testament are memorized by students. After practicing in their churches, several times during the year students attend meets within their area in order to test their ability to memorize and understand God's Word.	6
Blessed Hope—the expectation of all believers of their joyful meeting with Jesus at the Rapture	1
candid—honest; open and sincere; impartial	6
condescend—to put aside one's dignity or superiority and be equal with a person on a lower level	6
Crete—the largest island in the Mediterranean Sea, straight south of the Aegean Sea. After Paul's first release from prison in Rome, he and Titus started a church in Crete. Paul left Titus to oversee the work there.	5
Dalmatia—the southern portion of the Roman province of Illyricum, on the eastern shore of the Adriatic Sea;. modern Yugoslavia, Bosnia, Herzegovina, and Croatia; Writing from Rome to Timothy during his second imprisonment (66 or 67 A.D.), Paul records the departure of Titus to Dalmatia (2 Tim. 4:10) for some unknown purpose.	5
Day of the Lord—Old Testament: a time that God judges the evil and rewards the righteous. New Testament: a period of time when God breaks into human history, so that His kingdom comes, and His will is done on earth, as it is in heaven—bringing judgment to the disobedient, but salvation, glorification, and reward to the obedient. The Day of the Lord includes such things as the Rapture, judgment of the Antichrist and his followers, Christ's reign on earth, and the Great White Throne judgment. Scholars agree that the Day of the Lord and its events extend beyond a normal day.	1
deacon—one who serves and ministers to help overseers; leaders in the local church	3
dead in Christ—believers who died before the return of Christ	1
doxology—words of glorious praise to God, often sung as a short hymn in a Christian worship service	4
Ephesus—an important center in Asia Minor. Paul lived there, worked with believers, and organized missionary trips into the regions nearby; Paul left his co-worker, Timothy, to oversee the churches in and around Ephesus	3
eschatological—refers to the last days of humans on earth, and final matters such as the Return of Christ, judgments, punishment and rewards, heaven and hell	6
eschatology—a study about last things, including teachings on final matters such as the Return of Christ, judgments, punishment and rewards, heaven and hell	1

eternal security—a false doctrine that claims if a person has been born again, he or she cannot do anything to lose salvation; often called "once saved, always saved" — 4

gangrene—the death of soft tissue in a body due to obstructed blood circulation, usually followed by decay and rot which result in the loss of body parts or death — 6

gospel—In the Pastoral Epistles, and all of Paul's writings, the gospel is **not** just good news for lost sinners. Rather, it **is** *the faith*—a fixed body of beliefs to embrace and live by.[11] The beliefs in the gospel include teaching on regeneration, justification, holy living, the kingdom of God, hope, retribution (punishment for the rebellious), and glorification (sharing eternity with our God and King). — 3

grace—the free, kind, and generous ways God relates to people. In Titus 2, Paul does not define grace but compares grace to a teacher from God. — 5

hyperbole—an over-statement; a figure of speech that exaggerates the truth to make a point. Example: *"You blind guides! You strain out a gnat but swallow a camel"* (Matt. 23:24). — 2

iceberg—a mountain of ice that has broken off of a glacier or ice shelf—and is floating in the sea; often only one-tenth of an iceberg is above water, while nine-tenths is hidden below the surface — 3

imminent—an event, like the Coming of Christ, that could happen at any moment — 1

imparted—given or bestowed; Isaac imparted his blessing to Jacob; Jesus imparted the Holy Spirit to believers at Pentecost; teachers impart knowledge to students. God imparts righteousness and holiness at regeneration, and these qualities increase as we are transformed into the image of Christ, day by day. — 1

imparted righteousness—holiness we experience (sanctification) as we submit to the Holy Spirit and partake in the nature of God at regeneration, and as we grow in the likeness of Christ (Rom. 8:29). Those whom God justifies by faith, He sanctifies and delivers from the love of sin in this life. — 1

imperative—a command—"Preach the Word!" — 1

imputed—credited, attributed, reckoned to, accounted to; the righteousness of Christ is imputed or credited to believers, apart from any works of their own, as we believe in Christ as Savior and Lord. — 1

imputed righteousness—right standing (justification) that God credits to us as we trust in Jesus as Savior and Lord — 1

inerrant—truthful and free from error — 6

infallible—absolutely trustworthy and sure; not capable of erring, deceiving, or leading people astray — 6

inspiration—the process by which God breathed His message into the writers of Scripture, and carried them along by the Holy Spirit—so that they wrote what He intended, free from error — 6

Last Days—a period of time that stretches from the First Coming of Jesus to His Second Coming; the perilous time near the Lord's return — 6

liberation theology—a movement that interprets Scripture through the eyes of the poor; defending the rights of the poor as the central aspect of the gospel; working toward a just society, and political change [even through violence]; Errors: it places social action on equal footing with regenration, and it discriminates *for* the poor and *against* the rich. — 4

Lystra—a city in Asia Minor where Paul was stoned after healing a man during his first missionary journey; Timothy's hometown; in south central present-day Turkey — 3

Missionettes—an Assemblies of God weekly church program for discipling and training girls of all ages; also called Girls Ministries — 6

motivational gifts—spiritual gifts that inspire and guide us to serve in certain ways—such as the spiritual gifts listed in Romans 12 — 4

overseer—one who supervises, like a steward or bishop who watches over God's household; *elder* stresses the spiritual maturity and dignity of an overseer; *pastor* emphasizes one who watches over God's sheep, following the example of the Chief Shepherd. — 3

Parousia—a Greek word for "the Second Coming of Christ" — 1

pre-Millenialist—one who believes that the Second Coming of Christ will precede the Millennium — 2

protasis—the clause expressing the condition in a conditional sentence, in English usually beginning with *if*—"If you will help, then I will..." — 6

ransom—payment on behalf of another; the price paid to free a slave; Jesus gave Himself as the payment for all people to go free. — 3

Rapture—an event within the Day of the Lord, when living believers are *caught up* to meet Christ in the clouds — 1

retribution—God's judgment and punishment of the wicked — 2

Royal Rangers—an Assemblies of God weekly church program for discipling and training boys of all ages — 6

Selah—pause and think about this — 2

siblings—two or more children having one or both parents in common — 4

Sovereign—God; the supreme ruler over supernatural beings, humans, and the entire universe — 2

synonym—a word that means the same as another word — 1

tetradrachm—a silver Greek coin with the head of Antiochus IV as if he were Zeus, crowned with laurel; The writing on the coin says: "King Antiochus, God Manifest (Epiphanes)." — 2

Timothy—a son in the faith to Paul; a fellow worker of Paul, whom he sent to help maintain order and doctrine in local churches, like Ephesus. — 3

Titus—a beloved Gentile co-worker of Paul. He was capable, resourceful, and skillful in handling believers and church affairs, as in Crete — 3

vessel of honor—a believer who has cleansed himself of what is unfit, has been sanctified by the Holy Spirit, and is useful to the Master for every good work — 6

God's Plan of Salvation

1. Introduction: God is holy, good, and pure—completely righteous. *"God is light; in him there is no darkness at all"* (1 John 1:5).

2. The Problem: Our sins have separated us from God. Because we have sinned—done things we know are wrong—we cannot fellowship with God. Our sins make us too dirty to come into God's holy presence. As we cannot enter a clean room with muddy shoes, we cannot come into God's presence with our sins. *"All have sinned"* (Rom. 3:23). The wages for our sin is death—spiritual death—which is separation from God, now and forever. Those who reject Jesus will die in their sins. They will spend eternity tormented in the flames of hell, away from the presence of God.

3. God's Solution: God loves us so much that he sent Jesus to rescue us. Jesus said, *"I am the way and the truth and the life. No one comes to the Father except through me"* (John 14:6). His name is Jesus, which means Savior, because He saves us from our sins (Matt. 1:21). Jesus saves us from both the penalty and the power of sin–now and forever. Jesus, the Son of God, became a man and lived a perfect, sinless life (Jn. 1:14; Heb. 4:15). He died on the cross as our substitute—He took the penalty for our sins (Rom. 6:23; 2 Cor. 5:21; 1 Pet. 2:24-25. Those who submit their lives to Jesus—God declares to be forgiven, clean and righteous (Rom. 5:1-2).

4. God's Invitation: Jesus says, *"Here I am! I stand at the door (of your heart) and knock. If anyone hears my voice and opens the door, I will come in"* (Rev. 3:20). God's favorite word is "Come". He wants to come to all people, and He wants them to come to him. *"The Spirit and the bride say, "Come!" And let him who hears say, "Come!" Whoever is thirsty, let him come; and whoever wishes, let him take the free gift of the water of life"* (Rev. 22:17). Accept God's invitation. Come to Jesus. Repent of your sins, that is, turn away from what you know is wrong. Put your trust in Jesus as your Savior and Lord. Believe that He died to save you from your sins. Ask Him to forgive your past sins and free you from being a slave to sin. *"If we confess our sins, He is faithful and just and will forgive us our sins, and cleanse us from all unrighteousness"* (1 John 1:9). Welcome Jesus into your life and He will enter. To all who receive Him, He gives the right to become God's children (1 John 1:12).

5. Your Commitment: Welcome to the family of God! God's plan of salvation has a beginning, a middle, and a completion–when we reach heaven. By walking through steps 1-4 above, you have begun to follow God's plan of salvation. Your name is now written in God's book of life (Ph. 4:3; Rev. 3:5; 20:12). The middle part of God's plan is following Jesus as we live on earth. As a child of God, seek to obey the teachings of Jesus in the Bible (Mt. 28:19-20). As you follow Him, He will lead and strengthen you in your relationship with God. As a baby grows into an adult, you will grow from a new child of God into to a mature family member. Be baptized in water (Mt 28:19; Acts 8:36-38; Rom. 6:4; Mk. 16:16). Become part of a local church that preaches and teaches the Bible (Acts 2:41; 9:31). Seek to be filled with the Holy Spirit (Acts 1:8; 2:4; 4:31; 8:17; 10:44-46; 19:1-7; Eph. 5:18-20). Learn to walk in the Spirit, so you can overcome sinful desires that come through the flesh (Rom. 8:5; Gal. 5:16). Grow in grace, and in the knowledge of our Lord and Savior Jesus Christ, and in maturity (2 Pet. 3:18; 2 Pet. 1:5-18). Fellowship with other believers who will encourage you. Share your testimony with others, and lead them to Jesus (Jn. 1:40-42; 4:39). The completion of salvation occurs when Jesus Christ returns. At that time, He will give you a new body, and complete His glorious plan of salvation in your life (Rom. 8:18-25;1 Cor. 15:20-58;1 Th. 4:13-17). We do not know the exact time Jesus will return. For now, enjoy the presence of God, and His Spirit in you, as you grow in grace. You have been saved from your past sins. You are being saved daily, as you abide and grow in Christ. And your salvation has a glorious completion ahead.

Scripture List

Genesis
1:27, 31 125
2:18 125
4:6-7 64
19:30-38 109

Exodus
18:13-24 186

Numbers
11:14-17, 25-29 186
22–24 85
23:19 158
32:23 145

Deuteronomy
19:15 143
25:4 142

Judges
16 139

1 Samuel
2:27-36 195
2:30 198
30:6 178

2 Samuel
11 139

1 Kings
12:8 141

2 Chronicles
15:2 64
16:9 64

Psalms
24:3-4 102
30:5 63
34:16 101
66:18 104
119:9 138
119:105 205

Proverbs
4:18-19 201
4:23 137
5:15 138
5:15-23 139
16:32 115
20:1 109
23:4-5 152
23:29-32 111
23:29-35 109
29:5 26
29:20 112

Ecclesiastes
4:12 . . . . 141, 185

Isaiah
1:15-20 103
3:16-25 106
11; 53; 65–66 67
14:12-14 113
28:16 101
40:29-31 27

Jeremiah
9:1 47
18:1-18 199
29:10-13 65
31:31-34 88

Ezekiel
18:4 100

Daniel
2:19-21 72
9:24-27 70
12:2 42

Amos
5:18-27 44

Habakkuk
3:17-19 55

Malachi
2:13-16 139

Matthew
4:16 165
6:12 207
7:23 88
7:24-25 76
9:13 92
10:34-36 25
12:18-21 195
19:19 204
20:28 98
22:39 204
24–25 47
24:4-5 71
24:9-14 73
24:12 96
24:31 43
24:35 153
24:36-41 49
24:42-44 49
24:45-51 49
25:1-13 49
25:13 23
25:31-46 133
25:36-40 24
26:13 61
28:19 158
28:20 208

Mark
2:17 30
10:45 112
12:30-31 127
12:31, 33 204
16:15-16 158

Luke
10:7 142
10:27 204
12:32 . . . . 63, 173
16:19-25 62
18:13 102
21:34-36 49
23:46 181

John
1:16-17 165
5:22-23 118
5:28-29 . . . . 42, 68
8:42-44 125
8:46 151
11:43 42
13:35 53
14:27 79
15:18-21 33

Acts
1:6-8 45
2:3 55
2:16-20 197
2:21 165
6:1-6 108
8:1 25
8:3 90
9:1-18 90
9:13-27 90
10:38 169
16:1, 3 83
16:16-24 24
17:1-9 21
17:5-10 21
17:7 21
17:9 25
17:11 86
17:11-12 31
17:21 77
18:26 106
20:17 108
20:28 108
20:28-31 85
20:30 86
20:31 86

Romans
1:21-32 75
3:19-20, 23 93
5:1 124
5:3 62
5:8 91
6:23 100
8:6-9 136
8:15 184
8:18 63
8:28 40
8:29 62
8:31 65
8:38-39 68
9:1 92
9:1-4 35
9:2-4 48
9:33 101
10:11 101
10:13 165
12:3-8 127
12:9 76
12:17-21 207
13:1-5 72
14:1-13 110
14:13, 20-21 111

1 Corinthians

2:12 184
5:9-13 198
6:9-11 . . . . 75, 103
6:11 29
7:39 134
9:14 142
9:24-27 188
10:12 135
10:13 136
11:5 106
11:30-32 33
12:1-11 127
14:39-40 55
15:51-52 170
15:51-58 43
15:52 49

2 Corinthians

1:14 45
3:2-3 164
4:7 184
4:16-18 63
5:17 172
10:3-5 95
10:5 137
12:7 33
13:1 143
13:5 76

Galatians

3:28 146
5:16 . . . . 38, 136
5:19-21 75

Ephesians

2:12 165
4:5-6 146
4:7-11 127
4:11-12 185
4:25–5:7 103
4:29 127
5:3 141
5:4 127
5:18 39
5:19 127
5:28 107
6:1-4 163
6:12 95

Philippians

1:1 108
1:6 45
1:9-11 110
2:19-23 84
3:14 189
3:20-21 42
4:8 . . . . 138, 194
4:11-13 148

Colossians

1:24 33
2:1-4 194
2:3 194
3:5-10 103
3:16 127
3:17 27
3:19 107
4:14 131

1 Thessalonians

1:2-3 . . . . 25, 26, 27
1:2-5 61
1:2-10 61
1:3-12 22
1:4-5 27
1:5 28
1:6 . . . . 28, 33
1:6-10 37
1:7-9 28
1:9 . . . . 27, 29, 61
2:1 29
2:1-6 29
2:1-16 22
2:2 . . . . 24, 25
2:2-7 35
2:5 28
2:6-12 . . . . 30, 31
2:11 35
2:13 31
2:13-16 31
2:14 21
2:14-16 21
2:17–3:10 22
2:17 35
2:17-18 35
2:17-20 34
2:18 25
2:19 35
3:1 35
3:1-5 22
3:1-5, 11 33
3:3-7, 11 33
3:5 21
3:6-10 21
3:6-13 34
3:8 35
3:9-13 35
3:10 35
4:1 . . . . 36, 38
4:1-8 . . . . 22, 24
4:1-12 36
4:3 36
4:4-6 37
4:6 38
4:7 38
4:8 . . . . 37, 38
4:9-10 38
4:10 38
4:11-12 . . . . 22, 39, 78
4:12 39
4:13-14 41
4:13-18 . . . . 22, 65
4:15-18 41
4:16 . . . . 42, 43
4:17 . . . . 42, 43, 46
4:18 44
5:1-2 44
5:1-3 47
5:1-11 . . . . 44, 47, 49, 65
5:1-24 22
5:2-3 49
5:3 66
5:4, 9 49
5:9 . . . . 50, 66
5:9-11 50
5:10 41
5:12-13 51
5:12-28 51
5:13, 26 52

[1 Thessalonians continued]

5:14 . . . . 53, 78
5:15 53
5:16 54
5:17 54
5:18 54
5:19 55
5:19-22 . . . . 55, 66
5:20 56
5:21-22 57
5:23-24 57

2 Thessalonians

1 61
1:3-5 61
1:4-10 22
1:5 62
1:5–2:12 76
1:5-10 22
1:6 68
1:6-7 63
1:6-9 50
1:6-10 . . . . 48, 62, 64, 68
1:7 68
1:8 24
1:9-10 64
1:9 66
1:11-12 64
2 66
2:1-2 . . . . 66, 79
2:1-5 56
2:1-8 . . . . 65, 70, 71, 72
2:1-12 . . . . 22, 46
2:2 66
2:3 . . . . 45, 70, 73, 74, 88
2:3-8 71
2:4 70
2:5 65
2:6-7 72
2:8 73
2:9 74
2:9-10 74
2:9-12 73
2:10 74
2:10-12 75
2:12 75
2:13–3:5 77
2:13–3:18 75
2:13 . . . . 46, 77
2:13-17 . . . . 22, 76
2:14 77
2:15 . . . . 69, 77
3:1-18 79
3:3-5 77
3:6-13 39
3:6-15 . . . . 22, 77, 78
3:10 40

1 Timothy

1:1 84
1:1-2 84
1:1-7 84
1:1-11 90
1:2 83
1:3 . . . . 84, 85
1:3-5 88
1:3-7 . . . . 85, 86, 87
1:4 . . . . 86, 87
1:5 . . . . 85, 87
1:5-6 127

1 Timothy continued

1:6 . . . . 84, 85
1:6-7 127
1:7 86
1:8 86
1:8-11 . . . . 87, 88
1:9 87
1:9-10 93
1:10 89
1:10-11 88
1:11 . . . . 86, 89
1:12-13 90
1:12-17 165
1:12, 17 94
1:13 . . . . 90, 93
1:13-14 91
1:15 . . . . 86, 92
1:15-16 . . . . 92, 93
1:16 93
1:18 85
1:18-20 94
1:19 . . . . 89, 95
2:1 98
2:1-7 97
2:2 98
2:3-7 93
2:4 . . . . 89, 98, 158
2:5-6 98
2:6 99
2:8 . . . . 102, 104
2:9, 10 105
2:9-15 104
2:11 106
2:13-14 106
2:15 107
3:1-7 109
3:2 . . . . 108, 109, 115, 116
3:3 . . . . 109, 111, 112, 114
3:4 117
3:5 117
3:6 113
3:8 . . . . 109, 112
3:9 . . . . 89, 116
3:10 113
3:11 115
3:12 . . . . 114, 117
3:14-15 118
3:14-16 117
3:15 117
3:16 . . . . 89, 118
4:1 . . . . 74, 89, 123, 190
4:1-5 . . . . 125, 126
4:1-8 95
4:2 125
4:3 . . . . 89, 125, 159
4:3-5 125
4:4 125
4:6 89
4:6-10 125
4:6-11 126
4:7-8 89
4:12 . . . . 93, 109, 126
4:12-16 84
4:13 161
4:14 . . . . 127, 128, 184
4:15 130
4:15-16 130
4:16 130
5–6 130
5:1 . . . . 141, 161
5:1-2 130

5:2 . . . . 131, 134
5:3 131
5:3-7 132
5:3-10 . . . . 131, 133
5:4-5 132
5:4, 8 132
5:5 132
5:6 132
5:8 89
5:9 132
5:9-10 132
5:10 132
5:11-13 133
5:11-16 133
5:12 134
5:13 105
5:14 134
5:14-16 134
5:15 105
5:16 134
5:17 142
5:17-18 142
5:17-25 141
5:18 142
5:19 143
5:20 . . . . 143, 161
5:21-25 144
5:22 144
5:24-25 145
6:1 146
6:1-2 145
6:2 . . . . 147, 161
6:3 89
6:3-5 147
6:3, 5-6 89
6:3-5, 9-10 150
6:3-10 147
6:5-10 . . . . 112, 147
6:6 148
6:7 148
6:8 148
6:9-10 148
6:10 . . . . 89, 112, 147
6:11 . . . . 84, 150
6:11-16 149
6:12 89
6:13 . . . . 84, 181
6:13-15 151
6:17 152
6:17-19 148
6:18-19 152
6:20 . . . . 84, 85, 89, 153, 194
6:20-21 153

2 Timothy

1:1–2:13 183
1:2 83
1:3-7 178
1:6 . . . . 55, 127, 128
1:6-7 84
1:6-8 183
1:7 . . . . 115, 179, 183, 184
1:8 181
1:8-10 190
1:8-12 . . . . 180, 182
1:9 . . . . 165, 181
1:11 . . . . 181, 182
1:12 . . . . 181, 182
1:13 89
1:14 . . . . 89, 183, 185
1:15 180

1:16-18 180
2:1-2 185
2:3-4 188
2:3-10 187
2:5 188
2:6-7 188
2:8 188
2:9 189
2:9-10 189
2:10 189
2:11-13 189
2:14–3:9 191
2:14 192
2:14-18 191
2:15 . . . . 86, 193, 201
2:16 85
2:17 88
2:19 193
2:19-22 193
2:20-21 190
2:22 150
2:23-26 . . . . 195, 204
2:24-25 195
2:25 89
2:26 195
3:1 196
3:1-5 74
3:1-9 197
3:5 197
3:6-7 105
3:7 . . . . 85, 89, 197
3:8 89
3:10-17 200
3:10-18 199
3:12 . . . . 33, 201
3:13 159
3:14 . . . . 199, 200
3:14-15 83
3:14-17 201
3:16 161
3:16-17 202
4:1-2 203
4:1-8 203
4:2 . . . . 161, 203, 204
4:2-4 85
4:3 89
4:3-8 205
4:7 89
4:9-22 206
4:10 131
4:14-15 206
4:16 207
4:16-17 207
4:18 208

Titus

1:1 . . . . 89, 158
1:1-4 157
1:2 158
1:3 158
1:4 158
1:5 . . . . 108, 158, 162
1:5-9 . . . . 109, 160
1:5-16 160
1:6 . . . . 114, 117, 160
1:6-7 109
1:7 . . . . 108, 109, 111, 112, 160
1:8 . . . . 115, 116
1:9 . . . . 89, 116, 161
1:10, 14 159
1:10-16 . . . . 158, 159, 161

1:11 . . . . 85, 147, 159, 161
1:12 . . . . 159, 171
1:12-13 . . . . 161, 162
1:13 . . . . 89, 161
1:14 . . . . 159, 161
1:15 . . . . 125, 159, 162
1:16 . . . . . . 127, 159, 160, 162, 193
2:1 . . . . 89, 163
2:1-5 163
2:1-10 . . . . 163, 164
2:1-14 162
2:2 168
2:3 168
2:4 . . . . 163, 168
2:4-5 . . . . 106 , 168
2:5 . . . . 169, 172
2:6 168
2:6-8 163
2:7 193
2:7-8 . . . . 168, 172
2:8 . . . . 89, 168, 169
2:9 168
2:9-10 . . . . 146, 163
2:9-11 75
2:10 . . . . 168, 169, 172
2:11 . . . . 164, 165
2:11-13 166
2:11-14 . . . . 100, 164, 167
2:12 . . . . 158, 166
2:12-13 166
2:13 . . . . 43, 169
2:14 . . . . 165, 169, 193
3:1 193
3:1-11 192
3:1-15 170
3:3 171
3:3-5 169
3:3-7 164
3:3-10 192
3:4 171
3:4-7 171
3:5 172
3:7 . . . . 165, 172, 173
3:8 . . . . 172, 193
3:9 174
3:9-15 173
3:10 174
3:14 . . . . 174, 193

Philemon
12-16 147
24 131

Hebrews
2:10 62
3:14 96
4:15 135
4:16 165
6:18 158
8:10 88
10:1-18 99
10:16 88
10:29 165
10:31 64
10:32-34 . . . . 25, 53
12:1 178
12:1-3 189
12:3-11 33
12:15 165
13:2 116
13:5 . . . . 148, 208
13:17 52

James
1:2-4 . . . . 33, 62
1:12 188
1:12-15 135
1:19 112
1:22-25 202
1:27 103
2:1-5 85
3:9-12 112
4:1-4 104
4:8 104
5:1-6 25
5:16 101

1 Peter
1:1-5 158
1:6-7 33
1:13 137
1:16 36
2:6 101
2:22-23 196
2:25 108
3:3-4 105
3:9 165

3:10-12 101
4:1-2 33
5:8 135

2 Peter
2:13 64
2:15 . . . . 85, 147
2:20 123
3:9 . . . . 63, 97

1 John
1:9 123
2:1 123
2:16 111
3:2 170
3:4 . . . . 70, 87
3:7-10 125

Jude
3 95
11 85
21 69

Revelation
1:16 73
2:10-11 190
2:14 85
2:15 85
2:18-23 144
2:20 85
3:4 103
5:6-10 100
6:2 73
6:10-11 63
11–15 69
12:11 190
13:1-8 74
13:3, 12 74
13:11-18 71
13:12-13 70
13:13 74
13:15 74
13:16-17 70
17:4 105
17:12 72
19:19-20 72
20:4-6 . . . . 67, 68, 69
20:10 72
21:2 105

Bibliography

Alcorn, Randy. "The real and untold cost: The exorbitant price of sexual sin," *Leadership: A Practical Journal for Church Leaders.* A Publication of Christianity Today, Summer 1996.

Allen, Kerry James, ed. *Exploring the Mind and Heart of the Prince of Preachers: Five-Thousand Illustrations Selected from the Works of Charles Haddon Spurgeon.* Oswego, Illinois: Fox River, 2005.

Anderson, J. N. D. *Morality, Law and Grace.* London, England: Tyndale Press, 1972.

Arndt, W. F. and F. W. Gingrich. *A Greek-English Lexicon of the New Testament and Other Early Christian Literature.* Chicago, Illinois: University of Chicago Press, 1957.

Arrington, French L. and Roger Stronstad. *Life in the Spirit New Testament Commentary.* Grand Rapids, Michigan: Zondervan Publishing House, 2003.

Barclay, William.. *The Daily Bible Study Series: The Letters to Timothy, Titus, and Philemon. rev. ed.* Philadelphia, Pennsylvania: Westminster Press, 1975.

_____. *The Daily Bible Study Series: The Letters to the Philippians, Colossians, and Thessalonians, rev. ed.* Philadelphia, Pennsylvania: Westminster Press, 1975

Barker, Kenneth, gen. ed. *The NIV Study Bible.* Grand Rapids, Michigan: Zondervan Publishing House, 1985.

Barlow, Fred. *"Adoniram Judson: Father of Baptist Missionaries" from Profiles in Evangelism.* Murfreesboro, TN: Sword of the Lord Publishers, 1976; available from www.wholesomewords.org; Internet accessed 11 September 2014.

Barrett, C. K. *The Pastoral Epistles—The New Clarendon Bible.* Oxford, England, Clarendon Press, 1963.

Barrett, David. *International Bulletin of Missionary Research.* January 2000.

Boteler, Mattie M. *Side Windows, Or, Lights on Scripture Truths.* Cincinnati, Ohio: The Standard Publishing Company, 1901.

Bruce, F. F. *1 & 2 Thessalonians, Word Biblical Commentary, vol. 45.* Waco, Texas: Word Books, 1982.

Burgess, David F. compiler. *Encyclopedia of Sermon Illustrations.* St. Louis, Missouri: Concordia Publishing House, 1988.

Corner, Daniel D. *The Believer's Conditional Security: Eternal Security Refuted.* Washington, Pennsylvania: Evangelical Outreach, 2000.

Dobson, James. *Straight Talk to Men and Their Wives.* Nashville, Tennessee: W Publishing Group, 1980.

Eutsler, Dr. Steve D. *Sermon: "What's the Biblical Portrayal of Love? You Can't Beat it."* available from www.wix.com/steveeutsler/reveut; Internet; accessed 4 September 2014.

Evans, Tony. *Tony Evans' Book of Illustrations: Stories, Quotes, and Anecdotes from More Than 30 Years of Preaching and Public Speaking.* Chicago, Illinois: Moody Press, 2009.

Fee, Gordon D. *New International Biblical Commentary: 1 & 2 Timothy, Titus.* Grand Rapids, Michigan: Baker Books, 1988.

_____. *The New International Commentary on the New Testament: The First and Second Letters to the Thessalonians.* Grand Rapids, Michigan: Wm. B. Eerdmans Publishing Co., 2009.

Foster, Elon. *6,000 Windows for Sermons: A Companion Volume to 6,000 Sermon Illustrations.* Grand Rapids, Michigan: Baker Book House, 1953.

Foster, Richard J. *Celebration of Discipline: The Path to Spiritual Growth.* San Francisco, California: HarperCollins Publishers, Inc, 1998.

Gilbrandt, Thoralf, ed. *The Complete Biblical Library, The New Testament Study Bible Galatians–Philemon, vol. 8.* Springfield, Missouri: World Library Press, 1989.

_____. *Complete Biblical Library, The New Testament Greek-English Dictionary, Alpha-Gamma.* Springfield, Missouri: World Library Press, Inc., 1991.

Gray, John. *Men Are From Mars, Women Are From Venus.* New York, New York: HarperCollins Publishers, 1992.

Green, Michael P., ed. *1500 Illustrations for Biblical Preaching.* Grand Rapids, Michigan: Baker Book House, 1989.

Guthrie, Donald. *Tyndale New Testament Commentaries: The Pastoral Epistles, vol. 14, paperback ed.* Grand Rapids, Michigan: IVP Academic/Wm. B. Eerdmanns Publishing Co., 2009.

Hayes, Steve. *Safe and Sound: Protecting Personal and Ministry Relationships.* Nashville: Tennessee: Broadman and Holman Press, 2002.

Horton, Stanley M. *The Ultimate Victory, An Exposition of the Book of Revelation.* Springfield, Missouri: Gospel Publishing House, 1991.

_____, ed. *Systematic Theology: A Pentecostal Perspective.* Springfield, Missouri: Logion Press, 2007.

Johnson, Van, Quentin McGhee, Edgardo Muñoz, and Steve Eutsler, *Romans & Galatians.* Springfield, Missouri: Faith & Action Team, 2012.

Jowett, John Henry. *The Passion for Souls.* CreateSpace Independent Publishing Platform, 2016.

Knight, Walter B. *Knight's Master Book of New Illustrations.* Grand Rapids, Michigan: Wm. B. Eerdmans Publishing Co., 1956.

Larson, Craig Brian. *Leadership Journal, 750 Engaging Illustrations for Preachers, Teachers, & Writers.* Grand Rapids, Michigan: Baker Book House, 1993.

_____, ed. *Perfect Illustrations for Every Topic and Occasion.* Compiled by the editors of PreachingToday.com, 2002.

Lawson, James Gilchrist, compiler. *Best Sermon Pictures: 2935 Anecdotes and Illustrations.* Chicago, Illinois: Moody Press, 1900.

Macartney, Clarence Edward. *Macartney's Illustrations: Illustrations from the Sermons of Clarence Edward Macartney.* Nashville, Tennessee: Abingdon Press, 1946.

MacDonald, Gordon. 'Feeling As God Feels,' *Preaching Today #196*; quoted by Craig Brian Larson in *Perfect Illustrations for Every Topic and Occasion,* Wheaton, Illinois: Tyndale House, 2002.

Martin, Sydney. *Beacon Bible Expositions, vol. 10: Thessalonians through Titus.* Kansas City, Missouri: Beacon Hill Press, 1977.

McKenzie, E. C. *Mac's Giant Book of Quips & Quotes.* Irvine, California: Harvest House, 1980.

Menzies, William W. and Stanley M. Horton. *Bible Doctrines: A Pentecostal Perspective.* Springfield, Missouri: Gospel Publishing House, 1994.

Michael, Larry J. *Spurgeon on Leadership: Key Insights for Christian Leaders from the Prince of Preachers.* Grand Rapids, Michigan: Kregel Publications, 2010.

Morris, Leon. *Tyndale New Testament Commentary The Epistles of Paul to the Thessalonians.* Grand Rapids, Michigan: Wm B. Eerdmans Publishing Co., 1977.

Mounce, Robert H. *The New International Commentary on the New Testament: The Book of Revelation, rev. ed.* Grand Rapids, Michigan: Wm. B. Eerdmans Publishing Co., 1998.

Naismith, A. *A Treasury of Notes, Quotes, & Anecdotes: For Sermon Building.* Grand Rapids, Michigan: Baker Book House, 1975.

National Council of Alcoholism, 2006, https://www.cdc.gov/features/alcoholconsumption/

Nicoll, W. Robertson. *The Expositor's Greek New Testament vol. IV.* Grand Rapids, Michigan, Wm. B. Eerdmans Publishing Co., 1974.

Orr, James. *The International Standard Bible Encyclopedia, (ISBE), vol. IV.* Grand Rapids, Michigan: Wm. B. Eerdmans Publishing Company, 1956.

Packer, James. *Your Father Loves You.* N.p.: Harold Shaw, 1986. Available from www.Bible.org; 'Infallible & Inerrant'.

Patterson, Ben. *He Has Made Me Glad: Enjoying God's Goodness with Reckless Abandon.* InterVarsity Press, 2005; quoted in Craig Brian Larson & Phyllis Ten Elshof, gen. eds., *1001 Illustrations That Connect: Compelling Stories, Stats, and News Items for Preaching, Teaching, and Writing.* Grand Rapids, Michigan: Zondervan Publishing House, 2008.

Reed, John W., compiler. *1100 Illustrations from the Writings of D. L. Moody: For Teachers, Preachers, and Writers.* Grand Rapids, Michigan: Baker Book House, 1996.

Richie, Tony. *Toward a Pentecostal Theology of Religions: Encountering Cornelius Today.* Cleveland Tennessee: CPT Press, 2013.

Rosberg, Gary and Barbara. *The Five Love Needs of Men and Women.* Tyndale House Publishers, 2001.

Sandford, John Loren. *Why Some Christians Commit Adultery.* Tulsa, Oklahoma: Victory House Publishers, 1989.

Steele, Richard A., Jr. and Evelyn Stoner, compilers. *Practical Bible Illustrations from Yesterday and Today.* Chattanooga, Tennessee: AMG Publishers, 1996.

Sugden, Edward H., ed. Wesley's *Standard Sermons, vol. 1.* London, England: Epworth Press, 1921.

Swindoll, Charles R. *Insights on 1 & 2 Timothy, Titus: Swindoll's Living Insights New Testament Commentary.* Grand Rapids, Michigan: Zondervan Publishing House, 2010.

_____. *Ultimate Book of Illustrations & Quotes: Over 1,500 Outstanding Ways to Effectively Drive Home Your Message.* Nashville, TN: Thomas Nelson, Inc., 2003.

Tan, Paul Lee. *Encyclopedia of 7,700 Illustrations: Signs of the Times.* Rockville, Maryland: Assurance Publishers, 1997.

Taylor, Cheryl. "The War Within: Maintaining Sexual Purity," in *Rapport.* Springfield, Missouri: Assemblies of God Theological Seminary, Summer 2004.

The Hinsons, "Lock Me Up In Prison," ["That I Could Still Go Free"], http://www.youtube.com/watch?v=j7CGANOMDP0 Recorded December 6, 1979 at the Old Broadmoor Theater in Shreveport, Louisiana.

Toplady, Augustus M. The hymn, *Rock of Ages.* 1776; https://www.hymnal.net/en/hymn/h/1058

Tuttle, Robert G., Jr. *John Wesley and the Gifts of the Holy Spirit.* http://ucmpage.org/articles/rtuttle1.html

Twelftree, Graham H. *Your Point Being? Powerful and Poignant Stories for Preachers, Teachers, Speakers, and Writers.* Grand Rapids, Michigan: Monarch Books, 2003.

Volf, Miroslav. *Exclusion & Embrace: A Theological Exploration of Identity, Otherness, and Reconciliation, 1st ed.* Nashville, Tennessee: Abingdon Press, 1996.

Wallis, Charles L., ed. *A Treasury of Sermon Illustrations.* Nashville, Tennessee: Abingdon Press, 1940.

White, Newport J. D. *The Expositor's Greek Testament: Volume Four.* Grand Rapids, Michigan: Wm. B. Eerdmans Publishing Co., 1974.

Williams, Morrris. *Declare His Righteousness.* Springfield, Missouri, Gospel Publishing House, 1975.

Wood, George O. "Down-to-Earth Living," *Sermon on 1 Thessalonians 4.* http://sermons.georgeowood.com/SiteFiles/102297/Content/Thessalonians/04%20DOWN-TO-EARTH%20LIVING.pdf

_____. "Holy Women," *Sermon on 1 Timothy 2:9-15.* http://sermons.georgeowood.com/SiteFiles/102297/Content/Timothy/04%20HOLY%20WOMEN.pdf

_____. "Please Pass the Praise," *Sermon on 1 Thessalonians 1.* http://sermons.georgeowood.com/SiteFiles/102297/Content/Thessalonians/01%20PLEASE%20PASS%20THE%20PRAISE.pdf

_____. "Relationships in the House of God." *Sermon on 1 Timothy 5.* http://sermons.georgeowood.com/SiteFiles/102297/Content/Timothy/07%20RELATIONSHIPS%20IN%20THE%20HOUSE%20OF%20GOD.pdf

_____., James Hernando, Floyd Woodworth, Edgardo Muñoz, and Quentin McGhee. *First and Second Corinthians.* Springfield, Missouri: Faith & Action Team, 2011.

Zuck, Roy. *The Speaker's Quote Book: Over 4,500 Illustrations and Quotations for All Occasions.* Grand Rapids, Michigan: Kregel Publications, 1997.

http://dukespace.lib.duke.edu/dspace/bitstream/handle/10161/7885/John_Wesley_on_Holistic_Health. pdf%3Fsequence%3D1; http://www.danielrjennings.org/tsoojw2.pdf

http://sermons.logos.com/submissions/15583-Prayer-as-a-Way-of-Life#content=/submissions/15583

http://time100.time.com/2013/04/18/time-100/slide/wilfredo-de-jesus/

http://www.247ag.com/WAGF/wp-content/uploads/2009/11/Application-Statement-of-Faith.pdf

http://www.christianitytoday.com/edstetzer/2016/december/stay-course-my-interview-with-wilfredo-de-jesus-on-his-rece.html

http://www.creationmoments.com/radio/transcripts/snake-fishes-desert

http://www.goodreads.com/quotes/332507-in-essentials-unity-in-non-essentials-liberty-in-all-things-charity

http://www.puritanfellowship.com/2008/05/charles-spurgeon-imparted-righteousness.html

http://www.sermoncentral.com/sermons/persecution--then--now-donna-kazenske-sermon-on-endurance-50096

http://www.whatchristianswanttoknow.com/21-awesome-christian-quotes-about-women/#ixzz2FR5zKLmx.

Endnotes

Chapter 1

1 Leon Morris, *Tyndale New Testament Commentary: The Epistles of Paul to the Thessalonians,* (Grand Rapids, Michigan: Wm B. Eerdmans Publishing Co., 1977), p. 60.

2 Roy Zuck, *The Speaker's Quote Book: Over 4,500 Illustrations and Quotations for All Occasions* (Grand Rapids, Michigan: Kregel Publications, 1997), p. 426.

3 Kenneth Barker, gen. ed., *The NIV Study Bible* (Grand Rapids, Michigan: Zondervan Publishing House, 1985), adapted from the Introduction to 1 Thessalonians, pp. 1821-1822.

4 Adapted from *The NIV Study Bible,* Introductions to 1 and 2 Thessalonians, pp. 1821-1822, 1829.

5 Paul Lee Tan, *Encyclopedia of 7,700 Illustrations: Signs of the Times* (Rockville, Maryland: Assurance Publishers, 1997), p. 1658.

6 Adapted from Michael P. Green, ed., *1500 Illustrations for Biblical Preaching* (Grand Rapids, Michigan: Baker Book House, 1989), p. 261.

7 French L. Arrington and Roger Stronstad, *Life in the Spirit New Testament Commentary* (Grand Rapids, Michigan: Zondervan Publishing House, 2003) p. 1167.

8 George O. Wood, "Please Pass the Praise," Sermon on 1 Thessalonians 1. http://sermons.georgeowood.com/SiteFiles/102297/Content/Thessalonians/01%20PLEASE%20PASS%20THE%20PRAISE.pdf

9 William Barclay, *The Daily Bible Study Series: The Letters to the Philippians, Colossians, and Thessalonians,* rev. ed. (Philadelphia, Pennsylvania: Westminster Press, 1975), p. 186.

10 John Henry Jowett, *The Passion for Souls* (CreateSpace Independent Publishing Platform, 2016), p. 12.

11 Tony Evans, *Tony Evans' Book of Illustrations: Stories, Quotes, and Anecdotes from More Than 30 Years of Preaching and Public Speaking* (Chicago, Illinois: Moody Press, 2009), p. 51.

12 http://www.sermoncentral.com/sermons/persecution--then--now-donna-kazenske-sermon-on-endurance-50096

13 Adapted from *Life in the Spirit New Testament Commentary,* p. 1176.

14 George O. Wood, James Hernando, Floyd Woodworth, Edgardo Muñoz, and Quentin McGhee, *First and Second Corinthians* (Springfield, Missouri: Faith & Action Team, 2011), Chapter 3, Lesson 9. pp. 53-59.

15 James Orr, *The International Standard Bible Encyclopedia,* (ISBE), vol. IV (Grand Rapids, Michigan: Wm. B. Eerdmans Publishing Company, 1956), p. 2682.

16 http://www.puritanfellowship.com/2008/05/charles-spurgeon-imparted-righteousness.html

17 George O. Wood, "Down-to-Earth Living," Sermon on 1 Thessalonians 4. http://sermons.georgeowood.com/SiteFiles/102297/Content/Thessalonians/04%20DOWN-TO-EARTH%20LIVING.pdf

18 Adapted from David F. Burgess, compiler, *Encyclopedia of Sermon Illustrations* (St. Louis, Missouri: Concordia Publishing House, 1988), p. 103.

19 Adapted from *Encyclopedia of Sermon Illustrations,* p. 194.

20 Diagram adapted from Morrris Williams, *Declare His Righteousness* (Springfield, Missouri, Gospel Publishing House, 1975), p. 50.

21 Arrington and Stronstad, p. 1190.

22 Thoralf Gilbrandt, *Complete Biblical Library, The New Testament Greek-English Dictionary, Alpha-Gamma* (Springfield, Missouri: World Library Press, Inc., 1991), p. 448.

23 F. F. Bruce, *1 & 2 Thessalonians, Word Biblical Commentary,* vol. 45 (Waco, Texas: Word Books, 1982), p. 100. [Information is from Arrington and Stronstad, p. 1218.]

24 For a discussion of *the gospel,* see Van Johnson, Quentin McGhee, Edgardo Muñoz, and Steve Eutsler, *Romans & Galatians,* Lesson 4, Point E (Springfield, Missouri: Faith & Action Team, 2012).

25 http://www.247ag.com/WAGF/wp-content/uploads/2009/11/Application-Statement-of-Faith.pdf

26 Adapted from *Life in the Spirit New Testament Commentary,* pp. 1217-1218.

27 Green p. 148.

28 http://sermons.logos.com/submissions/15583-Prayer-as-a-Way-of-Life#content=/submissions/15583

29 The Hinsons, "Lock Me Up In Prison," ["That I Could Still Go Free"], http://www.youtube.com/watch?v=j7CGANOMDP0 Recorded December 6, 1979 at the Old Broadmoor Theater in Shreveport, Louisiana.

30 Arrington and Stronstad, pp. 1197-1198.

31 Arrington and Stronstad, p. 1197.

32 Online article by Robert G. Tuttle, Jr., http://ucmpage.org/articles/rtuttle1.html

33 Burgess, pp. 49-50.

Chapter 2

1 http://www.creationmoments.com/radio/transcripts/snake-fishes-desert

2 Adapted from John W. Reed, compiler, *1100 Illustrations from the Writings of D. L. Moody: For Teachers, Preachers, and Writers* (Grand Rapids, Michigan: Baker Book House, 1996), pp. 85-86.

3 David Barrett, *International Bulletin of Missionary Research* (January 2000), p. 25.

4 Tony Richie, *Toward a Pentecostal Theology of Religions: Encountering Cornelius Today* (Cleveland Tennessee: CPT Press, 2013), p. 149.

5 Miroslav Volf, *Exclusion & Embrace: A Theological Exploration of Identity, Otherness, and Reconciliation,* 1st ed. (Nashville, Tennessee: Abingdon Press, 1996), pp. 299-302.

6 Adapted from *Encyclopedia of Sermon Illustrations*, p. 35.

7 Thoralf Gilbrandt, ed., *The Complete Biblical Library, The New Testament Study Bible Galatians–Philemon,* vol. 8 (Springfield, Missouri: World Library Press, 1989), p. 351.

8 Gordon D. Fee, *The New International Commentary on the New Testament: The First and Second Letters to the Thessalonians* (Grand Rapids, Michigan: Wm. B. Eerdmans Publishing Co., 2009), pp. 271-305.

9 Tan, p. 149.

10 Adapted from Tan, *Encyclopedia of 7,700 Illustrations: Signs of the Times,* p. 149.

11 W. F. Arndt and F. W. Gingrich, *A Greek-English Lexicon of the New Testament and Other Early Christian Literature* (Chicago, Illinois: University of Chicago Press, 1957), p. 97.

12 Adapted from James Gilchrist Lawson, compiler, *Best Sermon Pictures: 2935 Anecdotes and Illustrations* (Chicago, Illinois: Moody Press, 1900), p. 274.

Chapter 3

1 Gordon D. Fee, *New International Biblical Commentary: 1 & 2 Timothy, Titus* (Grand Rapids, Michigan: Baker Books, 1988), p. 37.

2 Fee, *New International Biblical Commentary: 1 & 2 Timothy, Titus,* p. 35.

3 Arrington and Stronstad, p. 1227.

4 Fee, *NIBC: 1 & 2 Timothy, Titus,* p. 39.

5 Fee, *NIBC: 1 & 2 Timothy, Titus,* p. 42.

6 Burgess, p. 77.

7 Reed, pp. 17-18.

8 Donald Guthrie, *Tyndale New Testament Commentaries: The Pastoral Epistles,* vol. 14, paperback ed. (Grand Rapids, Michigan: IVP Academic/Wm. B. Eerdmanns Publishing Co., 2009), p. 61.

9 Fee, *NIBC: 1 & 2 Timothy, Titus,* p. 46.

10 Guthrie, p. 62.

11 Fee, *NIBC: 1 & 2 Timothy, Titus,* p. 16.

12 J. N. D. Anderson, *Morality, Law and Grace* (London, England: Tyndale Press, 1972), p. 124.

13 Anderson, p. 124.

14 Fee, *NIBC: 1 & 2 Timothy, Titus,* p. 15.

15 Fee, *NIBC: 1 & 2 Timothy, Titus,* pp. 16-17.

16 Fee, *NIBC: 1 & 2 Timothy, Titus,* p. 50.

17 Guthrie, p. 63.

18 Fee, *NIBC: 1 & 2 Timothy, Titus,* p. 51.

19 Guthrie, p. 64.

20 Burgess, p. 105.

21 Burgess, pp. 92-93.

22 Jowett, pp. 12-18.

23 Fee, *NIBC: 1 & 2 Timothy, Titus,* p. 54.

24 http://time100.time.com/2013/04/18/time-100/slide/wilfredo-de-jesus/

25 http://www.christianitytoday.com/edstetzer/2016/december/stay-course-my-interview-with-wilfredo-de-jesus-on-his-rece.html

26 Fee, *NIBC: 1 & 2 Timothy, Titus,* p. 53.

27 Guthrie, p. 67.

28 Adapted from Charles L. Wallis, ed., *A Treasury of Sermon Illustrations* (Nashville, Tennessee: Abingdon Press, 1940), p. 148.

29 Guthrie, p. 69.

30 Fee, *NIBC: 1 & 2 Timothy, Titus,* p. 61.

31 Fee, *NIBC: 1 & 2 Timothy, Titus,* p. 64.

32 Fee, *NIBC: 1 & 2 Timothy, Titus,* p. 65.

33 Gilbrandt, *The New Testament Study Bible Galatians–Philemon,* p. 367.

34 Adapted from the hymn, *Rock of Ages,* by Augustus M. Toplady, 1776; https://www.hymnal.net/en/hymn/h/1058

35 James Orr, *The International Standard Bible Encyclopedia,* (ISBE), vol. II (Grand Rapids, Michigan: Wm. B. Eerdmans Publishing Company, 1955), p. 1263.

36 Craig Brian Larson, *Leadership Journal, 750 Engaging Illustrations for Preachers, Teachers, & Writers* (Grand Rapids, Michigan: Baker Book House, n.d.), pp.16-17.

37 Fee, *NIBC: 1 & 2 Timothy, Titus,* p. 70.

38 E. C. McKenzie, *Mac's Giant Book of Quips & Quotes* (Irvine, California: Harvest House, 1980), p. 556.

39 Richard J. Foster, *Celebration of Discipline: The Path to Spiritual Growth* (San Francisco, California: HarperCollins Publishers, Inc, 1998), p. 269.

40 Kerry James Allen, ed., *Exploring the Mind and Heart of the Prince of Preachers: Five-Thousand Illustrations Selected from the Works of Charles Haddon Spurgeon* (Oswego, Illinois: Fox River Press, 2005), p. 492.

41 George O. Wood, "Holy Women," Sermon on 1 Timothy. 2:9-15 http://sermons.georgeowood.com/SiteFiles/102297/Content/Timothy/04%20HOLY%20WOMEN.pdf

42 Fee, *NIBC: 1 & 2 Timothy, Titus,* p. 75.

43 Barclay, *The Daily Bible Study Series: The Letters to Timothy, Titus, and Philemon,* rev. ed. (Philadelphia, Pennsylvania: Westminster Press, 1975), p. 79.

44 National Council of Alcoholism, 2006, https://www.cdc.gov/features/alcoholconsumption/

45 Tan, p. 121.

46 Barclay, *The Letters to Timothy, Titus, and Philemon,* p. 236.

47 Larry J. Michael, *Spurgeon on Leadership: Key Insights for Christian Leaders from the Prince of Preachers* (Grand Rapids, Michigan: Kregel Publications, 2010), p. 169-70.

48 Charles R. Swindoll, *Swindoll's New Testament Insights: Insights on 1 & 2 Timothy, Titus* (Grand Rapids, Michigan: Zondervan, 2010), p. 574.

49 W. Robertson Nicoll, *The Expositor's Greek New Testament,* vol. four (Grand Rapids, Michigan, Wm. B. Eerdmans Publishing Co., 1974) p. 115

50 Fee, *NIBC: 1 & 2 Timothy, Titus,* p. 174.

51 Adapted from Charles R. Swindoll, *Swindoll's Ultimate Book of Illustrations & Quotes: Over 1,500 Outstanding Ways to Effectively Drive Home Your Message* (Nashville. Tennessee: Thomas Nelson, Inc., 1998), p. 389.

52 Guthrie, p. 83.

53 Green, p. 288.

54 Arrington and Stronstad, p. 1236.

55 Fee, *NIBC: 1 & 2 Timothy, Titus*, p. 81.

56 Adapted from Clarence Edward Macartney, *Macartney's Illustrations: Illustrations from the Sermons of Clarence Edward Macartney* (Nashville, Tennessee: Abingdon Press, 1946), p. 326.

57 Adapted from Walter B. Knight, *Knight's Master Book of New Illustrations* (Grand Rapids, Michigan: Wm. B. Eerdmans Publishing Co., 1956), p. 498.

58 Arrington and Stronstad, p. 1238.

59 Green, pp. 196-197.

60 Zuck, p. 375.

61 Fee, *NIBC: 1 & 2 Timothy, Titus*, p. 81.

62 Fee, *NIBC: 1 & 2 Timothy, Titus*, pp. 92-95).

63 Burgess, pp. 87-88.

Chapter 4

1 Daniel D. Corner, *The Believer's Conditional Security: Eternal Security Refuted* (Washington, Pennsylvania: Evangelical Outreach, 2000), pp. 258-302.

2 Fee, *NIBC: 1 & 2 Timothy, Titus*, pp. 43-44.

3 Burgess, p. 192.

4 http://dukespace.lib.duke.edu/dspace/bitstream/handle/10161/7885/John_Wesley_on_Holistic_Health. pdf%3Fsequence%3D1; http://www.danielrjennings.org/tsoojw2.pdf

5 This list is adapted from Phoenix First Assembly of God, which has over 200 ministries by church members.

6 Adapted from Graham H. Twelftree, *Your Point Being? Powerful and Poignant Stories for Preachers, Teachers, Speakers, and Writers* (Grand Rapids, Michigan: Monarch Books, 2003), p. 303.

7 Twelftree, p. 303.

8 Guthrie, p. 99.

9 Fee, *NIBC: 1 & 2 Timothy, Titus*, p. 109.

10 Swindoll, *Insights on 1 & 2 Timothy, Titus*, p. 95.

11 Fee, *NIBC: 1 & 2 Timothy, Titus*, pp. 112-113.

12 Barclay, *The Letters to Timothy, Titus, and Philemon*, p. 104.

13 Fee, *NIBC: 1 & 2 Timothy, Titus*, p. 115.

14 Guthrie, p. 100.

15 Guthrie, p. 101.

16 Fee, *NIBC: 1 & 2 Timothy, Titus*, p. 117.

17 http://www.whatchristianswanttoknow.com/21-awesome-christian-quotes-about-women/#ixzz2FR5zKLmx.

18 Many of the principles and thoughts in this lesson are adapted from an article, "The War Within: Maintaining Sexual Purity," by Dr. Cheryl Taylor in *Rapport* (Springfield, Missouri: Assemblies of God Theological Seminary, Summer 2004), Vol. 20, No. 2, pp. 6-9. Dr. Taylor is a professor at the Assemblies of God Theological Seminary and is available to teach seminars on how to overcome sexual temptation. You can access some of her articles on the Internet at www.agts.edu.

19 Adapted from John Loren Sandford's book, *Why Some Christians Commit Adultery* (Tulsa, Oklahoma: Victory House Publishers, 1989), and Steve Hayes, *Safe and Sound: Protecting Personal and Ministry Relationships* (Nashville: Tennessee: Broadman and Holman Press, 2002), p. 60.

20 James Dobson, *Straight Talk to Men and Their Wives* (Nashville, Tennessee: W Publishing Group, 1980).

21 See these two sources: *Men Are From Mars, Women Are From Venus* by John Gray (New York, New York: HarperCollins Publishers, 1992), pp. 135-137; *The Five Love Needs of Men and Women* by Gary and Barbara Rosberg (Tyndale House Publishers, 2001).

22 Adapted from an article by Randy Alcorn, "The real and untold cost: The exorbitant price of sexual sin," *Leadership: A Practical Journal for Church Leaders* (Summer 1996), p. 52.

23 Swindoll, *Insights on 1 & 2 Timothy, Titus,* p. 94.

24 Fee, *NIBC: 1 & 2 Timothy, Titus*, p. 112.

25 George O. Wood, "Relationships in the House of God." Sermon on 1 Timothy 5. http://sermons.georgeowood.com/SiteFiles/102297/Content/Timothy/07%20RELATIONSHIPS%20IN%20THE%20HOUSE%20OF%20GOD.pdf

26 Adapted from Gordon MacDonald, in the sermon 'Feeling As God Feels,' *Preaching Today* #196; quoted by Craig Brian Larson in *Perfect Illustrations for Every Topic and Occasion* (Wheaton, Illinois: Tyndale House, 2002), p. 257.

27 Fee, *NIBC: 1 & 2 Timothy, Titus*, p. 128.

28 Fee, *NIBC: 1 & 2 Timothy, Titus*, p. 128.

29 Arrington and Stronstad, p. 1254.

30 Adapted from Elon Foster, *6,000 Windows for Sermons: A Companion Volume to 6,000 Sermon Illustrations* (Grand Rapids, Michigan: Baker Book House, 1953), p. 695.

31 Green, p. 345.

32 Adapted from *6,000 Windows for Sermons: A Companion Volume to 6,000 Sermon Illustrations*, p. 698.

33 Barclay, *The Letters to Timothy, Titus, and Philemon*, p. 121.

34 Adapted from Charles Chu, quoted in *Perfect Illustrations for Every Topic and Occasion*, pp. 79-80.

35 Adapted from *Encyclopedia of Sermon Illustrations*, p. 50.

36 Adapted from *Encyclopedia of Sermon Illustrations*, p. 143.

37 Adapted from *6,000 Windows for Sermons: A Companion Volume to 6,000 Sermon Illustrations*, p. 727.

38 Gilbrandt, *Complete Biblical Library ... Alpha-Gamma*, pp. 91-92.

39 Fee, *NIBC: 1 & 2 Timothy, Titus*, pp. 152-154.

Chapter 5

1 Guthrie, p. 183.

2 Fee, *NIBC: 1 & 2 Timothy, Titus*, p. 169.

3 Fee, *NIBC: 1 & 2 Timothy, Titus*, pp. 4, 171-172.

4 Guthrie, p. 190.

5 Fee, *NIBC: 1 & 2 Timothy, Titus*, p. 178.

6 Guthrie, p. 188.

7 Fee, *NIBC: 1 & 2 Timothy, Titus*, p. 173.

8 Newport J. D. White, *The Expositor's Greek Testament: Volume Four* (Grand Rapids, Michigan: Wm. B. Eerdmans Publishing Co., 1974), p. 111.

9 Fee, *NIBC: 1 & 2 Timothy, Titus*, p. 173.

10 Guthrie, p. 186.

11 Adapted from Ben Patterson, *He Has Made Me Glad: Enjoying God's Goodness with Reckless Abandon* (InterVarsity Press, 2005); quoted in Craig Brian Larson and Phyllis Ten Elshof, gen. eds., *1001 Illustrations That Connect: Compelling Stories, Stats, and News Items for Preaching, Teaching, and Writing* (Grand Rapids, Michigan: Zondervan Publishing House, 2008), p. 226.

12 Arrington and Stronstad, p. 1280.

13 Adapted from *6,000 Windows for Sermons: A Companion Volume to 6,000 Sermon Illustrations*, p. 571.

14 Adapted from *Encyclopedia of Sermon Illustrations*, p. 212.

15 Fee, *NIBC: 1 & 2 Timothy, Titus*, p. 186.

16 Fee, *NIBC: 1 & 2 Timothy, Titus*, p. 203.

17 Arrington and Stronstad, p. 1281.

18 Guthrie, p. 205.

19 Stanley M. Horton, ed. *Systematic Theology: A Pentecostal Perspective* (Springfield, Missouri: Logion Press, p. 365.

Chapter 6

1 Fee, *NIBC: 1 & 2 Timothy, Titus*, p. 222.

2 Adapted from Dr. Steve D. Eutsler, sermon, "What's the Biblical Portrayal of Love? You Can't Beat it," p. 17; available from www.wix.com/steveeutsler/reveut; Internet; accessed 4 September 2014.

3 Adapted from A. Naismith, *A Treasury of Notes, Quotes, & Anecdotes for Sermon Building* (Grand Rapids, Michigan: Baker Book House, 1975), p. 179.

4 Adapted from Mattie M. Boteler, *Side Windows, Or, Lights on Scripture Truths* (Cincinnati, Ohio: The Standard Publishing Company, 1901), pp. 60-61.

5 Adapted from *1100 Illustrations from the Writings of D. L. Moody: For Teachers, Preachers, and Writers*, p. 52.

6 Tan, p. 239.

7 Stanley M. Horton, *The Ultimate Victory, An Exposition of the Book of Revelation* (Springfield, Missouri: Gospel Publishing House, 1991), p. 43.

8 Robert H. Mounce, *The New International Commentary on the New Testament: The Book of Revelation*, rev. ed. (Grand Rapids, Michigan: Wm. B. Eerdmans Publishing Co., 1998), p. 72.

9 Fee, *NIBC: 1 & 2 Timothy, Titus*, p. 226-227.

10 C. K. Barrett, *The Pastoral Epistles—The New Clarendon Bible* (Oxford, England, Clarendon Press, 1963), p. 102.

11 Fee, *NIBC: 1 & 2 Timothy, Titus*, p. 260.

12 Fee, *NIBC: 1 & 2 Timothy, Titus* p. 266.

13 http://www.goodreads.com/quotes/332507-in-essentials-unity-in-non-essentials-liberty-in-all-things-charity

14 Fee, *NIBC: 1 & 2 Timothy, Titus*, p. 272.

15 Fee, *NIBC: 1 & 2 Timothy, Titus*, p. 275.

16 Adapted from *Encyclopedia of 7,700 Illustrations: Signs of the Times*, p. 985.

17 William W. Menzies and Stanley M. Horton, *Bible Doctrines: A Pentecostal Perspective* (Springfield, Missouri: Gospel Publishing House, 1994), p. 26.

18 James I. Packer, *Your Father Loves You: Daily Insights for Knowing God* (Wheaton, Illinois: Harold Shaw Publishers, 1986), page for November 9; available from www.Bible.org; 'Infallible & Inerrant.'

19 Green, p. 31.

20 Adapted from *A Treasury of Notes, Quotes, & Anecdotes: For Sermon Building*, pp. 247-248.

21 Sydney Martin, *Beacon Bible Expositions, vol. 10: Thessalonians through Titus* (Kansas City, Missouri: Beacon Hill Press, 1977), pp. 192-194.

22 Adapted from *The Speaker's Quote Book: Over 4,500 Illustrations and Quotations for All Occasions*, p. 310.

23 Adapted from Fred Barlow, "Adoniram Judson: Father of Baptist Missionaries" from *Profiles in Evangelism* (Murfreesboro, Tennessee: Sword of the Lord Publishers, 1976); available from www.wholesomewords.org; Internet accessed 11 September 2014.

24 Edward H. Sugden, ed., *Wesley's Standard Sermons*, vol. 1 (London, England: Epworth Press, 1921), pp. 31-32.

25 Tan, p. 1559.

26 Richard A. Steele, Jr., and Evelyn Stoner, compilers, *Practical Bible Illustrations from Yesterday and Today* (Chattanooga, Tennessee: AMG Publishers, 1996), pp. 164-165.

27 James Bradford, sermon on 2 Timothy 4.

28 John R. W. Stott, *The Message of 2 Timothy* (Downers Grove, Illinois: Inter-Varsity Press Leicester, England, 1973), p. 123.

29 Bradford, sermon on 2 Timothy 4.

30 Tan, p. 465.